Autism Spectrum Disorders: Foundations, Characteristics and Effective Strategies

Autism Spectrum Disorders: Foundations, Characteristics and Effective Strategies

Editor: Draco Oldman

MURPHY & MOORE
www.murphy-moorepublishing.com

www.murphy-moorepublishing.com

MURPHY & MOORE

Cataloging-in-Publication Data

Autism spectrum disorders : foundations, characteristics and effective strategies / edited by Draco Oldman.
p. cm.
Includes bibliographical references and index.
ISBN 978-1-63987-800-0
1. Autism spectrum disorders. 2. Autism spectrum disorders--Diagnosis. 3. Autism spectrum disorders--Treatment.
4. Psychiatry. I. Oldman, Draco.
RC553.A88 A983 2023
616.858 82--dc23

Murphy & Moore Publishing
1 Rockefeller Plaza,
New York City,
NY 10020, USA

ISBN 978-1-63987-800-0 (Hardback)

Contents

Preface

Autism spectrum disorders (ASD) are a diverse group of medical conditions which are characterized by difficulties in interacting and communicating socially. Other characteristics include atypical patterns of behavior and activity, like difficulty in paying attention to details, switching from one activity to another and odd responses to sensations. These issues in ASD affected people might range from minor to severe. The initial symptoms of this disorder can be detected by parents, caregivers or pediatricians, before a child turns one year old. However, symptoms usually develop and become more noticeable by the time the child reaches two or three years of age. The quality of life and well-being of autistic persons and their caregivers can benefit from evidence-based psychosocial therapies that enhance social skills and communication. This book attempts to understand the characteristics of autism spectrum disorders as well as the different interventions used for their management. Those in search of information to further their knowledge will be greatly assisted by it.

This book has been the outcome of endless efforts put in by authors and researchers on various issues and topics within the field. The book is a comprehensive collection of significant researches that are addressed in a variety of chapters. It will surely enhance the knowledge of the field among readers across the globe.

It gives us an immense pleasure to thank our researchers and authors for their efforts to submit their piece of writing before the deadlines. Finally in the end, I would like to thank my family and colleagues who have been a great source of inspiration and support.

Editor

Fundamental Motor Skills Intervention for Children with Autism Spectrum Disorder: A 10-Year Narrative Review

Silvia Busti Ceccarelli [1], Camilla Ferrante [2], Erica Gazzola [2], Gian Marco Marzocchi [2], Maria Nobile [1], Massimo Molteni [1] and Alessandro Crippa [1,*]

[1] Child Psychopathology Unit, Scientific Institute, IRCCS E. Medea, 23842 Bosisio Parini, Italy; silvia.busti@lanostrafamiglia.it (S.B.C.); maria.nobile@lanostrafamiglia.it (M.N.); massimo.molteni@lanostrafamiglia.it (M.M.)

[2] Department of Psychology, University of Milano-Bicocca, 20126 Milan, Italy; c.ferrante1@campus.unimib.it (C.F.); e.gazzola1@campus.unimib.it (E.G.); gianmarco.marzocchi@unimib.it (G.M.M.)

* Correspondence: alessandro.crippa@lanostrafamiglia.it

Abstract: In the past decade, converging evidence has suggested that motor impairment is one of the most consistent markers, alongside sociocommunicative difficulties, for autism spectrum disorder (ASD). Indeed, widespread anomalies of movement have been described in the ASD context. These motor abnormalities could have critical implications for subsequent cognitive and social development. Nevertheless, this area of development is particularly underexamined in the autism-related context, and early intervention programs commonly focus on the core symptoms of the condition. In the present work, we review and discuss the findings from recent studies that investigated the effect of interventions regarding fundamental motor skills in autistic children. Although the limited nature of the literature prevents researchers from drawing definitive conclusions, the results from the studies discussed here demonstrated potentially significant improvements in the motor abilities of autistic children after the interventions. Only a subset of the reviewed studies explored possible changes in the sociocommunicative domain after the motor skills improvements, and they had not concordant, although promising, conclusions. Overall, in consideration of the well-documented motor impairment people with the condition, the present findings highlight the importance of including motor skills training within the rehabilitation programs designed for autistic children. Furthermore, this narrative review encourages future interventional trials to consider motor skills as a possible target for reducing activity limitations and participation restrictions of autistic children.

Keywords: autism spectrum disorder; fundamental motor skills; intervention; treatment; rehabilitation

---

1. Introduction

Autism spectrum disorder (ASD) is a pervasive neurodevelopmental condition that is characterized by an impairment in social interaction and communicative skills, as well as the presence of repetitive and restricted behaviors. Although not included in the Diagnostic and Statistical Manual of Mental Disorders-Fifth Edition (DSM-5) criteria [1], ASD is frequently associated with extensive motor abnormalities (see [2], for a review). From the comprehensive meta-analysis of Fournier and colleagues [3] that suggested a remarkable effect size of 1.20 for motor deficits, the study of motor function in ASD has gained increasing momentum over the last decade. Indeed, a very recent analysis of the SPARK (Simons Foundation Powering Autism Research for Knowledge) study database [4] indicated that 86.9% of autistic children/adolescents are also at risk of a developmental coordination disorder. Motor difficulties in ASD occur in the first years of life, even preceding the social-communication deficits, and tend to increase with age, reducing the possibility of social interaction [5,6]. A number of studies also suggested that motor difficulties could be one of the earliest identifiable manifestations of ASD in clinical settings [7–12]. Early motor disturbances could even provide crucial information for delineating the different trajectories for typical development as well as early-onset and regressive forms of ASD that start from six months of age [13–15].

In this framework, the term "fundamental motor skills" (FMS) is often used to indicate the essential movements that allow a person to successfully perform a variety of physical activities—such as walking, running, jumping, reaching, catching, and throwing [16]. The development of FMS has been associated with active play throughout the childhood [17]. The stage of rhythmic stereotypies in infancy, for example, indicates neuromuscular maturation and promotes the subsequent control of specific motor patterns, whereas rough-and-tumble behavior during childhood serves as a basis for social interaction [17]. Poor motor skills represent a barrier to participation in physical activities, and the difficulty in engaging in active play prevents favorable occasions for the development of motor functions. Accordingly, motor delays in autistic children not only impact the motor domain but also may critically interfere with a range of abilities—such as cooperation, empathy, joint attention, self-regulation, and emotional well-being—that children with typical development acquire during free active play with parents, siblings, or other peers [6]. Conversely, it is important to bear in mind that also social functioning influences physical activity (even though to a lesser extent), as recently indicated by Reinders and colleagues [18]. For autistic people, social difficulties may indeed represent barriers to physical activity [18]. Although Esposito and Pasca [19] proposed that motor symptoms are an early biomarker of ASD and Leary and Hill [20] suggested that motor control is crucial for communication and social interaction, there is a lack of literature addressing this topic at this stage. Rehabilitation programs usually target social interaction, communicative skills, and behavioral difficulties as their primary foci. However, as discussed above, improving motor skills in autistic children could have a beneficial cascade effect on engagement in active play, thus offering remarkable opportunities for the social interactions mediated by physical activity [21–23].

Researchers [24] have proposed different strategies for interventions that help children cope with motor impairments in ASD. Most of the interventions involve FMS only marginally and instead focus on physical aerobic exercise, educational games, and sports, with moderately positive benefits reported in almost all studies (for reviews on this topic, see [6,25,26], for meta-analyses [24,27]). Interestingly, one systematic review [28] and one meta-analysis [29] have been performed in the last year focusing on the effect of specific interventions on FMS and gross motor skills. While reporting a positive effect of motor interventions on FMS and gross motor skills, both works provided useful insights to start developing a specific guideline for building future interventional studies. Namely, Colombo-Dagouvito and Block [28] very precisely defined a motor intervention as "an intentional and directed manipulation of motor skills through a set procedure taking place over a defined period of time to develop an overall change in motor skill performance" (p. 162). On the other hand, Case and Yun [29] clearly demonstrated that interventions that were 16 total hours or longer had a significantly larger effect than those shorter than 16 h. Furthermore, the authors also indicated that interventions in experimental settings were more effective than ones in practical settings [29].

Given the current stage of literature and starting from these recent suggestions, the primary goal of the present study was to summarize the studies on FMS interventions in autistic children in the past 10 years to delineate the strengths and weaknesses of the previous programs and to continue encouraging future research in this field. Being exploratory in nature, this work did not plan to exhaustively review all interventional studies addressing FMS as recently done [28,29]. Our focus was rather to discuss the most recent evidence also in light of the advances in autism-related research in the last 10 years. A secondary objective of this narrative review was to investigate whether interventions that have specifically addressed FMS included measures related to autistic core features and, in case, to explore the possible effect of FMS interventions on the sociocommunicative domain of autistic children. Given the above-mentioned literature [18], it would be plausible to expect some improvements in the social domain after FMS motor intervention. Moreover, exploring the potential effect of FMS programs beyond the motor domain is particularly relevant when considering the International Classification of Functioning, Disability, and Health for Children and Youth (ICF-CY; [30]) perspective. Indeed, ICF-CY assumes that the degree of functioning of a child is the result of a complex interaction between body functions and structures, activities, and participation, and that changes in one of these levels may influence the others. Accordingly, significant modifications of body functions (i.e., motor skills) after FMS intervention could significantly affect also "interpersonal interactions and relationships" within the level of activity and participation, a component significantly impaired in ASD [31].

2. Methods

A comprehensive search of three databases (PubMed, PsychInfo, Web Of Science) from January 2010 up to September 2020 was performed by two reviewers (S.B.C. and E.G.) using a combination of indexing terms with free text searching. The form of the general search strategy was the following: ([motor] AND [intervention] AND [autism] OR [autism spectrum disorders]). In the present review, studies were included if they involved motor intervention that fulfilled the definition provided by Colombo-Dagouvito and Block [28] and that specifically addressed FMS. Other inclusion criteria were (a) participants were 3–12 years old and (b) specific fine and/or gross motor intervention. Exclusion criteria were: (a) participants were above 12 years old; (b) general sport and physical activity intervention; (c) rehabilitation treatment or programs not specifically developed to involve motor intervention targets (e.g., Early Start Denver Model, JASPER); (d) single case studies. Despite a number of advantages, single case studies were not included because of the lack of generality of obtained effects.

The search and inclusion/exclusion criteria were specified before conducting the review but were not registered online. The search process through electronic databases identified a total of 147 studies. The electronic search was supplemented by hand searches of journals and individual article reference lists. Five additional articles were identified. Of the total 152 studies, 115 were excluded after reading the title and the abstract. The two reviewers then carried out a full-text screening of the remaining 37 articles. A total of ten articles were identified that met all inclusion/exclusion criteria and were included for analysis. Figure 1 depicts a flow diagram showing the procedure for the present review and the number of articles examined.

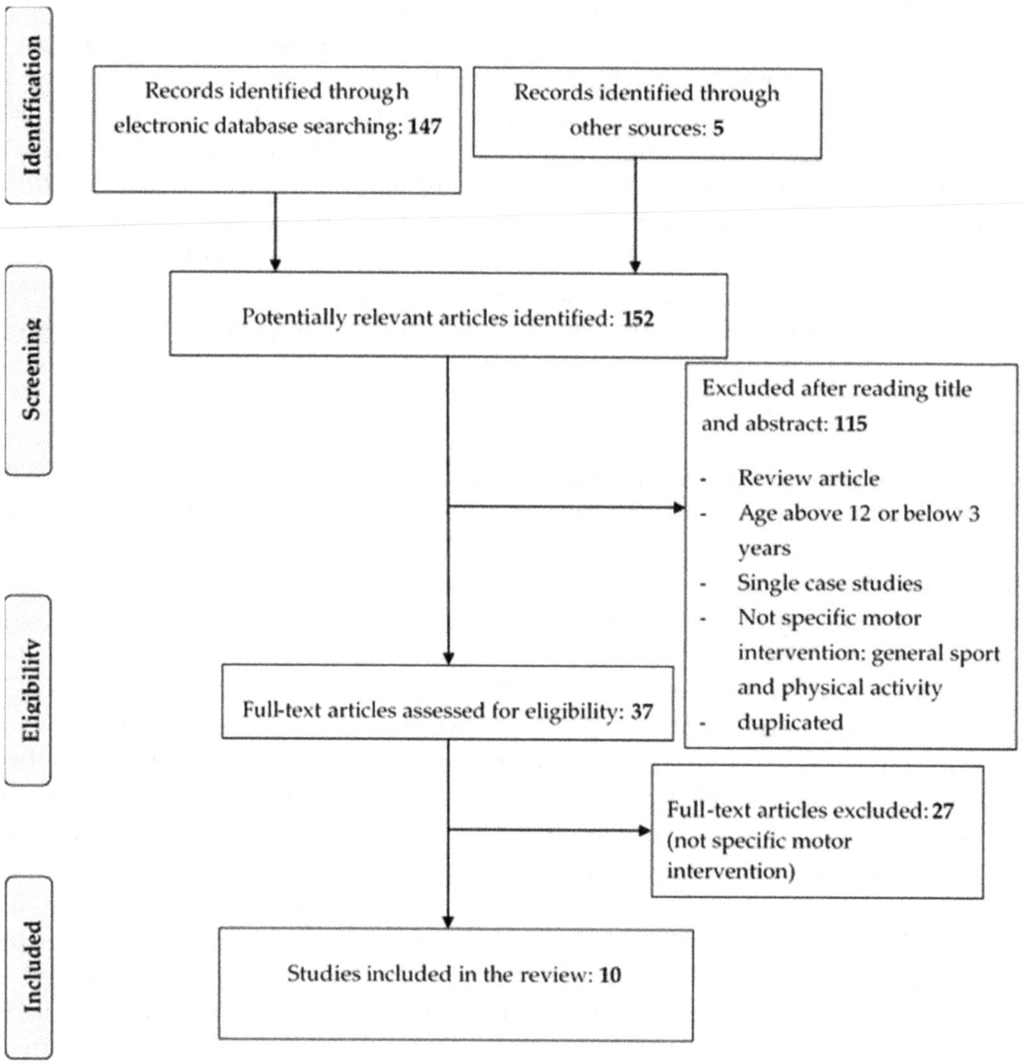

Figure 1. Flow diagram of the study selection process.

The included studies are summarized in Table 1.

Table 1. Main characteristics of studies included in the present review.

Study	Location	Study Type	Participants (N, Groups)	Age Range (Mean ± SD)	Intervention Approach	Intervention Length	Setting	Outcome Measures	Results
Bremer et al. [6]	Canada	Multiple-method study with pre-/posttest	N = 5 (4 ASD, 1 autism-like characteristics) One group (1f/4m)	3–7 years (5.46 ± 1.49)	Fundamental motor skill intervention (FMSI): each session focused on teaching and strengthening of both locomotor and object control skills. Each week focused on teaching one core skill with previously learned skills integrated into the sessions.	12 weeks split into two blocks (each block: 45 min per day for 3 days per week) for a total of 36 sessions	Local elementary school	• Test of Gross Motor Development-2 (TGMD-2); • Social Skills Improvement System (SSIS); Motor-skill proficiency and social skills were assessed at 3 times: baseline, after Block 1 of the intervention, and after Block 2 of the intervention.	Improvements on the majority of the individual TGMD-2 items, 4 of the participants showed improvements in locomotor skills, furthermore 3 of the participants in object-control from Assessments 1–3. Improvements in SSIS on all items. The special education teacher noted the increase of motor skills and knowledge in the participants, the treatment program could be easily generalized and her own perception of her ability to teach physical education improved.
Bremer et al. [32]	Canada	Wait-list control experimental design with pre-/post-follow up test	N = 9 ASD 2 groups: EG N = 5 (5m); CG N = 4 (1f/3m)	4 years (EG = 4.30 ± 0.25; CG = 4.33 ± 0.22)	Fundamental motor skill intervention (FMSI): each session focused on teaching and strengthening of both locomotor and object control skills (they progressed in difficulty over the intervention period), while integrating previously learned skills into the review period and obstacle course.	Phase I: group 1 attended a 12-week FMS intervention for 1 h per week, while group 2 acted as a control. Phase II: group 2 attended a 6-week FMS intervention for 2 h each week (1 h per day on 2 separate days)	Local Children's Treatment Centre	• Peabody Developmental Motor Scales-2 (PDMS-2), considering the total motor quotient score provided as the primary outcome for the study; • Vineland Adaptive Behavior Scales-2 (VABS-2); • Social Skills Improvement System (SSIS); • Behavioral video coding using Social Behavior Codes.	Intervention effectiveness: higher scores on object manipulation and total motor quotient PDMS-2 for EG compared to CG. No significant differences between two groups regarding adaptive behavior (VABS-2) and social skills (SSIS). Intensity effectiveness: time played a role on all PDMS-2 variables but not on adaptive behavior and social skills. No differences were found on outcomes between the two intervention intensities.

Table 1. *Cont.*

Study	Location	Study Type	Participants (N, Groups)	Age Range (Mean ± SD)	Intervention Approach	Intervention Length	Setting	Outcome Measures	Results
Edwards et al. [33]	Australia	Pre- and posttest experimental design	N = 30 (11 ASD, 8m/3f; 19 TD, 10m/9f)	6–10 years (ASD = 7.64 ± 1.12; TD = 7.89 ± 1.45)	Active Video Games (AVGs) like Kinect Sports Season 1, Kinect Sports Season 2, Sports Rivals and Kinect Adventures (TD group only).	ASD = 6 session (45/60 min each one, 3 times per week for 2 weeks) TD = 6 session (50 min each one, once a week for 6 weeks)	For ASD at home, for TD group at school during lunchtime	• Test of Gross Motor Development-3 (TGMD-3) for OC (object control) skill improvement; • Pictorial Scale of Perceived Movement Skill Competence (PMSC) for perceived OC skills.	There was no increase between pre- and postintervention for actual OC skill both in ASD and in TD group. Only in children with ASD, there was an increase of perception of skill.
Felzer-Kim and Lynn Hauck [34]	USA	RCT; pre-/posttest design	N = 14 ASD 2 groups: EG (1f/7m); CG (3f/3m)	4 years (EG = 4.5 ± 0.6; CG = 4.5 ± 0.6)	Fundamental motor skill intervention (FMSI): each session focused on training one of the 13 FMS. Each trial consisted of viewing a tablet-displayed video of the FMS, a picture task card and a verbal instruction. Then participants completed one trial of the skill, with physical prompt and reinforcement.	20 weeks split into two blocks (each block: 15 min per day for 4 days per week) for a total of 20 h	Campus of an ABA EIBI clinic	• Test of Gross Motor Development-3 (TGMD-3) • Anthropometrics (height; weight; BMI) • Assessment at 4 times: baseline, at mid-intervention (10 weeks), post-intervention and follow up. Results presented here are only relative to the first two assessment points.	No significant interaction between time*group was found: 10 h of intervention did not alter FMS in this sample. Time*group interaction approached significance for ball skills and total but more time is necessary. Overall, locomotor skill improvement seems to be lower than ball skills and total skills.

Table 1. *Cont.*

Study	Location	Study Type	Participants (N, Groups)	Age Range (Mean ± SD)	Intervention Approach	Intervention Length	Setting	Outcome Measures	Results
Guest et al. [35]	Canada	Pre-/posttest quasi-experimental design with follow-up 8 weeks later.	15 ASD (13f)	8–11 (9.76 ± 1.00)	Special Olympics FUNdamentals program based on Long Term Athlete Development Model (LTAD) focused on locomotor skills and object control skills. Motor skills were incorporated into active group games and became difficult throughout the week.	Five full-day	School gymnasium	• Test of Gross Motor Development-2 (TGMD-2) • Time-stamped pedometer for physical activity • Physical self-perceptions. The Children and Youth Physical Self-Perception • Profile (CY-PSPP) • Children's Self-Perceptions of Adequacy in and Predilection for Physical • Activity (CSAPPA) • Social Skills Improvement System (SSIS) • Adaptive Behavior Scales, 2nd edition (VABS-2)	Significant improvement after the intervention in Test of Gross Motor Development-2, physical self-perception in CY-PSPP, and social skills domain in VABS
Hassani et al. [36]	IRAN	Pre-/posttest design	30 ASD (10f/20m) 3 groups: EG-training 1 (4f/6m); EG-training 2 (3f/8m); CG (3f/6m)	8–11 years (EG-training 1 = 9.10 ± 0.87; EG-training 2 = 8.55 ± 0.68; CG = 8.70 ± 0.70)	• Training 1- SPARK: this protocol consisted of ten minutes for warm-up and 40 min for MS like balance skills, locomotor skills such • Training 2—I Can Have a Physical Literacy (ICPL): this program focuses on MS like locomotor, balance, kicking, throwing and using of various tools such as visual cards	Sixteen indoor sessions, with two sessions of 60 min each per week performed after school.	Sport arena	• Bruininks-Oseretsky Test of Motor Proficiency (BOT-2)	Both treatments incremented gross MS in comparison with the control group, with a major effect of ICPL group. Interestingly ICPL training also improved fine MS, unlike SPARK training.

Table 1. *Cont.*

Study	Location	Study Type	Participants (N, Groups)	Age Range (Mean ± SD)	Intervention Approach	Intervention Length	Setting	Outcome Measures	Results
Henderson et al. [37]	USA	Pre-/posttest design	37 ASD (35m, 2f)	5–12 (8.4 ± 2.06)	Physical education program targeting the six locomotor and six object control skills of the TGMD-2	40 min twice a week for six months, total: 40 classes	Gymnasium at a center for children with ASD	• Test of Gross Motor Development-2 (TGMD-2)	Significant improvement after intervention for both gross motor skills and object control skills.
Ketcheson et al. [38]	USA	Pre-/post-follow-up test design	N = 20 ASD 2 groups: EG N = 11 (2f/9m); CT N = 9 (3f/6m)	4–6 years (EG = 4.87 ± 0.61; CG = 5.04 ± 0.61)	The intervention implies a weekly rotation between the Test of Gross Motor Development-2 (TGMD-2) subtests: locomotor skills and object control skills, using the eight components from the Classroom Pivotal Response Teaching (CPRT) manual as the framework for delivery of instruction.	4 h per day, 5 days per week for 8 weeks	Gymnasium and outdoor environment	• Test of Gross Motor Development-2 (TGMD-2); • Physical Activity monitor wearable; • Playground Observation of Peer Engagement (POPE), only for EG.	Significant increase in motor proficiency in EG (locomotor skills, object control and gross quotient TGMD-2) compared with CG. A decrease in solitary scale in POPE was found. For all levels of PA, no significant group differences were observed. For joint engagement, parallel play and onlooking, no significant effects of time were found.
Pfeiffer et al. [39]	USA	Pilot study for subsequent randomized controlled trial; pre-/posttest design	N = 37 (21 ASD; 16 PDD-NOS) 2 groups: EG N = 20 (3f/17m); CG N = 17 (2f/15m)	6–12 years (EG = 8.3 ± 2.06; CG = 9.21 ± 2.06)	• Sensory Integration (SI) based treatment: therapeutic activities characterized by enhanced sensation, especially tactile, vestibular, and proprioceptive, active participation, and adaptive interaction; • Fine Motor (FM) intervention: focus on three main activity areas: (1) constructional, (2) drawing and writing, (3) FM crafts.	18 treatment interventions of 45 min each for 6 weeks	Three areas with appropriate equipment for SI; a separate room for FM.	• Sensory Processing Measure (SPM); • Social Responsiveness Scale (SRS); • Quick Neurological Screening Test (QNST–II); • Goal Attainment Scaling (GAS).	Decrease in mannerisms (a subscale of the SRS) in SI group; both groups showed significant improvement on the GAS, although the improvement was significantly greater in SI group. No significant differences between the two groups on sensory processing standardized scores (SPM), other subscales of SRS and the QNST–II.

Table 1. *Cont.*

Study	Location	Study Type	Participants (N, Groups)	Age Range (Mean ± SD)	Intervention Approach	Intervention Length	Setting	Outcome Measures	Results
Srinivasan et al. [5]	USA	RCT; pre-/posttest	N = 36 ASD 3 groups: EG1 N = 12 (2f/10m); EG2 N = 12 (1f/11m); CG N = 12 (1f/11m).	5–12 years (EG1 = 7.88 ± 2.56; EG2 = 7.52 ± 2.22; CG = 7.36 ± 2.02)	In the Rhythm and Robot group, gross motor skills including balance, bilateral coordination, imitation, interpersonal synchrony, and manual dexterity were trained whereas in the comparison group fine motor skills such as symmetrical and asymmetrical grips and pinches, coloring, drawing, cutting, and gluing were promoted. In all three groups, training enhanced social communication skills.	32 sessions (16 expert and 16 parent sessions) of 45 min each one over 8 weeks	Participants' home	• Bruininks-Oseretsky Test of Motor Proficiency (BOT-2); • Training-Specific Test of Imitation/Praxis; • Training-Specific Test of Interpersonal Synchrony.	Improvements in body coordination for both rhythm and robot group. Improvements on the fine manual control composite for the control group. Improvements on Imitation/praxis for all groups and on interpersonal synchrony for the two EGs. No improvement in fine motor performance for both rhythm and robot group. No improvement in the body coordination composite for the control group.

Note: EG = experimental group; CG = control group; ASD = autism spectrum disorder; m = male; f = female; RCT = randomized controlled trial; PDD-NOS = pervasive developmental disorder not otherwise specified; PA = physical activity; FMSI = fundamental motor skill intervention.

3. Results

3.1. Participants: Clinical and Demographic Characteristics

All the participants of the studies included had a diagnosis of either autism or pervasive developmental disorder not otherwise specified, or ASD, except one case that was included in the sample due to his ASD-like characteristics [6]. Diagnoses were confirmed by a family physician, pediatrician, psychiatrist, psychologist, school psychologist or psychological associate according to DSM-IV or DSM-5 criteria in 80% of studies. In the remaining studies, the diagnostic assessment was done by two graduate-level students [38] and by the rehabilitation campus staff [34], respectively.

The age range of the participants in the reviewed studies was 3–12 years. The mean age of the studies included was seven years. The majority of the participants were male (80%).

3.2. Studies Designs

With respect to the experimental designs, 80% of studies were pre-/posttest quasi-experimental or experimental design. Two studies were randomized clinical trials [5,34].

3.3. Types of the Interventions

As for the types of interventions, 70% of studies [6,32,34–38] proposed a program mainly based on FMS that involved teaching and strengthening locomotor and object-control skills—such as balance, running, underhand rolling, galloping, leaping, underhand throwing, jumping, dribbling and bouncing, overhand throwing, catching, hopping, kicking, and striking. Another study focused on whole-body movements [5], but it differed from the above-mentioned works because it used the innovative support of a robot in one of the two experimental conditions. The study implemented rhythmic training as one condition and robot training as another, whereas the control training group worked on activities at a table. More precisely, the rhythm intervention included the following: imitation; praxis tasks—such as action songs with finger play, discrete whole-body movements, a xylophone game; interpersonal synchrony-based joint-action games—such as beat keeping and music making; and movements such as jumping, stomping, marching, clapping, and skipping. The robot training included the same motor activities and interpersonal joint-action games; the only difference was that, instead of having the human trainer of the rhythm intervention, the robot intervention had robots that guided the participants through the activities of the sessions. Whereas the rhythm and robot conditions of the intervention focused mainly on whole-body and gross motor skills, the control condition focused on promoting academic and fine motor skills (by building creations using Play-Doh or LEGO blocks or engaging in arts and craft activities—such as drawing, coloring, and cutting) to resemble the training that autistic children typically receive in special education programs. Pfeiffer et al. [39] also used training in fine motor skills that focused on construction, drawing, writing, and crafts activities and compared it to a sensory integration treatment that was characterized by tactile, vestibular, and proprioceptive experiences and promoted enhanced sensations, adaptive responses from the child, and a good therapist–child relationship. In another innovative study, Edwards et al. [33] used active video games (AVGs) to improve actual and perceived object control in autistic children. For this intervention, the authors used the games Kinect Sports Season 1, Kinect Sports Season 2, Sports Rivals, and Kinect Adventures for Microsoft's Kinect platform, which is associated with Xbox 360 and Xbox One.

3.4. Durations of the Interventions

On average, each training session lasted 45–60 min, apart from the study of Felzer-Kim and Lynn Hauck [34] that implemented sessions of 15 min each. Eighty percent of studies had an intensity of 1–3 h/week [5,6,32–34,36,37,39] and 60% had a total duration of 6–12 weeks [5,6,32,36,38,39]. Other two studies had higher intensity. The first one consisted in 20 h/week, five days/week [38]. The second one was defined as "five full days' program" [35]: it was a camp curriculum inspired by Special Olympics Fundamentals program and training on motor skills was integrated in active group games in order to promote a high level of practice in more naturalistic situations. Lastly, another three studies presented durations which differed from the average: Edwards and colleagues' study [33] lasted two weeks, whereas the studies of Felzer-Kim and Lynn Hauck [34] and of Henderson and colleagues [37] lasted 20 and 24 weeks, respectively. It is worth noting that only Bremer et al.'s study [32] had a crossover design, though the two arms had different intensities: in the first phase, the experimental group received an FMS intervention in one 1 h session per week over 12 weeks (12 sessions), whereas the control group received the same FMS intervention in 2 h sessions per week for six weeks (12 sessions) in the second phase, so that has been possible comparing groups for the efficacy of different intensities.

3.5. Settings

The interventions took place in different settings. Seventy percent of interventions took place at the participants' schools [6,35,38], or at rehabilitation centers [32,34,37,39]. Two studies involved participants' homes [5,33], and one study performed the program at a sports arena [36]. The interventions were implemented by therapists [5,34,39], researchers (either principal investigators or research assistants; [6,32–34,38]), teachers/sport coaches [35,37], or parents [5,33].

3.6. Outcome Measures and Results

Motor outcomes were assessed in the considered studies using different test of motor development: Peabody Developmental Motor Scales-2 (PDMS-2), the Test of Gross Motor Development-2 and -3 (TGMD-2, -3), and the Bruininks–Oseretsky Test of Motor Proficiency-2 (BOT-2). All the considered studies revealed statistically significant differences between the experimental and control groups or a significant within-group improvement in at least one of the outcome measures after the interventions, apart from the study of Felzer-Kim and Lynn Hauck [34], which, nevertheless, presented midpoint results of a larger, ongoing intervention. With respect to the motor domain, results presented here are organized in macroareas for the sake of simplicity. However, it is important to consider that each of the above mentioned motor assessment measures has different underlying assumptions, according to the theoretical perspective from which the test was developed [40]. The results showed significant improvements in:

(a) fine motor abilities, including fine motor precision and fine motor integration, tested by BOT-2 [36];
(b) object control, intended as developmental abilities needed to catch and throw objects as assessed with PDMS-2 [32], and grouping a set of components, such as striking a stationary ball, stationary dribble, kick, catch, overhand throw, and underhand roll as tested by TGMD-2 [6,35,37,38];
(c) locomotor skills, as measured with TGMD-2 [6,35,37,38];
(d) global gross motor skills, as quantified by the overall composite score of TGMD-2 [35], by four subtests of PDMS-2 (reflexes, stationary, locomotion, and object manipulation) [32], and by total motor composite score of BOT-2 [36]);
(e) body coordination, as assessed with BOT-2 [5].

Edwards et al. [33] observed increased self-perceptions of proficiency in object-control skills after AVG training only in the ASD group, even though neither the TGMD-3 scores nor the quantitative measures of the object-control skills showed a significant increase after the intervention across participants (both autistic and typically developing). With respect to the possible effects of the FMS programs on social skills, the results are discordant. Some studies reported positive outcomes in the participants' social abilities, as measured with the Social Skills Improvement System scales [6] and the Solitary Playground Observation of Peer Engagement scale [38]. Guest and colleagues [35] observed an improvement in the social skills domain in the Vineland Adaptive Behavior Scale-2 (VABS-2) but not in Social Skills Improvement System scores. This last result was in line with the study of Bremer et al. [32], although they reported no significant effects on the VABS-2 as well. Comparing fine motor and sensory integration interventions, Pfeiffer et al. [39] reported a significant decrease of mannerisms, as rated by parents with the Social Responsiveness Scale, in the sensory integration group. Lastly, the study that compared the outcomes of rhythm and robot interventions to those of an intervention with activities at a table [5] revealed no intergroup difference in imitation, as assessed with a program-specific test of imitation and praxis.

Interestingly, three of the reviewed studies also collected follow-up measures to evaluate the persistence of the interventions' effects. Bremer and colleagues [32] performed a follow-up assessment six weeks after the end of intervention and observed a retention of motor improvements, as assessed with the Peabody Developmental Motor Scales-2, for one experimental group (the one had the longer treatment but less intense treatment) but not for the other one (the one that had the shorter but more intense treatment). Ketcheson et al. [38] confirmed a significant persistence in the improvements identified with the TGMD-2 scales four weeks after the end of treatment. Last, Guest and colleagues [35] had a follow-up eight weeks later that showed the retention of the improvements identified with TGMD-3.

4. Discussion

The purpose of the present narrative review was twofold. First, we aimed to provide an up-to-date overview of the findings from the studies that have used specific FMS interventions in autistic children over the past 10 years. Second, we intended to explore whether interventions that have specifically addressed FMS also included measures of autistic core characteristics and, in case, to consider the possible effect of FMS interventions on the sociocommunicative domain of autistic children. These issues have been representing emerging fields of interest for autism-related research through the last decade, given the systematic observations of motor deficits in autistic children (e.g., [3,4]) and following the hypothesis that early motor difficulties could significantly interfere with the development of sociocommunicative skills (e.g., [20]).

Although the literature is at a very early stage, some preliminary qualitative suggestions can be drawn from the reviewed studies. With respect to the first goal, the results of the present review are in line and extend those of Colombo-Dugovito and Block [28] and of Case and Yun [29], suggesting that specific FMS interventions could have a beneficial effect on the motor proficiency of autistic children. Indeed, nine of the ten reviewed studies reported significant improvements in a range of fine motor skills, gross motor skills, locomotor activity, and body coordination. Furthermore, the three studies which included follow-up evaluations of motor skills suggested a significant retention of FMS improvements four weeks [38], eight weeks [35], and even five months [32] after the end of the intervention. As highlighted by Colombo-Dugovito and Block [28], long-term maintenance of motor skills over time is a crucial question for FMS interventions, not sufficiently addressed at this stage. On the other hand, it is also important to acknowledge that only two works [5,34] among the reviewed studies were randomized clinical trials. Of these, the study of Felzer-Kim and Lynn Hauck [34] did not report statistically significant FMS improvements after intervention (although the authors reported, at this stage, only the partial interim results of a larger ongoing intervention). Thus, the limited evidence available from randomized clinical trials does not allow at this stage any definitive conclusions. More randomized clinical studies are warranted to replicate the predominantly positive results of the reviewed studies.

As for the systematic review of Colombo-Dagouvito and Block [28] and for the meta-analysis of Case and Yun [29], the studies included in the present work also differed in many methodological aspects, such as sample size, study duration, type and dosage of intervention. These variations limited the possibility to identify a direct link between a specific intervention and different behavioral outcomes. However, it is interesting to consider, also in light of the recent advances of autism-related research, that two of the reviewed studies made additional use of technologies, beyond the mediation of therapists, to implement the rehabilitation programs. In Srinivasan et al.'s study [5], children engaged with two robots: Nao—a humanoid robot used for imitation and synchrony-based games—and Rovio—a mobile robot that involved the children in walking games. The results showed greater improvements in the body-coordination composite score of the BOT-2 and in imitation in participants in the robot-mediated intervention compared to participants who received standard treatments. Edwards et al. [32] tested the effect of sports AVGs on FMS. The results revealed a lack of after-training improvements in the participants' skill scores—as measured with quantitative measures—but a significant improvement in their self-perceptions of their motor skills. Beyond providing those preliminary—though discordant—results [5,32], those innovative studies showed the feasibility of an FMS intervention that includes technology to engage autistic children. The use of the technology—in particular, robots and virtual reality environments—in interventions for autistic individuals has rapidly increased in recent years [41]. Robots offer a unique type of interaction for autistic children, as they are highly attractive and more predictable than human partners [42–44]. Virtual reality can actively support learning by allowing autistic children to systematically manipulate sensory feedback and control the environment, which prevents social anxiety and distress [45–47]. Accordingly, more studies need to explore the feasibility and validity of technology-mediated FMS interventions. Indeed, as stated by Case and Yun [29], the current stage of literature seems to indicate that the use of technology and robots within motor environments is not yet fully understood.

With respect to the secondary aim of the present work, we became concerned about the lack of a clear relationship between the improvement in FMS reported in the reviewed studies and subsequent potential benefits in the socio-communicative domain. Only six out of ten studied included an assessment of social and communication skills [5,6,32,35,38,39]. This was concerning in consideration of the increasing evidence that early difficulties in basic motor skills could significantly hinder the development of sociocommunicative skills and could even have a role in the pathogenesis of the disorder [18,48,49]. Among these studies, five [6,32,35,38,39] reported some positive effects of motor training on social skills and mannerism, as assessed by parents, and on imitation skills and engagement in peer interaction, as rated through direct observation. One study did not find any positive effect [5]. Altogether, these findings are in line with the recent suggestions of Reinders and colleagues [18] which further documented the bidirectional relationship between social functioning and physical activity. However, considering the studies that described positive findings, we observed a number of inconsistencies between the scores of the different measures used to assess social and communicative skills. Thus, the available evidence about the potential effects of FMS interventions on core difficulties of ASD is still insufficient for drawing any conclusion. Beyond the scarcity of studies that measure sociocommunication outcome after FMS and small sample sizes of the reviewed ones, one reason for the results' inconsistency could be directly related to the nature of the assessment process of ASD. Dimensions such as sociocommunication and adaptive functioning are complex to be quantified and the measures currently used for evaluating core features of ASD could be not sensitive enough to detect immediate changes after a specific, brief FMS training. From the ICF-CY perspective, the interconnection between motor skills and social abilities is a complex system rather than a linear causal relationship, as stated also by Reinders and colleagues [18]. This system can develop into a virtuous circle and it is important that future research on FMS intervention in ASD could find the best way to disentangle it. As recently suggested by Ruggeri and colleagues [50], it is crucial to identify the proper way to assess the impact of a body function improvement on the level of activity and participation of an individual as defined by ICF-CY. These dimensions are the actual indicators of the person's adaptation and functioning in its own context. On the other hand, it could also be critical to individuate facilitators and barriers in the child's environment, as factors to keep into consideration when quantifying activity and participation. Lastly, it is important that future studies include an assessment of the participants' quality of life after treatment because it could be a reliable indicator of the intervention's effectiveness [51].

The present review had some limitations. The goal of this work was to provide an up-to-date, narrative overview of recent findings on FMS interventions in autistic children. To do this, we limited our search to the literature published in the last 10 years that involved autistic participants between the ages of 3 and 12. In addition, even though we did not have any a priori language limitations, we considered only papers in English. Furthermore, we did not include single-case studies in consideration of the lack of generalizability of obtained effects. However, this decision could have significantly limited the present findings, because single-case designs formed a pivotal role in early motor skill development work. Given the exploratory nature of the present narrative review, we did not take into account the possible confounding role of co-occurring conditions or intellectual impairments. Some methodological aspects of the reviewed studies also limited our findings. Many interventions had small sample sizes, and only Felzer-Kim and Lynn Hauck [33] reported the effect size of their studies. Although small samples are frequent in daily clinical practice and the rehabilitation of autistic children, this could have limited the power of the studies considered by preventing the detection of even more significant behavioral outcomes. Further, only four studies indicated whether the pre- and posttreatment examiners were blind about the status of interventions. Remarkably, only three of ten interventions had follow-up assessments. Because the retention of learning skills for a significant period of time is a pivotal aspect of any treatment, future research on FMS interventions should systematically include a follow-up visit to evaluate the maintenance of possible behavioral benefits. Finally, future studies should consider exploring the validity of the video-modeling approach for developing FMS due to its demonstrated benefits for other skills such as sociocommunicative and daily living skills [52,53].

Despite these limitations, the present review preliminary suggests that FMS interventions could have some beneficial effects in autistic children, highlighting the importance of including motor skills training within the rehabilitation programs designed for children with this condition. This is particularly relevant because of the well-documented existence of motor impairments in autistic people. More work is needed to ascertain the possible impact of the positive motor outcomes on the participants' social abilities.

Author Contributions: Conceptualization, S.B.C. and A.C.; methodology, S.B.C., C.F., E.G. and A.C.; resources, A.C.; writing—original draft preparation, S.B.C., C.F., E.G. and A.C.; writing—review and editing, G.M.M., M.N. and M.M.; supervision, A.C.; funding acquisition, M.N. and A.C. All authors have read and agreed to the published version of the manuscript.

References

1. American Psychiatric Association. *Diagnostic and Statistical Manual of Mental Disorders (DSM-V-TR)*; American Psychiatric Association: Washington, DC, USA, 2013.
2. Gowen, E.; Hamilton, A. Motor abilities in autism: A review using a computational context. *J. Autism Dev. Disord.* **2013**, *43*, 323–344. [CrossRef]
3. Fournier, K.A.; Hass, C.J.; Naik, S.K.; Lodha, N.; Cauraugh, J.H. Motor coordination in autism spectrum disorders: A synthesis and meta-analysis. *J. Autism Dev. Disord.* **2010**, *40*, 1227–1240. [CrossRef] [PubMed]
4. Bhat, A.N. Is Motor Impairment in Autism Spectrum Disorder Distinct from Developmental Coordination Disorder? A Report from the SPARK Study. *Phys. Ther.* **2020**, *100*, 633–644. [CrossRef]
5. Srinivasan, S.M.; Kaur, M.; Park, I.K.; Gifford, T.D.; Marsh, K.L.; Bhat, A. The Effects of Rhythm and Robotic Interventions on the Imitation/Praxis, Interpersonal Synchrony, and Motor Performance of Children with Autism Spectrum Disorder (ASD): A Pilot Randomized Controlled Trial. *Autism Res. Treat.* **2015**, *2015*, 736516. [CrossRef] [PubMed]
6. Bremer, E.; Crozier, M.; Lloyd, M. A systematic review of the behavioural outcomes following exercise interventions for children and youth with autism spectrum disorder. *Autism* **2016**, *20*, 899–915. [CrossRef] [PubMed]
7. Bryson, S.E.; Zwaigenbaum, L.; Brian, J.; Roberts, W.; Szatmari, P.; Rombough, V.; McDermott, C. A Prospective Case Series of High-risk Infants who Developed Autism. *J. Autism Dev. Disord.* **2007**, *37*, 12–24. [CrossRef] [PubMed]
8. Esposito, G.; Venuti, P. Analysis of Toddlers' Gait after Six Months of Independent Walking to Identify Autism: A Preliminary Study. *Percept. Mot. Ski.* **2008**, *106*, 259–269. [CrossRef] [PubMed]
9. Phagava, H.; Muratori, F.; Einspieler, C.; Maestro, S.; Apicella, F.; Guzzetta, A.; Prechtl, H.F.R.; Cioni, G. General movements in infants with autism spectrum disorders. *Georgian Med. News* **2008**, *156*, 100–105.

10. Esposito, G.; Venuti, P.; Apicella, F.; Muratori, F. Analysis of unsupported gait in toddlers with autism. *Brain Dev.* **2011**, *33*, 367–373. [CrossRef]
11. Sacrey, L.-A.R.; Bennett, J.A.; Zwaigenbaum, L. Early Infant Development and Intervention for Autism Spectrum Disorder. *J. Child Neurol.* **2015**, *30*, 1921–1929. [CrossRef]
12. Iverson, J.M. Early Motor and Communicative Development in Infants with an Older Sibling with Autism Spectrum Disorder. *J. Speech Lang. Heart Res.* **2018**, *61*, 2673–2684. [CrossRef] [PubMed]
13. Landa, R.J.; Gross, A.L.; Stuart, E.A.; Bauman, M. Latent class analysis of early developmental trajectory in baby siblings of children with autism. *J. Child Psychol. Psychiatry* **2012**, *53*, 986–996. [CrossRef]
14. Landa, R.J.; Gross, A.L.; Stuart, E.A.; Faherty, A. Developmental Trajectories in Children with and without Autism Spectrum Disorders: The First 3 Years. *Child Dev.* **2013**, *84*, 429–442. [CrossRef] [PubMed]
15. Lloyd, M.; Macdonald, M.; Lord, C. Motor skills of toddlers with autism spectrum disorders. *Autism* **2013**, *17*, 133–146. [CrossRef] [PubMed]
16. Ulrich, D. *Test of Gross Motor Development*, 2nd ed.; Examiner's Manual: Austin, TX, USA, 2000.
17. Pellegrini, A.D.; Smith, P. Physical Activity Play: The Nature and Function of a Neglected Aspect of Play. *Child Dev.* **1998**, *69*, 577–598. [CrossRef]
18. Reinders, N.J.; Branco, A.; Wright, K.; Fletcher, P.C.; Bryden, P.J. Scoping Review: Physical Activity and Social Functioning in Young People with Autism Spectrum Disorder. *Front. Psychol.* **2019**, *10*, 120. [CrossRef]
19. Esposito, G.; Paşca, S.P. Motor abnormalities as a putative endophenotype for Autism Spectrum Disorders. *Front. Integr. Neurosci.* **2013**, *7*, 43. [CrossRef]
20. Leary, M.R.; Hill, D.A. Moving on: Autism and movement disturbance. *Ment. Retard.* **1996**, *34*, 39–53.
21. Baranek, G.T. Efficacy of Sensory and Motor Interventions for Children with Autism. *J. Autism Dev. Disord.* **2002**, *32*, 397–422. [CrossRef]
22. Scharoun, S.M.; Wright, K.T.; Robertson-Wilson, P.C.F.J.E.; Bryden, P.J. Physical Activity in Individuals with Autism Spectrum Disorders (ASD): A Review. In *Autism: Paradigms, Recent Research and Clinical Applications*; BoD—Books on Demand: Norderstedt, Germany, 2017.
23. Bishop, J.C.; Pangelinan, M.M. Motor skills intervention research of children with disabilities. *Res. Dev. Disabil.* **2018**, *74*, 14–30. [CrossRef]
24. Healy, S.; Nacario, A.; Braithwaite, R.E.; Hopper, C. The effect of physical activity interventions on youth with autism spectrum disorder: A meta-analysis. *Autism Res.* **2018**, *11*, 818–833. [CrossRef] [PubMed]
25. Lang, R.; Koegel, L.K.; Ashbaugh, K.; Regester, A.; Ence, W.; Smith, W. Physical exercise and individuals with autism spectrum disorders: A systematic review. *Res. Autism Spectr. Disord.* **2010**, *4*, 565–576. [CrossRef]
26. Sorensen, C.; Zarrett, N. Benefits of Physical Activity for Adolescents with Autism Spectrum Disorders: A Comprehensive Review. *Rev. J. Autism Dev. Disord.* **2014**, *1*, 344–353. [CrossRef]
27. Sowa, M.; Meulenbroek, R. Effects of physical exercise on Autism Spectrum Disorders: A meta-analysis. *Res. Autism Spectr. Disord.* **2012**, *6*, 46–57. [CrossRef]
28. Colombo-Dougovito, A.M.; Block, M.E. Fundamental Motor Skill Interventions for Children and Adolescents on the Autism Spectrum: A Literature Review. *Rev. J. Autism Dev. Disord.* **2019**, *6*, 159–171. [CrossRef]
29. Case, L.; Yun, J. The Effect of Different Intervention Approaches on Gross Motor Outcomes of Children with Autism Spectrum Disorder: A Meta-Analysis. *Adapt. Phys. Act. Q.* **2019**, *36*, 501–526. [CrossRef]
30. World Health Organization. *International Classification of Functioning, Disability and Health: Children and Youth Version: ICF-CY*; World Health Organization: Geneva, Switzerland, 2007.
31. Mahdi, S.; Albertowski, K.; Almodayfer, O.; Arsenopoulou, V.; Carucci, S.; Dias, J.C.; Khalil, M.; Knüppel, A.; Langmann, A.; Lauritsen, M.B.; et al. An International Clinical Study of Ability and Disability in Autism Spectrum Disorder Using the WHO-ICF Framework. *J. Autism Dev. Disord.* **2018**, *48*, 2148–2163. [CrossRef]
32. Bremer, E.; Balogh, R.; Lloyd, M. Effectiveness of a fundamental motor skill intervention for 4-year-old children with autism spectrum disorder: A pilot study. *Autism* **2014**, *19*, 980–991. [CrossRef]
33. Edwards, J.; Jeffrey, S.; May, T.; Rinehart, N.J.; Barnett, L.M. Does playing a sports active video game improve object control skills of children with autism spectrum disorder? *J. Sport Health Sci.* **2017**, *6*, 17–24. [CrossRef]
34. Felzer-Kim, I.T.; Hauck, J.L. How Much Instructional Time Is Necessary? Mid-intervention Results of Fundamental Movement Skills Training within ABA Early Intervention Centers. *Front. Integr. Neurosci.* **2020**, *14*, 24. [CrossRef]
35. Guest, L.; Balogh, R.; Dogra, S.; Lloyd, M. Examining the Impact of a Multi-Sport Camp for Girls Ages 8–11 with Autism Spectrum Disorder. *Ther. Recreat. J.* **2017**, *51*, 109–126. [CrossRef]

36. Hassani, F.; Shahrbanian, S.; Shahidi, S.H.; Sheikh, M. Playing games can improve physical performance in children with autism. *Int. J. Dev. Disabil.* **2020**, 1–8. [CrossRef]
37. Henderson, H.; Fuller, A.; Noren, S.; Stout, V.M.; Williams, D. The effects of a physical education program on the motor skill performance of children with autism spectrum disorder. *Palaestra* **2016**, *30*, 41–50.
38. Ketcheson, L.; Hauck, J.; Ulrich, D. The effects of an early motor skill intervention on motor skills, levels of physical activity, and socialization in young children with autism spectrum disorder: A pilot study. *Autism* **2017**, *21*, 481–492. [CrossRef]
39. Pfeiffer, B.A.; Koenig, K.; Kinnealey, M.; Sheppard, M.; Henderson, L. Effectiveness of sensory integration interventions in children with autism spectrum disorders: A pilot study. *Am. J. Occup. Ther.* **2011**, *65*, 76–85. [CrossRef]
40. Wiart, L.; Darrah, J. Review of four tests of gross motor development. *Dev. Med. Child Neurol.* **2001**, *43*, 279–285. [CrossRef]
41. Odom, S.L.; Thompson, J.L.; Hedges, S.; Boyd, B.A.; Dykstra, J.R.; Duda, M.A.; Szidon, K.L.; Smith, L.E.; Bord, A. Technology-Aided Interventions and Instruction for Adolescents with Autism Spectrum Disorder. *J. Autism Dev. Disord.* **2015**, *45*, 3805–3819. [CrossRef]
42. Srinivasan, S.M.; Lynch, K.A.; Bubela, D.J.; Gifford, T.D.; Bhat, A.N. Effect of Interactions between a Child and a Robot on the Imitation and Praxis Performance of Typically Devloping Children and a Child with Autism: A Preliminary Study. *Percept. Mot. Ski.* **2013**, *116*, 885–904. [CrossRef]
43. Pennisi, P.; Tonacci, A.; Tartarisco, G.; Billeci, L.; Ruta, L.; Gangemi, S.; Pioggia, G. Autism and social robotics: A systematic review. *Autism Res.* **2016**, *9*, 165–183. [CrossRef]
44. Casellato, C.; Gandolla, M.; Crippa, A.; Pedrocchi, A. Robotic set-up to quantify hand-eye behavior in motor execution and learning of children with autism spectrum disorder. In Proceedings of the 2017 International Conference on Rehabilitation Robotics (ICORR), London, UK, 17–20 July 2017; pp. 953–958.
45. Bellani, M.; Fornasari, L.; Chittaro, L.; Brambilla, P. Virtual reality in autism: State of the art. *Epidemiol. Psychiatr. Sci.* **2011**, *20*, 235–238. [CrossRef]
46. Biffi, E.; Costantini, C.; Ceccarelli, S.B.; Cesareo, A.; Marzocchi, G.M.; Nobile, M.; Molteni, M.; Crippa, A. Gait Pattern and Motor Performance During Discrete Gait Perturbation in Children With Autism Spectrum Disorders. *Front. Psychol.* **2018**, *9*. [CrossRef] [PubMed]
47. Yang, D.Y.-J.; Allen, T.; Abdullahi, S.M.; Pelphrey, K.A.; Volkmar, F.R.; Chapman, S.B. Neural mechanisms of behavioral change in young adults with high-functioning autism receiving virtual reality social cognition training: A pilot study. *Autism Res.* **2018**, *11*, 713–725. [CrossRef] [PubMed]
48. Donnellan, A.M.P.; Hill, D.A.M.; Leary, M.R.M. Rethinking autism: Implications of sensory and movement differences for understanding and support. *Front. Integr. Neurosci.* **2013**, *6*, 124. [CrossRef]
49. Trevarthen, C.; Delafield-Butt, J.T. Autism as a developmental disorder in intentional movement and affective engagement. *Front. Integr. Neurosci.* **2013**, *7*, 49. [CrossRef]
50. Ruggeri, A.; Dancel, A.; Johnson, R.; Sargent, B. The effect of motor and physical activity intervention on motor outcomes of children with autism spectrum disorder: A systematic review. *Autism* **2019**, *24*, 544–568. [CrossRef] [PubMed]
51. Crippa, A.; Tesei, A.; Sangiorgio, F.; Salandi, A.; Trabattoni, S.; Grazioli, S.; Agostoni, C.; Molteni, M.; Nobile, M. Behavioral and cognitive effects of docosahexaenoic acid in drug-naïve children with attention-deficit/hyperactivity disorder: A randomized, placebo-controlled clinical trial. *Eur. Child Adolesc. Psychiatry* **2018**, *28*, 571–583. [CrossRef]
52. Piccin, S.; Crippa, A.; Nobile, M.; Hardan, A.Y.; Brambilla, P. Video modeling for the development of personal hygiene skills in youth with autism spectrum disorder. *Epidemiol. Psychiatr. Sci.* **2017**, *27*, 127–132. [CrossRef]
53. Rosenberg, N.; Schwartz, I.; Davis, N.C.A. Evaluating the Utility of Commercial Videotapes for Teaching Hand Washing to Children with Autism. *Educ. Treat. Child.* **2010**, *33*, 443–455. [CrossRef]

2

Effective Strategies for Managing COVID-19 Emergency Restrictions for Adults with Severe ASD in a Daycare Center in Italy

Natascia Brondino *, Stefano Damiani and Pierluigi Politi

Department of Brain and Behavioral Sciences, University of Pavia, via Bassi 21, 27100 Pavia, Italy; stefano.damiani01@ateneopv.it (S.D.); pierluigi.politi@unipv.it (P.P.)

* Correspondence: natascia.brondino@unipv.it

Abstract: The COVID-19 pandemic has posed a serious challenge for the life and mental health of people with autism spectrum disorder (ASD). COVID-19 sanitary restrictions led to significant changes in the lives of people with ASD, including their routines; similarly, these modifications affected the daily activities of the daycare centers which they attended. The present retrospective study evaluated the impact of COVID-19 restrictions on challenging behaviors in a cohort of people with severe ASD attending a daycare center in Italy at the beginning of the pandemic. During the first two weeks of the pandemic, we did not observe variations in challenging behaviors. This suggests that adaptations used to support these individuals with ASD in adapting to the COVID-19 emergency restrictions were effective for managing their behavior.

Keywords: autism spectrum disorder; COVID-19; challenging behavior

1. Introduction

Autism spectrum disorders (ASDs) are complex neurodevelopmental conditions characterized not only by impairment in socio-emotional reciprocity and communication, but also by restrictive and repetitive patterns of behaviors (RRB) and interests [1]. Until recently, the RRB domain has received little attention compared to the social domain. Several mechanisms may underlie RRB, as they can act as a method of communicating needs or obtaining attention. In addition, RRB may often represent a self-regulatory system to modulate anxiety and the level of activation. While the exact mechanism underlying specific types of RRB may be relevant to guide treatment, the impact of RRB, irrespective of the etiopathogenesis, is particularly relevant in severe ASD with comorbid cognitive impairment: Individuals in this group often present an unpostponable adhesion to routines, rituals, and repetitive behaviors which could significantly impair the quality of life of both ASD subjects and caregivers [2]. Additionally, disruption of routines or, more generally, changes to expectations are usually correlated with a worsening in challenging behaviors [2,3] leading to bouts of self- and other-directed aggressiveness.

The emergence of the COVID-19 pandemic in Italy started in February and is still ongoing. At the beginning of the emergency, the Italian government promulgated several restrictions of increasing severity, starting on 23 February 2020, in order to flatten the curve of contagions. Firstly, the government closed schools, restaurants, malls (on the weekends), swimming pools, and gyms, forbade gatherings (no more than 8 people per room), and recommended social distancing of at least 1 m between each other. It was also recommended to frequently wash hands in order to contain the virus.

It is evident that the COVID-19 emergency restrictions resulted in many relevant changes in the lives of people with ASD and their families. Such a complex situation was extremely difficult to share with service users, especially when learning disabilities were present. Understanding why things were changing, why the sanitary limitations should be scrupulously followed, without losing hope that the emergency would end if everyone cooperates, has been a real challenge for people with developmental disabilities. Additionally, the recommended use of personal protective equipment (PPE) has been controversial among this population. In this paper we focus on a peculiar issue, the impact of COVID-19 restrictions on the routine of daycare centers for adults with ASD and cognitive impairment, which rely on maintaining predictability and an ecologically structured context. The application of governmental restrictions determined significant changes in the activities of the daycare center and a great effort from the healthcare workers to maintain the quality and specificity of services provided to people with ASD. In the end, the difficulties in applying COVID-19 emergency restrictions led to the closure of all daycare centers for people with developmental disabilities one week before total lockdown of the country, which happened on 10 March 2020. These changes may have had the potential to increase distress in our patients and, consequently, challenging behaviors and the need of psychotropic medications [4]. The countermeasures and modifications of daycare center activities were put in place in order to comply to COVID-19 restrictions. In spite of having been dictated by necessity, these restrictions were implemented and inspired by knowledge on management of RRB and problem behaviors. For instance, differential reinforcement of variability was put in place in order to reinforce changes in routine activities or in behavioral responding to ordinary situations. As the spontaneous rate of variability is extremely low in autism, therapists firstly reinforced non-repetitions, moving subsequently to reinforcing of behaviors that were not previously observed.

The aim of the present study is to evaluate the impact of restrictions on challenging behaviors in a sample of individuals with ASD and cognitive impairment attending a daycare center before complete lockdown.

2. Materials and Methods

We conducted a retrospective study evaluating medical charts in a daycare center for adolescents and adults with ASD.

The daycare center "Il Tiglio" is a day center specifically designed for individuals with severe ASD and comorbid cognitive impairment, located in the Lombardy Region, Italy, near a regional nature park. It accommodates 18 individuals with ASD, and the staff is composed of 7 therapists, 1 psychologist, 1 kinesiologist, 2 care assistants, 1 nurse, and 1 consultant psychiatrist. Weekly schedules for each individual are strictly monitored and kept consistent. Planned activities consist of physical activity (water-based activities in a nearby swimming pool once a week, trekking once a week, judo lessons once a week, adaptive physical activity twice a week—both at the daycare center and in a nearby gym), horticultural therapy (once a week), cognitive training for language production and augmentative and alternative communication (AAC) use (every day), occupational therapy (every day), and art therapy (twice a week). The center is open five days a week from 8:00 a.m. to 5:00 p.m.

To comply with COVID-19 emergency restrictions, several adjustments were adopted in order to maintain the best quality of life for individuals with ASD. Specifically, as swimming and physical contact sports were no longer possible to perform, we implemented trekking (which was done every day for at least 1–2 h). Laboratories were split so that no more than 4–5 people were in the same room at the same time. AAC and social stories were implemented in order to provide information about the virus and about specific restrictions (for instance, some of them usually went to malls on the weekends with their parents as part of their routine and, as shops were closed, this could have resulted in potential problem behaviors). All individuals with ASD had already learned how to wash their hands thanks to a behavioral treatment and positive reinforcement; therefore, this routine was increased in frequency and inserted in a visual agenda for each of them. To increase changes in routine behaviors, differential reinforcement of variability was implemented: During the time between the arrival at the day center and the beginning of activities, everyone had a specific routine which could include doing puzzles, drawing, or running in the field outside. Every time the individual with ASD changed his/her arrival routine, a reinforcement (consisting in the possibility to listen to music or watching preferred parts of movies or social reinforcement) was given.

2.1. *Measures*

As general clinical practice, each day care workers filled out the aberrant behavior checklist (ABC) [5] for each individual with ASD. The ABC is a scale empirically designed to measure psychiatric symptoms and problem behaviors in subjects with developmental disabilities. It is composed of 58 items, evaluating 5 domains: Irritability; lethargy/social withdrawal; stereotypic behavior; hyperactivity; and inappropriate speech. Higher scores indicate a higher level of problem behaviors. The ABC is generally completed by the primary caregiver and informants can complete the scale in 10–15 min the first time they fill it in; subsequently it is more rapid, and it is used in our daycare center on a daily basis. The ABC was specifically designed for subjects living in institutions and residential settings, and therefore appeared appropriate for our center.

2.2. *Design*

We retrospectively evaluated the effect of COVID-19 emergency restrictions and daycare center implementation on problem behaviors using our registry. We evaluated changes in ABC total scores between 19 February 2020 (the last day free from restrictions) and 4 March 2020 (two weeks after the full restrictions were applied).

2.3. *Statistical Analysis*

Differences between the two time points were evaluated by means of a paired-sample *t*-test after the normality of data was ascertained. To account for multiple comparison, Bonferroni's correction was applied. IBM SPSS Statistics for Windows, version 23 (IBM Corp., Armonk, NY, USA) was used for all statistical analyses. Two-tailed p-value < 0.06 was regarded as statistically significant.

3. Results

General characteristics of the sample are reported in Table 1. Our sample was composed of 18 young adults, of which 13 are males. All presented severe ASD; four individuals with ASD occasionally showed self-injurious behavior, while seven had severe bouts of aggression. All individuals were diagnosed during childhood. However, each of them was also re-evaluated by a senior psychiatrist with specific expertise in ASD in adulthood, according to the DSM 5 criteria. All individuals were rated as Level 3 of severity (requiring very substantial support). Diagnosis was supported by ADI-R [6] in all cases. ADOS 2 module 4 [7] was also performed in a verbal subject with mild cognitive impairment ($n = 1$). Cognitive impairment was evaluated by means of the Leiter 3 scale and by clinical judgment. Most of the sample subjects received stable psychiatric medications. Antipsychotics were administered to more than half of the sample (aripiprazole $n = 4$, risperidone $n = 1$, olanzapine $n = 1$, levomepromazine $n = 2$, clotiapine $n = 4$), while mood stabilizers were less frequently prescribed (valproate $n = 3$, gabapentin $n = 2$).

Overall, no significant differences in ABC scores were observed between the two time-points (24.83 ± 11.75 vs. 22.33 ± 12.18, $t = -1.07$, $p = 0.29$). In order to evaluate the generalizability of our findings, our baseline data (t0: 19 February 2020) were compared to the same period of the previous two years (19 February 2019 and 19 February 2018). No significant differences were found (2019 $t = -0.09$, $p = 0.43$; 2018 $t = 0.03$, $p = 0.46$). Additionally, we compared the 19 February 2020 ABC scores with ABC scores of the previous five days to determine if our baseline data were consistent with the previous week: No significant differences were found (p not significant for all the comparisons). We evaluated differences in ABC subscales: No statistically significant differences were found (see Table S1).

Table 1. General characteristics of the sample.

Variables	Mean ± SD or % (*n*)
Age	22.72 ± 4.75
Gender, male	72.2% (13)
DSM 5 level of severity	
Level 3	100% (18)
Verbal behavior	
Verbal	44.4% (8)
Minimally verbal	27.8% (5)
Non-verbal	27.8% (5)
Cognitive impairment	
Mild	5.6% (1)
Moderate	50% (9)
Severe	22.2% (4)
Profound	22.2% (4)
Medications	83.3% (15)
Antipsychotics	66.6% (12)
Mood stabilizers	27.8% (5)

4. Discussion

Our retrospective study did not show a significant change in problem behaviors in our individuals with ASD after COVID-19 restrictions were initiated. We could cautiously hypothesize that the preventive countermeasures we adopted were effective in reducing distress in individuals with ASD. This could be due to several reasons: First, maintaining the same amount of physical activity (increasing trekking over water-based activity or group contact sports) could have played a key role in controlling problem behaviors in individuals with ASD: It is well-known that physical activity can reduce aggressiveness, stereotyped and self-injurious behaviors, as well as self-stimulation [8]. Walking/trekking could be feasible for almost everyone, irrespective of physical fitness. It is cost-effective and it could be performed outdoors (both in winter and in summer), minimizing the risk of contagion connected with closed indoor environments, while enhancing health benefits connected with exposure to nature. Second, splitting the initial laboratory group into smaller groups (4 individuals or less) could have helped in maintaining the daily schedule without major deviations, allowing for social distancing at the same time. Third, smaller groups increased the ratio between therapists and individuals with ASD, leading to more personalized interventions. Fourth, reducing transfers to other facilities (like swimming pools, gyms) may have led to a lower sensory stimulation and therefore lower anxiety. Finally, AAC as well as social stories could have been a powerful instrument for changing the visual agenda of each individual and teaching new routines (i.e., wearing a facial mask) or enhancing already learned skills (i.e., hand washing).

Our retrospective study presents several limitations: The sample size is small, even if compatible with the average sample size of a daycare center. Another limitation is the lack of a control group. Unfortunately, the absence of a control group is inevitable, as sanitary restrictions were mandatory for all centers in the country. In the future we could design retrospective studies in order to evaluate time fluctuation in problem behaviors before and after the pandemic of COVID-19. In fact, the impact of COVID-19 after the lockdown and closure of daycare centers is yet to be determined. During lockdown, online interventions were implemented as suggested in [9] in order to help parents in caring for their loved ones, who did not have access to their daycare center. Additionally, the need for emergency home interventions, as well as dose-increases of psychiatric medications, were required in several cases. Another potential limitation regarded the care workers who filled the ABC and performed the intervention: Our implementation was designed by the coordinator of the daycare center who did not care directly for individuals with ASD and did not complete the ABC scores. All care workers were blind to the subsequent evaluation leading to the present study. Finally, the time interval chosen for the evaluation of the impact of COVID-19 restriction could have been longer in order to detect changes in behaviors; however, the ABC is designed to detect changes in a shorter period of time and the worsening of problem behaviors usually appear more rapidly than improvement.

At present, the COVID-19 emergency is still representing a massive psychological overload for all individuals, among whom we should not forget individuals with ASD, with their peculiar needs. Despite its limitations, our study may provide some important suggestions for the re-opening phase and the return to a "new normal": Daycare centers in Italy are still struggling to find a compromise between minimizing the risk of contagion and providing adequate care for individuals with severe ASD. In fact, the long-term lack of specific interventions in this group may have resulted in loss of skills, reduction of positive behaviors, and increases in maladaptive behaviors. Additionally, returning to the same level of activity as before the COVID-19 pandemic may not be easy. For instance, changes due to restrictions and the general disempowerment of the public care services may slow the return to normality for individuals with ASD. On the other hand, the slow progress may be supportive for individuals with ASD, allowing them to re-adapt to a full daycare schedule at a slower pace.

Author Contributions: Conceptualization, formal analysis, and investigation, N.B.; writing—review and editing, N.B., S.D., P.P. All authors have read and agreed to the published version of the manuscript.

Acknowledgments: We thank all health workers and therapists from our day center for their precious efforts. We thank all people with ASD and their families for their strength during this unprecedented crisis.

References

1. American Psychiatric Association. *Diagnostic and Statistical Manual of Mental Disorders*, 5th ed.; American Psychiatric Association: Washington, DC, USA, 2013.
2. Gomot, M.; Wicker, B. A challenging, unpredictable world for people with Autism Spectrum Disorder. *Int. J. Psychophysiol.* **2012**, *83*, 240–247. [CrossRef] [PubMed]
3. Bull, L.E.; Oliver, C.; Callaghan, E.; Woodcock, K.A.; Oliver, C. Increased Exposure to Rigid Routines can Lead to Increased Challenging Behavior Following Changes to Those Routines. *J. Autism Dev. Disord.* **2015**, *45*, 1569–1578. [CrossRef] [PubMed]
4. Courtenay, K.; Perera, B. COVID-19 and people with intellectual disability: Impacts of a pandemic. *Ir. J. Psychol. Med.* **2020**, 1–21. [CrossRef] [PubMed]
5. Aman, M. *Aberrant Behavior Checklist Manual*; Slosson Publications: East Aurora, NY, USA, 1986.
6. Lord, C.; Rutter, M.; Le Couteur, A. Autism Diagnostic Interview-Revised: A revised version of a diagnostic interview for caregivers of individuals with possible pervasive developmental disorders. *J. Autism Dev. Disord.* **1994**, *24*, 659–685. [CrossRef] [PubMed]
7. Lord, C.; Rutter, M.; DiLavore, P.C.; Risi, S.; Gotham, K.; Bishop, S.L. *Autism Diagnostic Observation Schedule*, 2nd ed.; Western Psychological Services: Torrance, CA, USA, 2012.
8. Srinivasan, S.M.; Pescatello, L.S.; Bhat, A.N. Current Perspectives on Physical Activity and Exercise Recommendations for Children and Adolescents with Autism Spectrum Disorders. *Phys. Ther.* **2014**, *94*, 875–889. [CrossRef] [PubMed]
9. Narzisi, A. Handle the Autism Spectrum Condition during Coronavirus (COVID-19) Stay at Home Period: Ten Tips for Helping Parents and Caregivers of Young Children. *Brain Sci.* **2020**, *10*, 207. [CrossRef] [PubMed]

3

Autism in Adulthood: Clinical and Demographic Characteristics of a Cohort of Five Hundred Persons with Autism Analyzed by a Novel Multistep Network Model

Roberto Keller [1], Silvia Chieregato [1], Stefania Bari [1], Romina Castaldo [1], Filippo Rutto [2], Annalisa Chiocchetti [3] and Umberto Dianzani [3,*]

1 Adult Autism Center, Mental Health Department, Health Unit ASL Città di Torino, 10138 Turin, Italy; rokel2003@libero.it (R.K.); chieregato.s@gmail.com (S.C.); stefania.bari@aslcittaditorino.it (S.B.); romina.castaldo@aslcittaditorino.it (R.C.)

2 Department of Psychology, University of Turin, 10100 Turin, Italy; filipporutto@gmail.com

3 Department of Health Sciences, Universita' del Piemonte Orientale, 28100 Novara, Italy; annalisa.chiocchetti@med.uniupo.it

* Correspondence: umberto.dianzani@med.uniupo.it

Abstract: Autism spectrum disorder (ASD) is a neurodevelopmental disorder characterized by deficits in communication and relational skills, associated with repetitive verbal and motor behaviors, restricted patterns of interest, need for a predictable and stable environment, and hypo- or hypersensitivity to sensory inputs. Due to the challenging diagnosis and the paucity of specific interventions, persons with autism (PWA) reaching the adult age often display a severe functional regression. In this scenario, the Regional Center for Autism in Adulthood in Turin seeks to develop a personalized rehabilitation and enablement program for PWA who received a diagnosis of autism in childhood/adolescence or for individuals with suspected adulthood ASD. This program is based on a Multistep Network Model involving PWA, family members, social workers, teachers, and clinicians. Our initial analysis of 500 PWA shows that delayed autism diagnosis and a lack of specific interventions at a young age are largely responsible for the creation of a "lost generation" of adults with ASD, now in dire need of effective psychosocial interventions. As PWA often present with psychopathological co-occurrences or challenging behaviors associated with lack of adequate communication and relational skills, interventions for such individuals should be mainly aimed to improve their self-reliance and social attitude. In particular, preparing PWA for employment, whenever possible, should be regarded as an essential part of the intervention program given the social value of work. Overall, our findings indicate that the development of public centers specialized in assisting and treating PWA can improve the accuracy of ASD diagnosis in adulthood and foster specific habilitative interventions aimed to improve the quality of life of both PWA and their families.

Keywords: autism spectrum disorder; adulthood; diagnosis; intervention

1. Introduction

Autism spectrum disorder (ASD) is a neurodevelopmental disorder with a prevalence ranging from 1% in the general population to ~1.9% in specific population groups [1,2]. ASD is typically characterized by deficits in socio-emotional reciprocity, impaired verbal and non-verbal communication skills, and an inability to develop and maintain adequate social relationships with peers, often associated with repetitive verbal and motor behaviors, restricted patterns of interest, need for a predictable and stable environment, and hypo- or hypersensitivity to sensory inputs. The onset of clinical symptoms occurs during the early years of life [1].

A large number of persons with autism (PWA) also meet criteria for co-occurring psychiatric conditions at a significantly higher rate compared to non-autistic populations [3,4]. Consequently, the socio-economic impact of ASD has become an increasing concern for public healthcare systems, which are now oriented toward an early diagnosis and intervention to improve ASD patient management while reducing the costs related to ASD care. However, there is paucity of guidelines for the diagnosis and management of PWA in adulthood. This aspect is of particular relevance in light of the detrimental effect that functional regression in these patients can exert on their psychosocial and work wellbeing. Indeed, PWA and their families are exposed to a "lifetime of difficult transitions" due to a limited number of service providers and resources alongside stringent and restrictive program funding criteria. As a result, there is widespread concern about the ability of some individuals with ASD to establish meaningful lives in adulthood [5].

Adolescents and adults with ASD are largely an underserved population. In a survey in Poland, the vast majority of parents of young PWA complained about the lack of assistance and support for PWA (93.5%) and the many difficulties in accessing the available services (82.7%) [6]. Indeed, low-income families and those living outside large cities have to deal more frequently with barriers to service access. This is particularly important in light of the fact that adult ASD patients need targeted psychosocial support to meet increasing social demands related to independent living, personal relationships, and successful employment. It is estimated that no more than 20% of adults with ASD have good or very good outcomes in these areas [7–9].

Studies from the US and Canada have reported that the number of outpatient services used by PWA decreases from childhood to adulthood and continues to decrease until late adulthood, while the use of medications and in-patient services increases [7–9], with very limited social integration, poor job prospects and high rates of mental health problems [10]. Indeed, the ensuing social isolation and unemployment further contribute to high rates of depression, anxiety, and other psychiatric disorders [11,12].

Qualitative studies have shown that transition outcomes among ASD patients are negatively affected by several factors such as poor person-environment fit, uncertainty about the roles of parents and the lack of comprehensive or integrated services. These findings have also revealed the aspects of familial, organizational and policy contexts that may be targeted for interventions. In this regard, stakeholders emphasize that supports should be individualized and focused on the changing aspects of the young adult's social and physical environment rather than on behavioral changes [12–14]. Thus, there is widespread consensus that policymakers should address economic, regional, and age-related inequities in access to services among PWA [6,15]. Furthermore, adult-oriented healthcare services should work directly with PWA and their support networks to facilitate successful engagement with services and enable adults to manage their mental health needs [16].

To address these challenges, in 2009, a specialized Regional Center for Autism in Adulthood has been established at the department of Mental Health in Turin. The aim of the Center is to follow up PWA who received a diagnosis of autism in childhood/adolescence or individuals with suspected adulthood ASD, with the aim of improving the accuracy of ASD diagnosis and identifying a personalized rehabilitation and enablement program and this study describes the clinical and demographic characteristics of the participants in the survey outcomes of the diagnostic path.

2. Materials and Methods

Participants were adults referred to the Regional Center for Autism in Adulthood in Turin by general psychiatrists across the Piedmont region—the region has an adult population of 3,600,000 inhabitants—due to ASD or suspected autism, with the aim of designing a personalized intervention plan. Each participant was evaluated using a model developed by the center, namely the Multistep Network Model. This tool consists of a multistep diagnostic and evaluation assessment that combines diagnostic evaluation with a personalized life project devised by a team of psychiatrists and psychologists of the center, the PWA and their family members, social workers, members of the educational and vocational services (i.e., teachers and job trainers) and employment agencies (i.e., job-brokers). The main goal of the approach is to set up a network of integrated services to serve the needs of PWA in the Piedmont region.

All clinical evaluations, testing and treatments were conducted in the center upon written informed consent signed directly by the participants or their guardians, authorizing data collection and processing as well. Not requiring a specific authorization from the Ethics Committee during the course of daily clinical activity, all clinical and research activities described in this study were authorized by the Medical Director of the Local Health Unit DSM To2 in 2009. Such authorization was subsequently confirmed by the Director of the Local Health Unit Città di Torino in 2019. The research was also authorized by the Institutional Board of the Piedmont Public Health Agency by means of two Regional Council Resolutions (DGR) No. 22-7178, 3 March 2014 and No. 88-8997, 16 May 2019.

Multistep Network Model:

Step required for diagnosis and individualized project:

(a) First meeting with the parents: (i) careful collection of life history, (ii) all interventions carried out, (iii) needs and expectations—the direct meeting with the subject to be evaluated takes place only in the case of suspected high functioning PWA;
(b) Meeting with the PWA or individual with suspected autism: (i) welcoming and creating a human supporting relationship, (ii) clinical evaluation of the symptoms presented, (iii) clinical evaluation of any psychopathological symptom in co-occurrence, (iv) objective neurological evaluation, and (v) clinical evaluation of cognitive functioning;
(c) Assessment of the intellectual profile by using appropriate tests for the level of clinical functioning (Wechsler Adult Intelligence Scale IV edition; Raven; Leiter) and, if necessary, neuropsychological testing [17–19];
(d) Evaluation tests for suspected autism. The choice of tests to be performed is based on the clinical functioning and cognitive profile—Autism Diagnostic Interview-revised (ADIr) for all; Ritvo Autism and Asperger's Diagnostic Scale-revised (RAADS) or Autism Diagnostic Observation Shedule-2nd Edition (ADOS 2) or Childhood Autism Rating Scale, Second Edition (CARS2-ST)depending on the level of functioning defined according to the clinical level and cognitive profile) [20–23];
(e) Evaluation of the adaptive functioning profile (e.g., Vineland/Adaptive Behavior Assessment System – Second Edition) [24,25]; Test evaluation of psychopathological functioning—if there is a clinical suspicion—with scales for intellectual functioning evaluation (Structured Clinical Interview, Minnesota Multiphasic Personality Inventory-2, Systematic Psychopathological Assessment for persons with Intellectual and Developmental Disabilities - General screening, Rorschach) [26];
(f) Medical evaluation focused on general health and specific conditions of neurodevelopment, including neuroimaging, genetic, metabolic evaluation, Electroencephalogram (EEG), depending on the individual's situation;
(g) Network meetings between operators of the Center for Autism in Adulthood and the patient's family members. When possible, there should also be meetings between the PWA and the operators involved in the clinical management of the patient, i.e., the child neuropsychiatrist, and if in transition age, social workers, school teachers, job trainers, and educators. In addition, all personal information and that related to the life context should be collected. These meetings should ultimately lead to the creation of a life project through the integration of clinical information and that derived from the care network, above all taking into account the preferences and wishes of the PWA and their families;

(h) The activation of a habilitative path provided directly by the center and/or presentation of the project to a Medico-Legal/Social Health Assessment Committee for evaluation of its appropriateness and allocation of the budget for the projects that will be delivered by accredited private healthcare centers.

3. Results

We performed a descriptive analysis of our cohort consisting of 500 participants. The sample of participants is described in Table 1.

Table 1. Description of the participants.

Sample	*n*	%	
Male	388	77.5	
Female	112	22.5	
Age	M = 31.7	SD = 10.7	Range: 18–82 years
Place of Residence	*n*	%	
Turin	262	52.9	
(Rural) Canavese Area	34	6.9	
Nichelino/Moncalieri and Carmagnola (Periurban areas)	55	11.1	
Medico-Legal Assessment of Professional Competences	*n*	%	
	302	65.4	
In Details			
46% civil disability level (CD)		2.1	
67% civil disability level (CD)		0.9	
75% civil disability level (CD)		7.1	

According to DSM5 criteria, ASD levels diagnosed in adult patients were as follows: level 1 in 39% ($n = 193$), level 2 in 27.1% ($n = 135$), level 3 in 18% ($n = 90$), neurodevelopmental disorder NOS not otherwise specified in 3% ($n = 15$), personality disorder (no autism) in 2.8% ($n = 14$) and psychosis (no autism) in 2.2% ($n = 11$). Additionally, 67.2% ($n = 336$) of participants displayed psychiatric and neurological co-occurrences, as shown in Tables 2 and 3 [1].

Intellectual disability was found in 53% ($n = 265$), which was mild in 35.8% of cases ($n = 95$), moderate in 34% ($n = 90$), and severe in 30.2% ($n = 80$), while 11% of the sample ($n = 55$) had a speech disorder.

Concerning therapies, 42% ($n = 207$) received psychotropic drugs and 14% anti-epileptic drugs ($n = 69$). Relevant medical comorbidities were epilepsy (16.6%; $n = 82$), allergies (8.4%; $n = 39$), and gastrointestinal complaints (21.3%; $n = 99$).

Table 2. Psychopathological and neurological co-occurrence in the study participants with autism.

Co-Occurrence	*n*	%
personality disorders	79	24%
challenging/problem behaviour	66	19.6%
Attention Deficit Hyperactivity Disorder (ADHD)	32	9.5%
epilepsy	23	6.8%
obsessive compulsive disorder	23	6.8%
major depressive disorder	21	6.3%
psychosis	19	5.7%
bipolar disorder	8	2.4%
anxiety disorder	6	1.8%

Table 2. *Cont.*

Co-Occurrence	*n*	%
specific learning disorder.	6	1.8%
tic disorder	6	1.8%
oppositional defiant disorder	5	1.5%
deafness	5	1.5%
Down syndrome	5	1.5%
social phobia	5	1.5%
Tourette syndrome	5	1.5%
eating disorder	4	1.2%
blindness	3	0.9%
movement disorder	3	0.9%
substance abuse disorder	3	0.9%
dyspraxia	2	0.6%
language disorder	2	0.6%
X fragile syndrome	2	0.6%
tuberous sclerosis	1	0.3%
Turner syndrome	1	0.3%
XXY syndrome	1	0.3%

Table 3. Personality disorders in the study participants with autism.

Personality Disorders Co-Occurrence in ASD (PD)	*n*	%
paranoid PD	19	5.7%
borderline PD	18	5.4%
personality disorder not otherwise specified	7	2.1%
schizotypical PD	7	2.1%
avoidant PD	6	1.8%
obsessive PD	6	1.8%
narcissistic PD	5	1.5%
schizoid PD	5	1.5%
aggressive passive PD	3	0.9%
histrionic PD	2	0.6%
dependant PD	1	0.3%
Total	**79**	**24%**

The parent's age at the time of birth ranged 17–48 years (mean ± SD: 30.72 ± 5.4) for the mothers, and 18–60 (mean ± SD: 34.21 ± 6.3) for the fathers; 15.5% of mothers experienced complications during pregnancy ($n = 72$) (Table 4). Moreover, 27.8% of the mothers had complications during delivery ($n = 130$).

Table 4. Prenatal and perinatal complications.

Complications	*n*	%	Note
During pregnancy	72	15.5	including 5.8% risk of abortion ($n = 27$)
Gestosis	12	2.5	
Twin pregnancy	7	1.5	
Depressive disorder	3	0.6	
Diabetes	1	0.2	
Thyroid disorder	1	0.2	
Toxoplasmosis	2	0.4	

With regard to neurodevelopmental stages, language skills on average appeared at 25.1 months (SD 19.94, range 6–180 months), and walking skills were achieved at 15.7 months (SD 6.3, range 8–60 months).

Table 5 reports the ages of PWA when the first symptoms became worrisome for the PWA's family. The average age of symptom recognition was 41.6 months (SD 54.3), with the most delayed recognition occurring at the age of 50 years.

Table 5. Age of PWA when the first ASD symptoms worried the family.

The Age When Symptoms Worried the Family	% PWA
6 Months	3.8
12 Months	11.3
18 Months	19.5
24 Months	42.6
30 Months	47.2
42 Months	80.3
48 Months	84.3
60 Months	97.8
72 Months	93.8

Symptoms at onset ranged from social-relational isolation in 38.1% of cases (n = 166), delay in the appearance of language in 25.7% (n = 112), inadequate relationship with peers in 15.1% (n = 66), stereotypies in 8.7% (n = 38), loss of language in 5.5% (n = 24), subjective experience of diversity (in individuals with high functioning autism in 3.2% (n = 14), and motor-coordination difficulties in 3.2% (n = 14).

First diagnosis of autism was made at the average age of 10.8 years (SD 12.3), but the diagnosis was revised in 49.4% of cases (n = 246), with an average of 26.5 years (SD 10.5). In 24.8% of cases (n = 123) the diagnosis was changed. Of note, during childhood only a small proportion of participants received medical assessment: 26.1% (n = 126) were evaluated with MRI (Magnetic resonance imaging) brain scan, 13.5% (n = 65) with cranial computed axial tomography, 16.8 (n = 81) with genetic analysis, and 16.2 (n = 78) with metabolic screening.

The types of intervention administered during childhood and adolescence are described in Table 6. No specific interventions were prescribed in 23.4% of cases (n = 117).

Table 6. Intervention administered during childhood and adolescence.

Intervention Type	n	%
Psychotherapy	143	29.9
Speech Therapy	200	42.1
Educational Interventions	117	24.6
Psychomotor skills Treatment	183	38.6
Delacato method	4	0.8
Portage method	13	2.7

The analysis of schooling revealed that 6 out of 500 participants had an elementary education degree without completing middle school (1.2%), whereas 137 subjects (27.4%) finished middle school but did not pursue secondary education. Fifty-seven participants (11.4%) started a secondary education program but dropped out. Thus, 38.8% of participants earned a middle school diploma, while 52.2% of them completed successfully a secondary school program. Only 4.4% of subjects enrolled in a post-secondary program. Notably, 70.1% of participants (n = 337) needed additional teaching support at school, and 31.7% of subjects were bullied (n = 146). Unfortunately, bullying occurred in almost all situations related to Level 1 Autism (DSM5 criteria, ASD Requiring support) [1].

Neuropsychiatric disorders were reported in 53% of family members—familiarity up to III degree—n = 265. The most frequent disorders were depression (21%; n = 56), autism (16.2%; n = 43), psychosis (14%; n = 37), intellectual disability (13.2%; n = 35), dementia (5.3%; n = 14), Parkinson's disease (4.2%; n = 11), specific learning disability (3.8%; n = 10), drug abuse 3.8% (n = 10) and Down syndrome (3.4%; n = 9).

After the evaluation, 189 out of 500 people (37.8%) received interventions directly delivered by the Center for Autism in Adulthood. Specifically, study participants were administered social skills interventions (37%; $n = 69$), cognitive-behavioral psychotherapy (26%; $n = 50$), expressiveness through visual art (9%; $n = 17$), parenting support group programs (9%; $n = 17$), body-vocal expressiveness (7%; $n = 13$), cognitive enhancement (Feuerstein method) (6%; $n = 12$), neuropsychological rehabilitation (3%; $n = 6$), habilitative intervention with animals (2%; $n = 3$) and musical expressiveness (1%; $n = 2$).

Indirect interventions were provided by accredited private centers as follows: 50.4% of patients ($n = 143$) attended a daily center, 31% ($n = 88$) underwent psychoeducational intervention and 7.4% ($n = 21$) followed a work-oriented training path. From the psychiatric standpoint, 6% ($n = 17$) were assisted by a mental health center due to the presence of severe psychopathological co-occurrences.

Finally, analyzing the housing situation, most PWA still lived with their families, with only 8.1% ($n = 40$) living in a residential structure offering around-the-clock assistance. Only 1% ($n = 5$) shared an apartment with few other disabled people, whereas 11% ($n = 54$) lived independently.

4. Discussion

Autism in adulthood is a complex condition that should be distinguished from ASD in childhood and adolescence, especially for high level of co-occurrence and specific needs [9,27,28]. In this regard, there are several reasons that prompted us to develop a new integrated assessment models, termed the Multistep Network Model, able to improve the accuracy of autism diagnosis in adults, a growing concern for public healthcare systems, with the ultimate goal of developing personalized rehabilitation and enablement programs. Firstly, there are a number of undiagnosed PWA, especially among women with ASD, that need to be detected [29–31]. Secondly, the transition to adulthood needs to be built by means of a habilitative program specific for adult (personalized life-project). Thirdly, we can clinically observe high rates of psychiatric comorbidities, requiring specific treatment. Finally, as caregivers become older, there is a marked decrease in family resources, which translates into a higher level of concern for the future of PWA [9,27].

Currently, PWA can follow a wide range of pathways during their transition to adulthood, such as attending college, entering the labor force, and achieving a degree of independent living. Less cognitively able individuals, on the other hand, may be eligible for state benefits or may access supported employment programs. Thus, clinicians need to familiarize with the unique needs of adults with ASD to be able to administer specific supports and interventions to these patients to ensure their best possible social integration in the community [28].

Among high functioning PWA, our study shows that these patients, especially women, are more likely to experience feeling different. This awareness begins at an early age—"I have always felt different from others" is a frequently used expression among adults with autism—, suggesting a more internalized autism syndrome [31]. Considering the possibility to decrease the risk of ASD, we can observe that prenatal, perinatal, and postnatal factors have been associated with autism [32]. The average age of parents at the time of birth, which could have increased the genetic risk in our sample, is in line with that of the general population—i.e., 30 years for the mother and 34 years for the father in PWA vs. 30.6 years for the mother and 34.2 years for the father in the general population. The role of pregnancy and delivery with respect to the pathogenesis appears to be relevant as 15.5% of PWA had complicated pregnancies and 27.8% had complications at delivery. These elements may therefore have been decisive for the development of hypoxic brain injuries with neuronal damages. According to a meta-analysis by Wang et al., during the prenatal period, the factors associated with autism risk were maternal and paternal age > 35 years, mother's and father's ethnicity (i.e., Caucasian and Asian), gestational hypertension, gestational diabetes, maternal and paternal education level (i.e., college graduation), threatened abortion and antepartum hemorrhage. During the perinatal period, the factors associated with autism risk were caesarian delivery, gestational age ≤ 36 weeks, parity ≥ 4, spontaneous labor, induced labor, no labor, breech presentation, preeclampsia, and fetal distress. During the postnatal period, the factors associated with autism risk were low birth weight, postpartum hemorrhage, male gender, and brain anomaly [32]. Thus, health policy programs aimed at improving pre-natal and peri-natal conditions, including environmental factors that may preclude a safe pregnancy, may play an important role in decreasing ASD incidence.

Therefore, the implementation of training programs for teachers of nursery and primary schools together with routine screening by pediatricians is highly recommended to improve ASD diagnosis at an early age.

It is also important to point out that language problems in ASD patients are not only related to onset delay but also to semantic deficits: children with ASD produced more global, rather than local, semantic features in their definitions than children with normal language. An over-reliance on global, rather than local, features in children with ASD may reflect in-depth deficits of word knowledge [33].

The need for a diagnostic revaluation over time during the transition to adulthood is clearly documented by the fact that almost half of the PWA (49.4%) required revision of diagnosis—mostly due to changes of the clinical picture, nosographic reference parameters, cognitive functioning, psychopathological co-occurrences, etc.—, which was modified in 24.8% of PWA. The revaluation is particularly useful in detecting not only modifications of cognitive level of functioning but also the co-occurrence of a psychiatric disorder. Consistently, ASD diagnoses were confirmed in all PWA if made previously. Co-occurring mental health conditions are more prevalent in ASD than in the general population and a careful assessment of mental health is an essential component of care for all PWA and should be integrated into clinical practice with specific assessment [34–38]. Given that the co-occurrence of personality disorders is typically related to young adulthood but not childhood, the assessment should also explore personality in ASD. Psychopathological co-occurrences were present in 67.2% of the sample. They included the high prevalence of challenging behavior/problem behavior, which constitutes one of the main issues in family management. For this purpose, adequate diagnostic methods should be implemented, aimed primarily at excluding organic causes, with a subsequent activation of response programs, possibly behavioral, limiting psychopharmacological intervention as much as possible. The co-occurrence of Attention Deficit Hyperactivity Disorder (ADHD, 9.5%) is likely underestimated because of difficulty in making ADHD diagnosis in severe cases of autism and the presence of overlapping symptoms in both disorders. However, these should be regarded as continuous neurodevelopmental disorders instead of categorical comorbidities [39]. Generally, obsessive-compulsive disorders (OCD, 6.8%) are difficult to diagnose in PWA due to the presence of autistic rituals that, even though they may seem obsessive, represent an epiphenomenon of the primary disorder [40]. Major depressive disorder (6.3%) has a lower prevalence in our sample than what reported in the literature. This may be due to an increase in diagnostic performance that allowed us to rule out major depression forms belonging to other nosographic pictures. However, we did find a co-occurrence of psychosis and paranoid personality disorder in 5.7% of cases: psychotic forms were represented by both reactive forms with paranoid characteristics, often activated by triggers, such as bullyism and mobbing, and an interpretative deficit of reality, alongside rare forms of the schizophrenic type [41]. The latter is probably ascribable to a common genetic load with respect to the neurodevelopmental disorder, which expresses a first autistic phase and a second phase of schizophrenic deterioration [42–44]. Concerning the structuring of a paranoid personality disorder, we identified several situations fueling a chronic persecutory reading of the external human environment, such as the inability to read the surrounding environment, experience of exclusion, distress originated from bullying and mobbing episodes, and problems with social and work insertion. Use of psychotropic drugs is reported in 42% of the sample, and antiepileptics in 14%, with the presence of comorbidity for epilepsy in 16.6% of subjects. In a large cohort in the UK, approximately one-third of the identified cohort was prescribed at least one psychotropic medication and the prevalence increased 3.3-fold from 0.109 per 100 persons in 2009 to 0.355 per 100 persons [45]. More recently, a survey carried out in the Emilia Romagna region in Italy showed that 74.5% of adults with ASD were being treated with a psychotropic drug, with 41.6% of the participants using an antipsychotic drug, 15.19% two or more antipsychotic drugs and 5.17% a long-acting antipsychotic drug [46]. This large increase in psychotropic drug use among PWA calls for strict monitoring of drug prescriptions by healthcare services. Regarding psychopathology, in particular neurodevelopmental disorders, we found that a high proportion (53%) of family members of PWA (up to the third degree) report neuropsychiatric disorders, with one family member out of five expressing a depressive disorder, partly reactive to chronic stress and partly independent. With respect to neurodevelopmental disorders, 16% of family members display forms of autism—therefore, at least 16 folds more frequently than the general population—, while others show intellectual disability, specific learning disorders, Down syndrome, ADHD, stereotypes, with a cumulative percentage for neurodevelopment disorders reaching 39.6%. These data underscore the importance of providing genetic-metabolic evaluation also in adulthood PWA, since a transgenerational transmission of the vulnerability to neurodevelopmental disorders is highly likely [47,48]. Psychotic disorders were reported in 14% of family members, raising a question with respect to common biological/genetic factors shared between autism spectrum disorders and psychotic disorders [49]. Another interesting observation regards the high incidence of neurodegenerative disorders, such as dementia—Parkinson's disease is present in 4.2% of the participants—which warrants further in-depth studies aimed to elucidate its potential pathogenetic ramifications.

At the somatic level, the most evident finding is the lower prevalence of allergies in PWA compared to that of the general population (8.4% vs. ~30%, respectively), indicating substantial differences in the immune system response to allergens between the two groups. Furthermore, we recorded gastrointestinal disorders in 21.3% of cases, which are often the basis of behavioral disturbances, especially in seriously affected PWA experiencing difficulties in communicating. Medical evaluation plays a key role in ASD, especially during the developmental age, since it can rule out secondary forms of autism that could be specifically treated. Metabolic and genetic evaluations were observed in 6.2% and 16.8% of PWA, respectively. This may be the result of both the scarce attention paid to the organic aspects of autism and the attribution of autism pathogenesis to poor parental relationships in that historical period [50]. Consequently, even the interventions that PWA received during their developmental age often lacked specificity. In our sample, we recorded the following types of intervention: psychotherapy—rarely cognitive behavioral and more frequently psychoanalytic—in 29.9% of cases, speech therapy in 41.1%, psychomotor skill training in 38.6%, and non-specific psychoeducational interventions in 24.6%. In this context, speech and psychomotor therapies represented for years the standardized response offered by public services to autistic or disabled children.

A relevant finding in this study is represented by the high levels of co-occurrence of intellectual disability in more than a half of PWA. This percentage is seemingly higher than that recently reported by a study on childhood autism. If confirmed, this co-occurrence may be ascribable to the inadequate treatments received by PWA during their childhood, which presumably contributed to worsen their cognitive and functional abilities. This percentage may also indicate a general improvement in the diagnosis of high functioning forms of autism, which probably went undiagnosed in the past, especially in females [3].

Bullying is a trigger for psychopathology in adolescence and adulthood. One-third (31.7%) of PWA reported to have been bullied. This occurred to almost all PWA with the best functioning level (ASD level 1, DSM 5), which appear to be at high risk of psycho-traumatic events especially if undiagnosed. In keeping with other studies, autism severity did not significantly predict bullying-related behaviors. Consequently, secondary psychopathological comorbidity (e.g., anxiety, depression, etc.) may arise. Furthermore, this represents the level of autism in which the diagnostic evaluation is often lacking, as shown by those children mistaken for "little geniuses", whose socio-relational deficit is seen as a side effect of academic excellence [51,52]. With regard to the severity of the ASD, since we are a public health assessment center, our PWA sample included all forms of autism, with 39% of minor forms, i.e., ASD level 1 DSM 5, including previously defined forms of high-functioning autism and Asperger's syndrome—27.1% of level 2 autism (DSM 5), and 18% of severe forms of autism (ASD level 3 DSM 5) [1]. A small proportion included participants with neurodevelopmental disorders but with no sufficient information to categorize them in a specific subtype. The lack of information was due, for example, to the old age of PWA, which made it extremely difficult to gain information about his/her childhood from the parents. The few participants that did not meet the diagnostic criteria for autism were found to match those related to personality disorders (2.8%) and psychosis (2.2%), thus providing a bona fide of the assessment carried out by the Regional Center for Autism in Adulthood and the screening made by the general psychiatrists. Our organization is in fact based on a screening performed by a general psychiatrist to detect relevant psychiatric disorders before sending the patients to the Center. This triage policy has allowed us to save a considerable amount of clinical resources that would have otherwise been used to assess non-ASD patients. Our results also point out that the transition from childhood to adulthood in PWA represents a critical step for their families, whose management requires an overall re-evaluation, both at the clinical and project level. Consistently, the clinical evaluation model applied in this study is based not just on a process of progressive and deeper evaluation of the PWA or people with suspected autism and their families, but also on the available network of services that may be involved to formulate a personalized life-project (multistep network model). This personalized project is based on the information collected during the evaluation and may be delivered by the Regional Center for Autism in Adulthood or accredited private social centers. In the latter case, the project would need to be evaluated by a commission composed by members of the Health Public Agency and Public Social Services of the municipality of residence, which verifies the validity of the project and allocates a budget to support the external project. The interventions delivered directly by the Regional Center for Autism in Adulthood included paths for the improvement of social skills (social skill training) and cognitive-behavioral therapy. Group or individual support paths were activated for parents upon request. Another area of intervention concerned the improvement of expression and relationship skills, with activities aimed at improving communication through figurative arts—particularly for people with verbal communication impairment—and vocal-bodily expressive activities, using theater-based techniques. A subgroup of PWA, with medium-level autistic functioning and cognitive difficulties, followed a path specifically dedicated to improving cognitive functioning through structured learning techniques, such as Feuerstein or neuropsychological rehabilitation. Only in specific and selected exceptional situations, in the presence of severe communication deficits, interventions included the support of animals (three participants included) or communication through music (two participants). By analyzing the interventions provided indirectly by the accredited private partner, most PWA attended an educational activity covering most of the day and organized in groups (daily center; 50.4%), offering educational qualification courses and laboratories. In 31% of the participants, the activated path was instead based on individual educational activities or performed in small groups, delivering projects targeting specific skills of individual autonomy. For 7.4% of PWA, pre-work paths were activated: these consisted of training courses dedicated to PWA, lasting one to two years, made up of a theoretical part delivered in a classroom and a practical part via company internships. This type of path was dedicated to PWA with real job placement opportunities, thus needing less support, and managed by a professional school with teachers trained on autism and specifically dedicated to this type of course. In addition, the courses were prescribed provided that the PWA had followed a clinical path to improve and test his/her social skills and abilities to avoid stress deriving from real-life failures. Indeed, a person with autism needs to be adequately trained before being exposed to potentially harmful situations [53,54]. A small percentage of PWA (6%) was also followed by a Mental Health Center because these patients displayed a level of severity of the psychopathological comorbidity requiring a second parallel intervention dedicated to its management. This usually took place in outpatient clinics or day hospitals, but it may sometime require admission to the psychiatric ward. With regard to the housing situation, most PWA lived with their family of origin, whereas a small fraction (8%) lived in a community for disabled people with round-the-clock assistance. Only 1% of PWA resided in an apartment with other disabled people, while 11% achieved enough skills to live an independent life. Based on our findings, we propose a model for ASD in adulthood where public health and private services are integrated, and where the Regional Center for Autism in Adulthood plays a key role in managing PWA patients thanks to a joint effort between the private and public health sectors.

5. Conclusions

Among the several important aspects highlighted by our PWA analysis, the late age of autism diagnosis and the non-specific interventions provided during the developmental age are of particular relevance. As the current adult generation of PWA is apparently "lost", it urgently needs a very complex intervention program [34]. Indeed, these are PWA who have often developed other psychopathological co-occurrences or manifest a challenging behavior/problem behavior usually associated with lack of adequate communication and relational skills, never taught to them during their educational path.

Altogether, our findings call for a radical improvement of the accuracy and timeliness of the diagnosis of ASD in adulthood and the implementation of specific interventions in favor of this often-neglected population. Such interventions should address as much as possible the autonomy and communication dimensions, especially in those individuals that did not received any specific interventions during their developmental age. Also, preparing PWA for employment is of the utmost importance, if possible, given the social value of work. In conclusion, the implementation of public centers dedicated to PWA represents a viable solution for improving the diagnosis of ASD in adulthood and ameliorating the quality of life of PWA and their families through specific habilitative interventions. These interventions, in accordance with the Autism Guidelines, should merge multidisciplinary professional teams, formed by psychiatrists, clinical psychologists, educators and rehabilitation therapists, with other entities, such as social services, schools and job agencies, all forming a network capable of assisting autistic children and adults along their social integration path. In light of hypotheses regarding developmental and environmental influences on the course of ASD, future studies should compare the changes in symptoms and presentation across adulthood to those occurring in childhood.

Author Contributions: Conceptualization R.K.; methodology R.K.; software F.R., S.C.; validation, U.D., A.C.; formal analysis F.R.; investigation, S.B., R.C., R.K.; resources, A.C., U.D.; data curation, F.R., R.K., S.C.; writing—original draft preparation, R.K.; writing—review and editing, R.K., U.D., A.C., S.B.; visualization, R.K., F.R.; supervision, U.D., A.C.; project administration R.K., U.D., A.C.; funding acquisition, U.D., A.C. All authors have read and agreed to the published version of the manuscript.

References

1. American Psychiatric Association. *Author Diagnostic and Statistical Manual of Mental Disorders*, 5th ed.; American Psychiatric Association: Arlington, VA, USA, 2013.
2. Maenner, M.J.; Shaw, K.A.; Baio, J. Prevalence of Autism Spectrum Disorder Among Children Aged 8 Years—Autism and Developmental Disabilities Monitoring Network, 11 Sites, United States, 2016. *MMWR Surveill. Summ.* **2020**, *69*, 1–12. [CrossRef]
3. Bertelli, M.O. Autism spectrum disorder and intellectual disability. In *Psychopathology in Adolescents and Adults with Autism Spectrum Disorders*; Keller, R., Ed.; Springer Nature Switzerland: Basel, Switzerland, 2019; pp. 111–130.
4. Simonoff, E.; Jones, C.R.G.; Baird, G.; Pickles, A.; Happé, F.; Charman, T. The persistence and stability of psychiatric problems in adolescents with autism spectrum disorders: Stability of psychiatric symptoms in autism spectrum disorders. *J. Child Psychol. Psychiatry* **2013**, *54*, 186–194. [CrossRef]
5. Milen, M.T.; Nicholas, D.B. Examining transitions from youth to adult services for young persons with autism. *Soc. Work Health Care* **2017**, *56*, 636–648. [CrossRef]
6. Płatos, M.; Pisula, E. Service use, unmet needs, and barriers to services among adolescents and young adults with autism spectrum disorder in Poland. *BMC Health Serv. Res.* **2019**, *19*, 587. [CrossRef]
7. Eaves, L.C.; Ho, H.H. Young adult outcome of autism spectrum disorders. *J. Autism Dev. Disord.* **2008**, *38*, 739–747. [CrossRef]
8. Howlin, P.; Moss, P.; Savage, S.; Rutter, M. Social outcomes in mid- to later adulthood among individuals diagnosed with autism and average nonverbal IQ as children. *J. Am. Acad. Child Adolesc. Psychiatry* **2013**, *52*, 572–581. [CrossRef]
9. Howlin, P.; Magiati, I. Autism spectrum disorder: Outcomes in adulthood. *Curr. Opin. Psychiatry* **2017**, *30*, 69–76. [CrossRef]

10. Lugnegård, T.; Hallerbäck, M.U.; Gillberg, C. Psychiatric comorbidity in young adults with a clinical diagnosis of Asperger syndrome. *Res. Dev. Disabil.* **2011**, *32*, 1910–1917. [CrossRef]
11. Hofvander, B.; Delorme, R.; Chaste, P.; Nydén, A.; Wentz, E.; Ståhlberg, O.; Herbrecht, E.; Stopin, A.; Anckarsäter, H.; Gillberg, C.; et al. Psychiatric and psychosocial problems in adults with normal-intelligence autism spectrum disorders. *BMC Psychiatry* **2009**, *9*, 1–9. [CrossRef]
12. Anderson, K.A.; Sosnowy, C.; Kuo, A.A.; Shattuck, P.T. Transition of Individuals With Autism to Adulthood: A Review of Qualitative Studies. *Pediatrics* **2018**, *141*, S318–S327. [CrossRef]
13. Cidav, Z.; Lawer, L.; Marcus, S.C.; Mandell, D.S. Age-Related Variation in Health Service Use and Associated Expenditures Among Children with Autism. *J. Autism Dev. Disord.* **2013**, *43*, 924–931. [CrossRef] [PubMed]
14. Turcotte, P.; Mathew, M.; Shea, L.L.; Brusilovskiy, E.; Nonnemacher, S.L. Service needs across the lifespan for individuals with autism. *J. Autism Dev. Disord.* **2016**, *46*, 2480–2489. [CrossRef] [PubMed]
15. Lord, C.; Elsabbagh, M.; Baird, G.; Veenstra-Vanderweele, J. Autism spectrum disorder. *Lancet* **2018**, *392*, 508–520. [CrossRef]
16. King, C.; Merrick, H.; Le Couteur, A. How should we support young people with ASD and mental health problems as they navigate the transition to adult life including access to adult healthcare services. *Epidemiol. Psychiatr. Sci.* **2020**, *29*, e90. [CrossRef]
17. Wechsler, D. *Wechsler Adult Intelligence Scale-Fourth Edition (WAIS-IV)*; NCS Pearson: San Antonio, TX, USA, 2008.
18. Raven, J.C. Standardization of progressive matrices, 1938. *Br. J. Med. Psychol.* **1941**, *19*, 137–150. [CrossRef]
19. Roid, G.H.; Miller, L.J. *Leiter International Performance Scale-Revised (Leiter-R)*; Stoelting: Wood Dale, IL, USA, 1997.
20. Rutter, M.; Le Couteur, A.; Lord, C. *ADI-R. Autism Diagnostic Interview Revised. Manual*; Western Psychological Services: Los Angeles, CA, USA, 2003.
21. Ritvo, R.A.; Ritvo, E.R.; Guthrie, N.; Ritvo, M.J.; Hufnagel, D.H.; McMahon, W.; Tonge, B.J.; Mataix-Cols, D.; Jassi, A.; Attwood, T.; et al. The Ritvo Autism Asperger Diagnostic Scale-Revised (RAADS-R): A Scale to Assist the Diagnosis of Autism Spectrum Disorder in Adults: An International Validation Study. *J. Autism Dev. Disord.* **2011**, *41*, 1076–1089. [CrossRef]
22. Lord, C.; Rutter, M.; DiLavore, P.C.; Risi, S.; Gotham, K.; Bishop, S. *Autism Diagnostic Observation Schedule: ADOS*; Western Psychological Services: Los Angeles, CA, USA, 2002.
23. Schopler, E.; Reichler, R.J.; DeVellis, R.F.; Daly, K. Toward objective classification of childhood autism: Childhood Autism Rating Scale (CARS). *J. Autism Dev. Disord.* **1980**, *10*, 91–103. [CrossRef]
24. Sparrow, S.S.; Cicchetti, D.V.; Balla, D.A. The Vineland Adaptive Behavior Scales. *Major Psychol. Assess. Instrum.* **1989**, *2*, 199–231.
25. Harrison, P.; Oakland, T. *ABAS-3: Adaptive Behavior Assessment System*; Western Psychological Services: Los Angeles, CA, USA, 2015.
26. Keller, R.; Bari, S.; Fratianni, B.; Piedimonte, A.; Freilone, F. Response to Rorschach test in autism spectrum disorders in adulthood: A pilot study. *J. Psychopathol.* **2018**, *24*, 224–229.
27. Bennett, A.E.; Miller, J.S.; Stollon, N.; Prasad, R.; Blum, N.J. Autism Spectrum Disorder and Transition-Aged Youth. *Curr. Psychiatry Rep.* **2018**, *20*, 103. [CrossRef]
28. Van Schalkwyk, G.I.; Volkmar, F.R. Autism Spectrum Disorders: Challenges and Opportunities for Transition to Adulthood. *Child Adolesc. Psychiatr. Clin. N. Am.* **2017**, *26*, 329–339. [CrossRef]
29. Baron-Cohen, S. Empathizing, systemizing, and the extreme male brain theory of autism. *Prog. Brain Res.* **2010**, *186*, 167–175.
30. Rynkiewicz, A.; Janas-Kozik, M.; Słopień, A. Girls and women with autism. *Psychiatr. Pol.* **2019**, *53*, 737–752. [CrossRef]
31. Lai, M.-C.; Lombardo, M.V.; Auyeung, B.; Chakrabarti, B.; Baron-Cohen, S. Sex/gender differences and autism: Setting the scene for future research. *J. Am. Acad. Child Adolesc. Psychiatry* **2015**, *54*, 11–24. [CrossRef]
32. Wang, C.; Geng, H.; Liu, W.; Zhang, G. Prenatal, perinatal, and postnatal factors associated with autism. *Medicine* **2017**, *96*, e6696. [CrossRef]
33. Gladfelter, A.; Barron, K.L. How Children with Autism Spectrum Disorder, Developmental Language Disorder, and Typical Language Learn to Produce Global and Local Semantic Features. *Brain Sci.* **2020**, *10*, 231. [CrossRef]

34. Lai, M.-C.; Baron-Cohen, S. Identifying the lost generation of adults with autism spectrum conditions. *Lancet Psychiatry* **2015**, *2*, 1013–1027. [CrossRef]
35. Valkanova, V.; Rhodes, F.; Allan, C.L. Diagnosis and management of autism in adults. *Practitioner* **2013**, *257*, 13–16.
36. Luciano, C.; Keller, R. Misdiagnosis of High Function Autism Spectrum Disorders in Adults: An Italian Case Series. *Autism Open Access* **2014**, *4*, 2. [CrossRef]
37. Sistema Italiano Linee Guida. *Linea Guida n. 21, Il Trattamento dei Disturbi Dello Spettro Autistico nei Bambini e Negli Adolescent*; Sistema Italiano Linee Guida: Roma, Italy, 2011.
38. Lai, M.C.; Kassee, C.; Besney, R.; Bonato, S.; Hull, L.; Mandy, W.; Szatmari, P.; Ameis, S.H. Prevalence of co-occurring mental health diagnoses in the autism population: A systematic review and meta-analysis. *Lancet Psychiatry* **2019**, *6*, 819–829. [CrossRef]
39. Craig, F.; Lamanna, A.L.; Margari, F.; Matera, E.; Simone, M.; Margari, L. Overlap Between Autism Spectrum Disorders and Attention Deficit Hyperactivity Disorder: Searching for Distinctive/Common Clinical Features. *Autism Res.* **2015**, *8*, 328–337. [CrossRef] [PubMed]
40. Postorino, V.; Kerns, C.M.; Vivanti, G.; Bradshaw, J.; Siracusano, M.; Mazzone, L. Anxiety Disorders and Obsessive-Compulsive Disorder in Individuals with Autism Spectrum Disorder. *Curr. Psychiatry Rep.* **2017**, *19*, 92. [CrossRef] [PubMed]
41. Keller, R.; Bari, S. Psychosis and Autism Spectrum Disorder. In *Psychopathology in Adolescents and Adults with Autism Spectrum Disorders*; Keller, R., Ed.; Springer Nature Switzerland: Basel, Switzerland, 2019; pp. 51–65.
42. Cauda, F.; Nani, A.; Costa, T.; Palermo, S.; Tatu, K.; Manuello, J.; Duca, S.; Fox, P.T.; Keller, R. The morphometric co-atrophy networking of schizophrenia, autistic and obsessive spectrum disorders. *Hum. Brain Mapp.* **2018**, *39*, 1898–1928. [CrossRef] [PubMed]
43. Cauda, F.; Costa, T.; Nani, A.; Fava, L.; Palermo, S.; Bianco, F.; Duca, S.; Tatu, K.; Keller, R. Are schizophrenia, autistic, and obsessive spectrum disorders dissociable on the basis of neuroimaging morphological findings?: A voxel-based meta-analysis. *Autism Res.* **2017**, *10*, 1079–1095. [CrossRef]
44. Keller, R.; Piedimonte, A.; Bianco, F.; Bari, S.; Cauda, F. Diagnostic Characteristics of Psychosis and Autism Spectrum Disorder in Adolescence and Adulthood. A Case Series. *Autism Open Access* **2015**, *6*, 159. [CrossRef]
45. Alfageh, B.H.; Man, K.K.C.; Besag, F.M.C.; Alhawassi, T.M.; Wong, I.C.K.; Brauer, R. Psychotropic Medication Prescribing for Neuropsychiatric Comorbidities in Individuals Diagnosed with Autism Spectrum Disorder (ASD) in the UK. *J. Autism Dev. Disord.* **2020**, *50*, 625–633. [CrossRef]
46. Di Sarro, R.; Varrucciu, N.; Di Santantonio, A.; Fioritti, A. Indagine sulle terapie farmacologiche e sulle diagnosi psichiatriche nei pazienti con diagnosi di disturbo dello spettro autistico registrati nei sistemi informativi territoriali. *G. Ital. Disturbi Neurosviluppo* **2020**, *5*, 100–107.
47. Keller, R.; Basta, R.; Salerno, L.; Elia, M. Autism, epilepsy, and synaptopathies: A not rare association. *Neurol. Sci.* **2017**, *38*, 1353–1361. [CrossRef]
48. Biamino, E.; Di Gregorio, E.; Belligni, E.F.; Keller, R.; Riberi, E.; Gandione, M.; Calcia, A.; Mancini, C.; Giorgio, E.; Cavalieri, S.; et al. A novel 3q29 deletion associated with autism, intellectual disability, psychiatric disorders, and obesity. *Am. J. Med Genet. Part B Neuropsychiatr. Genet.* **2016**, *171*, 290–299. [CrossRef]
49. Bertelli, M.; Merli, M.P.; Bradley, E.; Keller, R.; Varrucciu, N.; Del Furia, C.; Panocchia, N. The diagnostic boundary between autism spectrum disorder, intellectual developmental disorder and schizophrenia spectrum disorders. *Adv. Ment. Heal. Intellect. Disabil.* **2015**, *9*, 243–264. [CrossRef]
50. Deslauriers, N. The Empty Fortress: Infantile Autism and the Birth of the Self. *Arch. Gen. Psychiatry* **1967**, *17*, 510–512. [CrossRef]
51. Fink, E.; Olthof, T.; Goossens, F.; Van Der Meijden, S.; Begeer, S. Bullying-related behaviour in adolescents with autism: Links with autism severity and emotional and behavioural problems. *Autism* **2018**, *22*, 684–692. [CrossRef]
52. Smith, I.C.; White, S.W. Socio-emotional determinants of depressive symptoms in adolescents and adults with autism spectrum disorder: A systematic review. *Autism* **2020**, *24*, 995–1010. [CrossRef] [PubMed]
53. Bari, S.; Tisci, R.; Burlando, R.; Keller, R. Caring for Autistic Adults. A Qualitative Analysis Under the Lens of Capability Approach. *Ital. Sociol. Rev.* **2018**, *8*, 243–264.
54. Gorenstein, M.; Giserman-Kiss, I.; Feldman, E.; Isenstein, E.L.; Donnelly, L.; Wang, A.T.; Foss-Feig, J. Brief Report: A Job-Based Social Skills Program (JOBSS) for Adults with Autism Spectrum Disorder: A Pilot Randomized Controlled Trial. *J. Autism Dev. Disord.* **2020**, 1–8. [CrossRef] [PubMed]

4

Whole Exome Sequencing in Females with Autism Implicates Novel and Candidate Genes

Merlin G. Butler [1,*], Syed K. Rafi [1,†], Waheeda Hossain [1,†], Dietrich A. Stephan [2,†] and Ann M. Manzardo [1,†]

1 Departments of Psychiatry & Behavioral Sciences, University of Kansas Medical Center, 3901 Rainbow Boulevard, MS 4015, Kansas City, KS 66160, USA; rafigene@yahoo.com (S.K.R.); whossain@kumc.edu (W.H.); amanzardo@kumc.edu (A.M.M.)

2 Department of Human Genetics, University of Pittsburgh, Pittsburgh, PA 15260, USA; dstephan@pitt.edu

* Author to whom correspondence should be addressed; mbutler4@kumc.edu

† These authors contributed equally to this work.

Academic Editor: William Chi-shing Cho

Abstract: Classical autism or autistic disorder belongs to a group of genetically heterogeneous conditions known as Autism Spectrum Disorders (ASD). Heritability is estimated as high as 90% for ASD with a recently reported compilation of 629 clinically relevant candidate and known genes. We chose to undertake a descriptive next generation whole exome sequencing case study of 30 well-characterized Caucasian females with autism (average age, 7.7 ± 2.6 years; age range, 5 to 16 years) from multiplex families. Genomic DNA was used for whole exome sequencing via paired-end next generation sequencing approach and X chromosome inactivation status. The list of putative disease causing genes was developed from primary selection criteria using machine learning-derived classification score and other predictive parameters (GERP2, PolyPhen2, and SIFT). We narrowed the variant list to 10 to 20 genes and screened for biological significance including neural development, function and known neurological disorders. Seventy-eight genes identified met selection criteria ranging from 1 to 9 filtered variants per female. Five females presented with functional variants of X-linked genes (*IL1RAPL1, PIR, GABRQ, GPRASP2, SYTL4*) with cadherin, protocadherin and ankyrin repeat gene families most commonly altered (e.g., *CDH6, FAT2, PCDH8, CTNNA3, ANKRD11*). Other genes related to neurogenesis and neuronal migration (e.g., *SEMA3F, MIDN*), were also identified.

Keywords: whole exome sequencing; females; autism spectrum disorder; genetic variants; X chromosome inactivation

1. Introduction

Classical autism or autistic disorder belongs to a group of genetically heterogeneous conditions known as Autism Spectrum Disorders (ASD) characterized by three clinical features: (1) marked impairments in verbal and non-verbal communication; (2) impairments in social interactions; and (3) restricted repetitive behaviors and interests [1,2]. Additional findings include lack of eye contact, tactile defensiveness and sleep disturbances with diagnosis validation at a young age requiring test instruments such as Autism Diagnostic Observation Schedule (ADOS) and Autism Diagnostic Interview-Revised (ADI-R) [3–5]. Latest estimates reveal that ASD affects about 1 of every 68 children by 8 years of age with a predominant male to female (4:1) ratio [6]. This occurrence rate is higher than that of epilepsy or Down syndrome. Congenital anomalies, intellectual disability, growth retardation and/or seizures can occur in a subset of children presenting with features related to autism. Regression of skills is observed in about 30% of cases with ASD and about 60% show intellectual disabilities [7,8].

Small or large head size is seen in about 30% of affected children with ASD with extreme macrocephaly associated with mutation of the *PTEN* tumor suppressor gene [9]. Heritability studies to identify the contribution of genetic factors in autism have shown an estimate as high as 90%. Recognized single gene conditions such as fragile X syndrome, Rett syndrome or tuberous sclerosis account for less than 20% of all cases with ASD [10].

Standard routine chromosome studies in individuals with ASD have shown abnormalities of over one dozen chromosomes. Various cytogenetic findings are reported including deletions, duplications, translocations and inversions often involving the chromosome 15q11-q13 region or the 22q11.2 band [10,11]. More advanced chromosome microarray studies are more powerful in finding cytogenetic abnormalities than routine chromosome studies. High resolution microarrays have detected recurrent small submicroscopic deletions or duplications in individuals with ASD indicating the presence of hundreds of candidate and/or known ASD genes localized to each human chromosome. In addition, there are numerous submicroscopic copy number changes, more often of the deletion type, seen in greater than 20% of patients with ASD using microarray analysis [11]. Many of these chromosome abnormalities contain genes playing a causative role in ASD. In a recent review of genetic linkage data, candidate genes and genome-wide association studies along with further advances in genetic technology including high resolution DNA microarray and next generation sequencing have led to a compilation of 629 clinically relevant candidate and known genes for ASD [12].

Given the fact that females with ASD are historically understudied, we performed whole exome sequencing of well-characterized females with classical autism from multiplex families in the search for existing or potentially new candidate genes for autism. We utilized a cohort of affected females recruited by the Autism Genetic Research Exchange (AGRE), a gene bank housing data and biospecimens from over 2000 families (www.AGRE.autismspeaks.org). Most families had two or more affected children with autism. Identification of causative mutations (e.g., serotonin-related gene mutations and disturbed biology) could be important to guide selection of treatment options and medication use as well as to manage medical co-morbidities such as seizures, developmental regression (e.g., *MECP2* gene) or for cancer (e.g., *PTEN* gene). A cursory autism data base search revealed a large body of publications, particularly since 2008, linking autism to a wide range of genetic and environmental factors found only 3 (0.48%) clinically relevant ASD genes to be located on the Y chromosome while 68 (10.81%) clinically relevant ASD genes were recognized on the X-chromosome [12].

The preponderance of males with ASD may be attributable to the single X chromosome in males depriving the normal allelic pair of genes due to the XY sex chromosome constitution. Hence, sex chromosomes illustrate the most obvious genetic difference between men and women. All female mammals have two X chromosomes and achieve a balanced X chromosome gene expression with males by inactivating one of their X chromosomes, a process known as X chromosome inactivation (XCI) [13]. This process occurs randomly and very early in embryonic development. Once an X chromosome is "selected" for inactivation within a cell, then the same X chromosome remains inactivated in each subsequent daughter cell. Therefore, females have a mixture of cells with random expression of genes on a single X chromosome. Occasionally, XCI represents a nonrandom pattern or high skewness which is usually defined by at least 80% preferential inactivation of one of the two X chromosomes [14,15]. Skewed XCI appears to play a role in the increased incidence and presentation of diseases in females with known X-linked gene involvement such as Rett syndrome [16], X-linked intellectual disability [14], X-linked adrenoleukodystrophy [17] and possibly autism [15]. Skewed XCI may also reflect an early disruption in the developing embryo causing cell death followed by a small number of dividing cells repopulating the embryo [18–20]. XCI can be measured by using the androgen receptor (*AR*) gene located at chromosome Xq13 which contains a highly polymorphic CAG repeat region and normally inactivated on one of the X chromosomes in females. The *AR* gene is used most often to determine the XCI status [21,22]. Disorders with an imbalance in the number of males versus females affected as in autism become a likely condition to study XCI and its impact on X-linked genes in females. We suspect additional autosomal and/or sex chromosome based ASD gene(s) that either overwhelms the protective normal alleles of the second X chromosome among females, or preferentially silences them due to a plausible skewed X chromosome inactivation among neural cell lineages. Therefore, the whole exome sequence of females with ASD from multiplex families having more than one family member affected was analyzed in our study with next generation sequencing and bioinformatics with a novel machine-learning classification engine applied to identify the contributing ASD genes and the proportion of disease contributing alleles from the X chromosomes versus autosomes. The inactivation status of the two X chromosomes was determined to identify significant deviation from randomness, taking into consideration whether the X chromosome gene is known to escape inactivation, or known to act as a dominant gene.

2. Results

Whole exome sequencing from DNA of 30 females with autism spectrum disorders from AGRE identified between 100 and 300 genes showing genomic variants of novel or candidate genes for autism per subject with an initial classification score >0.5. To further narrow the list of putative disease causing genes, we increased the level of selection criteria by adding cutoff levels for other predictive parameters (GERP2, PolyPhen2 and SIFT) and specifically increased the classification score from >0.5 to a more stringent score of >0.7. For example, the initial list of genes and genomic variants for Subject HI2898 consisted of 245 genes when using a classification score >0.5 alone and then reduced to 22 genes when the cutoff levels of other predictive parameters (GERP2, PolyPhen2 and SIFT) were included at the chosen final selection criteria level. Finally, the classification score was raised to >0.7 to generate the master list of 14 genes. For the 30 females with autism, the number of genes identified based on the final selection criteria ranged between 8 to 23 genes with 10 females presenting with an X-linked gene in the list of selected genes meeting the final selection criteria. The putative candidate genes and genomic variants were then subjected to further screening for biological significance and relevance for neural development, function and for causation of known neurological disorders based on published medical literature. In so doing, we identified two potentially causative genes for autism for Subject HI2898. See Table 1 for the list of genes meeting or exceeding the established final selection criteria level and screening for biological significance. Identical genomic variants were recognized for several subjects even after increasing the final level of selection criteria required to reduce the number of candidate genes and considered artifactual findings. These genes with identical genomic variants included *KCNJ12, MLL3, OR9G1* and *PCMTD1* with different mutations reported in other disease states and appeared to reflect artifacts in the present analysis of autism.

We report genomic coordinates, previously recognized SNPs (and their ID numbers), reference base to alternate base sequences (e.g., G→A), variant call format (VCF) information, SNP effects (synonymous vs non- synonymous), SNP codons, and GERP2, PolyPhen2, SIFT, Blosum, Blosum62 and the classification scores for each genomic variant identified per affected female (Table 1). Our analysis identified a total of 79 different genes containing variants (both known and novel) consisting of 12 (15%) known candidate genes for ASD, 24 (30%) paralogues of known candidate ASD genes and 43 (54%) novel genes with functional roles in nerve cell growth, adhesion and neurodevelopment or function as putative candidate ASD genes (See Table 2). The identified candidate ASD genes and paralogues were distributed across 11 (37%) and 16 (53%) of the females with autism, respectively.

Four females (HI0555, HI0890, HI1402 and HI2126) possessed a single variant of significance in clinically relevant candidate or known ASD genes considered conclusive for causality. Seventy-seven percent of subjects (N = 23) possessed multiple variants with possible influences on causation of ASD. Two (9%) of the 23 females (7% of the total sample population) possessed more than five variants/mutations of known candidate ASD genes, paralogues or other functionally relevant genes with presumed influence over the development of ASD. Three (10%) of the total females (HI1143, HI1884 and HI2278) possessed a single gene variant with possible functional relevance toward the development of ASD but no known candidate ASD genes or paralogues identified to be considered conclusive.

Table 1. Putative disease causing genes for autism identified using whole exome sequencing of females with autism spectrum disorder (ASD).

ID Number XCI	Gene Symbol (Category) *	Chromosome Position (Hg19)	Genomic Variant					Classification Score	GERP2	PolyPhen2 Score	SIFT Score	Blosum Score/Blosum62
			SNP Effect	Amino Acid	SNP Codon	SNP Function	VCF Allele Depth					
HI0405 46%:54%	*KCNC2* (P) [12]	12:75444895	Non-synon	p.F296C	tTt/tGt	Missense	162, 30	0.790	0	0.984	0	0.787/−2
	ASPM (F) [23]	1:197112823	Non-synon	p.R186G	Aga/Gga	Missense	69, 53	0.777	0.007	0.994	0	0.787/−2
	TAF3 (F) [24]	10:8006662	Non-synon	p.R396G	Cga/Gga	Missense	69, 60	0.740	0	0.956	0	0.787/−2
	FLRT2 (F) [25]	14:86089552	Non-synon	p.H564R	cAt/cGt	Missense	28, 29	0.736	0	0.958	0.02	0.787/0
	SYTL4 (F) [26]	X:99941091	Non-synon	p.H448D	Cat/Gat	Missense	36, 37	0.710	0.006	1	0.03	0.787/−1
HI0555/58%:42%	*SETD2* (A) [12,27,28]	3:47164293	Non-synon	p.K610O	aaG/aaT	Missense	23, 21	0.778	0	0.970	0	8.522/0
HI0558 52%:48%	*IFT122* (F) [29]	3:129238526	Non-synon	p.R986H	cGc/cAc	Missense	58, 61	0.795	0.008	0.989	0	0.074/0
	NUP98 (F) [30]	11:3756456	Non-synon	p.R519W	Cgg/Tgg	Missense	12, 9	0.793	0.006	0.999	0	24.449/−3
	ZKSCAN1 (F) [31]	7:99621487	Non-synon	p.R119C	Cgc/Tgc	Missense	8, 5	0.782	0.006	1	0	0.787/−3
	DNAH8 (F) [32]	6:38834433	Non-synon	p.M1971V	Atg/Gtg	Missense	8, 14	0.783	0.009	0.902	0	4.182/1
	CENPJ (F) [33]	13:25487103	Non-synon	p.M20L	Atg/Ttg	Missense	45, 42	0.761	0.007	0.991	0.01	4.312/2
	TRIM5 (F) [34]	11:5878550	Non-synon	p.R127P	cGc/cCc	Missense	42, 24	0.742	0.0089	0.971	0	0.787/−2
	PCDH8 (A) [35]	13:53421358	Non-synon	p.A404V	gCg/gTg	Missense	13, 14	0.731	0	0.924	0	0.787/0
	CTNNA3 (A) [36]	10:68381521	Non-synon	p.M434V	Atg/Gtg	Missense	30, 17	0.723	0.009	0.942	0.01	4.183/1
	PPP1R18 (P) [37]	6:30652604	Non-synon	p.S397P	Tct/Cct	Missense	12, 6	0.703	0.005	0.958	0	0.787/−1
HI0605 53%:47%	*CCDC64* (A) [38]	12:120428012	Non-synon	p.A113T	Gcc/Acc	Missense	13, 24	0.794	0.006	0.96	0	4.774/−1
	DCHS1 (F) [39]	11:6662745	Codon Change Plus Codon Insertion	p.L32LW	ctg/ctCTGg	None	11, 8	0.700	0	0.979	0.02	0/0
HI0714 40%:60%	*TRAK2* (F) [40]	2:202264189	Non-synon	p.R130G	Cga/Gga	Missense	31, 27	0.805	0.010	1	0	0.064/−2
	MPST (F) [41]	22:37425405	Utr_3_Prime	p.Null-1Null	Null	None	20, 21	0.731	0.008	1	0	0.787/−2
	FSTL3 (F) [42]	19:680331	Non-synon	p.R115H	cGc/cAc	Missense	7, 3	0.729	0.010	1	0.01	8.723/0
HI0751 16%:84%	*IST1* (F) [43,44]	16:71956522	Non-synon	p.P232R	cCc/cGc	Missense	63, 50	0.754	0.008	0.972	0.01	0.787/−2
	KIF27 (P) [43,44]	9:86474259	Non-synon	p.S921P	Tca/Cca	Missense	22, 25	0.730	0.009	0.970	0.01	0.787/−1
	PCDHGA1 (P) [45]	5:140870234	Non-synon	p.V475A	gTg/gCg	Missense	152, 141	0.713	0	0.995	0	0.787/0
HI0765 77%:23%	*SEMA3F* (P) [46]	3:50225525	Non-synon	p.R679W	Cgg/Tgg	Missense	21, 7	0.793	0.006	1	0	0.787/−3
	SCN11A (P) [47]	3:38968409	Frame-shift	p.-166SS?	-/TCTT CACT	None	23, 17	0.748	0.008	0.982	0	0/0
	GPRASP2 (F) [48]	X:101972234	Non-synon	p.R812C	Cgt/Tgt	Missense	69, 51	0.706	0	0.989	0.01	0.787/−3
HI0793 37%:64%	*ELTD1* (F) [49]	1:79356850	Non-synon	p.C687R	Tgt/Cgt	Missense	50, 25	0.807	0.008	0.998	0	10.199/−3
	DENND3 (F) [50]	8:142161854	Non-synon	p.S252L	tCg/tTg	Missense	40, 20	0.806	0.006	0.992	0	0.787/−2
	MIDN (F) [51]	19:1250353	Non-synon	p.C19G	Tgc/Ggc	Missense	8, 3	0.793	0.008	0.998	0	17.850/−3
	RADIL (F) [52]	7:4917586	Non-synon	p.P61R	cCt/cGt	Missense	42, 27	0.774	0.004	1	0	14.302/−2
	EXOC7 (P) [53,54]	17:74097856	Non-synon	p.R71Q	cGg/cAg	Missense	36, 46	0.755	0.006	0.992	0.01	0.059/1
	PLCE1 (F) [55]	10:96064250	Non-synon	p.H1515Y	Cat/Tat	Missense	22, 14	0.737	0.008	0.999	0.02	7.078/2
	KDM5A (F) [56]	12:416817	Non-synon	p.A1244T	Gcc/Acc	Missense	42, 25	0.706	0	0.993	0	0.157/0
	ARAP2 (F) [57]	4:36115873	Non-synon	p.D1358N	Gat/Aat	Missense	70, 53	0.702	0.008	0.907	0.02	12.052/1

Table 1. *Cont.*

ID Number XCI	Gene Symbol (Category) *	Chromosome Position (Hg19)	Genomic Variant					Classification Score	GERP2	PolyPhen2 Score	SIFT Score	Blosum Score/Blosum62
			SNP Effect	Amino Acid	SNP Codon	SNP Function	VCF Allele Depth					
HI0855 44%:56%	*CHAC1* (F) [58]	15:41247844	Frame- shift	p.-177?	-/T	None	23, 19	0.941	0.009	0.997	0	0.787/0
	MIDN (F) [59]	19:1250353	Non-synon	p.C19G	Tgc/Ggc	Missense	3, 7	0.793	0.008	0.998	0	17.85/−3
	CDH6 (P) [60]	5:31323179	Non-synon	p.R712G	Aga/Gga	Missense	76, 81	0.749	0.003	0.988	0.01	0.787/−2
HI0868 58%:42%	*CHST3* (P) [61]	10:73767391	Non-synon	p.Y200C	tAc/tGc	Missense	43, 30	0.759	0	0.998	0.02	17.489/−2
	FBXO5 (P) [62]	6:153296090	Non-synon	p.H256R	cAt/cGt	Missense	103, 76	0.756	0.003	1	0	0.787/0
HI0890/NI	*BTAF1* (A) [63]	10:93719892	Non-synon	p.Y414F	tAt/tTt	Missense	29, 16	0.765	0.005	0.997	0	3/3
HI1143/14%:86%	*CLPTM1* (F) [64]	19:45476442	Non-synon	p.N94I	aAc/aTc	Missense	30, 27	0.744	0.007	1	0	0.787/−3
HI1157 61%:39%	*AMIGO1* (F) [65]	1:110050220	Non-synon	p.R438W	Cgg/Tgg	Missense	42, 28	0.806	0	0.994	0	0.787/−3
	PEX5 (P) [66]	12:7362354	Non-synon	p.R560C	Cgc/Tgc	Missense	71, 50	0.801	0.006	1	0	0.787/−3
	KIF23 (P) [67]	15:69718474	Non-synon	p.E266A	gAa/gCa	Missense	52, 48	0.775	0.007	0.998	0	0.787/−1
HI1228 42%:58%	*FOXA3* (P) [68]	19:46376266	Non-synon	p.G334R	Gga/Aga	Missense	30, 29	0.801	0.004	0.975	0	26.000/−2
	FRMD4A (F) [69]	10:13698719	Non-synon	p.S941L	tCg/tTg	Missense	6, 8	0.775	0	0.957	0	0.064/−2
HI1305 73%:27%	*PIR* (F) [70]	X:15474053	Non-synon	p.E132G	gAa/gGa	Missense	32, 28	0.811	0.007	0.962	0	0.213/−2
	DNAH2 (F) [71]	17:7637815	Non-synon	p.I255T	aTa/aCa	Missense	25, 20	0.793	0.010	0.942	0	7.006/−1
HI1375 17%:83%	*LHX2* (F) [72]	9:126777468	Non-synon	p.A130P	Gct/Cct	Missense	50, 34	0.775	0.006	0.998	0	0.787/−1
	EPHA4 (P) [73]	2:222428829	Non-synon	p.A148T	Gct/Act	Missense	18, 25	0.744	0	0.977	0	0.787/0
HI1402/85%:15%	*IL1RAPL1* (A) [12,74]	X:29973282	Non-synon	p.P478Q	cCa/cAa	Missense	57, 42	0.761	0	0.999	0	7.684/−1
HI1422 56%:44%	*RTN4R* (F) [75]	22:20230387	Non-synon	p.S89L	tCg/tTg	Missense	11, 18	0.778	0.004	0.998	0	0.064/−4
	DHX8 (F) [76]	17:41606990	Non-synon	p.R282H	cGc/cAc	Missense	4, 8	0.724	0.010	1	0	0.787/0
HI1433 93%:7%	*FAT2* (P) [77–79]	5:150947258	Non-synon	p.T411I	aCt/aTt	Missense	32, 29	0.757	0	0.992	0	6.276/−1
	FITM2 (F) [80,81]	20:42939631	Non-synon	p.R52H	cGc/cAc	Missense	6, 5	0.750	0.008	0.999	0.02	8.723/0
	RALGPS2 (F) [82,83]	1:179064186	Non-synon	p.V342M	Gtg/Atg	Missense	69, 73	0.734	0.010	0.970	0	0.787/1
HI1739 31%:69%	*ASB3* (F) [84]	2:53941656	Non-synon	p.S208N	aGc/aAc	Missense	53, 30	0.773	0.007	0.980	0	0.403/1
	AKAP6 (F) [85]	14:33291533	Non-synon	p.D1504P	gAt/gTt	Missense	43, 41	0.761	0	0.983	0.01	0.787/−3
	GRM4 (A) [86]	6:34100940	Non-synon	p.D111N	Gac/Aac	Missense	58, 51	0.726	0.005	0.993	0.02	0.787/1
HI1884/48%:52%	*TRAF3IP1* (F) [87]	2:239306221	Non-synon	p.M537T	aTg/aCg	Missense	13, 19	0.759	0.007	0.999	0.01	0.033/−1
HI1954 23%:77%	*DDX5* (P) [88]	17:62500102	Non-synon	p.S146C	tCt/tGt	Missense	88, 91	0.788	0.007	0.950	0	0.787/−1
	KIF5A (P) [89]	12:57974875	Non-synon	p.R891Q	cGg/cAg	Missense	25, 19	0.767	0.005	0.989	0	0.787/1
HI2126/41%:59%	*ANKRD11* (A) [90,91]	16:89351565	Non-synon	p.T461R	aCa/aGa	Missense	20, 11	0.767	0	0.961	0	0.787/−1
HI2172 61%:39%	*TNFRSF21* (F) [92]	6:47221105	Non-synon	p.W465R	Tgg/Agg	Missense	8, 16	0.805	0.004	1	0	10.610/−3
	LRSAM1 (F) [93,94]	9:130253524	Non-synon	p.L484M	Ctg/Atg	Missense	18, 23	0.796	0.010	0.935	0	0.787/−1
	CYFIP1 (A) [95]	15:22960872	Non-synon	p.D716N	Gac/Aac	Missense	28, 30	0.767	0.009	0.999	0	0.067/1

Table 1. *Cont.*

ID Number XCI	Gene Symbol (Category) *	Chromosome Position (Hg19)	Genomic Variant						Classification Score	GERP2	PolyPhen2 Score	SIFT Score	Blosum Score/Blosum62
			SNP Effect	Amino Acid	SNP Codon	SNP Function	VCF Allele Depth						
HI2215 60%:40%	*FPGT- TNNI3K* (F) [96]	1:74836022	Non-synon	p.G673V	gGc/gTc	Missense	34, 53		0.802	0.009	0.998	0	0.787/−3
	MAP1A (P) [96]	15:43820377	Non-synon	p.P2235S	Ccc/Tcc	Missense	65, 67		0.793	0	0.998	0	0.787/−1
	MAP1A (P) [96]	15:43819396	Non-synon	p.Y1908H	Tac/Cac	Missense	13, 21		0.782	0.004	0.994	0	0.787/2
HI2244 32%:68%	*KDM5B* (P) [97–99]	1:202724501	Non-synon	p.Y320K	aTa/aAa	Missense	52, 47		0.808	0.007	0.988	0	0.787/−4
	TRPM2 (P) [97–99]	21: 45826549	Non-synon	p.I954F	Atc/Ttc	Missense	17, 16		0.786	0.008	0.997	0	12.615/−3
	RAI1 (A) [100]	17:17699284	Non-synon	p.P959A	Ccc/Gcc	Missense	37, 26		0.763	0	0.992	0	0.787/−1
HI2278 8%:92%	*DCHS1* (F) [39]	11:6662745	Codon Change Plus Codon Insertion	p.L32LW	Ctg/ctCTGg	None	12, 11		0.700	0	0.979	0.02	0/0
HI2843 25%:75%	*UBE2E2* (P) [101]	3:23631311	Non-synon	p.Y198H	Tac/Cac	Missense	64, 33		0.787	0	0.994	0	0.787/2
	PCDHB15 (P) [45]	5:140625618	Non-synon	p.R157W	Cgg/Tgg	Missense	33, 61		0.754	0.007	0.942	0	24.449/−3
	SCG2 (F) [102]	2:224463227	Non-synon	p.E257D	gaG/gaC	Missense	70, 64		0.750	0	0.993	0.01	0.787/2
HI2879 18%:82%	*TRIM9* (F) [103]	14:51448554	Non-synon	p.R623Q	cGg/cAg	Missense	64, 69		0.774	0	1	0	0.787/1
	SOX7 (A) [104]	8:10583274	Non-synon	p.Y432H	Tac/Cac	Missense	25, 33		0.766	0	0.997	0	0.787/2
	ANKFN1 (P) [105]	17:54559849	Non-synon	p.G744R	Ggg/Agg	Missense	28, 16		0.715	0	0.995	0.04	26.000/−2
	DCHS1 (F) [39]	11:6662745	Codon Change Plus Codon Insertion	p.L32LW	ctg/ctCTGg	None	11, 12		0.700	0	0.979	0.02	0/0
HI2898 85%:15%	*MPHOSPH8* (F) [106]	13:20242552	Non-synon	p.Y736C	tAc/tGc	Missense	39, 28		0.779	0.007	0.999	0	0.787/−2
	GABRQ (A) [107]	X:151819020	Non-synon	p.S292F	tCc/tTc	Missense	9, 16		0.749	0.008	0.963	0	0.787/−2

ID Number represents the AGRE identifier. For the 30 females with ASD in this table, the average age ± standard deviation was 7.7 ± 2.6 years and age range was 5–16 years. Final selection criteria: Classification Score > 0.7; GERP2 < 0.01; PolyPhen2 > 0.9; SIFT < 0.03. * (A) = Known clinically relevant gene for autism; (F) = Neurodevelopment functional gene for autism; (P) = Known paralogue of an autism gene; NI = not informative; XCI = X chromosome Inactivation (%); ? indicates an unspecified amino acid variation; [ ] represents literature citations for each gene description.

Table 2. Summary of Putative Disease Causing Gene Variants Identified by Exome Sequencing.

Gene Variant Category	Number of Subjects (%)	Number of Genes (%)	Range
Known ASD Genes	11 (37%)	12 (15%)	0–2
Paralogues of Known ASD Genes	16 (53%)	23 (30%)	0–2
Neurodevelopmental Function Genes	23 (77%)	43 (54%)	0–7

Six females (HI0605, HI2898, HI1739, HI2172, HI2244 and HI2879) possessed a single variant of a known candidate ASD gene meeting our final selection criteria for pathogenicity in addition to one or more paralogues of ASD genes or gene variants with functional influence over cell growth and neurodevelopment. Fourteen females (HI0714, HI0751, HI0765, HI0855, HI0868, HI1157, HI1228, HI1305, HI1375, HI1422, HI1433, HI1954, HI2215 and HI2843) possessed 2 to 4 variants of ASD gene paralogues or variants with functional roles of influence over ASD but without a conclusive or definable causal mutation. Variants of multiple putative candidate genes for ASD were identified for Subjects HI0405, HI0558 and HI0793.

Using XCI data, we found that eight of the 30 females had high skewness (XCI > 80%:20%) and an additional six females showed moderate skewness (XCI 65%:35% to 80%:20%). Two of the eight females with high skewness and two females with moderate skewness possessed an X-linked gene variant meeting the final selection criteria. When considering the 78 total genes identified meeting our final selection criteria, X-linked gene variants were disproportionally more likely to be found among the females with autism spectrum disorder who exhibited moderate to high level XCI skewness than females without XCI skewness ($OR = 6.4$, 95% CI: 0.68, 60.5, $p = 0.1$) but this relationship did not achieve statistical significance. Similarly, females who exhibited XCI skewness were more likely to possess an X-linked gene variant than females without XCI skewness, ($OR = 6.0$, 95% CI: 0.58, 61.8, $p = 0.132$).

3. Discussion

We chose females with ASD to study from the age of 5 to 16 years from multiplex families with more than one affected family member in order to increase the likelihood of identifying a single gene as a causative factor using a descriptive case study approach. The females were selected from the AGRE, a biorepository of specimens and clinical data from well-characterized families with children with ASD enrolled for genetic research studies. Females with ASD from multiplex families were also examined to determine whether an overabundance of X-linked genes could be identified contributing to ASD by using whole exome sequencing and XCI assays and if X-linked genes were more frequently disturbed in those females with XCI skewness.

3.1. Single Gene Variants

Our investigation identified four females (HI0555, HI0890, HI1402 and HI2126) with single gene variants of clinically relevant candidate or known genes for ASD with a high likelihood of causality. Subject HI0555 possessed a non-synonymous, missense mutation of the *SETD2* gene located on chromosome 3 with high likelihood to have a deleterious effect on gene expression and/or function. The *SETD2* encodes a Huntingtin-interacting protein B related to Huntington disease and known expression in the brain [27,28]. The *SETD2* gene is known as an autism susceptibility gene reported in autism [12] and was the highest rated and most likely candidate gene in this case. Subject HI0890 possessed a non-synonymous, missense mutation of the *BTAF1* gene located on chromosome 10 which is implicated as a helicase and sequence-specific binding transcription factor activity [63]. Subject HI2126 possessed a non-synonymous, missense mutation in a known candidate gene for ASD, *ANKRD11* which is located on chromosome 16 and likely to be causative in this case. The *ANKRD11* gene encodes an ankryin repeat domain-containing protein which inhibits ligand-dependent activation of transcription with mutations causing the KBG syndrome characterized by craniofacial features, short stature, skeletal anomalies, seizures and intellectual disability [90,91]. No physical examination or cognitive data were available from AGRE on this 12 year old female diagnosed with autism.

3.2. Involvement of Skewness of X Chromosome Inactivation and Putative Disease Causing Genes

High XCI skewness (>80%:20%) was observed for eight of our females with autism and two of these females possessed putative variants of X-linked genes (HI1402 and HI2898) which may contribute to the phenotype. Skewing of X-chromosome inactivation may increase expression of recessive disease causing variants on the X-chromosome. Subject HI1402 with an XCI status of 85%:15% indicating high skewness also possessed a non-synonymous, missense mutation of an X-linked gene (*IL1RAPL1*) which is a recognized candidate gene for ASD [12]. *IL1RAPL1* had the highest criteria selection score of the four genes meeting initial selection criteria and the most likely cause of ASD in this female. The *IL1RAPL1* gene encodes a protein with the highest expression in brain neurons and participates in the regulation of neurite outgrowth via interaction with neuronal calcium sensors thereby regulating synaptic formation and modulation of synaptic transmission [74].

Subject HI2898 with an XCI status of 85%:15% showing high skewness possessed a variant of the X-linked gene (*GABRQ*) found to be in the top two genes in the selection process. The *GABRQ* (gamma-aminobutyric acid A receptor theta) gene encodes a receptor protein for GABAergic neurotransmission in the mammalian central nervous system [107]. GABA is a major inhibitory neurotransmitter. *GABRQ* expression is distributed in the amygdala, hippocampus, anterior hypothalamus and cortex [107]. Subject HI2278 with an XCI status of 8%:92% possessed an X-linked gene (*PAK3*) in the top 25 genes but was excluded due to strict filtering requirements (*i.e.*, PolyPhen 2) and a correct classification score of >0.50. However, the *DCHS1* gene was identified which encodes a transmembrane cell adhesion molecule that belongs to the protocadherin superfamily and acts as a ligand for FAT4, another protocadherin protein. Both DCHS1 and FAT4 form an apically located adhesive complex in the developing brain [39].

The five remaining females (HI0751, HI1143, HI1375, HI1433 and HI2879) with high XCI skewness ranging from 93%:7% to 82%:18% showed no X-linked gene variants meeting the final selection criteria for pathogenicity. Other variations of possible clinical relevance in autosomal chromosomes were observed for these subjects. Subject HI1433 with an XCI status of 93%:7% indicating extreme skewness possessed a variant of the *FAT2* gene located on chromosome 5 which is a member of the cadherin-related FAT tumor suppressor homolog 2 (Drosophila) [77–79]. Subject HI2879 with an XCI status of 18%:82% showing high skewness possessed a variant of the *SOX7* (SRY-Box 7) gene which encodes a SOX protein, acting as a transcription factor regulating diverse developmental processes [104]. Based upon our investigation, XCI skewness in these females did not contribute to the presentation of autism.

Moderate skewness (65%:35% to 80%:20%) was observed for six females (HI0765, HI1305, HI1739, HI1954, HI2244 and HI2843). Two of these females possessed putative variants of X-linked genes that may have contributed to their phenotype. Subject HI1305 with an XCI status of 73%:27% possessed a variant for *PIR*, a highly conserved X-linked iron-binding nuclear protein gene which functions as a transcriptional co-regulator and contributes to regulation of cellular processes and may promote apoptosis when over expressed [70]. An associated disorder for this gene when disturbed is extratemporal epilepsy. Three genes were identified for Subject HI0765 with an XCI status of 77%:23% with moderate skewness including *GPRASP2* located on the X chromosome which encodes a protein that may regulate a variety of G-protein coupled receptors associated with autism spectrum disorders and schizophrenia [48], as an X-linked gene approaching high skewness becomes an important candidate for causation of ASD in this female. The *KCNC2* and *ASPM* genes were the highest rated and became likely candidates

3.3. Other Autosomal Putative Disease Causing Genes

The cadherin, protocadherin and ankyrin repeat gene families were the most commonly altered putative disease causing gene variants identified in our study. Subject HI0558 possessed a variant of *PCDH8*, a member of the cadherin superfamily of genes and functions in cell adhesion in a CNS-specific manner possibly playing a role in activity-induced synaptic reorganization underlying memory with down-regulation of dendritic spines, primarily in the hippocampal area [35]. In addition this affected female possessed a variant of the *CTNNA3* gene which is located on chromosome 10 and encodes an alpha-t-catenin which plays a role in functional cadherin-mediated cell adhesion. A possible association of this gene in Alzheimer disease has been proposed [36]. Subject HI0855 possessed a variant of *CDH6* located on chromosome 5 encoding a known cadherin playing a role in cell-cell adhesion and implicated in autism [60]. Subject HI0605 possessed a non-synonymous, missense mutation of the *CCDC64* (coiled-coil domain containing, 64), a recognized ASD gene on chromosome 12 [12,38]. CCDC64 is a component of the secretory vesicle machinery in developing neurons that acts as a regulator of neurite outgrowth in the early phase of neuronal differentiation which when disturbed is associated with neuronitis [38]. Subject HI1739 possessed a non-synonymous missense mutation of the *ASB3* gene located on chromosome 2 and related to the ankryin repeat gene family known to play a role in brain development and function including autism [88]. *GRM4* (glutamate receptor, metabotropic, 4) is a known ASD gene involved with glutamate, a major excitatory neurotransmitter in the central nervous system [86]. Subject HI2172 possessed a non-synonymous, missense mutation of the *CYFIP1* (cytoplasmic FMRP-interacting protein 1) gene located on chromosome 15 which encodes a protein that interacts with the familial mental retardation protein (FMRP) that when disturbed, causes the fragile X syndrome by impacting on development and maintenance of neuronal structures [108,109]. Individuals with the 15q11.2 BP1-BP2 microdeletion or Burnside-Butler syndrome are known to have developmental and speech delay involving the *CYFIP1* gene with an increased rate of aberrant behavior and autism [95].

4. Experimental Section

4.1. Samples from Females with Autism

Thirty Caucasian females (average age, 7.7 ± 2.6 years; age range, 5 to 16 years) were selected with confirmed diagnosis of autism. We chose to undertake whole exome sequencing from well-characterized females with autism with a positive family history (e.g., affected brothers) classified as multiplex families with autism and having a high probability of causation due to gene disturbances. We selected affected females from the Autism Genetic Research Exchange (AGRE) repository (www.agre.autismspeaks.org) for a descriptive next generation whole exome sequencing case study. The family members with autism in the AGRE were recruited and enrolled after screening and diagnostic assessments were performed with autism-related testing instruments (e.g., ADOS). Medical examinations and neurology evaluations were undertaken to collect family, pregnancy and medical history data along with physical and anthropometric measures and neurological recordings. Blood was also collected at AGRE for lymphoblastoid cell line development, plasma storage and DNA isolation. Normal chromosome analysis (karyotype) and fragile X syndrome DNA testing were completed previously in all female subjects selected from AGRE. DNA from parents or other family members were not analyzed as a component of our study.

4.2. Whole Exome Sequencing

4.2.1. Exome Sequencing Methods

Genomic DNA (5 µg) samples were sent to the Silicon Valley Biosystems, Foster City, CA, USA for whole exome sequencing via paired-end next generation sequencing (NGS) approach using standard protocols with the Illumina HiSeq2000 platform (http://www.service.Illumina.com) and Agilent

SureSelect Human All Exon v4–51Mb (http://www.genomics.agilent.com). The primary sequence raw data produced by the sequencing phase of our study was aligned to reference, the variants called and functional significance of each variant determined and rank-ordered into a list of functional variants (in order of decreasing pathology) that were correlated with or causative for the autism phenotype. The raw data was in the form of *fastq* files, containing the sequence reads and quality scores of the NGS sequencing runs. The individual reads were initially aligned by mapping to the reference genome using Burrows-Wheeler aligner (BWA), a software program for mapping low-divergent genomic sequences of up to 100 base pairs against a large reference genome (http://www.bio-bwa.sourceforge.net). Variant calling procedures then identified genomic sequence variants from the NGS sequencing runs or the absence of variants in the sample of interest relative to a reference sequence. The platform used to produce variant calls was an amalgamation of tools and methods uniquely combined and specifically calibrated for enhanced performance incorporating *Genome Analysis Toolkit* (*GATK*) V2.39 (https://www.broadinstitute.org/gatk/). A number of intermediate steps were applied to improve the quality/accuracy of the alignment and variant calling results prior to the creation of the final list of variants. Sequence reads that were likely to represent duplicates were marked to be ignored by the downstream variant-calling tools. Additionally, realignment around known insertions and deletions was performed, and quality scores recalibrated based upon the number of reads. The list of variants was produced in the form of a .vcf file annotated to reflect the results of quality control filters. This established and calibrated alignment and variant calling platform performs well and can reliably predict calls for single insertion and deletion events (up to 50 bp with between 97% and 99.9% sensitivity and specificity). The average number of reads per generated fragment was 64 for each of the 30 females with autism.

4.2.2. Data Analysis

The resulting .vcf file contained annotated variants with scientific features, including sequence, gene-, variant-, and transcript-level annotations. Annotations include characteristics of the observed variant such as the genomic coordinates or the variant's genomic region (e.g., exonic, upstream *etc.*), predicted effects on the various transcripts (e.g., missense, frame-shift, *etc.*), observed frequencies of the variant in control populations and affected individuals, curated knowledge from both proprietary and public databases, and pathogenicity predictions (e.g., Polyphen and SIFT). The machine learning tool utilized both the 2012 April 1K Genome release reflecting the frequency at the position and variant levels and the European Exome Sequencing Project (ESP6500) (https://esp.gs.washington.edu/drupal/) at the variant level which reflects the frequency of variants as observed in the ESP6500 dataset of healthy individuals in generating the correct classification score. The regulatory significance of variants were derived from ENCODE data. A classification engine developed by Silicon Valley Biosystems was used to create a pathogenicity score based on a machine learning technique approach. The model is trained and validated using 150,000 gene polymorphisms and mutations from a large set of variants with known pathogenicity. The classification accuracy exceeds 99% and thus the score provides the probability that a particular variant has an effect on gene expression or protein structure. The classifier was trained using known disease-causing mutations and known benign polymorphisms, each of which was annotated with attributes such as location relative to splice junctions, type of non-synonymous amino acid substitution and allele frequency in the population. The classifier was validated on a similarly sized set of variants and was shown to perform with 93% sensitive and 97% specificity. Prioritization of putative functionally relevant variants based on the classification score was performed and these variants were additionally classified with other means of determining pathogenicity such as SIFT, PolyPhen2, Blosum and Blosum62. The variants that were the most highly predicted to be functionally significant were examined across the study cohort for clustering within and around genes hypothesized as relevant to the phenotype.

4.2.3. Gene Filtration/Selection Parameters

A high filter system was utilized whereby the indels and quality disqualified (QD) parameters were identified and removed based on the bioinformatics outlined in our study approach. The classification score (range 0 to 1) was generated as our primary delimiting factor in identifying novel or candidate genes for autism in the affected females. The classifier uses machine learning algorithms to predict a variant's functional impact on a gene with higher scores for genomic variants considered more pathogenic or disease-causing changes at the gene level. Thus, we applied an initial classification cutoff of >0.5 with final selection criteria >0.7. Genomic Evolutionary Rate Profiling (GERP2), an indicator of the prevalence of the genomic variants in the general population, was assigned a cutoff value of <0.01 and remained at <0.01 as final selection criteria. GERP2 identifies constrained elements in multiple alignments by quantifying substitution deficits. These deficits represented substitutions that would have occurred if the element was neutral DNA, but did not occur because the element was under functional constraint. The initial Polymorphism Phenotyping v2 (PolyPhen2) cutoff value was >0.85 with the final selection criteria >0.9 and the initial Sorts Intolerant From Tolerant (SIFT) cutoff valuewas <0.05 with a final selection criteria <0.03 were predictors of pathogenicity or disease causing changes. The Blosum (BLOcks SUbstitution Matrix) score reports the ratio between the frequency of an amino acid substitution in the Human Gene Mutation Database (HGMD) to the frequency of this amino acid substitution in known polymorphism data sets. Numbers greater than 1 indicate this variant was observed more in diseased individuals than in controls and less likely to be tolerated. We also used the Blosum62 matrix to score alignments between evolutionarily divergent protein sequences based on local alignments. Blosum62 is a log-odds score for each possible substitution of the 20 standard amino acids. Higher Blosum62 numbers represent more closely related species comparisons and provide a general indication of frequency of the substitution. Negative numbers indicate less frequent substitutions and a lower likelihood to be tolerated (e.g., negative values = unexpected or rare substitutions).

The list of disease causing genes were developed using the primary selection criteria (*i.e.*, classification score) and then adding cutoff levels for other predictive parameters (GERP2, PolyPhen2, and SIFT). The initial list of genes and genomic variants used the classification score >0.5 alone and then the cutoff levels of the other predictive parameters (GERP2, PolyPhen2 and SIFT) were included. The classification score was then raised to >0.7 to generate the final list of genes. These putative candidate genes and genomic variants were then subjected to further screening for biological significance for neural development, function and known neurological disorders using Online Mendelian Inheritance in Man (OMIM, http://www.ncbi.nlm.nih.gov/omim), GeneCards (http://www.genecards.org/), PubMed and other online websites and databases.

4.2.4. Clinical Relevance to ASD

Following the recommendations of the American College of Medical Genetics and Genomics (ACMGG) in reporting clinical exome and genome sequencing data, we analyzed only the primary findings, in depth, which is termed as the pathogenic alteration in a gene or genes relevant to the diagnostic indication for sequencing study, *i.e.*, causation of autism in females. Only clinically relevant candidate or known existing genes for autism were included for extended analysis. Incidental findings are those pathogenic or likely pathogenic alterations in genes that are disease associated or causing but not apparently relevant to a diagnostic indication for which sequencing was undertaken (*i.e.*, in our study on autism [12]) and were not further investigated in our study. We did not include mutations of recognized autosomal recessive genes causing human disorder (e.g., *GJB2* or *GJB6*, gene mutations causing hearing loss). It is estimated that about 1% of sequencing reports would include an incidental variant.

4.3. X Chromosome Inactivation in Females with Autism

Genomic DNA isolated from blood was used as a template for polymerase chain reaction (PCR) amplification, to identify the CAG polymorphic region of the *AR* gene. Prior to the PCR amplification, 200 ng of genomic DNA was digested with the methyl-sensitive restriction enzyme *Hpa*II [21]. Approximately 50 ng of digested or undigested genomic DNA was used as a template for PCR amplification to determine the peak height of the polymorphic PCR fragment of the *AR* gene using the following primers: forward 5' TCCAGAATCTGTTCCAGAGCGTGC 3' and reverse 5' GCTGTGAAGGTTGCTGTTCCTCAT 3' with the forward primer fluorescently labeled with 6-FAM. The lengths and peak heights of the resulting PCR fragments are determined with the use of capillary electrophoresis and fragment separation software with the ABI 3100 DNA sequencer (Applied Biosystems, Carlsbad, CA, USA) using established protocols [18,22].

The digestion process preferentially degrades activated (unmethylated) over inactivated (methylated) DNA. Undigested DNA is preferentially amplified and produces larger peak heights. The peak height values for digested DNA is normalized using peak height values for the undigested DNA for each subject. The percentage of XCI for each *AR* allele was then calculated using the following formula: $(d1/u1)/[(d1/u1) + (d2/u2)]$; d1 = peak height of digested DNA from the first allele and u1 = peak height of undigested DNA from the first allele; d2 = peak height of digested DNA from the second allele and u2 = peak height of undigested DNA from the second allele. Highly skewed XCI is defined as >80% calculated ratio for either one of the *AR* gene alleles in the digested DNA sample. To ensure the reproducibility of XCI results and equal amplification of both alleles, the digestion, PCR amplification, and genotyping were repeated up to three times in several samples.

XCI status for each subject was assigned to one of the three mutually exclusive categories: (i) randomly selected inactivation of either allele from each X chromosome (XCI = 50%:50% to 64%:36%); (ii) moderately skewed inactivation favoring 1 allele of one of the X chromosomes (XCI = 65%:35% to 80%:20%); and (iii) highly skewed inactivation of a single allele representing one X chromosome (XCI > 80%:20%). The relative frequency of random, moderate, and highly skewed XCI categories was determined for the females with autism. The binomial frequency distribution of X-linked gene variants (present or absent) among females with autism spectrum disorder exhibiting moderate and high levels of XCI skewness were approximated using Yates' chi-squire test and odds ratios were calculated with 95% confidence intervals.

The top genes chosen were based on the final selection criteria identified for each female and evaluated for biologic function and whether each gene was previously reported as a clinically relevant candidate or known gene for autism [12]. The X chromosome inactivation data and XCI status on each female were used to support whether an X-linked gene played a role in the causation of autism in the affected female if XCI skewness was found.

5. Conclusions

In summary, we shared our experience using a descriptive next generation whole exome sequencing case study approach examining 30 well-characterized Caucasian females with autism between 5 and 16 years of age recruited from multiplex families enrolled at the AGRE for research purposes. Interpretation of DNA findings are limited due to an inability to study other affected and non-affected family members to determine whether the gene variants were de-novo or inherited in origin for correlation with clinical phenotypes and lack of Sanger sequencing confirmation. Using strict selection criteria, four females (13%) were found to possess single gene variants of known candidate genes for ASD with a high likelihood of causality. We also identified multiple plausible candidate genes [some known (e.g., *CCDC64* in subject HI0605) and some novel (e.g., *CHAC1* in subject HI0855)] in 77% of the remaining females. In most females, we found more than one gene that could contribute to the causation of autism. This compares with a recent report of molecular findings among 2000 consecutive patients (primarily pediatric age) referred for clinical whole exome sequencing for evaluation of suspected genetic disorders at a large USA medical center in which 25% received a molecular diagnosis. About 60% of the diagnostic mutations were not previously reported [110]. By phenotypic category, 36% of those presenting with neurological involvement were found to have a molecular diagnosis while 20% of those from the non-neurological group had a diagnosis. We not only performed whole exome sequencing in our females with autism but also performed X chromosome inactivation (XCI) studies for evidence of X-linked genes in the females showing non-random XCI skewness. Moderate and high XCI skewness was seen in 14 of the 30 females and those with skewness were 4 times more likely to show a gene variant on the X chromosome.

Acknowledgments: The authors thank Carla Meister for manuscript preparation. Partial grant support was provided by the University of Kansas Medical Center and Center of Translational Science through the NIH National Center for Advancing Translational Sciences (Grant# UL1TR000001) and from NICHD (HD02528).

Author Contributions: Merlin G. Butler conceived the study, analyzed data and wrote the manuscript. Syed K. Rafi reviewed literature, assessed the function of gene variants and contributed to the content of the manuscript. Waheeda Hossain carried out DNA isolation and X-chromosome inactivation studies with data analysis. Dietrich A. Stephan carried out whole exome sequencing experiments, data analysis and interpretation and contributed to the content of the manuscript. Ann M. Manzardo carried out and summarized data analysis and interpretation and contributed to the text of the manuscript.

References

1. American Psychiatric Association. *Diagnostic and Statistical Manual of Mental Disorders*, 4th ed.; American Psychiatric Association Press: Washington, DC, USA, 2000.
2. Johnson, C.P.; Myers, S.M. The Council on Children With Disabilities. Identification and evaluation of children with autism spectrum disorders. *Pediatrics* **2007** *120*, 1183–1215. [CrossRef] [PubMed]
3. Lord, C.; Risi, S.; Lambrecht, L.; Cook, E.H., Jr.; Leventhal, B.L.; DiLavore, P.C.; Pickles, A.; Rutter, M. The autism diagnostic observation schedule-generic: A standard measure of social and communication deficits associated with the spectrum of autism. *J. Autism Dev. Disord.* **2000**, *30*, 205–223. [CrossRef] [PubMed]
4. Le Couteur, A.; Lord, C.; Ruter, M. *Autism Diagnostic Interview-Reviewed (ADI-R)*; Western Psychological Services: Los Angeles, CA, USA, 2003.
5. Constantino, J.N.; Davis, S.A.; Todd, R.D.; Schindler, M.K.; Gross, M.M.; Brophy, S.L.; Metzger, L.M.; Shoushtari, C.S.; Splinter, R.; Reich, W. Validation of a brief quantitative measure of autistic traits: Comparison of the social responsiveness scale with the autism diagnostic interview-revised. *J. Autism Dev. Disord.* **2003**, *33*, 427–433. [CrossRef] [PubMed]
6. Developmental Disabilities Monitoring Network Surveillance Year 2010 Principal Investigators; Centers for Disease Control and Prevention (CDC). Prevalence of autism spectrum disorder among children aged 8 years—autism and developmental disabilities monitoring network, 11 sites, United States, 2010. *MMWR Surveill. Summ.* **2014**, *63*, 1–21.
7. Rapin, I.; Dunn, M. The neurology of autism: Many unanswered questions. *Eur. J. Neurol.* **1995**, *2*, 151–162. [CrossRef] [PubMed]
8. Geschwind, D.H.; Levitt, P. Autism spectrum disorders: Developmental disconnection syndromes. *Curr. Opin. Neurobio.* **2007**, *17*, 103–111. [CrossRef]
9. Butler, M.G.; Dasouki, M.J.; Zhou, X.P.; Talebizadeh, Z.; Brown, M.; Takahashi, T.N.; Miles, J.H.; Wang, C.H.; Stratton, R.; Pilarski, R.; *et al.* Subset of individuals with autism spectrum disorders and extreme macrocephaly associated with germline PTEN tumour suppressor gene mutations. *J. Med. Genet.* **2005**, *42*, 318–321. [CrossRef] [PubMed]
10. Herman, G.E.; Henninger, N.; Ratliff-Schaub, K.; Pastore, M.; Fitzgerald, S.; McBride, K.L. Genetic testing in autism: How much is enough? *Genet. Med.* **2007**, *9*, 268–274. [CrossRef] [PubMed]
11. Roberts, J.L.; Hovanes, K.; Dasouki, M.; Manzardo, A.M.; Butler, M.G. Chromosomal microarray analysis of consecutive individuals with autism spectrum disorders or learning disability presenting for genetic services. *Gene* **2014**, *535*, 70–78. [CrossRef] [PubMed]
12. Butler, MG; Rafi, S.K.; Manzardo, AM. Clinically relevant candidate and known genes for autism spectrum disorders (ASD) with representation on high resolution chromosome ideograms. *OA Autism* **2014**, *2*, 5–28.

13. Lyon, M.F. X-chromosome inactivation and human genetic disease. *Acta Paediatr.* **2002**, *91*, 107–112. [CrossRef]
14. Plenge, R.M.; Stevenson, R.A.; Lubs, H.A.; Schwartz, C.E.; Willard, H.F. Skewed X-chromosome inactivation is a common feature of X-linked mental retardation disorders. *Am. J. Hum. Genet.* **2002**, *71*, 168–173. [CrossRef] [PubMed]
15. Talebizadeh, Z.; Bittel, D.C.; Veatch, O.J.; Kibiryeva, N.; Butler, M.G. Brief report: Non-random X chromosome inactivation in females with autism. *J. Autism Dev. Disord.* **2005**, *35*, 675–681. [CrossRef] [PubMed]
16. Buyse, I.M.; Fang, P.; Hoon, K.T.; Amir, R.E.; Zoghbi, H.Y.; Roa, B.B. Diagnostic testing for Rett syndrome by DHPLC and direct sequencing analysis of the MECP2 gene: Identification of several novel mutations and polymorphisms. *Am. J. Hum. Genet.* **2000**, *67*, 1428–1436. [CrossRef] [PubMed]
17. Maier, E.M.; Kammerer, S.; Muntau, A.C.; Wichers, M.; Braun, A.; Roscher, A.A. Symptoms in carriers of adrenoleukodystrophy relate to skewed X inactivation. *Ann. Neurol.* **2002**, *52*, 683–688. [CrossRef] [PubMed]
18. Butler, M.G.; Theodoro, M.F.; Bittel, D.C.; Kuipers, P.J.; Driscoll, D.J.; Talebizadeh, Z. X-chromosome inactivation patterns in females with Prader-Willi syndrome. *Am. J. Med. Genet. A* **2007**, *143*, 469–475. [CrossRef]
19. Butler, M.G.; Sturich, J.; Myers, S.E.; Gold, J.A.; Kimonis, V.; Driscoll, D.J. Is gestation in Prader-Willi syndrome affected by the genetic subtype? *J. Assist. Reprod. Genet.* **2009**, *26*, 461–466. [CrossRef] [PubMed]
20. Cassidy, S.B.; Lai, L.W.; Erickson, R.P.; Magnuson, L.; Thomas, E.; Gendron, R.; Herrmann, J. Trisomy 15 with loss of the paternal 15 as a cause of Prader-Willi syndrome due to maternal disomy. *Am. J. Hum. Genet.* **1992**, *51*, 701–708. [PubMed]
21. Allen, R.C.; Zoghbi, H.Y.; Moseley, A.B.; Rosenblatt, H.M.; Belmont, J.W. Methylation of HpaII and HhaI sites near the polymorphic CAG repeat in the human androgen-receptor gene correlates with x chromosome inactivation. *Am. J. Hum. Genet.* **1992**, *51*, 1229–1239. [PubMed]
22. Bittel, D.C.; Theodoro, M.F.; Kibiryeva, N.; Fischer, W.; Talebizadeh, Z.; Butler, M.G. Comparison of X-chromosome inactivation patterns in multiple tissues from human females. *J. Med. Genet.* **2008**, *45*, 309–313. [CrossRef] [PubMed]
23. Bond, J.; Roberts, E.; Mochida, G.H.; Hampshire, D.J.; Scott, S.; Askham, J.M.; Springell, K.; Mahadevan, M.; Crow, Y.J.; Markham, A.F.; *et al.* ASPM is a major determinant of cerebral cortical size. *Nat. Genet.* **2002**, *32*, 316–320. [CrossRef]
24. Vermeulen, M.; Mulder, K.W.; Denissov, S.; Pim Pijnappel, W.W. M.; van Schaik, F.M.A.; Varier, R.A.; Baltissen, M.P.A.; Stunnenberg, H.G.; Mann, M.; Timmers, H.T.M. Selective anchoring of TFIID to nucleosomes by trimethylation of histone H3 lysine 4. *Cell* **2007**, *131*, 58–69. [CrossRef] [PubMed]
25. Lacy, S.E.; Bonnemann, C.G.; Buzney, E.A.; Kunkel, L.M. Identification of FLRT1, FLRT2, and FLRT3: A novel family of transmembrane leucine-rich repeat proteins. *Genomics* **1999**, *62*, 417–426. [CrossRef] [PubMed]
26. Wang, J.; Takeuchi, T.; Yokota, H.; Izumi, T. Novel rabphilin-3-like protein associates with insulin-containing granules in pancreatic beta cells. *J. Biol. Chem.* **1999**, *274*, 28542–28548. [CrossRef] [PubMed]
27. Faber, P.W.; Barnes, G.T.; Srinidhi, J.; Chen, J.; Gusella, J.F.; MacDonald, M.E. Huntingtin interacts with a family of WW domain proteins. *Hum. Mol. Genet.* **1998**, *7*, 1463–1474. [CrossRef] [PubMed]
28. Nagase, T.; Kikuno, R.; Hattori, A.; Kondo, Y.; Okumura, K.; Ohara, O. Prediction of the coding sequences of unidentified human genes. XIX. The complete sequences of 100 new cDNA clones from brain which code for large proteins *in vitro*. *DNA Res.* **2000**, *7*, 347–355. [CrossRef] [PubMed]
29. Claudio, J.O.; Liew, C.C.; Ma, J.; Heng, H.H.Q.; Stewart, A.K.; Hawley, R.G. Cloning and expression analysis of a novel WD repeat gene, WDR3, mapping to 1p12-p13. *Genomics* **1999**, *59*, 85–89. [CrossRef] [PubMed]
30. Iwamoto, M.; Asakawa, H.; Hiraoka, Y.; Haraguchi, T. Nucleoporin Nup98: A gatekeeper in the eukaryotic kingdoms. *Genes Cells* **2010**, *15*, 661–669. [CrossRef] [PubMed]
31. Tommerup, N.; Vissing, H. Isolation and fine mapping of 16 novel human zinc finger-encoding cDNAs identify putative candidate genes for developmental and malignant disorders. *Genomics* **1995**, *27*, 259–264. [CrossRef] [PubMed]
32. Chapelin, C.; Duriez, N.; Magnino, F.; Goossens, M.; Escudier, E.; Amselem, S. Isolation of several human axonemal dynein heavy chain genes: Genomic structure of the catalytic site, phylogenetic analysis and chromosomal assignment. *FEBS Lett.* **1997**, *412*, 325–330. [CrossRef] [PubMed]

33. Bond, J.; Roberts, E.; Springell, K.; Lizarraga, S.B.; Scott, S.; Higgins, J.; Hampshire, D.J.; Morrison, E.E.; Leal, G.F.; Silva, E.O.; *et al.* A centrosomal mechanism involving CDK5RAP2 and CENPJ controls brain size. *Nat. Genet.* **2005**, *37*, 353–355. [CrossRef]
34. Pertel, T.; Hausmann, S.; Morger, D.; Zuger, S.; Guerra, J.; Lascano, J.; Reinhard, C.; Santoni, F.A.; Uchil, P.D.; Chatel, L.; *et al.* TRIM5 is an innate immune sensor for the retrovirus capsid lattice. *Nature* **2011**, *472*, 361–365. [CrossRef]
35. Strehl, S.; Glatt, K.; Liu, Q.M.; Glatt, H.; Lalande, M. Characterization of two novel protocadherins (PCDH8 and PCDH9) localized on human chromosome 13 and mouse chromosome 14. *Genomics* **1998**, *53*, 81–89. [CrossRef] [PubMed]
36. Miyashita, A.; Arai, H.; Asada, T.; Imagawa, M.; Matsubara, E.; Shoji, M.; Higuchi, S.; Urakami, K.; Kakita, A.; Takahashi, H.; *et al.* Genetic association of CTNNA3 with late-onset Alzheimer's disease in females. *Hum. Mol. Genet.* **2007**, *16*, 2854–2869. [CrossRef]
37. Kao, S.C.; Chen, C.Y.; Wang, S.L.; Yang, J.J.; Hung, W.C.; Chen, Y.C.; Lai, N.S.; Liu, H.T.; Huang, H.; Chen, H.C.; *et al.* Identification of phostensin, a PP1 F-actin cytoskeleton targeting subunit. *Biochem. Biophys. Res. Commun.* **2007**, *356*, 594–598. [CrossRef] [PubMed]
38. Leidinger, P.; Backes, C.; Deutscher, S.; Schmitt, K.; Mueller, S.C.; Frese, K.; Haas, J.; Ruprecht, K.; Paul, F.; Stahler, C.; *et al.* A blood based 12-miRNA signature of Alzheimer disease patients. *Genome Biol.* **2013**, *14*. [CrossRef]
39. Cappello, S.; Gray, M.J.; Badouel, C.; Lange, S.; Einsiedler, M.; Srour, M.; Chitayat, D.; Hamdan, F.F.; Jenkins, Z.A.; Morgan, T.; *et al.* Mutations in genes encoding the cadherin receptor-ligand pair DCHS1 and FAT4 disrupt cerebral cortical development. *Nat. Genet.* **2013**, *45*, 1300–1308.
40. Grishin, A.; Li, H.; Levitan, E.S.; Zaks-Makhina, E. Identification of gamma-aminobutyric acid receptor-interacting factor 1 (TRAK2) as a trafficking factor for the K^+ channel Kir2.1. *J. Biol. Chem.* **2006**, *281*, 30104–30111. [CrossRef] [PubMed]
41. Billaut-Laden, I.; Rat, E.; Allorge, D.; Crunelle-Thibaut, A.; Cauffiez, C.; Chevalier, D.; Lo-Guidice, J.M.; Broly, F. Evidence for a functional genetic polymorphism of the human mercaptopyruvate sulfurtransferase (MPST), a cyanide detoxification enzyme. *Toxicol. Lett.* **2006**, *165*, 101–111. [CrossRef] [PubMed]
42. Hayette, S.; Gadoux, M.; Martel, S.; Bertrand, S.; Tigaud, I.; Magaud, J.P.; Rimokh, R. FLRG (follistatin-related gene), a new target of chromosomal rearrangement in malignant blood disorders. *Oncogene* **1998**, *16*, 2949–2954. [CrossRef] [PubMed]
43. Bajorek, M.; Morita, E.; Skalicky, J.J.; Morham, S.G.; Babst, M.; Sundquist, W.I. Biochemical analyses of human IST1 and its function in cytokinesis. *Mol. Biol. Cell.* **2009**, *20*, 1360–1373. [CrossRef] [PubMed]
44. Klejnot, M.; Kozielski, F. Structural insights into human Kif7, a kinesin involved in hedgehog signalling. *Acta Crystallogr.* **2012**, *68*, 154–159.
45. Wu, Q.; Maniatis, T. A striking organization of a large family of human neural cadherin-like cell adhesion genes. *Cell* **1999**, *97*, 779–790. [CrossRef] [PubMed]
46. Tran, T.S.; Rubio, M.E.; Clem, R.L.; Johnson, D.; Case, L.; Tessier-Lavigne, M.; Huganir, R.L.; Ginty, D.D.; Kolodkin, A.L. Secreted semaphorins control spine distribution and morphogenesis in the postnatal CNS. *Nature* **2009**, *462*, 1065–1069. [CrossRef] [PubMed]
47. Zhang, X.Y.; Wen, J.; Yang, W.; Wang, C.; Gao, L.; Zheng, L.H.; Wang, T.; Ran, K.; Li, Y.; Li, X.; *et al.* Gain-of-function mutations in SCN11a cause familial episodic pain. *Am. J. Hum. Genet.* **2013**, *93*, 957–966. [CrossRef] [PubMed]
48. Piton, A.; Gauthier, J.; Hamdan, F.F.; Lafreniere, R.G.; Yang, Y.; Henrion, E.; Laurent, S.; Noreau, A.; Thibodeau, P.; Karemera, L.; *et al.* Systematic resequencing of X-chromosome synaptic genes in autism spectrum disorder and schizophrenia. *Mol. Psychiatry* **2011**, *16*, 867–880. [CrossRef] [PubMed]
49. Agrawal, A.; Pergadia, M.L.; Saccone, S.F.; Lynskey, M.T.; Wang, J.C.; Martin, N.G.; Statham, D.; Henders, A.; Campbell, M.; Garcia, R.; *et al.* An autosomal linkage scan for cannabis use disorders in the nicotine addiction genetics project. *Arch. Gen. Psychiatry* **2008**, *65*, 713–721. [CrossRef] [PubMed]
50. Yoshimura, S.; Gerondopoulos, A.; Linford, A.; Rigden, D.J.; Barr, F.A. Family-wide characterization of the DENN domain Rab GDP-GTP exchange factors. *J. Cell Biol.* **2010**, *191*, 367–381. [CrossRef] [PubMed]
51. Le Meur, N.; Martin, C.; Saugier-Veber, P.; Joly, G.; Lemoine, F.; Moirot, H.; Rossi, A.; Bachy, B.; Cabot, A.; Joly, P.; *et al.* Complete germline deletion of the *STK11* gene in a family with Peutz-Jeghers syndrome. *Eur. J. Hum. Genet.* **2004**, *12*, 415–418. [CrossRef] [PubMed]

52. Smolen, G.A.; Schott, B.J.; Stewart, R.A.; Diederichs, S.; Muir, B.; Provencher, H.L.; Look, A.T.; Sgroi, D.C.; Peterson, R.T.; Haber, D.A. A Rap GTPase interactor, RADIL, mediates migration of neural crest precursors. *Genes Dev.* **2007**, *21*, 2131–2136. [CrossRef] [PubMed]
53. Zuo, X.; Zhang, J.; Zhang, Y.; Hsu, S.C.; Zhou, D.; Guo, W. Exo70 interacts with the Arp2/3 complex and regulates cell migration. *Nat. Cell Biol.* **2006**, *8*, 1383–1388. [CrossRef] [PubMed]
54. Oeffner, F.; Moch, C.; Neundorf, A.; Hofmann, J.; Koch, M.; Grzeschik, K.H. Novel interaction partners of Bardet-Biedl syndrome proteins. *Cell Motil. Cytoskelet.* **2008**, *65*, 143–155. [CrossRef]
55. Lopez, I.; Mak, E.C.; Ding, J.; Hamm, H.E.; Lomasney, J.W. A novel bifunctional phospholipase C that is regulated by Galpha 12 and stimulates the Ras/mitogen-activated protein kinase pathway. *J. Biol. Chem.* **2001**, *276*, 2758–2765. [CrossRef] [PubMed]
56. Liefke, R.; Oswald, F.; Alvarado, C.; Ferres-Marco, D.; Mittler, G.; Rodriguez, P.; Dominguez, M.; Borggrefe, T. Histone demethylase KDM5A is an integral part of the core Notch-RBP-J repressor complex. *Genes Dev.* **2010**, *24*, 590–601. [CrossRef] [PubMed]
57. Chen, P.W.; Jian, X.; Yoon, H.Y.; Randazzo, P.A. ARAP2 signals through Arf6 and Rac1 to control focal adhesion morphology. *J. Biol. Chem.* **2013**, *288*, 5849–5860. [CrossRef] [PubMed]
58. Chi, Z.; Zhang, J.; Tokunaga, A.; Harraz, M.M.; Byrne, S.T.; Dolinko, A.; Xu, J.; Blackshaw, S.; Gaiano, N.; Dawson, T.M.; *et al.* Botch promotes neurogenesis by antagonizing Notch. *Dev. Cell* **2012**, *22*, 707–720. [CrossRef] [PubMed]
59. Tsukahara, M.; Suemori, H.; Noguchi, S.; Ji, Z.S.; Tsunoo, H. Novel nucleolar protein, midnolin, is expressed in the mesencephalon during mouse development. *Gene* **2000**, *254*, 45–55. [CrossRef] [PubMed]
60. Suzuki, S.; Sano, K.; Tanihara, H. Diversity of the cadherin family: Evidence for eight new cadherins in nervous tissue. *Cell Regul.* **1991**, *2*, 261–270. [PubMed]
61. Unger, S.; Lausch, E.; Rossi, A.; Megarbane, A.; Sillence, D.; Alcausin, M.; Aytes, A.; Mendoza-Londono, R.; Nampoothiri, S.; Afroze, B.; *et al.* Phenotypic features of carbohydrate sulfotransferase 3 (CHST3) deficiency in 24 patients: Congenital dislocations and vertebral changes as principal diagnostic features. *Am. J. Med. Genet. A* **2010**, *152A*, 2543–2549. [CrossRef]
62. Reimann, J.D.; Freed, E.; Hsu, J.Y.; Kramer, E.R.; Peters, J.M.; Jackson, P.K. Emi1 is a mitotic regulator that interacts with Cdc20 and inhibits the anaphase promoting complex. *Cell* **2001**, *105*, 645–655. [CrossRef] [PubMed]
63. Van Der Knaap, J.A.; van Den Boom, V.; Kuipers, J.; van Eijk, M.J.; van Der Vliet, P.C.; Timmers, H.T. The gene for human TATA-binding-protein-associated factor (TAFII) 170: Structure, promoter and chromosomal localization. *Biochem. J.* **2000**, *345*, 521–527. [CrossRef] [PubMed]
64. Yoshiura, K.; Machida, J.; Daack-Hirsch, S.; Patil, S.R.; Ashworth, L.K.; Hecht, J.T.; Murray, J.C. Characterization of a novel gene disrupted by a balanced chromosomal translocation t(2;19)(q11.2;q13.3) in a family with cleft lip and palate. *Genomics* **1998**, *54*, 231–240. [CrossRef] [PubMed]
65. Kuja-Panula, J.; Kiiltomaki, M.; Yamashiro, T.; Rouhiainen, A.; Rauvala, H. AMIGO, a transmembrane protein implicated in axon tract development, defines a novel protein family with leucine-rich repeats. *J. Cell Biol.* **2003**, *160*, 963–973. [CrossRef] [PubMed]
66. Dammai, V.; Subramani, S. The human peroxisomal targeting signal receptor, Pex5p, is translocated into the peroxisomal matrix and recycled to the cytosol. *Cell* **2001**, *105*, 187–196. [CrossRef] [PubMed]
67. Iwamori, T.; Iwamori, N.; Ma, L.; Edson, M.A.; Greenbaum, M.P.; Matzuk, M.M. TEX14 interacts with CEP55 to block cell abscission. *Mol. Cell. Biol.* **2010**, *30*, 2280–2292. [CrossRef] [PubMed]
68. Friedman, J.R.; Kaestner, K.H. The Foxa family of transcription factors in development and metabolism. *Cell Mol. Life Sci.* **2006**, *63*, 2317–2328. [CrossRef] [PubMed]
69. Yoon, D.; Kim, Y.J.; Cui, W.Y.; Van der Vaart, A.; Cho, Y.S.; Lee, J.Y.; Ma, J.Z.; Payne, T.J.; Li, M.D.; Park, T. Large-scale genome-wide association study of asian population reveals genetic factors in FRMD4A and other loci influencing smoking initiation and nicotine dependence. *Hum. Genet.* **2012**, *131*, 1009–1021. [CrossRef] [PubMed]
70. Licciulli, S.; Cambiaghi, V.; Scafetta, G.; Gruszka, A.M.; Alcalay, M. Pirin downregulation is a feature of AML and leads to impairment of terminal myeloid differentiation. *Leukemia* **2010**, *24*, 429–437. [CrossRef] [PubMed]
71. Pazour, G.J.; Agrin, N.; Walker, B.L.; Witman, G.B. Identification of predicted human outer dynein arm genes: Candidates for primary ciliary dyskinesia genes. *J. Med. Genet.* **2006**, *43*, 62–73. [CrossRef] [PubMed]

72. Chou, S.J.; O'Leary, D.D. Role for Lhx2 in corticogenesis through regulation of progenitor differentiation. *Mol. Cell. Neurosci.* **2013**, *56*, 1–9. [CrossRef] [PubMed]
73. Leighton, P.A.; Mitchell, K.J.; Goodrich, L.V.; Lu, X.; Pinson, K.; Scherz, P.; Skarnes, W.C.; Tessier-Lavigne, M. Defining brain wiring patterns and mechanisms through gene trapping in mice. *Nature* **2001**, *410*, 174–179. [CrossRef] [PubMed]
74. Piton, A.; Michaud, J.L.; Peng, H.; Aradhya, S.; Gauthier, J.; Mottron, L.; Champagne, N.; Lafreniere, R.G.; Hamdan, F.F.; team, S.D.; *et al.* Mutations in the calcium-related gene IL1RAPL1 are associated with autism. *Hum. Mol. Genet.* **2008**, *17*, 3965–3974. [CrossRef] [PubMed]
75. Sinibaldi, L.; De Luca, A.; Bellacchio, E.; Conti, E.; Pasini, A.; Paloscia, C.; Spalletta, G.; Caltagirone, C.; Pizzuti, A.; Dallapiccola, B. Mutations of the Nogo-66 receptor (RTN4R) gene in schizophrenia. *Hum. Mutat.* **2004**, *24*, 534–535. [CrossRef] [PubMed]
76. Ono, Y.; Ohno, M.; Shimura, Y. Identification of a putative RNA helicase (HRH1), a human homolog of yeast Prp22. *Mol. Cell. Biol.* **1994**, *14*, 7611–7620. [PubMed]
77. Katoh, Y.; Katoh, M. Comparative integromics on FAT1, FAT2, FAT3 and FAT4. *Int. J. Mol. Med.* **2006**, *18*, 523–528. [PubMed]
78. Neale, B.M.; Kou, Y.; Liu, L.; Ma'ayan, A.; Samocha, K.E.; Sabo, A.; Lin, C.F.; Stevens, C.; Wang, L.S.; Makarov, V.; *et al.* Patterns and rates of exonic de novo mutations in autism spectrum disorders. *Nature* **2012**, *485*, 242–245. [CrossRef] [PubMed]
79. Kenny, E.M.; Cormican, P.; Furlong, S.; Heron, E.; Kenny, G.; Fahey, C.; Kelleher, E.; Ennis, S.; Tropea, D.; Anney, R.; *et al.* Excess of rare novel loss-of-function variants in synaptic genes in schizophrenia and autism spectrum disorders. *Mol. Psychiatry* **2014**, *19*, 872–879. [CrossRef] [PubMed]
80. Kadereit, B.; Kumar, P.; Wang, W.J.; Miranda, D.; Snapp, E.L.; Severina, N.; Torregroza, I.; Evans, T.; Silver, D.L. Evolutionarily conserved gene family important for fat storage. *Proc. Natl. Acad. Sci. USA* **2008**, *105*, 94–99. [CrossRef] [PubMed]
81. Bai, S.W.; Herrera-Abreu, M.T.; Rohn, J.L.; Racine, V.; Tajadura, V.; Suryavanshi, N.; Bechtel, S.; Wiemann, S.; Baum, B.; Ridley, A.J. Identification and characterization of a set of conserved and new regulators of cytoskeletal organization, cell morphology and migration. *BMC Biol.* **2011**, *9*, 54. [CrossRef] [PubMed]
82. Liu, F.; Arias-Vasquez, A.; Sleegers, K.; Aulchenko, Y.S.; Kayser, M.; Sanchez-Juan, P.; Feng, B.J.; Bertoli-Avella, A.M.; van Swieten, J.; Axenovich, T.I.; *et al.* A genomewide screen for late-onset Alzheimer disease in a genetically isolated Dutch population. *Am. J. Hum. Genet.* **2007**, *81*, 17–31. [CrossRef] [PubMed]
83. Jin, J.; Smith, F.D.; Stark, C.; Wells, C.D.; Fawcett, J.P.; Kulkarni, S.; Metalnikov, P.; O'Donnell, P.; Taylor, P.; Taylor, L.; *et al.* Proteomic, functional, and domain-based analysis of *in vivo* 14–3-3 binding proteins involved in cytoskeletal regulation and cellular organization. *Curr. Biol.* **2004**, *14*, 1436–1450. [CrossRef] [PubMed]
84. Kile, B.T.; Viney, E.M.; Willson, T.A.; Brodnicki, T.C.; Cancilla, M.R.; Herlihy, A.S.; Croker, B.A.; Baca, M.; Nicola, N.A.; Hilton, D.J.; *et al.* Cloning and characterization of the genes encoding the ankyrin repeat and SOCS box-containing proteins asb-1, asb-2, asb-3 and asb-4. *Gene* **2000**, *258*, 31–41. [CrossRef] [PubMed]
85. Dodge-Kafka, K.L.; Soughayer, J.; Pare, G.C.; Michel, J.J.C.; Langeberg, L.K.; Kapiloff, M.S.; Scott, J.D. The protein kinase A anchoring protein mAKAP coordinates two integrated cAMP effector pathways. *Nature* **2005**, *437*, 574–578. [CrossRef] [PubMed]
86. Wu, S.; Wright, R.A.; Rockey, P.K.; Burgett, S.G.; Arnold, J.S.; Rosteck, P.R., Jr.; Johnson, B.G.; Schoepp, D.D.; Belagaje, R.M. Group III human metabotropic glutamate receptors 4, 7 and 8: Molecular cloning, functional expression, and comparison of pharmacological properties in RGT cells. *Brain Res. Mol. Brain Res.* **1998**, *53*, 88–97. [CrossRef] [PubMed]
87. Berbari, N.F.; Kin, N.W.; Sharma, N.; Michaud, E.J.; Kesterson, R.A.; Yoder, B.K. Mutations in Traf3ip1 reveal defects in ciliogenesis, embryonic development, and altered cell size regulation. *Dev. Biol.* **2011**, *360*, 66–76. [PubMed]
88. Davis, B.N.; Hilyard, A.C.; Lagna, G.; Hata, A. SMAD proteins control DROSHA-mediated microRNA maturation. *Nature* **2008**, *454*, 56–61. [CrossRef] [PubMed]
89. Goizet, C.; Boukhris, A.; Mundwiller, E.; Tallaksen, C.; Forlani, S.; Toutain, A.; Carriere, N.; Paquis, V.; Depienne, C.; Durr, A.; *et al.* Complicated forms of autosomal dominant hereditary spastic paraplegia are frequent in SPG10. *Hum. Mutat.* **2008**, *30*, E376–E385. [CrossRef]
90. Youngs, E.L.; Hellings, J.A.; Butler, M.G. ANKRD11 gene deletion in a 17-year-old male. *Clin. Dysmorphol.* **2011**, *20*, 170–171. [CrossRef] [PubMed]

91. Sirmaci, A.; Spiliopoulos, M.; Brancati, F.; Powell, E.; Duman, D.; Abrams, A.; Bademci, G.; Agolini, E.; Guo, S.; Konuk, B.; *et al.* Mutations in ANKRD11 cause KBG syndrome, characterized by intellectual disability, skeletal malformations, and macrodontia. *Am. J. Hum. Genet.* **2011**, *89*, 289–294. [CrossRef] [PubMed]
92. Mi, S.; Lee, X.; Hu, Y.; Ji, B.; Shao, Z.; Yang, W.; Huang, G.; Walus, L.; Rhodes, K.; Gong, B.J.; *et al.* Death receptor 6 negatively regulates oligodendrocyte survival, maturation and myelination. *Nat. Med.* **2011**, *17*, 816–821. [CrossRef] [PubMed]
93. Guernsey, D.L.; Jiang, H.; Bedard, K.; Evans, S.C.; Ferguson, M.; Matsuoka, M.; Macgillivray, C.; Nightingale, M.; Perry, S.; Rideout, A.L.; *et al.* Mutation in the gene encoding ubiquitin ligase LRSAM1 in patients with Charcot-Marie-Tooth disease. *PLoS Genet.* **2010**, *6*. [CrossRef]
94. Weterman, M.A.; Sorrentino, V.; Kasher, P.R.; Jakobs, M.E.; van Engelen, B.G.; Fluiter, K.; de Wissel, M.B.; Sizarov, A.; Nurnberg, G.; Nurnberg, P.; *et al.* A frameshift mutation in LRSAM1 is responsible for a dominant hereditary polyneuropathy. *Hum. Mol. Genet.* **2012**, *21*, 358–370. [CrossRef] [PubMed]
95. Burnside, R.D.; Pasion, R.; Mikhail, F.M.; Carroll, A.J.; Robin, N.H.; Youngs, E.L.; Gadi, I.K.; Keitges, E.; Jaswaney, V.L.; Papenhausen, P.R.; *et al.* Microdeletion/microduplication of proximal 15q11.2 between BP1 and BP2: A susceptibility region for neurological dysfunction including developmental and language delay. *Hum. Genet.* **2011**, *130*, 517–528. [CrossRef] [PubMed]
96. Pastuszak, I.; Ketchum, C.; Hermanson, G.; Sjoberg, E.J.; Drake, R.; Elbein, A.D. GDP-L-fucose pyrophosphorylase. Purification, cDNA cloning, and properties of the enzyme. *J. Biol. Chem.* **1998**, *273*, 30165–30174. [CrossRef] [PubMed]
97. Xu, C.; Li, P.P.; Cooke, R.G.; Parikh, S.V.; Wang, K.; Kennedy, J.L.; Warsh, J.J. TRPM2 variants and bipolar disorder risk: Confirmation in a family-based association study. *Bipolar Disord.* **2009**, *11*, 1–10. [CrossRef] [PubMed]
98. Bueno, M.T.; Richard, S. SUMOylation negatively modulates target gene occupancy of the KDM5B, a histone lysine demethylase. *Epigenetics* **2013**, *8*, 1162–1175. [CrossRef] [PubMed]
99. Catchpole, S.; Spencer-Dene, B.; Hall, D.; Santangelo, S.; Rosewell, I.; Guenatri, M.; Beatson, R.; Scibetta, A.G.; Burchell, J.M.; Taylor-Papadimitriou, J. PLU-1/JARID1B/KDM5B is required for embryonic survival and contributes to cell proliferation in the mammary gland and in ER+ breast cancer cells. *Int. J. Oncol.* **2011**, *38*, 1267–1277. [PubMed]
100. Carmona-Mora, P.; Walz, K. Retinoic acid induced 1, RAI1: A dosage sensitive gene related to neurobehavioral alterations including autistic behavior. *Curr. Genomics* **2010**, *11*, 607–617. [CrossRef] [PubMed]
101. Van Wijk, S.J.; Timmers, H.T. The family of ubiquitin-conjugating enzymes (E2s): Deciding between life and death of proteins. *FASEB J.* **2010**, *24*, 981–993. [CrossRef] [PubMed]
102. Kirchmair, R.; Hogue-Angeletti, R.; Gutierrez, J.; Fischer-Colbrie, R.; Winkler, H. Secretoneurin—A neuropeptide generated in brain, adrenal medulla and other endocrine tissues by proteolytic processing of secretogranin II (chromogranin C). *Neuroscience* **1993**, *53*, 359–365. [CrossRef] [PubMed]
103. Tanji, K.; Kamitani, T.; Mori, F.; Kakita, A.; Takahashi, H.; Wakabayashi, K. TRIM9, a novel brain-specific E3 ubiquitin ligase, is repressed in the brain of Parkinson's disease and dementia with Lewy bodies. *Neurobiol. Dis.* **2010**, *38*, 210–218. [CrossRef] [PubMed]
104. Takash, W.; Canizares, J.; Bonneaud, N.; Poulat, F.; Mattei, M.G.; Jay, P.; Berta, P. SOX7 transcription factor: Sequence, chromosomal localisation, expression, transactivation and interference with Wnt signalling. *Nucleic Acids Res.* **2001**, *29*, 4274–4283. [CrossRef] [PubMed]
105. Agrawal, A.; Lynskey, M.T.; Hinrichs, A.; Grucza, R.; Saccone, S.F.; Krueger, R.; Neuman, R.; Howells, W.; Fisher, S.; Fox, L.; *et al.* A genome-wide association study of DSM-IV cannabis dependence. *Addict. Biol.* **2011**, *16*, 514–518. [CrossRef] [PubMed]
106. Kokura, K.; Sun, L.; Bedford, M.T.; Fang, J. Methyl-H3K9-binding protein MPP8 mediates E-cadherin gene silencing and promotes tumour cell motility and invasion. *EMBO J.* **2010**, *29*, 3673–3687. [CrossRef] [PubMed]
107. Bonnert, T.P.; McKernan, R.M.; Farrar, S.; le Bourdelles, B.; Heavens, R.P.; Smith, D.W.; Hewson, L.; Rigby, M.R.; Sirinathsinghji, D.J.; Brown, N.; *et al.* Theta, a novel γ-aminobutyric acid type a receptor subunit. *Proc. Natl. Acad. Sci. USA* **1999**, *96*, 9891–9896. [CrossRef] [PubMed]
108. Kobayashi, K.; Kuroda, S.; Fukata, M.; Nakamura, T.; Nagase, T.; Nomura, N.; Matsuura, Y.; Yoshida-Kubomura, N.; Iwamatsu, A.; Kaibuchi, K. P140Sra-1 (specifically rac1-associated protein) is a novel specific target for rac1 small GTPase. *J. Biol. Chem.* **1998**, *273*, 291–295. [CrossRef] [PubMed]

109. Schenck, A.; Bardoni, B.; Moro, A.; Bagni, C.; Mandel, J.L. A highly conserved protein family interacting with the fragile X mental retardation protein (FMRP) and displaying selective interactions with fmrp-related proteins FXR1P and FXR2P. *Proc. Natl. Acad. Sci. USA* **2001**, *98*, 8844–8849. [CrossRef] [PubMed]

110. Yang, Y.; Muzny, D.M.; Xia, F.; Niu, Z.; Person, R.; Ding, Y.; Ward, P.; Braxton, A.; Wang, M.; Buhay, C.; *et al.* Molecular findings among patients referred for clinical whole-exome sequencing. *JAMA* **2014**, *312*, 1870–1879. [CrossRef] [PubMed]

5

Delineating the Common Biological Pathways Perturbed by ASD's Genetic Etiology: Lessons from Network-Based Studies

Oded Oron and Evan Elliott *

Molecular and Behavioral Neurosciences Lab, Bar-Ilan University, Faculty of Medicine, 13215 Safed, Israel; odedoron@gmail.com

* Correspondence: evan.elliott@biu.ac.il

Academic Editor: Merlin G. Butler

Abstract: In recent decades it has become clear that Autism Spectrum Disorder (ASD) possesses a diverse and heterogeneous genetic etiology. Aberrations in hundreds of genes have been associated with ASD so far, which include both rare and common variations. While one may expect that these genes converge on specific common molecular pathways, which drive the development of the core ASD characteristics, the task of elucidating these common molecular pathways has been proven to be challenging. Several studies have combined genetic analysis with bioinformatical techniques to uncover molecular mechanisms that are specifically targeted by autism-associated genetic aberrations. Recently, several analysis have suggested that particular signaling mechanisms, including the Wnt and Ca^{2+}/Calmodulin-signaling pathways are often targeted by autism-associated mutations. In this review, we discuss several studies that determine specific molecular pathways affected by autism-associated mutations, and then discuss more in-depth into the biological roles of a few of these pathways, and how they may be involved in the development of ASD. Considering that these pathways may be targeted by specific pharmacological intervention, they may prove to be important therapeutic targets for the treatment of ASD.

Keywords: ASD; autism; networks; genetics; Fragile-X Syndrome; Wnt; mTOR; Calmodulin; Calcium; NGF

1. The Genetic Basis of Autism

Autism Spectrum Disorder (ASD) is a developmental disorder characterized by persistent deficits in social communication, as well as restricted and repetitive patterns of behavior. It has been well characterized that genetic aberrations have a prominent role in the etiology of ASD [1]. Among the first studies to support a genetic etiology were twin studies published in the 1970s by Folstein and Rutter [2,3]. A recent meta-analysis by Rutter, encompassing a total of 6413 twins, showed that the heritability rate in families with an autistic proband was in the range of 64–91% [4]. Furthermore, it has been well-established that ASD overlaps at both the behavioral and genetic levels with other disorders such as social anxiety, Attention Deficit and Hyperactivity Disorder (ADHD), Intellectual Disability (ID), bipolar disorder and schizophrenia [5–8]. For example, Khazanda et al. discovered 23 genes, many of which are involved in circadian entrainment, that are associated with ASD, bipolar disorder and schizophrenia, therefore demonstrating shared genes and genetic pathways between various psychiatric disorders [7]. As such, common behavioral phenotypes of these disorders may have a root in shared genetic etiology.

A heterogeneous genetic etiology for ASD has been firmly established. Historically, some of the first genes that were successfully associated to autism were those responsible for syndromic forms of autism. Thus far, approximately 35 such syndromes have been documented [9]. A sub-group of these syndromic autisms are mendelian monogenic, and consistently develop due to rare mutations. For example, in the case of Fragile-X Syndrome (FXS), which develops due to aberrations in the Fragile-X Mental Retardation 1 (*FMR1*) gene, up to 30% of these male patients also develop ASD [10]. Cortical Dysplasia-focal Epilepsy (CDFE) syndrome is caused by mutations in Contactin Associated Protein 2 (*CNTNAP2*), where a subgroup of patients express autistic behavior [11]. Tuberous sclerosis is caused by mutations in either Tuberous Sclerosis 1/2 (*TSC1/TCS2*), where up to 61% of patients express autistic behaviors [12]. Rett syndrome, which includes autistic behavior, is caused by mutations in the Methyl CpG binding protein 2 (*MECP2*) [13]. Another group of syndromic autisms arise from Copy Number Variations (CNV) [14], which contain large duplication/deletion loci that usually encompass several genes, yet the causative gene is often not known. One such example is Phelan-McDermid syndrome where up to 9 Mb are deleted at Chr22q13 encompassing up to 130 genes [15]. The most notable gene in this CNV is *SHANK3/PROSAP2*, where mutations in this gene alone have been shown to be associated with ASD [16,17]. Additional CNVs include the 15q11-13 deletion or duplication syndromes [18], the chromosome 16p11.2 deletion or duplication syndromes [19,20] and the 2q23.1 microdeletion syndrome [7]. Most syndromic autisms, such as CDFE, TSC or the 2q23.1 microdeletion syndrome are considered extremely rare, however the highest discovery rate observed in FXS accounts for no more than 2% of autistic cases [9].

A wider search for ASD's genetic etiology started with linkage studies, which uncovered several candidate loci, including 2q, 3q 7q and 20p. However, it was primarily through Next Generation Sequencing (NGS) technologies that majority of genes were discovered, and by 2012, 10–20% of ASD cases had a known genetic link [9]. One approach for locating new genetic candidates involved in ASD development is to determine de-novo mutations in gene coding regions, usually found in sporadic familial cases. In 2011, O'Roak et al. conducted the first exome-wide sequencing study in ASD on 20 sporadic cases, revealing de-novo mutations in *FOXP1*, *GRIN2B*, *SCN1A* and *LAMC3* [21]. In 2012, in an effort to discover de-novo mutations, the Simons Simplex Collection conducted three large exome-sequencing trails which included approximately 750 families with affected and unaffected siblings. Many promising genes were identified, including *SCN2A*, *CHD8* and *NTNG1* [22–24]. By that time, it had become increasingly clear that genetic mutations involved in ASD do not fall into one particular biological category, but seem to be found in genes involved in several different biological systems. In recent years, whole genome sequencing studies are also beginning to appear, which aim to discover genetic aberrations in both coding and noncoding regions. One such study, by Yuen et al., found genetic aberrations in *STXBP1*, *UBE3A*, *KATNAL2*, *THRA*, *KCNQ4*, *MYH14*, *GJB6* and *COL11A1*, some of which have been previously associated with ASD and some with overlapping conditions such as hearing loss [25]. In addition, several Genome-Wide Association Studies (GWAS) emphasized the significance of common genetic variation to the inheritance of autistic traits [26].

To this day, over 800 genes have been identified and associated with ASD development [27]. Given this heterogeneous genetic reality, it has been hypothesized that the multitude of genetic aberrations are affecting specific molecular pathways that might be in common across the autistic spectrum, and are responsible for dysregulated neurodevelopment [28]. Discovering such common pathways has proven to be challenging. To address this difficulty, it is appropriate to perform network-based analysis of autism associated genes [29]. In the following chapters, we will discuss attempts at using network-based approaches to discover candidate signaling pathways that are effected by ASD-associated genetic aberrations, and how these signaling pathways may be involved in dysregulated neurodevelopment and the phenotypes of ASD.

2. Searching for Common Molecular Targets of Autism Mutations

2.1. Protein–Protein Network Analysis and Pathways Enrichment Tools

One approach to discovering molecular pathways that are commonly targeted by autism-associated mutations is to perform Protein-Protein Interaction (PPI) network analysis to identify groups of proteins within a given list of proteins that physically interact with each other. This analysis uses different databases that curate experimentally validated or predicted protein-protein interactions [29]. PPI also identifies hubs, highly interconnected proteins, which might prove to be central in the molecular pathway. However, this approach has some disadvantages and biases. First, tissue specific PPI databases are scarce, which are necessary to understand protein interactions in specific tissues, such as the brain. A very partial solution to this problem is to combine PPI databases with RNA expression from the specific tissue, therefore making sure that you only take into account proteins which are found in that specific tissue. Additional tools used to reveal biologically-relevant pathways within a gene list are gene ontology databases and signaling pathway enrichment tools. The Gene Ontology project initiated by the Gene Ontology Consortium (GOC) strives to provide a unifying vocabulary to genes and their biological roles [30]. In addition, there is a growing number of signaling pathway enrichment tools available for free or through commercial license [31]. There are several differences that should be considered when using these tools, such as method of data curation (manually and computerized), algorithms used to generate signaling pathway maps, types of pathway maps (e.g., disease specific, kinase signaling, hormone mediated) and breadth of knowledgebase. For example, in the next section, we mention studies which used KEGG and IPA pathway enrichment tools to generate pathways that might be affected in ASD. Due to the fact that IPA is a commercial tool, it is difficult to thoroughly compare it to other tools, and thus, reviews conducting such comparisons lack information about IPA. However, one important difference between KEGG and IPA is the size of their knowledgebase. KEGG mainly curates interaction and reactions of molecular pathways from the literature, while IPA also imports data from several external databases, which increases its knowledgebase substantially [32,33]. Therefore, it is necessary to integrate knowledge from several different pathway analysis tools in order to discover biological pathways that are commonly targeted by autism-associated mutations.

2.2. Autism-Associated Signaling Pathways Discovered Using Network Analysis and Pathway Enrichment Tools

As part of the effort conducted by the SSC in 2012, O'Roak et al. sequenced the exome of 209 families with sporadic cases of ASD, revealing 126 genes which had truncation or missense mutations, followed by PPI analysis, to determine if these genes form a biologically-relevant network [23]. They discovered one highly interconnected cluster of mutated genes, which included genes involved both in chromatin-binding and β-catenin function. An additional network analysis conducted with the IPA tool enriched 8 Wnt-signaling regulators, which are involved in the regulation of β-catenin, as we will explain later. Therefore, combination of exome sequencing with downstream network analysis revealed an autism-associated molecular pathway, the Wnt-β-catenin pathway. This was not the first study to suggest the involvement of Wnt-signaling in ASD [34,35], however it strongly demonstrated that network analysis may reveal pathways that are highly important for further research. In a 2014 follow up bioinformatics study which included the combined data for the O'Roak et al. study, and two other de-novo ASD mutation studies that were published in the same issue of *Nature*, a subset of these de-novo mutations were enriched for genes involved in chromatin-binding [36]. A separate study collected genome association data of rare CNVs from 6742 ASD patients, and constructed PPI networks based on the genes deleted or duplicated due to the CNVs. Calmodulin1, which is a major regulator of Calcium-signaling, was found as a central hub in the PPI network [37]. An additional network analysis of autism-associated genes has suggested a role for both Wnt and calcium pathways in ASD. Wen et al. performed KEGG pathway analysis on the SFARI annotated list of autism-associated genes. They found that these genes were particularly enriched for biological pathways including Calcium-signaling, Wnt-signaling, mTOR, and cellular adhesion molecules [38].

A different strategy to identify molecular pathways that are dysregulated by autism-associated mutations is to use publicly available data of gene expression patterns in the human brain to build gene expression networks and PPI networks that are found in specific brain regions, and then to probe if any of these networks are enriched for autism-associated genes, and are therefore likely to be perturbed by autism-related mutations. Lin et al. used such an approach to identify PPI networks in the brain that are effected by the autism-associated CNV at chromosome 16p11.2 [39]. Using published databases of gene expression and protein interaction data, the authors built protein interaction networks that appear in specific brain regions, and at specific developmental time points. The authors then discovered that four of these protein interaction networks would be disrupted by the CNV, particularly during mid-fetal stage and in early childhood. Gene ontology analysis of these protein networks showed enrichment for Wnt-signaling and NGF-signaling. A similar method was used to discover human brain protein networks dysregulated by rare or common variants associated with autism. Ben-David et al., built brain-region specific gene co-expression modules using WGCNA [40]. They found that a co-expression module that was highly effected by both rare and common autism-associated variants was enriched for genes involved in synaptic transmission and the Calmodulin-binding pathway. To summarize, these studies used different methodologies to uncover molecular pathways targeted by ASD mutations and implicated the Wnt-signaling and Ca^{2+}/Calmodulin-signaling [37–40]. Therefore, we will focus on defining these two specific pathways and how they may be related to the autism phenotype, followed by a short discussion of some of the other pathways identified.

3. Wnt-Signaling

3.1. *Roles for Wnt-Signaling in Neurodevelopment and Adult Brain*

Wnt-signaling pathways orchestrate cellular proliferation, polarity and differentiation; processes that are crucial for healthy tissue morphogenesis, especially in the embryonic stage [41]. Dysregulation of these pathways have been implicated in a wide variety of cancers, as well as in other pathologies, such as type II diabetes, osteoporosis and heart conditions [41,42]. In humans there are 19 Wnt glycoprotein ligands, which activate signal transduction pathways through binding to one of the 10 Frizzled receptors. As of today, there are two extensively researched Wnt pathways; a canonical pathway and a non-canonical pathway. In the canonical pathway the secreted Wnt glycoproteins bind to Frizzled receptors, as well as either the LRP6 or LRP5 co-receptors, to initiate a signaling cascade. The activated receptor recruits the scaffolding protein Dishevelled, which recruits and sequesters the Axin-GSK3β-APC destruction complex, thus preventing its role in phosphorylating β-catenin, leaving it stable for downstream activity. Stabilized β-catenin is transported to the nucleus where it fulfills its role as a co-transcription factor by binding to the TCF/LEF transcription factors, or it relocates to the cellular membrane where it maintains cell-cell adhesion complexes [41,42]. The two non-canonical Wnt pathways are independent of β-catenin, and include the Wnt/JNK pathway, which drives polarized cell movements such as neuronal crest migration, as well as the Wnt/Calcium pathway that has been shown to be involved in cardiac development [43].

Canonical Wnt-signaling has a pivotal role both in the developing and mature brain. Much evidence has indicated that during development the Wnt pathway regulates the balance between proliferation and differentiation of neuronal progenitor and precursor cells, as was recently reviewed by Noelanders and Vleminckx [44]. In transgenic mice with overexpression of stabilized β-catenin, neuronal precursor cells in the ventricular zone continue to divide beyond their natural timeframe, resulting in enlarged brains and deeper sulci folds that resemble higher mammals [45]. Concurrently, inhibition of β-catenin during embryonic development leads to premature differentiation of precursors to neurons [46]. These studies suggest that Wnt-signaling promotes proliferation of neuronal precursors and delays their differentiation. There is some evidence suggesting Wnt-signaling may inhibit proliferation in certain circumstances.

For example, as shown in developing zebrafish, induced activation of Wnt8 reduced the population of neuronal progenitor in the hypothalamus; reduction in neuronal progenitors was also induced by the canonical Wnt pathway activator, BIO [47]. These studies suggest that Wnt-signaling can regulate neuronal precursor proliferation in a manner that is either species-specific, or cell type-specific.

In addition to its roles in development, Wnt-signaling also affects Neuronal Stem Cell (NSC) proliferation and differentiation in the mature brain. One study of Wnt-signaling in NSCs used mice which express lacZ under the control of a TCF transcription response [48]. These mice received intraventricular infusions of the mitotic inhibitor Ara-C, which kills the dividing progenitor cells and decreases NSCs; followed with BrdU infusions, which allows the tracking of the regeneration of NSCs in the Subventricular Zone (SVZ). 30% of the BrdU positive cells displayed active Wnt-signaling (LacZ); and when Wnt-signaling was pharmacologically blocked, the number of neurospheres in the SVZ significantly decreased. Wnt-signaling has also been shown to induce NSC proliferation after injury [48]. Mice subjected to a stroke-inducing surgery (Pial Vessel Disruption, or PVD) displayed an increase in lacZ expressing neuronal stem cells of the SVZ after seven days. Other studies showed that Wnt-signaling is also involved in the differentiation of NSCs in the mature brain. For example, in adult NSCs of the SVZ, Wnt-signaling induces cell-cycle exit in the presence of Hipk1, an interactor of β-catenin. Furthermore, when overexpressing β-catenin and Hipk1, an increase of the cell-cycle inhibitor P16Ink4 was observed [49]. Therefore, Wnt has a role both in the proliferation and differentiation of NSCs cells in the adult brain.

Apart from its role in NSCs, Wnt-signaling has a positive developmental role in the maturation of dendrites and spines. The α-catenin/β-catenin/*N*-cadherin complex acts as a scaffold between intracellular actin and extracellular cadherin-dependent interactions [50,51]. This role is important for dendrite arborization in the developing brain, as demonstrated by the fact that overexpression of β-catenin, α-catenin and *N*-cadherin individually, and co-expression of β-catenin and *N*-cadherin in vitro, both induce increased dendritic branching [52]. In addition, β-catenin has also been implicated in spine pruning and maturation as part of the β-catenin/*N*-cadherin complex. By inducing a conditional knockout of β-catenin in the cerebral cortex and hippocampus of mice, spine density is increased and is comprised mostly from immature spines [53]. This suggests that pruning of immature spines may be dependent on β-catenin function.

In addition to the roles in neuronal differentiation and morphology, β-catenin has been suggested to have an additional role in neurotransmission through two distinct mechanisms. First, translocation of β-catenin to spines may increase the size of the post synaptic density (PSD) which leads to increased synaptic transmission [54]. This was shown by inducing a point mutation, which prevents the phosphorylation of Tyr654 in β-catenin, and results in its increased localization to spines. Considering the role of β-catenin in the α-catenin/β-catenin/*N*-cadherin complex, and the complex's importance in inducing cell-cell contacts [55], the authors deciphered if increased presence of β-catenin in spines might increase synaptic contacts, and affect other properties such as postsynaptic morphology and neurotransmission. Interestingly, they observed more intense and larger PSD-95 puncta and increased mEPSCs. Second, in the presynaptic neuron, β-catenin has been shown to have a role in recruiting vesicles to the presynaptic membrane: β-catenin has a PDZ domain used to recruit PDZ domain containing proteins such as Veli and Cadherin clusters [56]. Veli has been shown to create a tripartite complex with CASK and Mint1, which binds Munc18-1. This complex is essential for vesicle docking to the plasma membrane [57,58]. It has also been shown that regulation of synaptic vesicle release into the synaptic cleft is important for healthy development of synaptic plasticity in 4–8 day old rats [59]. In that regard, β-catenin is suggested to have an essential role. This has been shown by siRNA-mediated knockdown of synaptic β-catenin, which increased spillage of vesicle content into the synaptic cleft in nascent presynaptic terminals [60]. An additional study revealed that neuronal cultures treated with Wnt8A-conditioned media displayed increased PSD95 puncta, and that the co-receptor LRP6 selectively localizes to excitatory synapses where it takes part in regulating excitatory synaptic development [61]. These studies show that Wnt-signaling, and in particular β-catenin, is essential for normal brain development as well as adult brain performance.

3.2. *How Wnt-Signaling May Be Involved in ASD*

From the known roles of Wnt-signaling in neuronal differentiation, morphology, and neurotransmission, we can propose possible roles for dysregulated Wnt-signaling in the processes that are dysregulated in the brain of individuals diagnosed with ASD. Numerous studies have witnessed differences in cortical patterning or spine morphology in the brain of individuals with ASD. In some cases, it has been shown that cortical dendritic spine density is increased in the brain of individuals with autism [62]. This matches the phenotype of the β-catenin knockout mice, which displays increased spines [53]. However, it is not clear if the increase in spine density in the ASD brain is due to an increase in immature spines, as is in the case of the knockout mice. In addition, studies have shown dysregulation of cytoarchitecture in the cortex and in the architecture of the microcolumns in the cortex of individuals diagnosed with ASD [63,64]. A separate study, using the three dimensional imaging technique CLARITY, determined abnormal connections between axons in the brain of individuals with ASD [65]. Considering that dysregulation of Wnt-signaling affects development of normal cortical architecture, as well as neuronal morphology, it is possible that dysregulated Wnt-signaling is involved in these dysregulations in the ASD brain.

Experimentation in mouse models have also given more insight into the possible roles of Wnt in the development of ASD. Interestingly, a conditional knockdown of β-catenin in Parvalbumin (PV) neurons in mice induced increased repetitive behaviors and anxiety, decreased social interaction, and an increase in PV neuron density in the prefrontal cortex [66]. An additional Wnt-signaling component, Glycogen Synthase Kinase-3 (GSK3) was recently reviewed as a key driver of ASD development, as well as a therapeutic target for FXS [67,68]. GSK3 is hyperactive in several brain regions of the FXS mouse model [69] and impaired social preference and exaggerated anxiety during social interaction have been recorded in a GSK3 knockin mouse model [35]. So using this model, researchers inhibited GSK3 functioning in the hippocampus to explore how its hyperactivity contributes to FXS phenotypes. Both novel object detection and hippocampal learning, which are deficient in this mouse model, were rescued [70,71]. These studies suggest a direct link between Wnt-signaling and autism-like behavior in autism mouse models.

In addition, recent studies in mouse models have determined how autism-related mutations may induce autism-related behaviors through the dysregulation of Wnt-signaling. One such example is *CHD8*, a gene that was recently found to be strongly associated to ASD and encodes for a chromatin-binding protein. One of the first studies on CHD8 in the brain shows that it acts as a positive regulator of the Wnt pathway in the brain [72]. CHD8 binds to the promoter regions of Fzd1, Dvl3 and β-catenin. Knockdown of CHD8 during cortical development results in their downregulation, leading to the reduction of the TCF/LEF transcription factor family and ultimately defective brain development. By expressing a degradation-resistant β-catenin construct in CHD8-downregulated embryos, researchers rescued the aberrant dendritic arborization as well as increased spine density in the CHD8-downregulated mice. In addition, the study showed that inducing stable β-catenin restores the aberrant social and anxiogenic behaviors to the levels seen in control mice. The Shank scaffolding family is an additional group of high-risk ASD genes that have been suggested to interact with Wnt-signaling components. In a recent publication by Harris et al., a Shank-knockout drosophila model was used to study of the potential molecular pathways that the Shank family of genes regulate [73]. Surprisingly, the study revealed that the non-canonical Wnt-Frizzled Nuclear Import (FNI) pathway was affected. In this pathway, Wnt binding induces internalization of the Fz2 receptor, followed by proteolytic cleavage of the receptors' N-terminus to form Fz2-C, which translocates into the nucleus, where it regulates transcription necessary for synaptic development [74,75]. By knocking out Shank family genes, Harris et al. revealed reduction of the Fz2 internalization into the post-synaptic membrane, reduction of Fz2-C presence in the nucleus, and abnormal synaptic development. Therefore, there is accumulating evidence that autism-associated mutations affect abnormal cortical patterning, synaptic development, and autism-like behaviors through modulation of Wnt-signaling pathway.

4. Calcium and Calmodulin Signaling

4.1. Roles of Calcium-Signaling and the Calmodulin-Binding Pathway in the Brain

Shifts in Calcium (Ca^{2+}) concentrations have been shown to affect the function of several tissues and organs such as the heart, pancreas and components of the Central Nervous System (CNS). Therefore, it is of no surprise that disequilibrium in signaling leads to pathology [76]. In the brain, Ca^{2+} performs specific functions in the presynapse and postsynapse. In the presynapse, arrival of action potentials induce an increase of presynaptic Ca^{2+} levels through activation of the N and P/Q-voltage-gated channel. The influx of Ca^{2+} leads directly to the release of neurotransmitters [77]. However, the role of Ca^{2+} in postsynaptic signal transduction pathways has been found to be dysregulated in the autism genetic studies discussed previously.

Ca^{2+}-induced effects in postsynaptic neuronal function and excitability are mediated through its binding with the protein Calmodulin (CaM; Ca^{2+}-Modulated protein), which induces signaling to additional downstream CaM Kinases [77,78]. Glutamic acid induces Ca^{2+} influx at the postsynapse by binding to *N*-methyl-D-aspartate receptors (NMDARs) and metabotropic glutamate receptors such as mGlur1, which initiates the release of internal Ca^{2+} stores [77]. After binding Ca^{2+}, CaM may induce the activation of CaMKII or CaMKK2. CaMKII is a dodecamer holoenzyme which has 28 isoforms composed of four different subunits (CaMKIIα through δ), and resides mostly in spines and dendritic shafts of excitatory neurons [79–81]. The mandatory role of CaMKII in synaptic function has been well described [82]. Active CaM binds to CaMKII subunits and relieves them from autoinhibition, which leads to autophosphorylation and kinase activity [78]. CaMKIIα kinase activity is mandatory for long-term potentiation (LTP), the main electrophysiological determinant of experience-dependent synaptic strengthening, and is highly involved in behavioral processes, such as learning and memory. Deletion of *CAMKIIA*, or inhibiting the binding of CaM and Ca^{2+} to CaMKII, inhibits LTP induction [83]. CaMKIIβ has been shown to interact with cytoskeleton subunits such as F-actin, α-catinin and the PSD protein Densin-180 for the purpose of spine size regulation, as well as to affect long-term synaptic plasticity by binding and regulating receptors such as GluN2B and GluA1 [80,82]. Furthermore, accumulating evidence show that CaMKII phosphorylates the $GABA_A$ β, $\gamma2$ and $\alpha1$ subunits, and regulates $GABA_A$ trafficking to the synaptic membrane [84]. Since GABA is the major inhibitory neurotransmitter, these findings highlight that CaMKII plays important roles in both excitatory and inhibitory neurotransmission.

CaM also activates CaMKK2, whose activity is crucial for spatial memory formation, and the downstream activation of additional kinases: CaMKI is a positive transducer of growth cone motility which is essential for neurite elongation and arborization [85]; phosphorylation of CaMKIV increases gene expression and protein synthesis, and is also necessary for contextual fear [86]. CaMKK2 also phosphorylates other kinases such as the AMP-activated Protein Kinase (AMPK) who's activity is essential for regulating the energy intake necessary for typical brain function [87]. Interestingly, *CAMKIG* and *CAMKIV* are among the genes which were enriched in the Calmodulin-binding pathway in the Ben-David et al. publication, which looked for common molecular pathways affected by rare and common variations in ASD [40]. Overall, this data provides compelling evidence of how Ca^{2+} signaling and the CaM pathway are involved in neurological functions by affecting a variety of synaptic characteristics, neurotransmission via excitatory and inhibitory receptor regulation and important biological functions such as LTP and LTM. Deficits in the CaM pathway and its branching cascades have the potential to be involved in many neuropsychiatric conditions due to their broad influence on many biological systems, and more specifically by the way it regulates neurotransmission and synaptic characteristics.

4.2. How Calcium-Signaling and the Calmodulin-Binding Pathway May Be Involved in ASD

Considering the central role of Ca^{2+} and CaM signaling in synaptic function and neuronal connectivity, it is reasonable to presume that dysregulation of this pathway could lead to autism-related symptoms. However, it is technically challenging to decipher if there are any dysregulation in synaptic functions such as LTP in humans diagnosed with ASD, while evidence for such dysregulation have been frequently observed in several ASD mouse models [88,89]. Therefore, our understanding of the possible role of Ca^{2+} signaling in autism is still at its infancy, compared to more established role of the Wnt pathway. Of great interest, one human study has used Transcranial Magnetic Stimulation (TMS) to study changes in long term potentiation-like synaptic plasticity in humans diagnosed with ASD [90]. In this study, the researchers performed TMS in cortical regions followed by motor-evoked potentials. Individuals with ASD did not show any changes in motor-evoked potentials after TMS, unlike neurotypical controls. This study suggests deficits in plasticity that resemble deficits in LTP. Additional human studies have verified similar deficits in neuronal network connectivity in ASD patients, as has been recently reviewed [91]. These studies have often found changes in electroencephalographic signals after different sensory stimuli in ASD patients. Overall, these studies suggest deficits in synaptic and network activity that may be related to Calcium-signaling.

While studies of Ca^{2+} signaling in the human brain remains challenging, recent studies have determined disturbances in Ca^{2+} signaling in cells derived from individuals with ASD. Agonist-evoked Ca^{2+} signaling has been shown to be dysfunctional in skin fibroblasts derived from individuals diagnosed with autism [92]. An elegant study was performed on induced Pluripotent Stem Cells (iPSC) derived from individuals diagnosed with Timothy syndrome [93], a syndromic autism where 80% of individuals are diagnosed with ASD. These iPSCs were differentiated into neurons in vitro and displayed dysregulated Ca^{2+} signaling and changes in activity-dependent gene transcription. While these studies suggest that Ca^{2+} signaling and CaM may be involved in the biology of ASD, technological improvements of Ca^{2+} imaging in the human brain, and more high-throughput studies in individuals diagnosed with ASD, are necessary to understand the role of Ca^{2+} in the specific behaviors and brain regions that are particularly relevant to ASD.

Animal models and in vitro studies have given some additional insights into how dysregulation of Ca^{2+} and Calmodulin-binding may be involved in abnormal neurodevelopment. For example, CaMKIV positively regulates the transcription of FMRP (Fragile-X Mental Retardation Protein), the causative gene of FXS [94]. A follow-up study found that a Single Nucleotide Polymorphism (SNP) in the gene CaMKIV (rs25925) is associated with higher risk for ASD development in a European cohort. This SNP appears to be located on a splicing factor binding site, and is predicted to alter the balance of CaMKIV isoforms [95]. In addition, CaMKIIα has been shown to regulate the activity of mGluR5, which is a potential target in FXS treatment [96]. It is still unclear how CaMKIIα perturb mGluR5 activity in FXS, however one proposed mechanism suggests that CaMKIIα is significantly elevated in the synapse of FXS mouse models, which might cause the hyperphosphorylation of the Homer 1 (H1) and 2 (H2) scaffolding proteins, resulting in their dissociation from mGluR5. This dissociation allows the short Homer 1 isoform, H1α, to bind mGluR5 and induce ligand-independent activity of the receptor [97]. Inhibition of mGluR5 in *FMR1* knockout mice improved learning and memory, which highlighted this therapy as a promising pharmaceutical treatment [98]. However, clinical trials that were designed to inhibit mGluR5 and its downstream pathways in FXS patients described only partial success, as extensively reviewed by Schaefer, Davenport and Erickson [99]. In one clinical study, the mGluR5 selective antagonist fenobam induced improvement in prepulse inhibition, but had no effects on the excessive impulsivity observed in FXS patients [100]. In another clinical study, treatment of a small cohort of FXS patients with Lithium—which mitigates signaling pathways activated via mGluR5 signaling—resulted in significant behavioral improvements such in hyperactivity and inappropriate speech, however induced only a tendency for improvement in irritability, lethargy and repetitive behaviors [101].

An additional syndromic autism linked with Ca^{2+} signaling dysregulation is Angelman Syndrome (AS), which is characterized by the deletion of the maternal allele of 15q13-11, including the gene *UBE3A*. In the *UBE3A* maternal allele null mouse model, disruptions in the autophosphorylation of CaMKIIα, which is essential for its kinase activity, is responsible for LTP deficits of the hippocampus [102]. CaMKIIα has also been found to interact directly with scaffolding proteins associated with ASD development. Specifically, using immunoprecipitation to pull-down CaMKII from different neuronal cell fractions of the forebrain, it was determined that CaMKII binds Shank3, Dlgap2 and Syngap1 in the synapse [103]. In summary, various studies have identified CaMKIV and CaMKIIα as the two main Ca^{2+} signaling enzymes that are most likely to be involved in ASD. On one hand the Ca^{2+} and Calmodulin-binding pathways may be interesting targets for therapeutic interventions. However, future studies in mouse models, and electrophysiology studies in humans, are necessary to understand how and why the Ca^{2+} signaling pathway is involved in ASD. Further studies are particularly needed to clarify the potential roles of Ca^{2+} signaling in social behaviors or repetitive behaviors, which form the core features of ASD.

5. Additional Signaling Pathways

Thus far, we have discussed the Wnt-signaling and Calmodulin-binding pathways as potential molecular mechanisms that are involved in ASD, due to the fact that these pathways have been found to be enriched for ASD-associated genes in multiple network-based analysis. In addition to these pathways, the mTOR-signaling and NGF-signaling pathways have also appeared in some of the discussed bioinformatic publications, although not quite as often as the Wnt and Calmodulin pathways. The mTOR pathway has already gained significant attention in connection to autism due to its significant involvement in syndromic autisms, as explained below. There is yet little known connection between NGF and ASD, however it is worth shortly considering the possible connections, considering its roles in brain development and function.

5.1. The PI3K/Mtor-Signaling Pathway

Mammalian Target of Rapamycin (mTOR) is a serine/threonine kinase, which is considered a central kinase in organism development. Therefore it is of no surprise that ablation of mTOR results in in-utero death a short time after the implantation stage of the embryo in the uterus endometrium [104]. The mTOR pathway regulates brain development through two main cascades driven by two complexes: mTOR complex 1 (mTORC1) and mTOR complex 2 (mTORC2). In the developing brain each cascade seems to take part in unique developmental duties [105]. The mTORC2 cascade facilitates growth cone motility through its interaction with actin filaments. This role is essential for pathfinding dynamics of the neurite in the developing brain. Additionally, mTORC2 has an indirect influence on neuron size and morphology by regulating mTORC1 through RAC-alpha serine/threonine-protein kinase (AKT) activity. AKT activates mTORC1 which in turn phosphorylates p70 ribosomal protein S6 kinase (p70S6K) and eukaryotic Initiation Factor 4E (eIF4E)-binding protein (4EBP), which enhance a downstream cascade necessary for both protein synthesis and lipid synthesis. The products are used for plasma membrane expansion that is required for neurite elongation and arborization, and dendrite formation. This developmental mechanism driven by mTORC1 may also be directly activated by extracellular stimulation such as growth factors and neurotransmitters.

There is an abundance of publications linking mTOR-signaling to ASD, and it is considered to be one of the most promising converging signaling pathway candidates for ASD development. The involvement of mTOR-signaling in ASD and other neuropsychiatric conditions has been thoroughly reviewed previously [106]. However, unlike the previously described pathways in this review, and to the best of our knowledge, only one publication has described a link between the mTOR-signaling pathway and ASD using a network analysis-based approach [38]. Rather, the evidence for mTOR-signaling as a promising common ASD pathway candidate arise mostly from in vivo research into syndromic autisms such as Tuberous Sclerosis (TS), *PTEN*-related syndrome, Neurofibromatosis Type 1 (NF-1) and FXS [12,107–109]. In TS, the TSC1/2 complex has an inhibitory role on mTORC1, and knockdown of TSC2 results in over-activation of mTORC1 and mTORC2, leading to an increase in neuronal cell size of the fetal brain [110]. Interestingly, blocking mTOR activity in TSC2-haploinsufficient mice using rapamycin reversed social deficits, suggesting that mTOR-signaling has a role in the manifestation of overall autistic behaviors, and in TSC particularly [111]. PTEN is a phosphatase which also acts as a negative regulator of the mTOR-signaling pathway by reducing the activity of the PI3K/AKT pathway. As previously mentioned, AKT activates mTORC1 which is essential for protein synthesis of the developing neurite. Therefore, PTEN dysfunction might lead to increased protein synthesis and abnormal brain growth. Indeed, it has been shown that *PTEN* mutations in a subset of ASD cases are co-morbid with overgrowth and macrocephaly [112]. Mouse models with conditional knockout of *PTEN* in mature neurons of the cerebral cortex and hippocampus display axonal overgrowth, ectopic axonal projections, and abnormal synapses, as well as reduced social interaction, increased anxiety, and hyperexcitability [113]. In a recent publication by Cupolillo et al., conditional knockout of PTEN in cerebellar Purkinje cells led to a reduction in social interaction and repetitive behavior, paralleled with structural abnormalities in cerebellar axons and dendrites [114]. Neurofibromin (NF), a tumor suppressor through its GTPase-activating function, is an additional negative regulator of mTOR-signaling via TSC2 [115]. It is the key inducer of the familial cancer syndrome, NF-1, a pathology where autism-like social dysfunction has also been observed [108]. It is still unclear exactly how NF is specifically involved with the ASD-like phenotype observed in NF-1. However, considering that the disequilibrium of the negative regulation of mTOR-signaling both by TSC1/2 and PTEN has been shown to be impaired in syndromic autisms, it is possible to claim that NF has a role in ASD-like phonotype development through its regulation of mTOR. In the case of FXS, increased phosphorylation of mTOR and p70S6K was observed both in lymphocytes and brain samples of FXS patients, which suggest increased protein synthesis, which is the main avenue by which mTOR dysregulation is believe to induce ASD development [109].

In all of the examples given above, inability to downregulate mTOR-signaling is associated with the autism phenotype. In fact, studies determined that blocking mTOR through the use of Rapamycin improves social deficits in the TS and BTBR mouse models [111,116] which implies that Rapamycin might be a possible therapy for the social deficits in ASD.

5.2. Nerve Growth Factor

Nerve Growth Factor (NGF) is a primary neurotrophin for peripheral organ innervation and sensory neuron development. As the nervous system develops, target-organs secret NGF that is detected by elongating axons, and through receptor-mediated endocytosis it enhances survival, neurite outgrowth and synaptic plasticity and connectivity [117]. A role for NGF in the CNS was initially observed in the developing rat forebrain, as researchers injected exogenous NGF intraventricularly to neonatal rats, which resulted in an increase of Choline Acetyltransferase (ChAT) [118]. Further studies of NGF in the rat forebrain showed that NGF regulates cholinergic development and differentiation by binding Tropomyosin receptor kinase A (TrkA), which by a positive feedback loop, increases TrkA expression as well as ChAT in cholinergic neurons [119]. Since then, NGF, together with BDNF, have been shown to play an important role in orchestrating neuronal plasticity important for sociability in mice [117].

Given its important role in nervous system development, it is not surprising that dysregulation in NGF-signaling has been implicated in psychiatric disorders such as depression, schizophrenia and Alzheimer's disease [117]. Nevertheless, the number of publications linking NGF to ASD is scarce. In fact, some publications have shown that NGF levels in cerebral spinal fluid (CSF) and blood is typical in children with ASD [120,121]. However, more recent publications begin to present a different picture. A study analyzing Differential Alternative Splicing (DAS) in the blood mRNA of 2–4 year old boys diagnosed with ASD showed there was a significant difference in DAS for several genes involved in NGF-signaling, including the NGF receptors, Nerve Growth Factor Receptor (NGFR) and Neurotrophic Receptor Tyrosine Kinase 1 (NTRK1) [122]. A different study showed that SNPs in NTRK1 associated with ASD behavioral traits measured by the Empathy Quotient (EQ) and the Autism Spectrum Quotient (AQ) [123]. In an interesting study by Lu et al., researchers conducted a genome-wide Quantitative Trait Loci (QTL) study and found that several SNPs in NGF are significantly associated with deficits in non-verbal communication, which is an autistic trait [124]. The reasoning for the QTL approach was to focus on a specific trait and find the genetic loci associated to it and reduce some of the genetic heterogeneity that usually complicates ASD genetic research. Therefore, while there is scarce evidence for the role of NGF-signaling in ASD from animal studies, human genetic studies have actually found associations between the NGF pathway and behaviors that are dysregulated in ASD. Therefore, further research into the possible mechanistic roles for NGF in social behavior are needed [39].

6. Conclusions

ASD's elusive genetic etiology imposes a great challenge to our understanding of the disorder's pathology. The growing number of genes associated with ASD, both rare and common variants, and the fact that these genes are involved in a variety of biological processes, makes it difficult for the research community to find a specific target for therapy. Taking into account that there are currently no pharmacological agents that treat the core symptoms of ASD, there is great need to understand the biological pathways that are targeted by ASD-mutations, which can be novel pharmacological targets. Both Wnt and the Ca^{2+} signaling pathways that we discussed in-depth in this review are potential targets for pharmacological intervention. However, while these pathways have been well characterized, there is still a great need to understand exactly how dysregulation of these pathways are involved in the core characteristics of ASD, including social and repetitive behaviors. A more clear understanding of the specific roles of these pathways in specific brain region is also likely to shed some light into this issue.

Up until now, the only way to find common pathways affected by ASD-associated genes was by in-silico network analysis. However, with the creation of multiple mouse models based on these genetic aberrations, a current method can be to decipher common molecular dysregulations found in these multiple autism mouse models, and to correlate these dysregulations with the animal's behavioral and neurodevelopmental phenotypes. For example, Ellegood et al. revealed that autism mouse models can be clustered according to neuroanatomical differences such as changes in the volume of different brain regions [125]. In a recent review, Kim et al., compared publications on multiple mouse models, and searched for physiological dysregulations underlying the variety of repetitive behavior types observed in ASD mouse models. While Kim et al. deciphered that it is difficult to link repetitive behavior types to specific brain regions, they discovered a few common pathways that are often involved in ASD phenotypes [126]. One example is involvement of glutamatergic connections from the frontal cortex to the midbrain, involved in repetitive behaviors. Therefore, the spatial and temporal resolution of ASD-related molecular pathways cannot be determined by network analysis of genetic data, but rather through the analysis of in vivo models. Therefore, parallel investigation of molecular mechanisms dysregulated in multiple mouse models of autism genes is likely to reveal important mechanisms and novel therapeutic targets.

Acknowledgments: Our research is currently being supported by Israel Science Foundation grant 1047/12 and by a grant from Teva Pharmaceutical Industries.

Author Contributions: Both Oded Oron and Evan Elliott designed, wrote, and edited this review, according to own expertise. All authors have read and approved the final version of the manuscript.

Abbreviations

ADHD	Attention Deficit Hyperactivity Disorder
AKT	RAC-alpha serine/threonine-protein kinase
AMPK	AMP-activated Protein Kinase

AQ	Autism Spectrum Quotient
AS	Angelman Syndrome
ASD	Autism Spectrum Disorder
BDNF	Brain-derived Neurotrophic Factor
BIO	(2′*Z*,3′*E*)-6-Bromoindirubin-3′-oxime
CaM	Calmodulin
CAMK	Ca^{2+}/calmodulin-dependent protein kinase
CASK	Calcium/Calmodulin Dependent Serine Protein Kinase
CDFE	Cortical Dysplasia-focal Epilepsy
ChAT	Choline Acetyltransferase
CHD8	Chromodomain Helicase DNA Binding Protein 8
CNS	Central Nervous System
CNTNAP2	Contacting Associated Protein 2
CNV	Copy Number Variation
COL11A1	Collagen Type XI Alpha 1 Chain
DAS	Differential Alternative Splicing
Dlgap2	DLG Associated Protein 2
Dvl3	Dishevelled Segment Polarity Protein 3
eIF4E	Eukaryotic Translation Initiation Factor 4E
EQ	Empathy Quotient
FMR1	Fragile-X Mental Retardation 1
FNI	Frizzled Nuclear Import
FOXP1	Forkhead Box P1
FXS	Fragile-X Syndrome
Fzd1	Frizzled Class Receptor 1
GABA	Gamma-Aminobutyric
GJB6	Gap Junction Protein Beta 6
GOC	Gene Ontology Consortium
GRIN2B	Glutamate Ionotropic Receptor NMDA Type Subunit 2B
GSK3β	Glycogen Synthase Kinase 3 Beta
GWAS	Genome Wide Association Study
H1	Homer 1
H2	Homer 2
Hipk1	Homeodomain Interacting Protein Kinase 1
ID	Intellectual Deficiency
IPA	Ingenuity Pathway Analysis
iPSC	induced pluripotent stem cells
KATNAL2	Katanin Catalytic Subunit A1 Like 2
KCNQ4	Potassium Voltage-Gated Channel Subfamily Q Member 4
KEGG	Kyoto Encyclopedia of Genes and Genomes
LAMC3	Laminin Subunit Gamma 3
LEF	Lymphoid Enhancer Binding Factor
LRP5	LDL Receptor Related Protein 5
LRP6	LDL Receptor Related Protein 6
LTP	Long Term Potentiation
MECP2	Methyl CpG binding protein 2
mGluR5	Glutamate Metabotropic Receptor 5
mTOR	Mammalian Target of Rapamycin
mTORC1	Mammalian Target of Rapamycin complex 1
mTORC2	Mammalian Target of Rapamycin complex 2
MYH14	Myosin Heavy Chain 14
NF	Neurofibromin
NF-1	Neurofibromatosis Type 1

NGF	Nerve Growth Factor
NGFR	Nerve Growth Factor Receptor
NGS	Next Generations Sequencing
NMDAR	*N*-methyl-D-aspartate receptors
NSC	Neuronal Stem Cell
NTNG1	Netrin G1
NTRK1	Neurotrophic Receptor Tyrosine Kinase 1
p70S6K	p70 ribosomal protein S6 kinase
PI3K	Phosphatidylinositol-4,5-Bisphosphate 3-Kinase
PPI	Protein-Protein Interaction
PROSAP2	Proline Rich Synapse Associated Protein 2
PSD	Post Synaptic Density
PTEN	Phosphatase And Tensin Homolog
PV	Parvalbumin
PVD	Pial Vessel Disruption
QTL	Quantitative Trait Loci
SCN1A	Sodium Voltage-Gated Channel Alpha Subunit 1
SCN2A	Sodium Voltage-Gated Channel Alpha Subunit 2
SFARI	Simmons Foundation Autism Research Initiative
SHANK3	SH3 And Multiple Ankyrin Repeat Domains 3
SNP	Single Nucleotide Polymorphism
STXBP1	Syntaxin Binding Protein 1
SVZ	Subventricular Zone
Syngap1	Synaptic Ras GTPase Activating Protein 1
TCF	Transcription Factor
THRA	Thyroid Hormone Receptor, Alpha
TMS	Transcranial Magnetic Stimulation
TrkA	Tropomyosin receptor kinase A
TSC1	Tuberous Sclerosis 1
TSC2	Tuberous Sclerosis 2
UBE3A	Ubiquitin Protein Ligase E3A
WGCNA	Weighted Gene Co-expression Network Analysis
Wnt	Wingless-type

References

1. Grice, D.E.; Buxbaum, J.D. The Genetics of Autism Spectrum Disorders. *NeuroMol. Med.* **2006**, *8*, 451–460. [CrossRef]
2. Folstein, S.; Rutter, M. Infantile autism: A genetic study of 21 twin pairs. *J. Child Psychol. Psychiatry* **1977**, *18*, 297–321. [CrossRef] [PubMed]
3. Folstein, S.; Rutter, M. A Twin Study of Individuals with Infantile Autism. In *Autism: A Reappraisal of Concepts and Treatment*; Rutter, M., Schopler, E., Eds.; Springer: Boston, MA, USA, 1978; pp. 219–241.
4. Rutter, M. Heritability of autism spectrum disorders: A meta-analysis of twin studies. *J. Child Psychol. Psychiatry* **2016**, *57*, 585–595.
5. Taurines, R.; Schwenck, C.; Westerwald, E.; Sachse, M.; Siniatchkin, M.; Freitag, C. ADHD and autism: Differential diagnosis or overlapping traits? A selective review. *Atten. Defict Hyperact. Disord.* **2012**, *4*, 115–139. [CrossRef] [PubMed]
6. Hollocks, M.J.; Howlin, P.; Papadopoulos, A.S.; Khondoker, M.; Simonoff, E. Differences in HPA-axis and heart rate responsiveness to psychosocial stress in children with autism spectrum disorders with and without co-morbid anxiety. *Psychoneuroendocrinology* **2014**, *46*, 32–45. [CrossRef] [PubMed]
7. Talkowski, M.E.; Mullegama, S.V.; Rosenfeld, J.A.; Van Bon, B.W.M.; Shen, Y.; Repnikova, E.A.; Gastier-Foster, J.; Thrush, D.L.; Kathiresan, S.; Ruderfer, D.M.; et al. Assessment of 2q23.1 microdeletion syndrome implicates MBD5 as a single causal locus of intellectual disability, epilepsy, and autism spectrum disorder. *Am. J. Hum. Genet.* **2011**, *89*, 551–563. [CrossRef] [PubMed]

8. Khanzada, N.; Butler, M.; Manzardo, A. GeneAnalytics Pathway Analysis and Genetic Overlap among Autism Spectrum Disorder, Bipolar Disorder and Schizophrenia. *Int. J. Mol. Sci.* **2017**, *18*, 527. [CrossRef] [PubMed]
9. Buxbaum, J.D.; Hof, P.R. *The Neuroscience of Autism Spectrum Disorders*; Elsevier Science: Amsterdam, The Netherlands, 2012.
10. Hagerman, R.; Hoem, G.; Hagerman, P. Fragile X and autism: Intertwined at the molecular level leading to targeted treatments. *Mol. Autism* **2010**, *1*, 12. [CrossRef] [PubMed]
11. Strauss, K.A.; Puffenberger, E.G.; Huentelman, M.J.; Gottlieb, S.; Dobrin, S.E.; Parod, J.M.; Stephan, D.A.; Morton, D.H. Recessive symptomatic focal epilepsy and mutant contactin-associated protein-like 2. *N. Engl. J. Med.* **2006**, *354*, 1370–1377. [CrossRef] [PubMed]
12. Vignoli, A.; La Briola, F.; Peron, A.; Turner, K.; Vannicola, C.; Saccani, M.; Magnaghi, E.; Scornavacca, G.F.; Canevini, M.P. Autism spectrum disorder in tuberous sclerosis complex: Searching for risk markers. *Orphanet J. Rare Dis.* **2015**, *10*, 154. [CrossRef] [PubMed]
13. Percy, A.K. Rett syndrome: Exploring the autism link. *Arch. Neurol.* **2011**, *68*, 985–989. [CrossRef] [PubMed]
14. Leppa, V.M.; Kravitz, S.N.; Martin, C.L.; Andrieux, J.; Le Caignec, C.; Martin-Coignard, D.; DyBuncio, C.; Sanders, S.J.; Lowe, J.K.; Cantor, R.M.; et al. Rare Inherited and De Novo CNVs Reveal Complex Contributions to ASD Risk in Multiplex Families. *Am. J. Hum. Genet.* **2016**, *99*, 540–554. [CrossRef] [PubMed]
15. Wilson, H.L. Molecular characterisation of the 22q13 deletion syndrome supports the role of haploinsufficiency of SHANK3/PROSAP2 in the major neurological symptoms. *J. Med. Genet.* **2003**, *40*, 575–584. [CrossRef] [PubMed]
16. Durand, C.M.; Betancur, C.; Boeckers, T.M.; Bockmann, J.; Chaste, P.; Fauchereau, F.; Nygren, G.; Rastam, M.; Gillberg, I.C.; Anckarsäter, H.; et al. Mutations in the gene encoding the synaptic scaffolding protein SHANK3 are associated with autism spectrum disorders. *Nat. Genet.* **2007**, *39*, 25–27. [CrossRef] [PubMed]
17. Wang, X.; Xu, Q.; Bey, A.L.; Lee, Y.; Jiang, Y.-H. Transcriptional and functional complexity of SHANK3 provides a molecular framework to understand the phenotypic heterogeneity of SHANK3 causing autism and SHANK3 mutant mice. *Mol. Autism* **2014**, *5*, 30. [CrossRef] [PubMed]
18. Ornoy, A.; Liza, W.F.; Ergaz, Z. Genetic syndromes, maternal diseases and antenatal factors associated with autism spectrum disorders (ASD). *Front. Neurosci.* **2016**, *10*, 1–21. [CrossRef] [PubMed]
19. De Anda, F.C.; Rosario, A.L.; Durak, O.; Tran, T.; Gräff, J.; Meletis, K.; Rei, D.; Soda, T.; Madabhushi, R.; Ginty, D.D.; et al. Autism spectrum disorder susceptibility gene TAOK2 affects basal dendrite formation in the neocortex. *Nat. Neurosci.* **2012**, *15*, 1022–1031. [CrossRef] [PubMed]
20. Golzio, C.; Willer, J.; Talkowski, M.E.; Oh, E.C.; Taniguchi, Y.; Jacquemont, S.; Reymond, A.; Sun, M.; Sawa, A.; Gusella, J.F.; et al. KCTD13 is a major driver of mirrored neuroanatomical phenotypes of the 16p11.2 copy number variant. *Nature* **2012**, *485*, 363–367. [CrossRef] [PubMed]
21. O'Roak, B.J.; Deriziotis, P.; Lee, C.; Vives, L.; Schwartz, J.J.; Girirajan, S.; Karakoc, E.; Mackenzie, A.P.; Ng, S.B.; Baker, C.; et al. Exome sequencing in spordic autism spectrum disorders identifies severe de novo mutations. *Nat. Genet.* **2011**, *43*, 585–589. [CrossRef] [PubMed]
22. Iossifov, I.; Ronemus, M.; Levy, D.; Wang, Z.; Hakker, I.; Rosenbaum, J.; Yamrom, B.; Lee, Y.H.; Narzisi, G.; Leotta, A.; et al. De Novo Gene Disruptions in Children on the Autistic Spectrum. *Neuron* **2012**, *74*, 285–299. [CrossRef] [PubMed]
23. O'Roak, B.J.; Vives, L.; Girirajan, S.; Karakoc, E.; Krumm, N.; Coe, B.P.; Levy, R.; Ko, A.; Lee, C.; Smith, J.D.; et al. Sporadic autism exomes reveal a highly interconnected protein network of de novo mutations. *Nature* **2012**, *485*, 246–250. [CrossRef] [PubMed]
24. Sanders, S.J.; Murtha, M.T.; Gupta, A.R.; Murdoch, J.D.; Raubeson, M.J.; Willsey, A.J.; Ercan-Sencicek, A.G.; DiLullo, N.M.; Parikshak, N.N.; Stein, J.L.; et al. De novo mutations revealed by whole-exome sequencing are strongly associated with autism. *Nature* **2012**, *485*, 237–241. [CrossRef] [PubMed]
25. Yuen, R.K.C.; Thiruvahindrapuram, B.; Merico, D.; Walker, S.; Tammimies, K.; Hoang, N.; Chrysler, C.; Nalpathamkalam, T.; Pellecchia, G.; Liu, Y.; et al. Whole-genome sequencing of quartet families with autism spectrum disorder. *Nat. Med.* **2015**, *21*, 185–191. [CrossRef] [PubMed]
26. Gaugler, T.; Klei, L.; Sanders, S.J.; Bodea, C.A.; Goldberg, A.P.; Lee, A.B.; Mahajan, M.; Manaa, D.; Pawitan, Y.; Reichert, J.; et al. Most genetic risk for autism resides with common variation. *Nat. Genet.* **2014**, *46*, 881–885. [CrossRef] [PubMed]

27. Basu, S.N.; Kollu, R.; Banerjee-Basu, S. AutDB: A gene reference resource for autism research. *Nucleic Acids Res.* **2009**, *37*, D832–D836. [CrossRef] [PubMed]
28. Geschwind, D.H. Autism: Many genes, common pathways? *Cell* **2008**, *135*, 391–395. [CrossRef] [PubMed]
29. Parikshak, N.N.; Gandal, M.J.; Geschwind, D.H. Systems biology and gene networks in neurodevelopmental and neurodegenerative disorders. *Nat. Rev. Genet.* **2015**, *16*, 441–458. [CrossRef] [PubMed]
30. The Gene Ontology Consortium; Ashburner, M.; Ball, C.A.; Blake, J.A.; Botstein, D.; Butler, H.; Michael Cherry, J.; Davis, A.P.; Dolinski, K.; Dwight, S.S.; Eppig, J.T.; et al. Gene Ontology: Tool for the unification of biology. *Nat. Genet.* **2000**, *25*, 25–29.
31. Chowdhury, S.; Sarkar, R.R. Comparison of human cell signaling pathway databases—Evolution, drawbacks and challenges. *Database* **2015**, *2015*. [CrossRef] [PubMed]
32. Ogata, H.; Goto, S.; Sato, K.; Fujibuchi, W.; Bono, H.; Kanehisa, M. KEGG: Kyoto Encyclopedia of Genes and Genomes. *Nucleic Acids Res.* **1999**, *27*, 29–34. [CrossRef] [PubMed]
33. Ingenuity Systems Ingenuity Pathway Analysis (IPA). Available online: https://www.qiagenbioinformatics.com/ (accessed on 13 April 2017).
34. Mines, M.A.; Yuskaitis, C.J.; King, M.K.; Beurel, E.; Jope, R.S. GSK3 Influences Social Preference and Anxiety-Related Behaviors during Social Interaction in a Mouse Model of Fragile X Syndrome and Autism. *PLoS ONE* **2010**, *5*, e9706. [CrossRef] [PubMed]
35. Okerlund, N.D.; Cheyette, B.N.R. Synaptic Wnt signaling—A contributor to major psychiatric disorders? *J. Neurodev. Disord.* **2011**, *3*, 162–174. [CrossRef] [PubMed]
36. Iossifov, I.; O'roak, B.J.; Sanders, S.J.; Ronemus, M.; Krumm, N.; Levy, D.; Stessman, H.A.; Witherspoon, K.; Vives, L.; Patterson, K.E.; et al. The contribution of de novo coding mutations to autism spectrum disorder. *November* **2014**, *13*, 216–221. [CrossRef] [PubMed]
37. Hadley, D.; Wu, Z.-L.; Kao, C.; Kini, A.; Mohamed-Hadley, A.; Thomas, K.; Vazquez, L.; Qiu, H.; Mentch, F.; Pellegrino, R.; et al. The impact of the metabotropic glutamate receptor and other gene family interaction networks on autism. *Nat. Commun.* **2014**, *5*. [CrossRef] [PubMed]
38. Wen, Y.; Alshikho, M.J.; Herbert, M.R. Pathway network analyses for autism reveal multisystem involvement, major overlaps with other diseases and convergence upon MAPK and Calcium signaling. *PLoS ONE* **2016**, *11*, e0153329. [CrossRef] [PubMed]
39. Lin, G.N.; Corominas, R.; Lemmens, I.; Yang, X.; Tavernier, J.; Hill, D.E.; Vidal, M.; Sebat, J.; Iakoucheva, L.M. Spatiotemporal 16p11.2 Protein Network Implicates Cortical Late Mid-Fetal Brain Development and KCTD13-Cul3-RhoA Pathway in Psychiatric Diseases. *Neuron* **2015**, *85*, 742–754. [CrossRef] [PubMed]
40. Ben-David, E.; Shifman, S. Networks of neuronal genes affected by common and rare variants in autism spectrum disorders. *PLoS Genet.* **2012**, *8*, e1002556. [CrossRef] [PubMed]
41. MacDonald, B.T.; Tamai, K.; He, X. Wnt/β-Catenin Signaling: Components, Mechanisms, and Diseases. *Dev. Cell* **2009**, *17*, 9–26. [CrossRef] [PubMed]
42. Polakis, P. Wnt signaling and cancer. *Genes Dev.* **2000**, *14*, 1837–1851. [CrossRef] [PubMed]
43. Rao, T.P.; Kühl, M. An updated overview on Wnt signaling pathways: A prelude for more. *Circ. Res.* **2010**, *106*, 1798–1806. [CrossRef] [PubMed]
44. Noelanders, R.; Vleminckx, K. How Wnt Signaling Builds the Brain. *Neuroscientist* **2016**. [CrossRef] [PubMed]
45. Chen, A.; Walsh, C. Regulation of Cerebral Cortical Size by Control of Cell Cycle Exit in Neural Precursors. *Science* **2002**, *297*, 365–369. [CrossRef] [PubMed]
46. Woodhead, G.J.; Mutch, C.A.; Olson, E.C.; Chenn, A. Cell-Autonomous beta-Catenin Signaling Regulates Cortical Precursor Proliferation. *J. Neurosci.* **2006**, *26*, 12620–12630. [CrossRef] [PubMed]
47. Duncan, R.N.; Xie, Y.; McPherson, A.D.; Taibi, A.V.; Bonkowsky, J.L.; Douglass, A.D.; Dorsky, R.I. Hypothalamic radial glia function as self-renewing neural progenitors in the absence of Wnt/β-catenin signaling. *Development* **2015**, *143*, 45–53. [CrossRef] [PubMed]
48. Piccin, D.; Morshead, C.M. Wnt signaling regulates symmetry of division of neural stem cells in the adult brain and in response to injury. *Stem Cells* **2011**, *29*, 528–538. [CrossRef] [PubMed]
49. Marinaro, C.; Pannese, M.; Weinandy, F.; Sessa, A.; Bergamaschi, A.; Taketo, M.M.; Broccoli, V.; Comi, G.; Götz, M.; Martino, G.; et al. Wnt signaling has opposing roles in the developing and the adult brain that are modulated by Hipk1. *Cereb. Cortex* **2012**, *22*, 2415–2427. [CrossRef] [PubMed]
50. Huber, O.; Krohn, M.; Kemler, R. A specific domain in alpha-catenin mediates binding to beta-catenin or plakoglobin. *J. Cell Sci.* **1997**, *110 Pt 1*, 1759–1765. [PubMed]

51. Huber, A.H.; Weis, W.I. The structure of the B-catenin/E-cadherin complex and the molecular basis of diverse ligand recognition by β-catenin. *Cell* **2001**, *105*, 391–402. [CrossRef]
52. Yu, X.; Malenka, R.C. Beta-catenin is critical for dendritic morphogenesis. *Nat. Neurosci.* **2003**, *6*, 1169–1177. [CrossRef] [PubMed]
53. Bian, W.-J.; Miao, W.-Y.; He, S.-J.; Qiu, Z.; Yu, X. Coordinated Spine Pruning and Maturation Mediated by Inter-Spine Competition for Cadherin/Catenin Complexes. *Cell* **2015**, *162*, 808–822. [CrossRef] [PubMed]
54. Murase, S.; Mosser, E.; Schuman, E.M. Depolarization drives β-catenin into neuronal spines promoting changes in synaptic structure and function. *Neuron* **2002**, *35*, 91–105. [CrossRef]
55. Adams, C.L.; Nelson, W.J.; Smith, S.J. Quantitative Analysis of Cadherin-Catenin-Actin Reorganization during Development of Cell-Cell Adhesion. *J. Cell Biol.* **1996**, *135*, 1899–1911. [CrossRef] [PubMed]
56. Bamji, S.X.; Shimazu, K.; Kimes, N.; Huelsken, J.; Birchmeier, W.; Lu, B.; Reichardt, L.F. Role of β-catenin in synaptic vesicle localization and presynaptic assembly. *Neuron* **2003**, *40*, 719–731. [CrossRef]
57. Butz, S.; Okamoto, M.; Südhof, T.C. A Tripartite Protein Complex with the Potential to Couple Synaptic Vesicle Exocytosis to Cell Adhesion in Brain. *Cell* **1998**, *94*, 773–782. [CrossRef]
58. Han, G.A.; Malintan, N.T.; Collins, B.M.; Meunier, F.A.; Sugita, S. Munc18-1 as a key regulator of neurosecretion. *J. Neurochem.* **2010**, *115*, 1–10. [CrossRef] [PubMed]
59. Bolshakov, V.Y.; Siegelbaum, S.A. Regulation of hippocampal transmitter release during development and long-term potentiation. *Science* **1995**, *269*, 1730–1734. [CrossRef] [PubMed]
60. Taylor, A.M.; Wu, J.; Tai, H.C.; Schuman, E.M. Axonal translation of beta-catenin regulates synaptic vesicle dynamics. *J. Neurosci.* **2013**, *33*, 5584–5589. [CrossRef] [PubMed]
61. Sharma, K.; Choi, S.Y.; Zhang, Y.; Nieland, T.J.F.; Long, S.; Li, M.; Huganir, R.L. High-throughput genetic screen for synaptogenic factors: Identification of LRP6 as critical for excitatory synapse development. *Cell Rep.* **2013**, *5*, 1330–1341. [CrossRef] [PubMed]
62. Hutsler, J.J.; Zhang, H. Increased dendritic spine densities on cortical projection neurons in autism spectrum disorders. *Brain Res.* **2010**, *1309*, 83–94. [CrossRef] [PubMed]
63. Stoner, R.; Chow, M.L.; Boyle, M.P.; Sunkin, S.M.; Mouton, P.R.; Roy, S.; Wynshaw-Boris, A.; Colamarino, S.A.; Lein, E.S.; Courchesne, E. Patches of disorganization in the neocortex of children with autism. *N. Engl. J. Med.* **2014**, *370*, 1209–1219. [CrossRef] [PubMed]
64. Casanova, M.F.; van Kooten, I.; Switala, A.E.; van Engeland, H.; Heinsen, H.; Steinbusch, H.W.M.; Hof, P.R.; Schmitz, C. Abnormalities of cortical minicolumnar organization in the prefrontal lobes of autistic patients. *Clin. Neurosci. Res.* **2006**, *6*, 127–133. [CrossRef]
65. Chung, K.; Wallace, J.; Kim, S.-Y.; Kalyanasundaram, S.; Andalman, A.S.; Davidson, T.J.; Mirzabekov, J.J.; Zalocusky, K.A.; Mattis, J.; Denisin, A.K.; et al. Structural and molecular interrogation of intact biological systems. *Nature* **2013**, *497*, 332–337. [CrossRef] [PubMed]
66. Dong, F.; Jiang, J.; McSweeney, C.; Zou, D.; Liu, L.; Mao, Y. Deletion of CTNNB1 in inhibitory circuitry contributes to autism-associated behavioral defects. *Hum. Mol. Genet.* **2016**, *25*, 2738–2751. [CrossRef] [PubMed]
67. Mines, M.A.; Jope, R.S. Glycogen synthase kinase-3: A promising therapeutic target for fragile X syndrome. *Front. Mol. Neurosci.* **2011**, *4*, 35. [CrossRef] [PubMed]
68. Caracci, M.O.; Avila, M.E.; de Ferrari, G.V. Synaptic Wnt/GSK3β-Signaling Hub in Autism. *Neural Plast.* **2016**, *2016*. [CrossRef] [PubMed]
69. Min, W.W.; Yuskaitis, C.J.; Yan, Q.; Sikorski, C.; Chen, S.; Jope, R.S.; Bauchwitz, R.P. Elevated glycogen synthase kinase-3 activity in Fragile X mice: Key metabolic regulator with evidence for treatment potential. *Neuropharmacology* **2009**, *56*, 463–472. [CrossRef] [PubMed]
70. Guo, W.; Murthy, A.C.; Zhang, L.; Johnson, E.B.; Schaller, E.G.; Allan, A.M.; Zhao, X. Inhibition of GSK3β improves hippocampusdependent learning and rescues neurogenesis in a mouse model of fragile X syndrome. *Hum. Mol. Genet.* **2012**, *21*, 681–691. [CrossRef] [PubMed]
71. Franklin, A.V.; King, M.K.; Palomo, V.; Martinez, A.; Mcmahon, L.L.; Jope, R.S. Glycogen synthase kinase-3 inhibitors reverse deficits in long- term potentiation and cognition in Fragile X mice. *Biol. Psychiatry* **2014**, *75*, 198–206. [CrossRef] [PubMed]
72. Durak, O.; Gao, F.; Kaeser-Woo, Y.; Rueda, R.; Martorell, A.; Nott, A.; Liu, C.; Watson, L.; Tsai, L.-H. Chd8 mediates cortical neurogenesis via transcriptional regulation of cell cycle and Wnt signaling. *Nat. Neurosci.* **2016**, *19*, 1477–1488. [CrossRef] [PubMed]

73. Harris, K.P.; Akbergenova, Y.; Cho, R.W.; Baas-Thomas, M.S.; Littleton, J.T. Shank Modulates Postsynaptic Wnt Signaling to Regulate Synaptic Development. *J. Neurosci.* **2016**, *36*, 5820–5832. [CrossRef] [PubMed]
74. Budnik, V.; Salinas, P.C. Wnt signaling during synaptic development and plasticity. *Curr. Opin. Neurobiol.* **2011**, *21*, 151–159. [CrossRef] [PubMed]
75. Mathew, D.; Ataman, B.; Chen, J.; Zhang, Y.; Cumberledge, S.; Budnik, V. Wingless Signaling at Synapses Is through Cleavage and Nuclear Import of Receptor DFrizzled2. *Science* **2005**, *310*, 1344–1347. [CrossRef] [PubMed]
76. Carafoli, E. Special issue: Calcium signaling and disease. *Biochem. Biophys. Res. Commun.* **2004**, *322*, 1097. [CrossRef]
77. Berridge, M.J.; Lipp, P.; Bootman, M.D. The versatility and universality of Calcium signalling. *Nat. Rev. Mol. Cell Biol.* **2000**, *1*, 11–21. [CrossRef] [PubMed]
78. Clapham, D.E. Calcium Signaling. *Cell* **2007**, *131*, 1047–1058. [CrossRef] [PubMed]
79. Bossuyt, J.; Bers, D.M. Visualizing CaMKII and CaM activity: A paradigm of compartmentalized signaling. *J. Mol. Med.* **2013**, *91*, 907–916. [CrossRef] [PubMed]
80. Okamoto, K.-I.; Narayanan, R.; Lee, S.H.; Murata, K.; Hayashi, Y. The role of CaMKII as an F-actin-bundling protein crucial for maintenance of dendritic spine structure. *Proc. Natl. Acad. Sci. USA* **2007**, *104*, 6418–6423. [CrossRef] [PubMed]
81. Jalan-Sakrikar, N.; Bartlett, R.K.; Baucum, A.J.; Colbran, R.J. Substrate-selective and calcium-independent activation of CaMKII by α-actinin. *J. Biol. Chem.* **2012**, *287*, 15275–15283. [CrossRef] [PubMed]
82. Hell, J.W. CaMKII: Claiming center stage in postsynaptic function and organization. *Neuron* **2014**, *81*, 249–265. [CrossRef] [PubMed]
83. Lisman, J.; Schulman, H.; Cline, H. The molecular basis of CaMKII function in synaptic and behavioural memory. *Nat. Rev. Neurosci.* **2002**, *3*, 175–190. [CrossRef] [PubMed]
84. Houston, C.M.; He, Q.; Smart, T.G. CaMKII phosphorylation of the GABA A receptor: Receptor subtype-and synapse-specific modulation. *J. Physiol.* **2009**, *58710*, 2115–2125. [CrossRef] [PubMed]
85. Wayman, G.A.; Kaech, S.; Grant, W.F.; Davare, M.; Impey, S.; Tokumitsu, H.; Nozaki, N.; Banker, G.; Soderling, T.R. Regulation of axonal extension and growth cone motility by calmodulin-dependent protein kinase I. *J. Neurosci.* **2004**, *24*, 3786–3794. [CrossRef] [PubMed]
86. Mizuno, K.; Ris, L.; Sánchez-Capelo, A.; Godaux, E.; Giese, K.P. Ca^{2+}/calmodulin kinase kinase alpha is dispensable for brain development but is required for distinct memories in male, though not in female, mice. *Mol. Cell. Biol.* **2006**, *26*, 9094–9104. [CrossRef] [PubMed]
87. Marcelo, K.L.; Means, A.R.; York, B. The Ca^{2+}/Calmodulin/CaMKK2 Axis: Nature's Metabolic CaMshaft. *Trends Endocrinol. Metab.* **2016**, *27*, 706–718. [CrossRef] [PubMed]
88. Yun, S.H.; Trommer, B.L. Fragile X mice: Reduced long-term potentiation and *N*-Methyl-D-Aspartate receptor-mediated neurotransmission in dentate gyrus. *J. Neurosci. Res.* **2011**, *89*, 176–182. [CrossRef] [PubMed]
89. Moretti, P.; Levenson, J.M.; Battaglia, F.; Atkinson, R.; Teague, R.; Antalffy, B.; Armstrong, D.; Arancio, O.; Sweatt, J.D.; Zoghbi, H.Y. Learning and memory and synaptic plasticity are impaired in a mouse model of Rett syndrome. *J. Neurosci.* **2006**, *26*, 319–327. [CrossRef] [PubMed]
90. Jung, N.H.; Janzarik, W.G.; Delvendahl, I.; Münchau, A.; Biscaldi, M.; Mainberger, F.; Bäumer, T.; Rauh, R.; Mall, V. Impaired induction of long-term potentiation-like plasticity in patients with high-functioning autism and Asperger syndrome. *Dev. Med. Child Neurol.* **2013**, *55*, 83–89. [CrossRef] [PubMed]
91. Modi, M.E.; Sahin, M. Translational use of event-related potentials to assess circuit integrity in ASD. *Nat. Rev. Neurol.* **2017**, *13*, 160–170. [CrossRef] [PubMed]
92. Schmunk, G.; Nguyen, R.L.; Ferguson, D.L.; Kumar, K.; Parker, I.; Gargus, J.J. High-throughput screen detects calcium signaling dysfunction in typical sporadic autism spectrum disorder. *Sci. Rep.* **2017**, *7*, 40740. [CrossRef] [PubMed]
93. Paşca, S.P.; Portmann, T.; Voineagu, I.; Yazawa, M.; Shcheglovitov, A.; Paşca, A.M.; Cord, B.; Palmer, T.D.; Chikahisa, S.; Nishino, S.; et al. Using iPSC-derived neurons to uncover cellular phenotypes associated with Timothy syndrome. *Nat. Med.* **2011**, *17*, 1657–1662. [CrossRef] [PubMed]
94. Wang, H.; Wu, L.-J.J.; Zhang, F.; Zhuo, M. Roles of calcium-stimulated adenylyl cyclase and calmodulin-dependent protein kinase {IV} in the regulation of {FMRP} by group I metabotropic glutamate receptors. *J. Neurosci.* **2008**, *28*, 4385–4397. [CrossRef] [PubMed]

95. Waltes, R.; Duketis, E.; Knapp, M.; Anney, R.J.L.; Huguet, G.; Schlitt, S.; Jarczok, T.A.; Sachse, M.; Kämpfer, L.M.; Kleinböck, T.; et al. Common variants in genes of the postsynaptic FMRP signalling pathway are risk factors for autism spectrum disorders. *Hum. Genet.* **2014**, *133*, 781–792. [CrossRef] [PubMed]
96. Pop, A.S.; Gomez-Mancilla, B.; Neri, G.; Willemsen, R.; Gasparini, F. Fragile X syndrome: A preclinical review on metabotropic glutamate receptor 5 (mGluR5) antagonists and drug development. *Psychopharmacology* **2014**, *231*, 1217–1226. [CrossRef] [PubMed]
97. Guo, W.; Ceolin, L.; Collins, K.A.; Perroy, J.; Huber Correspondence, K.M.; Huber, K.M. Elevated CaMKIIα and Hyperphosphorylation of Homer Mediate Circuit Dysfunction in a Fragile X Syndrome Mouse Model. *Cell Rep.* **2015**, *13*, 2297–2311. [CrossRef] [PubMed]
98. Michalon, A.; Bruns, A.; Risterucci, C.; Honer, M.; Ballard, T.M.; Ozmen, L.; Jaeschke, G.; Wettstein, J.G.; von Kienlin, M.; Künnecke, B. Chronic Metabotropic Glutamate Receptor 5 Inhibition Corrects Local Alterations of Brain Activity and Improves Cognitive Performance in Fragile X Mice. *Biol. Psychiatry* **2013**, *75*, 189–197. [CrossRef] [PubMed]
99. Schaefer, T.L.; Davenport, M.H.; Erickson, C.A. Emerging pharmacologic treatment options for fragile X syndrome. *Appl. Clin. Genet.* **2015**, *2015*, 75–93.
100. Berry-Kravis, E.; Hessl, D.; Coffey, S.; Hervey, C.; Schneider, A.; Yuhas, J.; Hutchison, J.; Snape, M.; Tranfaglia, M.; Nguyen, D.V.; et al. A pilot open label, single dose trial of fenobam in adults with fragile X syndrome. *J. Med. Genet.* **2009**, *46*, 266–271. [CrossRef] [PubMed]
101. Berry-Kravis, E.; Sumis, A.; Hervey, C.; Nelson, M.; Porges, S.W.; Weng, N.; Weiler, I.J.; Greenough, W.T. Open-label treatment trial of lithium to target the underlying defect in fragile X syndrome. *J. Dev. Behav. Pediatr.* **2008**, *29*, 293–302. [CrossRef] [PubMed]
102. Weeber, E.J.; Jiang, Y.-H.; Elgersma, Y.; Varga, A.W.; Carrasquillo, Y.; Brown, S.E.; Christian, J.M.; Mirnikjoo, B.; Silva, A.; Beaudet, A.L.; et al. Derangements of hippocampal calcium/calmodulin-dependent protein kinase II in a mouse model for Angelman mental retardation syndrome. *J. Neurosci.* **2003**, *23*, 2634–2644. [PubMed]
103. Baucum, A.J.; Shonesy, B.C.; Rose, K.L.; Colbran, R.J. Quantitative Proteomics Analysis of CaMKII Phosphorylation and the CaMKII Interactome in the Mouse Forebrain. *ACS Chem. Neurosci.* **2015**, *6*, 615–631. [CrossRef] [PubMed]
104. Murakami, M.; Ichisaka, T.; Maeda, M.; Oshiro, N.; Hara, K.; Edenhofer, F.; Kiyama, H.; Yonezawa, K.; Yamanaka, S. mTOR is essential for growth and proliferation in early mouse embryos and embryonic stem cells. *Mol. Cell. Biol.* **2004**, *24*, 6710–6718. [CrossRef] [PubMed]
105. Takei, N.; Nawa, H. mTOR signaling and its roles in normal and abnormal brain development. *Front. Mol. Neurosci.* **2014**, *7*, 28. [CrossRef] [PubMed]
106. Chen, J.A.; Peñagarikano, O.; Belgard, T.G.; Swarup, V.; Geschwind, D.H. The Emerging Picture of Autism Spectrum Disorder: Genetics and Pathology. *Annu. Rev. Pathol. Mech. Dis.* **2015**, *10*, 111–144. [CrossRef] [PubMed]
107. McBride, K.L.; Varga, E.A.; Pastore, M.T.; Prior, T.W.; Manickam, K.; Atkin, J.F.; Herman, G.E. Confirmation study of PTEN mutations among individuals with autism or developmental delays/mental retardation and macrocephaly. *Autism Res.* **2010**, *3*, 137–141. [CrossRef] [PubMed]
108. Plasschaert, E.; Descheemaeker, M.-J.; Van Eylen, L.; Noens, I.; Steyaert, J.; Legius, E. Prevalence of Autism Spectrum Disorder symptoms in children with neurofibromatosis type 1. *Am. J. Med. Genet. Part B* **2015**, *168B*, 72–80. [CrossRef] [PubMed]
109. Hoeffer, C.A.; Sanchez, E.; Hagerman, R.J.; Mu, Y.; Nguyen, D.V.; Wong, H.; Whelan, A.M.; Zukin, R.S.; Klann, E.; Tassone, F. Altered mTOR signaling and enhanced CYFIP2 expression levels in subjects with Fragile X syndrome. *Genes Brain Behav.* **2012**, *11*, 332–341. [CrossRef] [PubMed]
110. Tsai, V.; Parker, W.E.; Orlova, K.A.; Baybis, M.; Chi, A.W.S.; Berg, B.D.; Birnbaum, J.F.; Estevez, J.; Okochi, K.; Sarnat, H.B.; et al. Fetal Brain mTOR Signaling Activation in Tuberous Sclerosis Complex. *Cereb. Cortex* **2014**, *24*, 315–327. [CrossRef] [PubMed]
111. Sato, A.; Kasai, S.; Kobayashi, T.; Takamatsu, Y.; Hino, O.; Ikeda, K.; Mizuguchi, M. Rapamycin reverses impaired social interaction in mouse models of tuberous sclerosis complex. *Nat. Commun.* **2012**, *3*, 1292. [CrossRef] [PubMed]

112. Butler, M.G.; Dasouki, M.J.; Zhou, X.; Talebizadeh, Z.; Brown, M.; Takahashi, T.N.; Miles, J.H.; Wang, C.H.; Stratton, R.; Pilarski, R.; et al. Subset of individuals with autism spectrum disorders and extreme macrocephaly associated with germline PTEN tumour suppressor gene mutations. *J. Med. Genet.* **2005**, *42*, 318–321. [CrossRef] [PubMed]
113. Kwon, C.H.; Luikart, B.W.; Powell, C.M.; Zhou, J.; Matheny, S.A.; Zhang, W.; Li, Y.; Baker, S.J.; Parada, L.F. Pten Regulates Neuronal Arborization and Social Interaction in Mice. *Neuron* **2006**, *50*, 377–388. [CrossRef] [PubMed]
114. Cupolillo, D.; Hoxha, E.; Faralli, A.; De Luca, A.; Rossi, F.; Tempia, F.; Carulli, D. Autistic-Like Traits and Cerebellar Dysfunction in Purkinje Cell PTEN Knock-Out Mice. *Neuropsychopharmacology* **2015**, *41*, 1–27. [CrossRef] [PubMed]
115. Johannessen, C.M.; Reczek, E.E.; James, M.F.; Brems, H.; Legius, E.; Cichowski, K. The NF1 tumor suppressor critically regulates TSC2 and mTOR. *Proc. Natl. Acad. Sci. USA* **2005**, *102*, 8573–8578. [CrossRef] [PubMed]
116. Burket, J.A.; Benson, A.D.; Tang, A.H.; Deutsch, S.I. Rapamycin improves sociability in the BTBR T+itpr3tf/J mouse model of autism spectrum disorders. *Brain Res. Bull.* **2014**, *100*, 70–75. [CrossRef] [PubMed]
117. Berry, A.; Bindocci, E.; Alleva, E. NGF, Brain and Behavioral Plasticity. *Neural Plast.* **2012**, *2012*, 1–9. [CrossRef] [PubMed]
118. Gnahn, H.; Hefti, F.; Heumann, R.; Schwab, M.E.; Thoenen, H. NGF-Mediated increase of choline acetyltransferase (ChAT) in the neonatal rat forebrain: Evidence for a physiological role of NGF in the brain? *Dev. Brain Res.* **1983**, *9*, 45–52. [CrossRef]
119. Li, Y.; Holtzman, D.M.; Kromer, L.F.; Kaplan, D.R.; Chua-Couzens, J.; Clary, D.O.; Knüsel, B.; Mobley, W.C. Regulation of TrkA and ChAT expression in developing rat basal forebrain: Evidence that both exogenous and endogenous NGF regulate differentiation of cholinergic neurons. *J. Neurosci.* **1995**, *15*, 2888–2905. [PubMed]
120. Riikonen, R.; Vanhala, R. Levels of cerebrospinal fluid nerve-growth factor differ in infantile autism and Rett syndrome. *Dev. Med. Child Neurol.* **1999**, *41*, 148–152. [CrossRef] [PubMed]
121. Nelson, K.B.; Grether, J.K.; Croen, L.A.; Dambrosia, J.M.; Dickens, B.F.; Jelliffe, L.L.; Hansen, R.L.; Phillips, T.M. Neuropeptides and neurotrophins in neonatal blood of children with autism or mental retardation. *Ann. Neurol.* **2001**, *49*, 597–606. [CrossRef] [PubMed]
122. Stamova, B.S.; Tian, Y.; Nordahl, C.W.; Shen, M.D.; Rogers, S.; Amaral, D.G.; Sharp, F.R. Evidence for differential alternative splicing in blood of young boys with autism spectrum disorders. *Mol. Autism* **2013**, *4*, 30. [CrossRef] [PubMed]
123. Chakrabarti, B.; Dudbridge, F.; Kent, L.; Wheelwright, S.; Hill-Cawthorne, G.; Allison, C.; Banerjee-Basu, S.; Baron-Cohen, S. Genes related to sex steroids, neural growth, and social-emotional behavior are associated with autistic traits, empathy, and asperger syndrome. *Autism Res.* **2009**, *2*, 157–177. [CrossRef] [PubMed]
124. Lu, A.T.-H.; Yoon, J.; Geschwind, D.H.; Cantor, R.M. QTL replication and targeted association highlight the nerve growth factor gene for nonverbal communication deficits in autism spectrum disorders. *Mol. Psychiatry* **2013**, *18*, 226–235. [CrossRef] [PubMed]
125. Ellegood, J.; Anagnostou, E.; Babineau, B.A.; Crawley, J.N.; Lin, L.; Genestine, M.; DiCicco-Bloom, E.; Lai, J.K.Y.; Foster, J.A.; Peñagarikano, O.; et al. Clustering autism: Using neuroanatomical differences in 26 mouse models to gain insight into the heterogeneity. *Mol. Psychiatry* **2015**, *20*, 118–125. [CrossRef] [PubMed]
126. Kim, H.; Lim, C.-S.; Kaang, B.-K. Neuronal mechanisms and circuits underlying repetitive behaviors in mouse models of autism spectrum disorder. *Behav. Brain Funct.* **2016**, *12*, 3. [CrossRef] [PubMed]

6

Association Analysis of Noncoding Variants in Neuroligins 3 and 4X Genes with Autism Spectrum Disorder in an Italian Cohort

Martina Landini [1], Ivan Merelli [1], M. Elisabetta Raggi [2], Nadia Galluccio [1], Francesca Ciceri [2], Arianna Bonfanti [2], Serena Camposeo [3], Angelo Massagli [3], Laura Villa [2], Erika Salvi [4], Daniele Cusi [1,5], Massimo Molteni [2], Luciano Milanesi [1], Anna Marabotti [2,6] and Alessandra Mezzelani [1,*]

1 Institute of Biomedical Technologies, National Research Council, Via Fratelli Cervi 93, 20090 Segrate, Italy; landinimartina@gmail.com (M.L.); ivan.merelli@itb.cnr.it (I.M.); nadiagalluccio@gmail.com (N.G.); daniele.cusi@unimi.it (D.C.); luciano.milanesi@itb.cnr.it (L.M.)

2 Scientific Institute, IRCSS Eugenio Medea, 23842 Bosisio Parini, Italy; mariaelisabetta.raggi@bp.lnf.it (M.E.R.); francesca.ciceri@bp.lnf.it (F.C.); arianna.bonfanti@bp.lnf.it (A.B.); laura.villa@bp.lnf.it (L.V.); massimo.molteni@bp.lnf.it (M.M.); amarabotti@unisa.it (A.M.)

3 Scientific Institute, IRCSS Eugenio Medea, 72100 Brindisi, Italy; serena.camposeo@libero.it (S.C.); angelo.massagli@gmail.com (A.M.)

4 Department of Health Sciences, University of Milan, 20142 Milan, Italy; erika.salvi@unimi.it

5 Sanipedia srl, via Ariosto 21, 20091 Bresso, Italy

6 Department of Chemistry and Biology, University of Salerno, Via Giovanni Paolo II 132, 84084 Fisciano, Italy

* Correspondence: alessandra.mezzelani@itb.cnr.it

Academic Editor: Merlin G. Butler

Abstract: Since involved in synaptic transmission and located on X-chromosome, neuroligins 3 and 4X have been studied as good positional and functional candidate genes for autism spectrum disorder pathogenesis, although contradictory results have been reported. Here, we performed a case-control study to assess the association between noncoding genetic variants in *NLGN3* and *NLGN4X* genes and autism, in an Italian cohort of 202 autistic children analyzed by high-resolution melting. The results were first compared with data from 379 European healthy controls (1000 Genomes Project) and then with those from 1061 Italian controls genotyped by Illumina single nucleotide polymorphism (SNP) array 1M-duo. Statistical evaluations were performed using Plink v1.07, with the Omnibus multiple loci approach. According to both the European and the Italian control groups, a 6-marker haplotype on *NLGN4X* (rs6638575(G), rs3810688(T), rs3810687(G), rs3810686(C), rs5916269(G), rs1882260(T)) was associated with autism (odd ratio = 3.58, p-value = 2.58×10^{-6} for the European controls; odds ratio = 2.42, p-value = 6.33×10^{-3} for the Italian controls). Furthermore, several haplotype blocks at 5-, 4-, 3-, and 2-, including the first 5, 4, 3, and 2 SNPs, respectively, showed a similar association with autism. We provide evidence that noncoding polymorphisms on *NLGN4X* may be associated to autism, suggesting the key role of *NLGN4X* in autism pathophysiology and in its male prevalence.

Keywords: autism; genetics; neuroligins; SNPs; haplotype analysis; noncoding regions

---

1. Introduction

Autism spectrum disorder (ASD) is a complex neurodevelopmental disorder with an early onset, typically prior to age 3, characterized by impaired social interactions, absent or limited verbal communication, and stereotyped and restricted pattern of interests [1]. Considering the great variability of clinical presentations, the definition of ASD includes autism, Asperger's syndrome, and pervasive developmental disorder not otherwise specified (PDD-NOS) [2]. A combination of both genetic and environmental causes, such as pesticides, heavy metals, dysbiosis, and mycotoxins, has been suggested for ASD pathogenesis but, despite approximately 5%–15% of ASDs cases being due to identified genetic or chromosomal alterations, the ASD etiology is still largely unknown [3–8]. Considering the higher occurrence of ASD in males than in females, with a ratio of roughly 4:1, a role for the X-chromosome in the ASD etiology has been also suggested [7,9]. In this regard, cytogenetic abnormalities highlight the putative involvement of the loci from Xq12 to Xq21 and Xp22 in autism pathogenesis [10,11], as well as associations with structural variants that have been reported for some X-chromosomal genes, such as *NLGN4X* and *MECP2* genes [12–15]. Since located on the X-chromosome and involved in synaptic plasticity, both Neuroligin3 (*NLGN3*) and Neuroligin4X (*NLGN4X*), mapped at Xq13.1 and Xp22.31, respectively, were extensively studied as good positional and functional candidates for ASD predisposing. Neuroligins are postsynaptic cell-adhesion molecules that interact with the presynaptic cell-surface receptors neurexins. Neurexins contain a single transmembrane domain, and together with neuroligins they form Ca^{2+}-dependent neurexin/neuroligin complexes. These transsynaptic complexes play a crucial role in modulating neurotransmission and differentiation [16–18]. Several ASD genetic studies have identified mutations affecting neuroligin proteins and influencing synaptic function [19–21]. The involvement of neuroligins in ASD has been firstly confirmed in two Swedish families by a de novo missense mutation (R451C) in *NLGN3* and a frameshift mutation (1186insT) in *NLGN4X* causing premature protein termination (D396X), respectively associated with typical autism and Asperger's syndrome [12]. Both these mutations resulted in an intracellular retention of the mutant proteins, with a consistent loss of the synaptic activity, leading to neurodevelopmental defects and mental retardation [22,23]. In mouse models, autism-associated *NLGN3* mutations induced repetitive behaviors, and R451C mutant mice showed impaired social interactions, but enhanced spatial learning abilities [24–26]. A loss-of-function mechanism has also been suggested for the point mutation R87W in *NLGN4X*, found in two brothers with classical ASD [27]. Recently, missense variations in *NLGN3* (G426S) and *NLGN4X* (G84R, Q162K, and A283T) in Chinese ASD patients have been associated to ASD predisposing, by causing abnormal synaptic homeostasis [28]. Deletion of exons 4, 5, and 6 in *NLGN4X* have been also found in autistic children, suggesting that alternative splicing variants might lead to abnormal neuroligin function in ASD [29,30]. Moreover, several noncoding genetic variants have been specifically found in ASD patients [31–37]. All these variations often segregate into ASD families [12,13] and can also be associated with different cognitive phenotypes, such as intellectual and language disabilities [32,37], highlighting the role of neuroligins in the ASD pathogenesis. In this regard, a de novo base pair substitution (−335G>A) in the promoter region of *NLGN4X*, has been found in one autistic child with nonsyndromic mental retardation (NSMR) [32]. Since associated with an increased level of *NLGN4X* transcripts, this variation probably affects the binding sites of transcription factors in the mutated promoter sequence [32]. Four novel synonymous substitutions, specific to ASD, have been reported in the coding sequences of the *NLGN3* (p.K566K) and *NLGN4X* (p.G99G; p.I172I; p.F530F) [34]. Despite the uncertainty of the physiological and clinical relevance, they might affect the protein structures by altering splicing sites [34] or affecting gene regulation, as they are located in conserved regulatory regions, such as enhancer- and promoter-associated histone modification sites [33]. Moreover, a positive association with ASD has been identified in a homogeneous autistic Chinese cohort (made of patients with typical phenotype), for a common intronic variant in *NLGN3* (rs4844285(G)) [6]. A three-marker haplotype (rs11795613(A), rs4844285(G), rs4844286(T)), with a significant male bias, has been suggested, supporting the hypothesis that defects of the synapse might have a role in ASD pathogenesis [6]. In addition, three haplotype sets in *NLGN4X* (rs3810686(T), rs1882260(C)), (rs6638575(G), rs3810686(T), rs18882260(T)) and (rs6638575(A), rs3810686(C), rs18882260(C)), have been positively associated with nonspecific mental retardation (Intelligence Quotients IQs < 70) and social disability scores ≤ 8 [36] and genetic variants in *NLGN4X* also have a significant effect on male cognitive abilities, highlighting the role of neuroligins in psychiatric conditions [37].

However, contradictory results have been also provided in validating the relevance and frequency of neuroligin genetic variants in ASD [38–41]. Wermenter and coworkers failed to find an involvement of *NLGN3* and *NLGN4X* with ASD in a study group of 107 probands with autistic disorders at a high-functioning level [40], and similar results have been reported in the Quebec population, after screening for neuroligin mutations in 96 individuals diagnosed with ASD [41]. Lastly, no association was found between *NLGN3/NLGN4X* alterations and ASD in a Chinese cohort [38]. However, the genetic heterogeneity of ASD, as well as differences in the ethnicity background of ASD samples, make it difficult to elucidate the involvement of neuroligin genes in autism pathogenesis.

Considering all these evidences and starting from an Italian ASD sample set, we assessed the effects of three noncoding genetic variants in *NLGN3*, already reported as associated with ASD in a Chinese cohort [6], and six common single nucleotide polymorphisms (SNPs) in *NLGN4X*, only partially described in literature [36], with the final aim to validate the selected genetic variants as susceptibility loci for ASD.

2. Results

2.1. Single-Locus Analysis

Association analyses have been performed considering SNPs located in the intronic and 3′ UTR regions of *NLGN3* and *NLGN4X*, considering both the European (EUR) population (1000 Genomes Project, Phase 2) [42] and the Italian population. Genotype counts of SNPs and results of the Hardy–Weinberg statistics, which do not present any significant disequilibrium, are shown in Tables S1 and S2. As shown in Table 1, a moderate statistical significance difference (odds ratio (OR) = 1.453, $p = 0.0456$) was identified in the single-locus analysis only for SNP rs3810688, with the minor allele T having frequency slightly lower in ASD cases in comparison to EUR controls (separate results for male and female analysis are provided in Tables S3 and S4). However, this association lost its significance after False Discovery Rate (FDR) correction for multiple testing (Table 1). As the number of samples was quite limited, Fisher's exact test has been chosen for comparing SNP allelic frequencies between cases and unrelated controls, always using the genetic data from the 1000 Genomes Project (Phase 2) as reference population [42]. We also verified that the allelic frequencies for all the SNPs analyzed do not statistically deviate in our control data set from those reported in the 1000 Genomes Project EUR population. The moderate statistical association of rs3810688(T) with autism disappeared when comparing ASD data with those from Italian controls.

Table 1. Single locus analysis for all the single nucleotide polymorphisms (SNPs) genotyped in *NLGN3* and *NLGN4X* (EUR control population).

Gene ID	SNP ID	Minor Allele	MAF Controls	MAF Case	*p*-Value	OR	95% CI	*p*-Corr
NLGN3	rs11795613	G	0.481	0.515	0.398	1.144	0.816–1.617	0.701
	rs4844285	A	0.4741	0.4895	0.701	1.064	0.755–1.496	0.701
	rs4844286	T	0.505	0.481	0.5396	0.908	0.646–1.280	0.701
NLGN4X	rs6638575	A	0.266	0.301	0.303	1.193	0.856–1.663	0.404
	rs3810688	T	0.2176	0.288	0.0456	1.453	1.018–2.074	0.152
	rs3810687	T	0.1086	0.1339	0.3369	1.269	0.805–2.000	0.404
	rs3810686	T	0.4466	0.4561	0.817	1.039	0.768–1.407	0.817
	rs5916269	A	0.1086	0.1339	0.3369	1.269	0.805–2.000	0.404
	rs1882260	C	0.2655	0.3347	0.0505	1.392	1.005–1.928	0.152

Statistical significance, for the single locus association analysis, was tested at $p < 0.05$, after Fisher's exact test. The *p*-values have been adjusted by false discovery rate (FDR) correction for multiple test analysis. MAF controls, frequency of the minor allele in controls ($n = 379$); MAF case, frequency of the minor allele in case ($n = 202$); OR, odds ratio; CI, confidence interval; *p*-corr, corrected *p*-value after FDR test.

2.2. Haplotype Analysis (EUR Control Population)

A 6-SNPs haplotype block in *NLGN4X* showed a strong significant association with ASD cases (odds ratio = 3.58, p-value = 2.58×10^{-6}), also after logistic regression and 100,000 permutation tests (empirical p-value < 1×10^{-5}, empirical q-value < 1×10^{-5}) (Table 2). This block (rs6638575(G), rs3810688(T), rs3810687(G), rs3810686(C), rs5916269(G), rs188260(T)) includes the SNP rs3810688(T), moderately associated with ASD in the single-locus analysis. Indeed, haplotypes on *NLGN4X* have been also analyzed as 5-, 4-, 3-, or 2-loci blocks, as reported in Table 2. A good statistical significance was obtained with blocks including the SNP rs3810688(T), especially together with the haplotype sets also including the SNPs rs3810687(G) and rs3810686(C)—both located in the 3′ UTR of *NLGN4X*—and with rs6638575(G), in the intron 5 of *NLGN4X* (Table 2). These variants are part of two 5-loci (rs6638575(G), rs3810688(T), rs3810687(G), rs381086(C), rs5916269(G)) and (rs3810688(T), rs3810687(G), rs381086(C), rs5916269(G), rs1882260(T)), two 4-loci (rs6638575(G), rs3810688(T), rs3810687(G), rs381086(C)) and (rs3810688(T), rs3810687(G), rs3810686(C), rs5916269(G)), two 3-loci (rs6638575(G), rs3810688(T), rs3810687(G)) and (rs3810688(T), rs3810687(G), rs3810686(C)) and two 2-loci (rs6638575(G), rs3810688(T)) and (rs3810688(T), rs3810687(G)) combinations, all with strong statistical association with ASD. Moreover, despite the single-locus analysis not showing any statistical difference for the SNPs rs1882260 and rs5916269, haplotype analysis showed that two 2-blocks (rs5916269(G), rs1882260(T)) and (rs3810686(C), rs5916269(G)), two 3-blocks (rs3810686(C), rs5916269(G), rs1882260(T)) and (rs3810687(G), rs3810686(C), rs5916269(G)) and one 4-block loci (rs3810687(G), rs3810686(C), rs5916269(G), rs1882260(T)), respectively, have also a very strong significant association with ASD (Table 2). Similar results have been obtained also comparing the ASD haplotype frequencies of *NLGN4X* with our unrelated controls, suggesting the reliability of the selected control population for the statistical analysis (EUR Phase 2, 1000 Genomes Project).

Table 2. Haplotype association analysis in *NLGN4X* (*EUR control population*).

N	SNPs in Haplotypes	Control Frequency	Case Frequency	Haplotype	p-Value	Emp. p-Value	Emp. q-Value
6	rs6638575-rs3810688-rs3810687-rs3810686-rs5916269-rs1882260	0.0335	0.1799	GTGCGT	2.58×10^{-6}	$<1 \times 10^{-5}$	$<1 \times 10^{-5}$
5	rs6638575-rs3810688-rs3810687-rs3810686-rs5916269	0.0805	0.1799	GTGCG	7.60×10^{-6}	$<1 \times 10^{-5}$	$<1 \times 10^{-5}$
5	rs3810688-rs3810687-rs3810686-rs5916269-rs1882260	0.0335	0.1799	TGCGT	2.58×10^{-6}	$<1 \times 10^{-5}$	$<1 \times 10^{-5}$
4	rs6638575-rs3810688-rs3810687-rs3810686	0.0805	0.1799	GTGC	7.6×10^{-6}	$<1 \times 10^{-5}$	2×10^{-5}
4	rs3810688-rs3810687-rs3810686-rs5916269	0.0801	0.1793	TGCG	7.6×10^{-6}	$<1 \times 10^{-5}$	2×10^{-5}
4	rs3810687-rs3810686-rs5916269-rs1882260	0.0943	0.1793	GCGT	1.3×10^{-5}	$<1 \times 10^{-5}$	2×10^{-5}
3	rs6638575-rs3810688-rs3810687	0.3538	0.4463	GTG	8.16×10^{-6}	$<1 \times 10^{-5}$	$<1 \times 10^{-5}$
3	rs3810688-rs3810687-rs3810686	0.0701	0.1793	TGC	7.6×10^{-6}	$<1 \times 10^{-5}$	$<1 \times 10^{-5}$
3	rs3810687-rs3810686-rs5916269	0.4062	0.4445	GCG	8.16×10^{-4}	6.99×10^{-4}	3.2×10^{-3}
3	rs3810686-rs5916269-rs1882260	0.0943	0.1793	CGT	1.3×10^{-5}	$<1 \times 10^{-5}$	3×10^{-4}
2	rs6638575-rs3810688	0.2109	0.2854	GT	1.08×10^{-4}	7×10^{-5}	8.3×10^{-4}
2	rs3810688-rs3810687	0.0943	0.1793	TG	1.3×10^{-5}	2×10^{-5}	1.5×10^{-4}
2	rs3810687-rs3810686	0.4062	0.4445	GC	8.16×10^{-4}	7.3×10^{-4}	5×10^{-3}
2	rs3810686-rs5916269	0.4062	0.4445	CG	8.16×10^{-4}	7.3×10^{-4}	5×10^{-3}
2	rs5916269-rs1882260	0.4314	0.6259	GT	2.4×10^{-8}	$<1 \times 10^{-5}$	$<1 \times 10^{-5}$

Haplotype combinations with significant p-values ($p < 0.05$), using the EUR control population, after permutation test, have been reported for all the SNPs located on *NLGN4X*. Empirical p-values and empirical q-values after 100,000 permutations are reported. Only haplotypes having case frequency >0.05 have been presented.

No statistically significant haplotypes have been found in the *NLGN3* after logistic regression and permutation analysis.

2.3. Haplotype Analysis (ITA control Population)

The analysis was then repeated comparing the frequencies of *NLGN4X* SNPs between ASD cases and 1061 healthy controls collected during the Hypergenes project [43]. The association with the 6-marker haplotype remained, although weaker than the EUR population (odds ratio = 2.42, p-value = 6.33×10^{-3}, empirical p-value = 6.79×10^{-3}, empirical q-value < 2.73×10^{-2}). A weaker association was also found for most of the 5-, 4-, 3- and 2-SNP haplotypes identified considering the EUR population. Data are reported in Table 3.

Table 3. Haplotype association analysis in *NLGN4X* (ITA control population).

N	SNPs in Haplotypes	Control Frequency	Case Frequency	Haplotype	p-Value	Empirical p-Value	Empirical q-Value
6	rs6638575-rs3810688-rs3810687-rs3810686-rs5916269-rs1882260	0.0678	0.1799	GTGCGT	6.33×10^{-3}	6.79×10^{-3}	2.73×10^{-3}
5	rs6638575-rs3810688-rs3810687-rs3810686-rs5916269	0.1349	0.1799	GTGCG	1.9×10^{-2}	1.87×10^{-2}	4.47×10^{-2}
5	rs3810688-rs3810687-rs3810686-rs5916269-rs1882260	0.0678	0.1799	TGCGT	6.33×10^{-3}	5.39×10^{-3}	2.78×10^{-2}
4	rs6638575-rs3810688-rs3810687-rs3810686	0.1189	0.1799	GTGC	1.66×10^{-2}	1.62×10^{-2}	4.41×10^{-2}
3	rs6638575-rs3810688-rs3810687	0.3782	0.4463	GTG	1.56×10^{-2}	1.29×10^{-2}	4.37×10^{-2}
3	rs3810688-rs3810687-rs3810686	0.0801	0.1793	TGC	1.17×10^{-2}	1.26×10^{-2}	4.78×10^{-2}
3	rs3810687-rs3810686-rs5916269	0.3360	0.4445	GCG	3.99×10^{-3}	4.10×10^{-3}	1.98×10^{-2}
2	rs3810687-rs3810686	0.3160	0.4445	GC	3.50×10^{-3}	3.20×10^{-3}	2.20×10^{-2}
2	rs3810686-rs5916269	0.3360	0.4445	CG	3.99×10^{-3}	3.70×10^{-3}	2.53×10^{-2}

Haplotype combinations with significant p-values ($p < 0.05$), using the ITA control population, after permutation test, have been reported for all the SNPs located on *NLGN4X*. Empirical p-values and empirical q-values after 100,000 permutations are reported. Only haplotypes having case frequency >0.05 have been presented.

2.4. Linkage Disequilibrium Analysis

The results for linkage disequilibrium (LD) analysis for the considered SNPs in *NLGN4X* are presented in Figure 1. Panel (a) represents the LD for SNPs in the EUR control populations; panel (b) shows the LD scores for the ITA control population patients; panel (c) reports the results achieved for ASD patients.

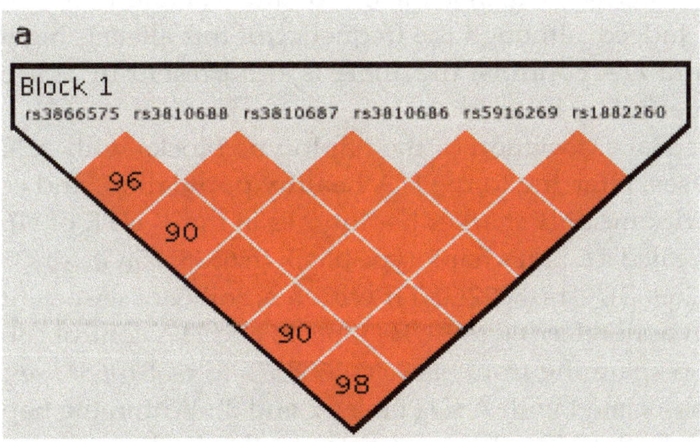

Figure 1. *Cont.*

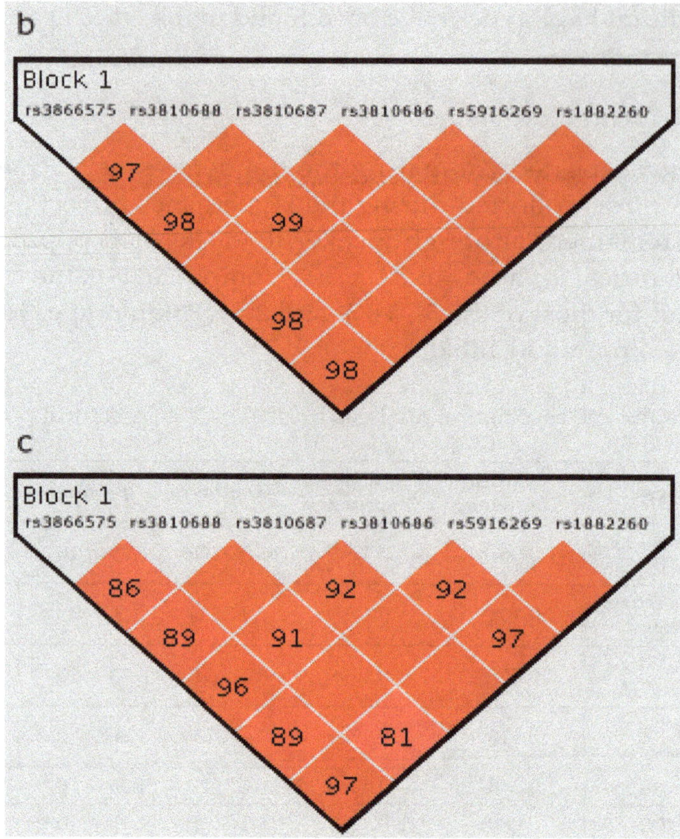

Figure 1. Linkage disequilibrium (LD) for the SNPs analyzed in *NLGN4X* calculated using Haploview: in panel (**a**) for the EUR population (1000 Genomes Project, Phase 2); in panel (**b**) for the Italian control population; and in panel (**c**) for the autistic patients enrolled in our study.

3. Discussion

According to our results, common noncoding variants in *NLGN4X* may play a role in ASD susceptibility. Starting from a relatively homogenous sample and a case-control study design, our results suggest that some SNP marker haplotype blocks, located in the 3′ UTR of *NLGN4X*, might be associated to ASD. After a first statistical analysis, referring to EUR 1000 Genomes Project population as control, the 3′ UTR of *NLGN3* did not show any association with ASD, nor at single SNP or at haplotype blocks. On the other hand, the 3′ UTR of *NLGN4X* displayed statistical association with the disease at single SNP rs3810688(T), which is the minor allele (Table 1), although this significance was lost after FDR correction. Indeed, although the frequency of this allele is higher in the ASD population in comparison to EUR and ITA controls, the allele is still present in 21% of EUR population, thus producing only a modest effect by itself.

To confirm the statistical association of the haplotype blocks with ASD, (Table 2), we repeated the same statistical analyses, referring to the ITA healthy population, and confirmed the association, although weaker, between some SNP marker haplotypes in the 3′ UTR of *NLGN4X* and ASD. Indeed, the haplotype analysis revealed a 6-SNPs haplotype block (rs6638575(G), −rs3810688(T), −rs3810687(G), −rs3810686(C), −rs5916269(G), −rs1882260(T)) with a significant association with ASD, even after correction by permutation both referring to EUR (Table 2) and ITA control cohort populations (Table 3). In particular, in the region spanning from SNPs rs6638575 to rs3810686, several multiloci haplotype blocks were found to be associated with ASD (Tables 2 and 3). Within the haplotype blocks containing rs3810687 and rs3810686, both SNPs always displayed the G allele. Interestingly, considering the LD analysis, we notice that the considered SNPs on *NLGN4X* are more in linkage than in control populations (Figure 1).

These results might imply that an approximately 4 kb region in the 3′ UTR of *NLGN4X*, spanning from SNPs rs66385775 to rs1882260, could be involved in autism susceptibility. This regulatory region in *NLGN4X* might have a role in modulating neuroligin biological function and, therefore, in causing or predisposing to neurological disorders. Since *NLGN4X* is involved in synaptic plasticity and X-linked, it might be a key gene in ASD pathogenesis and in its sex bias.

On the other hand, no associations were found for variants located on *NLGN3* at the single locus and haplotype analysis, despite Yu and coworkers (2011) reporting a positive association for the variants rs11795613(A), rs4844285(G), and rs4844286(T) with ASD [6]. Differences in sample ethnicity and size, as well as the ASD heterogeneity, might be taken into account for explaining such different results. Further studies, performed on a greater number of patients and with different genetic backgrounds, will be required to elucidate the role of *NLGN3* in autism susceptibility.

Nonetheless, our results are partially in agreement with Qi and collaborators (2009) that reported a positive association between SNPs in *NLGN4X* (rs6638575, rs3810686, rs1882260) and NSMR in a Chinese population [36]. In this regard, four putative haplotype combinations (rs3810686(T), rs1882260(T)), (rs3810686(C), −rs1882260(C)) and (rs6638575(G), rs3810686(T), rs18882260(T)) and (rs6638575(A), rs3810686(C), rs18882260(C)), in the sixth exon of *NLGN4X* have been reported as positively associated to NSMR in this Chinese cohort [36]. This genomic region, in fact, plays a crucial role for the biological function of *NLGN4X*, encoding for the transmembrane domain and postsynaptic density 95-disc large zone occludens-1 binding domain, both necessary for N-methyl aspartate receptors and downstream signal-transducing proteins. Furthermore, it has been reported that a target haplotype composed of the SNPs rs5916271(C) and rs6638575(A) had a significant effect in improving the general cognitive ability and especially verbal comprehension in male children, although further studies are required to highlight the role of these polymorphisms in ASD susceptibility [37].

As none of the analyzed SNPs on *NLGN4X* produce amino acid changes, two possible explanations should be taken into account for their association with ASD. First, considering the regulatory role of the 3′ UTR regions in modulating gene expression, the SNPs located in this region, correlated with ASD, might affect miRNA-binding sites, leading to impairments in *NLGN4X* expression. In this regard, the SNPs analyzed in this study might be located in or very close to putative miRNA regulatory regions, breaking or creating miRNA-binding sites with a possible effect on *NLGN4X* expression and thus on synaptic transmission. To this respect, it has been reported that a single nucleotide variant located in the 5′ UTR of *NLGN4X* is able to affect neuroligin expression [32], but further studies are required to validate if such a regulatory mechanism might also occur for the genetic variants in the 3′ UTR of neuroligin genes. Second, it might be also possible that other genetic variants, as putative predisposing loci or causative mutations, could exist in close linkage with the SNPs analyzed on *NLGN4X*, leading to differences in *NLGN4X* expression through alternative splicing or amino acid variations since each of these conditions can alter the biological function of *NLGN4X*.

Considering that males have higher predisposition in ASD etiology, an involvement of the X-chromosome in autism susceptibility has been suggested by genetic and cytogenetic studies [9–13] and several putative candidate genes, including neuroligins, have been largely investigated [7,8,23–37]. Nonetheless, taking advantages of the new sequencing technologies, further insights might be provided in discovering new X-linked genetic variants associated with ASD predisposition or its etiology.

Although the sample size of patients is quite limited for a genetic association study, statistical association between marker haplotype blocks located at 3′ UTR of *NLGN4X* and ASD was found referring both to EUR and ITA populations. Indeed, despite the stronger statistical significance found in reference to EUR controls, similar results were obtained in reference to ITA controls.

After all, considering the heterogeneity of ASD, in terms of symptoms, severity, and comorbidities, it sounds reasonable that several genes might be involved in ASD predisposition, as well as epigenetics or environmental factors. For this reason, a single genetic variant or haplotype, even if in a regulatory region or in a candidate gene, seems unlikely to be playing a major role in ASD predisposition. Thus, further functional and genetic studies coupled to these SNP profiles in a larger ASD cohort would be the next steps to elucidate the role of neuroligins and genetic variants in ASD etiology. Indeed, these SNPs could be the markers of other genetic variations or associated to specific phenotypes. Moreover, as gene–environment interaction has also been proposed for autism pathogenesis, further studies considering both the genetic and environmental risk factors should be designed.

As for clinical application, the relation between these genetic risk factors and symptoms or ASD characteristics could suggest molecular and epigenetic mechanisms triggering the disease and suggest possible preventive or therapeutic intervention.

In our study we found and discussed the association of several noncoding genetic variants in the *NLGN4X* gene with ASD in an Italian cohort. This implies that neuroligins and, therefore, impairments at the synaptic transmission, might play a role in ASD susceptibility and pathophysiology. To date, no other works have investigated the role of neuroligin noncoding variants in ASD susceptibility in an Italian autistic population, although Blasi and coworkers (2006) failed to find a significant association with ASD in neuroligin coding variants [39] when analyzing Italian ASD patients. Taking into account the contradictory results in validating the role of neuroligins in ASD predisposition as well as the complex etiology of this disease, our findings can be important for the characterization of this disease, although they need to be confirmed and replicated in different ethnic groups and to be associated with phenotypic and epigenetic data.

4. Materials and Methods

4.1. Subjects

The sample-sets consist of: 202 ASD patients (165 (81.7%) males; 37 (18.3%) females), recruited by IRCCS Eugenio Medea-La Nostra Famiglia in two different and far areas of Italy: Bosisio Parini (Lecco, Italy) in the North and Ostuni (BR, Italy) in the South. Patients had an age ranging between 2 and 12 years. Demographic characteristics are summarized in Table 4.

Table 4. Demographic data and diagnosis of autistic patients.

<table>
<tr><th colspan="3">Patients: 202; Age: 2–12; Males: 165; Females: 37</th></tr>
<tr><td rowspan="2">Patients from North Italy: $n = 157$</td><td>Males: 131, 83.44%</td><td>Young autism: 93 (71%)
PDD-NOS: 34 (26%)
Asperger's Syndrome: 4 (3%)</td></tr>
<tr><td>Females: 26, 16.56%</td><td>Young autism: 18 (69.2%)
PDD-NOS: 7 (27%)
Asperger's Syndrome: 1 (3.8%)</td></tr>
<tr><td rowspan="2">Patients from South Italy: $n = 45$</td><td>Males: 34, 75.55%</td><td>Young autism: 24 (70.6%)
PDD-NOS: 9 (26.5%)
Asperger's Syndrome: 1 (2.9%)</td></tr>
<tr><td>Females: 11, 24.45%</td><td>Young autism: 8 (72.7%)
PDD-NOS: 3 (27.3%)
Asperger's Syndrome: 0</td></tr>
</table>

The diagnosis for young autism (70.3%), Asperger's syndrome (3.5%), or PDD-NOS (26.2%) were performed according to DSM-IV TR (APA, 2000) and by the Autism Diagnostic Observation Scale (ADOS) and ADI-R. IQ, cognitive tests, and behavioral analyses were also done in all the patients, but 20, and are summarized in Table 5. Patients with genetic syndromes, epilepsy, and neuroradiological confirmed disorders were excluded.

One thousand sixty one healthy controls, collected during the Hypergenes Project [43] (European Network for Genetic-Epidemiological Studies; www.hypergenes.eu) were included in the study. These controls were from the same two areas of Italy from which patients were recruited and in similar proportion. The healthy subjects were genotyped at the University of Milan, using the Illumina

1M-duo array (San Diego, CA, USA) and imputed with Minimac software [44], a low-memory, fast, flexible, computationally efficient implementation of the Markov chain haplotyping method, using the haplotypes from the 1000 Genomes Project (March 2012) as reference [42].

Table 5. Cognitive and behavioral characteristics of autistic patients.

IQ		Hyperactivity	Language and Communication
>70 n = 71 (35.1%)	Level 1: IQ > 101; n = 15 (7.4%) Level 2: 100 > IQ> 70; n = 56 (27.7%)	Level 0: n = 136; (67.3%)	Level 1: n = 7 (3.5%) Level 2: n = 48 (23.7%)
≤69 n = 131 (64.6%)	Level 3: 69 > IQ > 50; n = 79 (39.1%) Level 4: 49 > IQ > 35; n = 28 (13.9%)	Level 1: n = 53 (26.2%)	Level 3: n = 65 (32.2%) Level 4: n = 64 (31.7%)
	Level 5: 34 > IQ> 20; n = 17 (8.4%) Level 6: IQ < 19; n = 7 (3.5%)	Level 2: n = 13 (6.5%)	Level 5: n = 3 (1.5%) 15 patients not evaluated (7.4%)

The data relative to the SNPs considered in the statistical analyses were obtained directly from genotyping for rs5916269, rs3810686, rs3810687, and rs663857 and by imputation for rs1882260 and rs3810688.

The Ethical committees of IRCCS Eugenio Medea-La Nostra Famiglia and of Hypergenes project approved the study.

Moreover, genotype data from the 1000 Genomes Project (Phase 2) [42] were also used as control cases, considering the 379 individuals with EUR genotype.

4.2. Selection of SNPs

The NCBI Accession Numbers, used as reference sequences for *NLGN3* and *NLGN4X* were, respectively, NG_015874 and NG_008881. Relying on literature [6,36], a selection of SNPs located in the intronic or 3′ UTR regions of both *NLGN3* and *NLGN4X* were genotyped. Furthermore, three additional SNPs, located in the 3′ UTR of *NLGN4X*, have been included since they are located in a putative regulatory region and have a close map distance with the previously selected SNPs. In this regard, the inter-SNP distance, for the SNPs analyzed in *NLGN3* and *NLGN4X*, was less than 5 kb. All the studied SNPs have a minor allele frequency (MAF) >0.05—as reported by the 1000 Genomes Project (Phase 2) in the EUR population—and are listed in the Table 6. Linkage disequilibrium for SNPs considered in this study has been calculated using Haploview [45], and the most relevant LD scores for these data are displayed in Figure 1. Figure S1 represents the LD scores (derived from the 1000 Genomes Project EUR population) of all the SNPs located in *NLGN4X*, including those selected for our analyses and the related TAG SNPs.

Table 6. List of SNPs analyzed in *NLGN3* and *NLGN4X*.

Genes	SNPs	Alleles	MAF	Position in Gene	References
NLGN3	rs11795613 rs4844285 rs4844286	(A/G) (A/G) (T/G)	G: 0.49 A: 0.48 T: 0.49	Intron 1 Intron 2 Intron 2	Yu et al., *Behav. Brain Funct.* 2011, *7*, 13 [6]
NLGN4X	rs6638575 rs3810686 rs1882260	(A/G) (T/C) (C/T)	A: 0.28 T: 0.44 C: 0.27	Intron 5 3′ UTR 3′ UTR	Qi et al., *Psychiatr. Genet.* 2009, *19*, 1 [36]
	rs3810687 rs3810688 rs5916269	(T/G) (T/C) (A/G)	T: 0.11 T: 0.29 A: 0.11	3′ UTR 3′ UTR 3′ UTR	–

All the SNPs analyzed as well as their position along the *NLGN3* and *NLGN4X* genes and MAF, are listed. MAF is referred to that reported for the EUR population (1000 Genomes Project, Phase 2). According to literature, their association to autism or psychiatric conditions, has been also reported. SNP: Single Nucleotide Polymorphism; MAF: Minor Allele Frequency; UTR: Untranslated Region.

4.3. SNPs Screening and Genotyping

Genomic DNA was extracted from peripheral blood samples, using commercial kit (Macherey-Nagel GmbH & Co. KG, Düren, Germany). SNPs located on both *NLGN3* and *NLGN4X* were amplified and genotyped by high-resolution melting analysis (HRM) (Rotor-Gene® Q-Pure detection, Qiagen, Venlo, The Netherlands). For each sample a total of 20 ng of genomic DNA was amplified in a 20 µL reaction mixture Phusion Flash High Fidelity PCR Master Mix (Thermo Fisher Scientific, Waltham, MA, USA), Stati Uniti of primer mix (0.7 each) and 5% of the intercalating dye EvaGreen (Biotium Inc., Fremont, CA, USA), with 1.4, as final concentration. HRM analysis primers were designed by PRIMER3plus software (http://bioinfo.ut.ee/primer3-0.4.0/primer3/). All samples were analyzed in duplicates, and for each selected SNP three internal controls—resembling all three possible genotypes, previously characterized by Sanger-sequencing—have been included. The temperature raising for the HRM analysis was of 0.1 °C/s. Normalized melting curves and differential graphs have been compared for the genotype analysis. Primers and amplification details are shown in the Table S5.

4.4. Statistical Analysis

A first screening was performed comparing the data obtained from ASD patients with those from the European subset of the 1000 Genomes Project (EUR Phase 2 population). SNP association analyses were performed first using Plink v1.07 [46] to test for possible associations between all the SNPs identified in *NLGN3* and *NLGN4X* and ASD. The two-tailed Fisher's exact test was chosen to compare the polymorphisms' distributions (cases vs. controls) and testing their significance at $p < 0.05$, under the null hypothesis of no association between each SNP and ASD. The p-values have been adjusted by false discovery rate (FDR) correction for multiple test analysis.

Using the same control data, haplotype tests were also performed using Plink v1.07. Omnibus multiple loci analyses were carried out for all the SNPs included in this study regarding *NLGN3* and *NLGN4X*, using logistic regression under the null hypothesis of no association between haplotypes and ASD. Permutation tests (100,000 permutations) were used to correct the p-values. Haplotypes with p-values equal or below the α threshold of 0.05 were considered as statistically significant.

The same statistical analyses were performed on SNPs in *NLGN4X*, which revealed a significant correlation with ASD, considering two groups of Italian healthy controls recruited in the same two areas of Italy in which patients were recruited.

Acknowledgments: This work has been supported by the Italian Ministry of Health (Targeted Research Funding in Public Health—Young Researchers; grant no. GR-2009-1570296), by the Italian Ministry of Education and Research (MIUR) through the Flagship project InterOmics (PB05), by IRCCS "Eugenio Medea" through the "5XMILLE" funds 2008, by the FP7-Health-F4-2007-201550 "HYPERGENES". The Flagship project InterOmics (PB05) covers costs to publish in open access. We specially thank all the parents and the children involved in this study.

Author Contributions: Alessandra Mezzelani and Martina Landini conceived and designed the experiments; Martina Landini and Nadia Galluccio performed the experiments; Ivan Merelli, Erika Salvi, Martina Landini and Alessandra Mezzelani analyzed the data; M. Elisabetta Raggi, Francesca Ciceri, Arianna Bonfanti and Serena Camposeo recruited the patients; Daniele Cusi recruited the controls; Angelo Massagli, Laura Villa and Massimo Molteni made the diagnosis; Martina Landini wrote the paper; Luciano Milanesi is the responsible of the Italian Flagship-project InterOmics (PB05); Anna Marabotti was the Principal Investigator of the project funded by Italian Ministry of Health. All the authors critically revised the manuscript.

Abbreviations

ASD	Autism spectrum disorder
EUR	European
FDR	False discovery rate
HRM	High resolution melting

IQ	Intelligence Quotient
ITA	Italian
MAF	Minor allele frequency
NLGN	Neuroligin
NSMR	Non-syndromic mental retardation
PDD-NOS	Pervasive developmental disorder-not otherwise specified
SNP	Single nucleotide polymorphism

References

1. Abrahams, B.S.; Geschwind, D.H. Advances in autism genetics: On the threshold of a new neurobiology. *Nat. Rev.* **2008**, *9*, 341–355. [CrossRef] [PubMed]
2. Johnson, C.P. Myers SM: Identification and evaluation of children with autism spectrum disorder. *Pediatrics* **2007**, *120*, 188–197. [CrossRef] [PubMed]
3. London, E.; Etzel, R.A. The environment as an etiologic factor in autism: A new direction for research. *Environ. Health Perspect.* **2000**, *108*, 401–404. [CrossRef] [PubMed]
4. Tordjman, S.; Somogyi, E.; Coulon, N.; Kermarrec, S.; Cohen, D.; Bronsard, G.; Bonnot, O.; Weismann-Arcache, C.; Botbol, M.; Lauth, B.; et al. Gene × environment interactions in autism spectrum disorders: Role of epigenetic mechanisms. *Front. Psychiatr.* **2014**, *5*, 1–17. [CrossRef] [PubMed]
5. Mezzelani, A.; Landini, M.; Facchiano, F.; Raggi, M.E.; Villa, L.; Molteni, M.; de Santis, B.; Brera, C.; Caroli, A.M.; Milanesi, L.; et al. Environment, dysbiosis, immunity and sex-specific susceptibility: An evidence-based translational hypothesis for regressive autism pathogenesis. *Nutr. Neurosci.* **2014**, *1*, 1–17. [CrossRef] [PubMed]
6. Yu, J.; He, X.; Yao, D.; Li, Z.; Zhao, Z. A sex specific association of common variants of neuroligin genes (*NLGN3* and *NLGN4X*) with autism spectrum disorders in a Chinese Han cohort. *Behav. Brain Funct.* **2011**, *7*, 13–23. [CrossRef] [PubMed]
7. David, B.; Scherer, S.W. Genetic architecture in autism spectrum disorder. *Curr. Opin. Genet. Dev.* **2012**, *22*, 229–237.
8. Talkowsky, M.E.; Minikel, E.V.; Gusella, J.F. Autism spectrum disorder genetics: Diverse genes with diverse clinical outcomes. *Harv. Rev. Psychiatr.* **2014**, *22*, 65–74. [CrossRef] [PubMed]
9. Piton, A.; Gauthier, J.; Hamdam, F.F.; Lafreniere, R.G.; Yang, Y.; Henrion, E.; Laurent, S.; Noreau, A.; Thibodeau, P.; Karemera, L.; et al. Systematic resequencing of X-chromosome synaptic genes in autism spectrum disorder ad schizophrenia. *Mol. Psychiatry* **2011**, *16*, 867–880. [CrossRef] [PubMed]
10. Vorstman, J.A.; Staal, W.G.; van Daalen, E.; van Engeland, H.; Hochstenbach, P.F.; Franke, L. Identification of novel autism candidate regions through the analysis of reported cytogenetic abnormalities associated with autism. *Mol. Psychiatr.* **2006**, *11*, 18–28. [CrossRef] [PubMed]
11. Betancur, C. Etiological heterogeneity in autism spectrum disorders: More than 100 genetic and genomic disorders and still counting. *Brain Res.* **2011**, *1380*, 42–77. [CrossRef] [PubMed]
12. Jamain, S.; Quach, H.; Betancur, C.; Råstam, M.; Colineaux, C.; Gillberg, I.C.; Soderstrom, H.; Giros, B.; Leboyer, M.; Gillberg, C.; et al. Paris autism research international sibpair study: Mutations of the X-linked genes encoding neuroligins NLGN3 and NLGN4 are associated with autism. *Nat. Genet.* **2003**, *34*, 27–29. [CrossRef] [PubMed]
13. Laumonnier, F.; Bonnet-Brilhault, F.; Gomot, M.; Blanc, R.; David, A.; Moizard, M.P.; Raynaud, M.; Ronce, N.; Lemonnier, E.; Calvas, P.; et al. X-linked mental retardation and autism are associated with a mutation in the *NLGN4* gene, a member of the neuroligin family. *Am. J. Hum. Genet.* **2004**, *74*, 552–557. [CrossRef] [PubMed]
14. Shibayama, A.; Cook, E.H.; Feng, J.; Glanzmann, C.; Yan, J.; Craddock, N.; Jones, I.R.; Goldman, D.; Heston, L.L.; Sommer, S.S. MECP2 structural and 3′ UTR variants in schizophrenia, autism and other psychiatric diseases; a possible association with autism. *Am. J. Med. Genet. B Neuropsychiatr. Genet.* **2004**, *128*, 50–53. [CrossRef] [PubMed]
15. Yan, J.; Oliveira, G.; Coutinho, A.; Yang, C.; Feng, J.; Katz, C.; Sram, J.; Bockholt, A.; Jones, I.R.; Craddock, N.; et al. Analysis of the neuroligin 3 and 4 genes in autism and other neuropsychiatric patients. *Mol. Psychiatr.* **2005**, *10*, 329–332. [CrossRef] [PubMed]

16. Chih, B.; Engelman, H.; Scheiffele, P. Control of excitatory and inhibitory synapse formation by neuroligins. *Science* **2005**, *307*, 1324–1328. [CrossRef] [PubMed]
17. Lisè, M.F.; El-Husseini, A. The neuroligin and neurexin families: From structure to function at the synapse. *Cell. Mol. Life Sci.* **2006**, *63*, 1833–1849. [CrossRef] [PubMed]
18. Varoqueaux, F.; Aramuni, G.; Rawson, R.L.; Mohrmann, R.; Missler, M.; Gottmann, K.; Zhang, W.; Südhof, T.C.; Brose, N. Neuroligins determine synapse maturation and function. *Neuron* **2006**, *51*, 741–754. [CrossRef] [PubMed]
19. Pettem, K.L.; Yokomaku, D.; Takahashi, H.; Ge, Y.; Craig, A.M. Interaction between autism-linked MDGAs and neuroligins suppresses inhibitory synapse development. *J. Cell Biol.* **2013**, *200*, 321–336. [CrossRef] [PubMed]
20. Südhof, T.C. Neuroligins and neurexins link synaptic function to cognitive disease. *Nature* **2008**, *455*, 903–911. [CrossRef] [PubMed]
21. Zoghbi, H.Y.; Bear, M.F. Synaptic dysfunction in neurodevelopmental disorders associated with autism and intellectual disabilities. *Cold Spring Harb. Perspect. Biol.* **2012**, *4*. [CrossRef] [PubMed]
22. Chih, B.; Afridi, S.K.; Clark, L.; Scheiffele, P. Disorder associated mutations lead to functional inactivation of neuroligins. *Hum. Mol. Genet.* **2004**, *13*, 1471–1477. [CrossRef] [PubMed]
23. Comoletti, D.; De Jaco, A.; Jennings, L.L.; Flynn, R.E.; Gaietta, G.; Tsigelny, I.; Ellisman, M.H.; Taylor, P. The Arg451Cys-neuroligin 3 mutation associated with autism reveals a defect in protein processing. *J. Neurosci.* **2004**, *24*, 4889–4893. [CrossRef] [PubMed]
24. Rothwell, P.E.; Fuccillo, M.V.; Maxeiner, S.; Hayton, S.J.; Gokce, O.; Lim, B.K.; Fowler, S.C.; Malenka, R.C.; Südhof, T.C. Autism-associated neuroligin 3 mutations commonly impair striatal circuits to boost repetitive behaviors. *Cell* **2014**, *158*, 198–212. [CrossRef] [PubMed]
25. Tabuchi, K.; Blundell, J.; Etherton, M.R.; Hammer, R.E.; Liu, X.; Powell, C.M.; Südhof, T.C. A neuroligin 3 mutation implicated in autism increases inhibitory synaptic transmission in mice. *Science* **2007**, *318*, 71–76. [CrossRef] [PubMed]
26. Jamain, S.K.; Hammerschmidt, R.K.; Granon, S.; Boretius, S.; Varoqueaux, F.; Ramanantsoa, N.; Gallego, J.; Ronnenberg, A.; Winter, D.; Frahm, J.; et al. Reduced social interaction and ultrasonic communication in a mouse model of monogenic heritable autism. *Proc. Natl. Acad. Sci. USA* **2008**, *105*, 1710–1715. [CrossRef] [PubMed]
27. Zhang, C.; Milunsky, J.M.; Newton, S.; Ko, J.; Zhao, G.; Maher, T.A.; Tager-Flusberg, H.; Bolliger, M.F.; Carter, A.S.; Boucard, A.A.; et al. A neuroligin 4 missense mutation associated with autism impairs neuroligin 4 folding and endoplasmic reticulum export. *J. Neurosci.* **2009**, *29*, 10843–10854. [CrossRef] [PubMed]
28. Hu, X.; Xiong, Z.; Zhang, L.; Liu, Y.; Lu, L.; Peng, Y.; Guo, H.; Zhao, J.; Xia, K.; Hu, Z. Variations analysis of *NLGN3* and *NLGN4X* gene in Chinese autism patients. *Mol. Biol. Rep.* **2014**, *41*, 4133–4140.
29. Talebizadeh, Z.; Lam, D.Y.; Theodoro, M.F.; Bittel, D.C.; Lushington, G.H.; Butler, M.G. Novel splice isoforms for NLGN3 and NLGN4 with possible implication in autism. *J. Med. Genet.* **2006**, *43*, e21. [CrossRef] [PubMed]
30. Lawson-Yuen, A.; Saldivar, J.S.; Sommer, S.; Picker, J. Familial deletion within *NLGN4* associated with autism and Tourette syndrome. *Eur. J. Hum. Genet.* **2008**, *16*, 614–618. [CrossRef] [PubMed]
31. Ylisaukko-oja, T.; Rehnström, K.; Auranen, M.; Vanhala, R.; Alen, R.; Kempas, E.; Ellonen, P.; Turunen, J.A.; Makkonen, I.; Riikonen, R.; et al. Analysis of four neuroligin genes as candidates for autism. *Eur. J. Hum. Genet.* **2005**, *13*, 1285–1292. [CrossRef] [PubMed]
32. Daoud, H.; Bonnet-Brilhault, F.; Vesdrine, S.; Demattei, M.V.; Vourc'h, P.; Bayou, N.; Andres, C.R.; Barthélémy, C.; Laumonnier, F.; Briault, S. Autism and nonsyndromic mental retardation associated with a de novo mutation in the *NLGN4X* gene promoter causing an increased expression level. *Soc. Biol. Psychiatry* **2009**, *66*, 906–910. [CrossRef] [PubMed]
33. Steinberg, K.M.; Ramachandran, D.; Patel, V.C.; Shetty, A.C.; Cutler, D.J.; Zwick, M.E. Identification of rare X-linked neuroligin variants by massively parallel sequencing in males with autism spectrum disorder. *Mol. Autism* **2012**, *3*, 8–20. [CrossRef] [PubMed]
34. Yanagi, K.; Kaname, T.; Wakui, K.; Hashimoto, O.; Fukushima, Y.; Naritomi, K. Identification of four novel synonymous substitutions in neuroligin 3 and neuroligin 4X in Japanese patients with autistic spectrum disorder. *Autism Res. Treat.* **2012**, *2012*, 724072–724077. [PubMed]

35. Volaki, K.; Pampanos, A.; Kitsiou-Tzeli, S.; Vrettou, C.; Oikonomakis, V.; Sofocleous, C.; Kanavakis, E. Mutation screening in the Greek population and evaluation of *NLGN3* and *NLGN4X* genes causal factors for autism. *Psychiatr. Genet.* **2013**, *23*, 198–203. [CrossRef] [PubMed]
36. Qi, H.; Xing, L.; Zhang, K.; Gao, X.; Zheng, Z.; Huang, S.; Guo, Y.; Zhang, F. Positive association of neuroigin-4 gene with non specific mental retardation in the Qinba mountains region of China. *Psychiatr. Genet.* **2009**, *19*, 1–5. [CrossRef] [PubMed]
37. Zhang, K.; Gao, X.; Qi, H.; Zheng, Z.; Zhang, F. Gender differencs in cognitive ability associated with genetic variants of *NLGN4*. *Neuropsychiatry* **2010**, *62*, 221–228.
38. Liu, Y.; Du, Y.; Liu, W.; Yang, C.; Liu, Y.; Wang, H.; Gong, X. Lack of association between *NLGN3*, *NLGN4*, *SHANK2* and *SHANK3* gene variants and autism spectrum disorder in a Chinese population. *PLoS ONE* **2013**, *8*, e56639. [CrossRef] [PubMed]
39. Blasi, F.; Bacchelli, E.; Pesaresi, G.; Carone, S.; Bailey, A.J.; Maestrini, E. International molecular genetic study of autism consortium (IMGAC): Absence of coding mutations in the X-linked genes neuroligin 3 and neuroligin 4 in individuals with autism from the IMGSAC collection. *Am. J. Med. Genet. B Neuropsychiatr. Genet.* **2006**, *141*, 220–221. [CrossRef] [PubMed]
40. Wermenter, A.K.; Kamp-Becker, I.; Strauch, K.; Schulte-Korne, G.; Remschmidt, H. No evidence for involvement of genetic variants in the X-linked neuroligin genes *NLGN3* and *NLGN4X* in probands with autism spectrum disorder on high functioning level. *Am. J. Med. Genet. B Neuropsychiatr. Genet.* **2008**, *147*, 535–537. [CrossRef] [PubMed]
41. Gauthier, J.; Bonnel, A.; St-Onge, J.; Karamera, L.; Laurent, S.; Mottron, L.; Fombonne, E.; Joober, R.; Rouleau, G.A. NLGN3/NLGN4 gene mutations are not responsible for autism in the Quebec population. *Am. J. Med. Genet. B Neuropsychiatr. Genet.* **2005**, *132*, 74–75. [CrossRef] [PubMed]
42. Altshuler, D.; Durbin, R.M.; Abecasis, G.R.; Bentley, D.R.; Chakravarti, A.; Clark, A.G.; Collins, F.S.; De La Vega, F.M.; Donnelly, P.; Egholm, M.; et al. A map of human genome variation from population-scale sequencing. *Nature* **2010**, *467*, 1061–1073.
43. Salvi, E.; Kutalik, Z.; Glorioso, N.; Benaglio, P.; Frau, F.; Kuznetsova, T.; Arima, H.; Hoggart, C.; Tichet, J.; Nikitin, Y.P.; et al. Genome wide association study using a high-density single nucleotide polymorphism array and case-control design identifies a novel essential hypertension susceptibility locus in the promoter region of endothelial NO synthase. *Hypertension* **2012**, *59*, 248–255. [CrossRef] [PubMed]
44. Howie, B.; Fuchsberger, C.; Stephens, M.; Marchini, J.; Abecasis, G.R. Fast and accurate genotype imputation in genome-wide association studies through pre-phasing. *Nat. Genet.* **2012**, *44*, 955–959. [CrossRef] [PubMed]
45. Barrett, J.C.; Fry, B.; Maller, J.; Daly, M.J. Haploview: Analysis and visualization of LD and haplotype maps. *Bioinformatics* **2005**, *21*, 263–265. [CrossRef] [PubMed]
46. Purcell, S.; Neale, B.; Todd-Brown, K.; Thomas, L.; Ferreira, M.A.R.; Bender, D.; Maller, J.; Sklar, P.; De Bakker, P.I.W.; Daly, M.J.; et al. PLINK: A toolset for whole-genome association and population-based linkage analysis. *Am. J. Hum. Genet.* **2007**, *81*, 559–575. [CrossRef] [PubMed]

Selection of Suitable Reference Genes for Analysis of Salivary Transcriptome in Non-Syndromic Autistic Male Children

Yasin Panahi [1], Fahimeh Salasar Moghaddam [2], Zahra Ghasemi [2], Mandana Hadi Jafari [1], Reza Shervin Badv [3,4], Mohamad Reza Eskandari [5,6] and Mehrdad Pedram [1,*]

1 Department of Genetics and Molecular Medicine, School of Medicine, Zanjan University of Medical Sciences (ZUMS), Zanjan 45139-56111, Iran; panahi.y@zums.ac.ir (Y.P.); mandana.hj@gmail.com (M.H.J.)
2 Department of Medical Biotechnology, School of Medicine, Zanjan University of Medical Sciences (ZUMS), Zanjan 45139-56111, Iran; f.moghaddam91@gmail.com (F.S.M.); zahra.ghasemi77@gmail.com (Z.G.)
3 Department of Pediatric Neurology, School of Medicine, Tehran University of Medical Sciences (TUMS), Tehran 14176-13151, Iran; badv@sina.tums.ac.ir
4 Children's Medical Center, Pediatric Center of Excellence, Tehran University of Medical Sciences (TUMS), Tehran 14176-13151, Iran
5 Metrowest CNS Research Center, Natick, MA 01760, USA; dr.eskandari@gmail.com
6 Department of Psychiatry, School of Medicine, Zanjan University of Medical Sciences (ZUMS), Zanjan 45139-56111, Iran
* Correspondence: mpedram@zums.ac.ir

Academic Editor: Stephen A. Bustin

Abstract: Childhood autism is a severe form of complex genetically heterogeneous and behaviorally defined set of neurodevelopmental diseases, collectively termed as autism spectrum disorders (ASD). Reverse transcriptase quantitative real-time PCR (RT-qPCR) is a highly sensitive technique for transcriptome analysis, and it has been frequently used in ASD gene expression studies. However, normalization to stably expressed reference gene(s) is necessary to validate any alteration reported at the mRNA level for target genes. The main goal of the present study was to find the most stable reference genes in the salivary transcriptome for RT-qPCR analysis in non-syndromic male childhood autism. Saliva samples were obtained from nine drug naïve non-syndromic male children with autism and also sex-, age-, and location-matched healthy controls using the RNA-stabilizer kit from DNA Genotek. A systematic two-phased measurement of whole saliva mRNA levels for eight common housekeeping genes (HKGs) was carried out by RT-qPCR, and the stability of expression for each candidate gene was analyzed using two specialized algorithms, geNorm and NormFinder, in parallel. Our analysis shows that while the frequently used HKG *ACTB* is not a suitable reference gene, the combination of *GAPDH* and *YWHAZ* could be recommended for normalization of RT-qPCR analysis of salivary transcriptome in non-syndromic autistic male children.

Keywords: childhood autism; non-syndromic; transcriptome; saliva; reverse transcriptase quantitative real-time PCR (RT-qPCR); housekeeping genes (HKGs); reference gene; stability of expression; geNorm; NormFinder

1. Introduction

Autism spectrum disorders (ASD) are serious, lifelong pervasive neurodevelopmental disorders characterized by impairments in reciprocal social interaction, including verbal and non-verbal communication, and also repetitive stereotyped behavioral patterns [1]. Childhood autism, which is the most severe form of ASD with an early life onset, is typically diagnosed between the ages of 2 and

3 years [2] and a male to female ratio of about 4:1 [3]. There is no doubt that genetic components play a key role in the pathogenesis of ASD with a high heritability index. However, the genes that have been associated with ASD only relate to only a small portion of the cases [4].

Due to the wide range of genetic heterogeneity reported in ASD, it is quite possible that different causes and various underlying molecular mechanisms may lead to a common set of changes in the brain resulting in a similar behavioral profile [5,6]. Nonetheless, analysis of the transcriptome, as an intermediate phenotype, still could provide valuable insights for investigation of such complex cases. Careful comparison of the gene expression profiles in autistic patients with normal subjects could provide important clues for the development of autism and also the molecular mechanisms and crossroads involved. Reverse transcriptase quantitative real-time PCR (RT-qPCR) is a highly sensitive technique for investigation of gene expression profile, and it is also used for confirmation of microarray results [7,8]. However, accurate analysis of gene expression with RT-qPCR requires proper normalization to stably expressed internal control or reference gene(s) [9]. An important caveat to consider for selection of reference genes, which are typically selected from housekeeping genes (HKGs), is that expression of HKGs could vary significantly under different biological conditions including disease states, age, sex, drug treatment. Furthermore, the stability of expression for a particular HKG could also be dependent upon the tissue type/source used for RNA isolation and experimental design [10,11]. Therefore, selection of appropriate reference genes for a complex neurodevelopmental disorder such as autism requires very careful design and planning.

A review of the literature shows that no single gene or particular set of genes has been used consistently as reference in gene expression studies in ASD, using either the brain or blood as the main RNA source (Table 1) [12–34]. Surprisingly, as we will further outline in the discussion, almost none of these studies have embarked on a systematic validation of the reference gene(s) prior to the start of the experiment. In the present study, we: (1) propose using saliva as a readily available biofluid and an alternative noninvasive sampling source for transcriptome analysis in childhood autism; and (2) provide a systematic evaluation for the expression levels of eight commonly used HKGs in whole saliva samples in drug naïve non-syndromic autistic male children, as a highly important yet defined subset of ASD patients, and healthy sex-, age-, and location-matched controls.

Table 1. Internal control genes used in ASD gene expression studies.

Reference	RNA/Protein Source	Reference Gene(s)	Age (Year)	N	Sex
Purcell et al. (2001) [12]	Brain tissue Cerebellum	ACTIN ^{WB} *GAPDH* ^{RP}	5–54	10	M/F [1]
Fatemi et al. (2001) [13]	Brain tissue Cerebellum	ACTIN ^{WB}	23.5 ± 4.8	5	M
Araghi-Niknam et al. (2003) [14]	Brain tissue Cerebellum, Frontal Cortex	ACTIN ^{WB}	23.8 ± 4.9	5	M
Samaco et al. (2004) [15]	Brain tissue Frontal Cortex	*TFRC* and *ACTIN* ^{IF} *GAPDH*, *H1*, and *TFRC* ^{FISH}	2–32	13	M/F [8]
Hu et al. (2006) [16]	LCL	*18s rRNA* ^{qP}	6–16	10	M
Nishimura et al. (2007 [17])	LCL	*HPRT1* ^{qP}	AGRE	42	M
Garbett et al. (2008) [18]	Brain tissue Sup. temporal gyrus	*ACTB* $^{MA-qP}$	4–30	6	M/F [2]
Gregg et al. (2008) [19]	Whole blood	*DDR1*, *RPL37A*, and *SMARC2* $^{MA-qP}$	CHARGE	35	M/F [6]
Enstrom et al. (2009) [20]	PBL, Natural killer cells	*DDR1*, *RPL37A*, and *SMARC2* $^{MA-qP}$	2.3–5.6	52	M
Hu et al. (2009a) [21]	LCL	*MDH1*, *ARF1*, *ACSL5* $^{MA-qP}$	12.3 ± 3.7	116	M
Hu et al. (2009b) [22]	LCL	*18s rRNA* $^{MA-qP}$	7.8 ± 3.4	20	NA
Sheikh et al. (2010) [23]	Brain tissue Frontal Cortex	ACTIN ^{WB}	8.9 ± 3.2	9	M/F [4]
Malik et al. (2011) [24]	PBL	ACTIN $^{WB, NB}$	8.4 ± 0.3	6	NA
Kuwano et al. (2011) [25]	Whole blood	*GAPDH* and *HDAC1* $^{MA-qP}$	26.7 ± 5.5	21	M/F [4]

Table 1. *Cont.*

Reference	RNA/Protein Source	Reference Gene(s)	Age (Year)	N	Sex
Ghahramani Seno et al. (2011) [26]	LCL	*TMEM32* qP *TUBB* WB	2–18	20	M/F [7]
Luo et al. (2012) [27]	LCL	*GAPDH* MA−qP	SSC	42	NA
Chow et al. (2012) [28]	Brain tissue Prefrontal Cortex	*ACTB*, *TBP*, and *RPL13A* MA−qP	2–56	20	M
Kong et al. (2012) [29]	Whole blood	*GAPDH* MA−qP	8.2 ± 3.0	170	M
Griesi-Oliveira et al. (2012) [30]	Dental pulp stem cells	*GAPDH*, *HPRT1*, *SDHA*, and *HMBS* qP	10	1	F
Anitha et al. (2012) [31]	Brain tissue Anterior cingulated gyrus, Motor Cortex, thalamus	*GAPDH* WB *B2M*, *HPRT1*, *RPL13A*, *GAPDH*, and *ACTB* qP	8–29	8	M/F [2]
Ginsberg et al. (2012) [32]	Brain tissue Occipital and cerebellar hemispheric cortices	*GAPDH* qP	2–60	9	M/F
Choi et al. (2014) [33]	Brain Tissue Cerebellum	*GAPDH* qP	4.5–82	29	M/F [8]
Nardone et al. (2014) [34]	Brain Tissue Anterior cingulated gyrus Prefrontal Cortex	*GAPDH*, *HPRT1*, *POLR2α*, and *SDHA* qP	18–51	13	M/F [2]

N, number of ASD samples; NA, not available; F ^{N}, number of female ASD samples; Regular capitalized abbreviations under the Reference Gene(s) columns are indicative of proteins, whereas the italicized ones denote RNA or mRNA. Sample sources: AGRE, Autism Genetic Resource Exchange; CHARGE, Childhood Autism Risks from Genetics and Environment; SSC, Simon Simplex Collection. Cell lines: LCL, Lymphoblastoid Cell Line; PBL, Peripheral Blood Lymphocyte. Techniques: FISH, Fluorescence in situ Hybridization; IF, Immunofluorescence; MA-qP, Microarray-RT-qPCR; qP, Reverse transcriptase quantitative real-time PCR; NB, Northern Blot; RP, semi-quantitative RT-PCR; WB, Western Blot.

2. Results

2.1. Selection of Candidate Reference Genes and Initial Screening

The present study was prompted by an earlier experiment, during which saliva samples were obtained from five lab members and β-actin gene (*ACTB*) mRNA levels were measured for RNA quality analysis. It should be noted that *ACTB* has been used previously by other investigators for RNA quality and transcriptome analysis by RT-qPCR in saliva [35–38], and that it also has been used as a common internal control for gene expression studies in ASD (Table 1). Interestingly, while *ACTB* *Cq* values were stable in the salivary transcriptome derived from the lab members (i.e., adults), the *Cq* values varied when examined in five samples (one autistic and four healthy control subjects) taken from children (Table S1).

There were limited amounts of saliva samples taken from our clinical groups, collected within a two-year period, available for future studies. Thus, in order to systematically evaluate potential reference genes for normalization of gene expression levels in whole saliva collected from patients with non-syndromic childhood autism and the healthy controls, a two-phase analysis was performed. In the first phase, for initial screening, mRNAs levels of eight candidate HKGs (Table 2) were examined by RT-qPCR using equal amounts of RNA templates extracted from four saliva samples: two samples taken from autistic patients, and two from healthy controls. The RT-qPCR procedures were designed and performed in line with the Minimum Information for Publication of Quantitative Real-Time PCR Experiments (MIQE) guidelines [10]. The mean *Cq* values ± SD (n = 2–4) for each candidate gene are presented on Table 3 (see Table S2 for detailed individual average *Cq* values of replicate qPCR reactions ± SD).

Table 2. List of the housekeeping genes evaluated as candidate reference genes during the first phase.

Gene Name	Function	Gene Symbol	mRNA Accession No.	Amplicon [2] Length (bp)
18S ribosomal RNA	Ribosomal RNA Subunit	*18s rRNA*	M10098 [1]	99 *
β-actin	Cytoskeletal structural protein	*ACTB*	NM_001101	94
Glyceraldehyde-3-phosphate dehydrogenase	Glycolytic enzyme	*GAPDH*	NM_002046	142 *
Ribosomal protein L13a	Structural component of large subunit of Ribosome	*RPL13A*	NM_012423	223 *
Succinate dehydrogenase complex subunit A, flavoprotein	Electron transporter in the Krebs cycle	*SDHA*	NM_004168	154 *
Transferrin receptor	Cellular iron uptake	*TFRC*	NM_003234	134
Ubiquitin C	Protein degradation	*UBC*	NM_021009	192 *
Tyrosine 3 monooxygenase activation protein, zeta polypeptide	Signal transduction	*YWHAZ*	NM_003406	150 *

[1] Non-coding RNA; [2] The numbers with asterisks given for *18s rRNA, GAPDH, RPL13A, SDHA, UBC*, and *YWHAZ* do not reflect exact Amplicon sizes. They are indicative of the "context sequence length" [39] information provided by PrimerDesign Ltd. (Southampton, UK).

To analyze the stability of expression for the candidate HKGs, the *Cq* values of each data set were exported to a Microsoft Office Excel sheet and then imported into the geNorm (qbasePLUS software v2.2, Biogazelle, Ghent, Belgium) and also NormFinder (Molecular Diagnostic Labrotory, Department of Clinical Biochemistry Molecular Medicine, Aarhus University Hospital, Skejby, Aarhus, Denmark) software. GeNorm, which is a strong algorithm for small sample sizes and also the most widely used algorithm to determine the most stable reference gene, calculates an expression normalization factor for each sample set by geometric averaging of a number of user-defined candidate reference genes. For each candidate gene, the geNorm algorithm determines an internal control stability measure (M), which is defined as the average pairwise variation of a particular gene compared with all other test genes. The lowest M value indicates the most stable gene [40]. By contrast, NormFinder that is also a visual basic application for Microsoft Excel focuses on the expression variation of each gene with the least intra- and inter-group values in a model-based approach. In addition to giving a direct measure for the estimated expression variation, the NormFinder algorithm evaluates the systematic error introduced when using the HKG of interest as internal control [41].

Table 3. The mean *Cq* values (±SD, $n = 2–4$) of samples studied in phase I.

Gene Symbol	Control			Autism			Overall SD
	Mean	SD	N	Mean	SD	N	
18s rRNA	16.06	1.78	2	14.58	0.66	2	1.04
ACTB	25.87	0.38	2	29.18	1.77	2	2.34
GAPDH	26.27	0.29	2	27.01	0.44	2	0.52
RPL13A	31.09	0.89	2	32.72	NA	1	1.15
SDHA	33.73	NA	1	28.93	0.32	2	3.40
TFRC	31.14	1.73	2	33.22	1.58	2	1.47
UBC	30.22	0.62	2	32.23	0.59	2	1.42
YWHAZ	27.54	0.61	2	28.07	1.11	2	0.37

N, number of samples (from independent individuals) with valid signals; NA, not applicable; SD, standard deviation.

According to the geNorm algorithm, the M values below the cut-off value of 1.5 (the recommended threshold) are acceptable in the selection of internal controls for normalization in RT-qPCR [40]. As it can be seen from Figure 1A, the data output from geNorm for the first phase of evaluation indicated that glyceraldehyde-3-phosphate dehydrogenase gene (*GAPDH*) was the best HKG in our panel of candidate reference genes followed by succinate dehydrogenase complex subunit A, flavoprotein

(*SDHA*), tyrosine 3 monooxygenase activation protein, zeta polypeptide (*YWHAZ*), and ubiquitin C (*UBC*). *ACTB*, a traditionally common reference gene in normalization of RT-qPCR data in ASD studies (Table 1) and salivary transcriptome analysis [35,37,38], was ranked among the least stable genes. The number of reference genes needed for optimal normalization was determined by geNorm based on the average pairwise variation ($Vn/n + 1$) below the recommended cut-off point value of 0.15. At this phase, the geNorm output indicated that the combination of the best three reference genes would be sufficient for normalization of RT-qPCR data (Figure S1).

The ranking of the best candidate genes by NormFinder algorithm in phase I was somewhat similar to the geNorm output. *GAPDH*, *YWHAZ*, and *UBC* were ranked as the best candidates, respectively (Figure 1B). However, *SDHA* was demoted to the 6th rank, while *ACTB* was promoted two steps from low to the intermediate ranking. It should be noted that, in phase I, the clinical identifier value was not included in the NormFinder analysis due to the small number of samples, and thus analysis was performed as a single clinical group. In both algorithms, two of the candidate genes, encoding for ribosomal protein L13a (RPL13A) and transferrin receptor (TFRC), were ranked as the least stable HKGs based on their high variation of relative expression values.

2.2. *Expression Profiling and Validation of Candidate Reference Genes*

Three of the candidate HKGs that had the best scores in phase I based on both geNorm and NormFinder algorithms (*GAPDH*, *YWHAZ*, and *UBC*) were selected for the second phase of analysis. Despite its low-intermediate ranking in phase I, *ACTB* was also taken for further analysis because of its common usage as an internal control HKG in saliva [35,38,42] and ASD studies (Table 1). In this phase, the expression levels of the final four candidate HKGs were examined in saliva samples from a panel of nine autistic and healthy boys (average age: 47.6 ± 21.9 vs. 41.2 ± 26.7 months, respectively). The amplification efficiency for each gene and linear regression coefficient (R2) values were calculated by performing standard curves (Table 4). The scatter plot representations of the *Cq* values recorded for the final four candidate HKGs in the autistic and healthy clinical groups are shown in Figure 2 (Table S3 for detailed average *Cq* values for replicate qPCR reactions $\pm$SD).

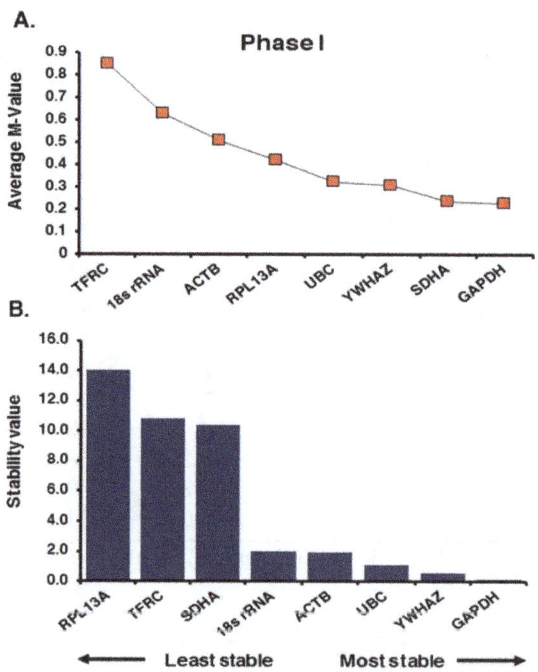

Figure 1. Expression stability analysis of the candidate reference genes in phase I. The stability of expression for 8 housekeeping genes tested in saliva is ranked (left to right) based on the least stable to the most stable gene by: (**A**) geNorm; and (**B**) NormFinder algorithms.

Table 4. Amplification efficiency data for candidate reference genes tested in phase II.

Gene Symbol	Slope	R^2	Efficiency (%)
ACTB	−3.400	0.981	96.8
GAPDH	−3.303	0.989	100.9
UBC	−3.747	0.974	84.8
YWHAZ	−3.398	0.984	97.2

Standard curves were used to calculate the reaction efficiency for each gene, using a five-point serial dilution made from pooled stock cDNAs. The amplification efficiency percentage for each gene was calculated using the equation $E = 10^{(-1/\text{Slope})} - 1$ multiplied by 100, where E stands for the efficiency and slope is the gradient of the best fit line. R^2: linear regression coefficient.

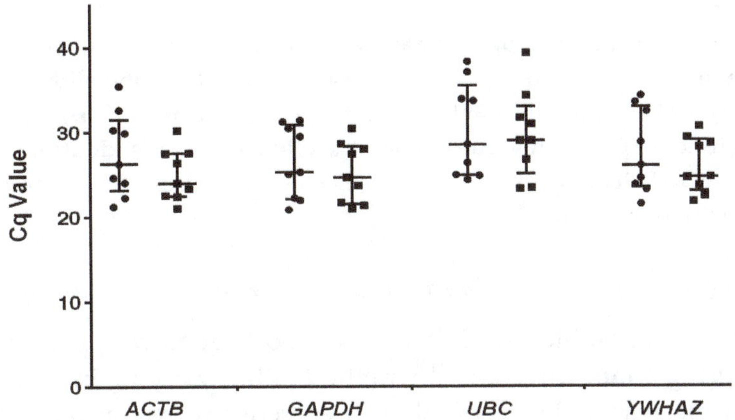

Figure 2. Scatter plot representations of the *Cq* values measured for the final four candidate genes. Filled squares and circles represent the control and autistic groups, respectively. The vertical bars indicate the median and interquartile range. The bottom and top of each bar represent the 25th and 75th percentiles, respectively, and the line bisecting each bar shows the median *Cq* value.

Noticeably, geNorm once again ranked *GAPDH* as the most stable HKG, and it ranked *ACTB* as the least stable gene (*M* values: 1.29 vs. 1.84, respectively). However, after the pairwise analysis, the combination of *GAPDH* and *YWHAZ* was selected as the best pair with an *M*-value of 1.02, followed by *UBC* and *ACTB* with *M*-values of 1.45 vs. 1.67, respectively (Figure 3A). An optimal number for reference genes was not determined by geNorm algorithm because the *V*-value was higher than recommended threshold (0.15). Similar to the geNorm analysis, NormFinder evaluated *GAPDH* as the most stable HKG, followed by *YWHAZ*, *UBC*, and *ACTB* (Stability values: 0.35, 0.60, 1.18, and 1.40, respectively). However, when the clinical subgroups were included in the analysis, the *GAPDH* and *YWHAZ* set was recommended as the best combination of two genes by NormFinder, followed by *UBC* (ranked third) and *ACTB*, ranked as the least stable gene once again (Figure 3B).

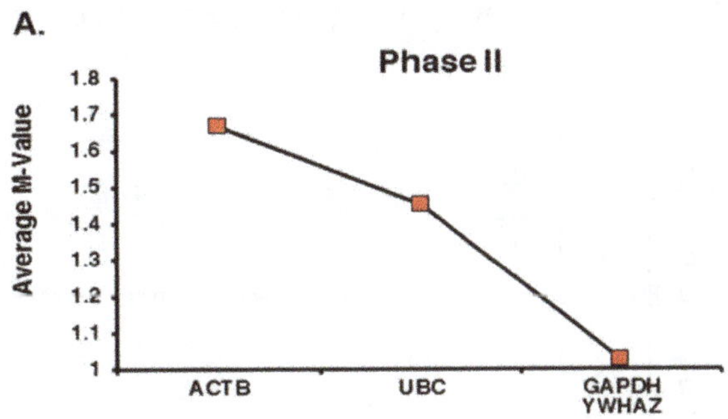

Figure 3. *Cont.*

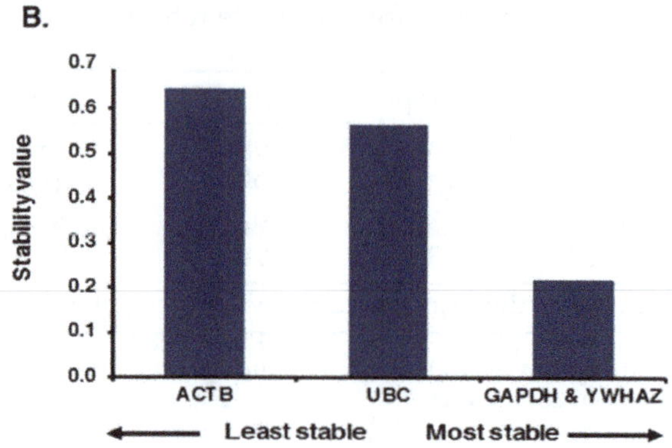

Figure 3. Expression stability analysis for the final four candidate reference genes in phase II. Expression of each candidate gene was examined in a total of 18 saliva samples (nine with childhood Autism and nine healthy controls) ranked compared with the rest by (**A**) geNorm and (**B**) NormFinder algorithms based on their stability of expression values; when the clinical group's identifier was included in the NormFinder analysis, *GAPDH* and *YWHAZ* were selected as the best genes combined, in agreement with the geNorm pair-wise ranking.

2.3. Relative Expression Levels of Candidate Reference Genes in Autistic vs. Healthy Subjects

Using *GAPDH*, the most stable HKG ranked by both geNorm and NormFinder algorithms, as reference, and employing an improved $2^{-\Delta Ct}$ method [43] (by taking into account the amplification efficiencies), the relative expression levels of other three genes were compared in the autistic children vs. the control group (Figure 4A). The results demonstrate that although *ACTB* shows a higher degree of variation compared with *UBC* and *YWHAZ* (p-values: 0.26, 0.45 and 0.82, respectively), as expected, there are no significant differences in the expression levels of any of these HKGs between the two clinical groups. By contrast, when *ACTB*, which was ranked as the least stable, was used as reference, the expression levels of *GAPDH*, *UBC*, and *YWHAZ* did not follow a normal distribution pattern, and in particular, the *UBC* expression levels and median values were significantly different ($p = 0.03$) between the autistic and control groups (Figure 4B).

The above observations are in support of the ranking validity of the candidate reference genes by geNorm and NormFinder algorithms, and they clearly demonstrate how selection of an inappropriate HKG as reference can bias interpretation of RT-qPCR data. Interestingly, examination of the *Cq* values obtained for the candidate HKGs using a third statistical algorithm applet, called BestKeeper [44], produced a similar ranking for the candidate reference genes, in particular for Phase II (Table S4). It should be noted that the BestKeeper algorithm works by calculating the SD for each gene of interest and Pearson's coefficient of correlation for each pair of the candidate genes. Thus, it would be best suited for our Phase II analysis, as BestKeeper cannot provide significant p-values for small sample sets (Table S4A,B). Nonetheless, based on the intra-variations for each candidate gene, the Phase I ranking by BestKeeper is not that far off from those produced by geNorm and NormFinder.

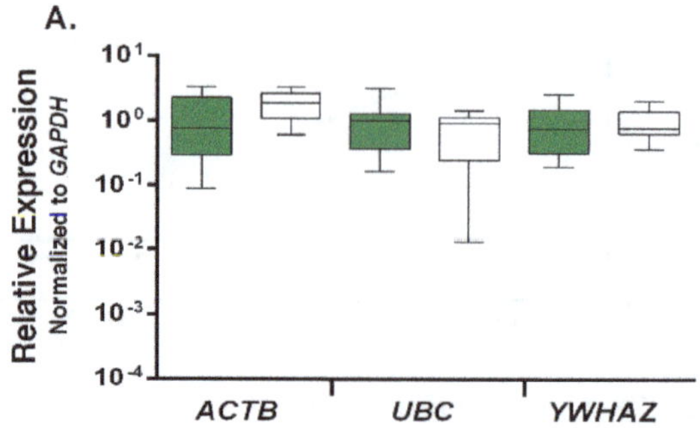

Figure 4. *Cont.*

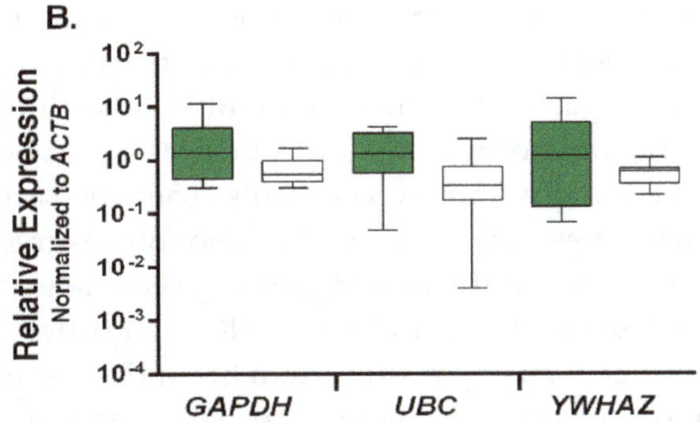

Figure 4. Comparison of the relative expression levels of candidate reference genes between the two groups. Colored and white boxes represent the autistic and control groups, respectively. The relative expression level for each gene was calculated by using either: (**A**) the *GAPDH* (glyceraldehyde-3-phosphate dehydrogenase); or (**B**) ACTB (β-actin) gene as the reference. Statistical analysis comparing the expression levels are done with Mann-Whitney *U* test (two-tailed), and the data are presented as the mean and interquartile range, with vertical bars representing the total range (**B**). *p*-values: (**A**) *ACTB* ($p = 0.26$), *UBC* ($p = 0.45$), *YWHAZ* ($p = 0.82$); and (**B**) *GAPDH* ($p = 0.26$), *UBC* ($p = 0.03$), *YWHAZ* ($p = 0.26$).

3. Discussion

To our knowledge, this is the first systematic evaluation of HKGs as reference for RT-qPCR analysis of salivary transcriptome in patients with autism reported so far. ASD encompass a heterogeneous set of complex and pervasive behaviorally-defined neurodevelopmental disorders, which brings up the possibility of different causes leading to similar brain deficits and behavioral patterns. In fact, there is a strong consensus on the involvement of various genetic and environmental components in the etiology of ASD [1,6]. Nonetheless, because of the high heritability reported in ASD, it should be quite plausible to search for a "common signature" at the level of gene expression profile. Thus, analysis of the transcriptome, as an intermediate phenotype for investigation, could provide insights into the molecular mechanism/s involved [5]. However, despite enormous number of research and concerted efforts at the international level during the past decade, as evident on Table 1, there is still an incoherent picture of a common gene expression profile signature/s for ASD, and the underlying molecular mechanisms are poorly understood.

A recent highly in depth meta-analysis of ASD gene expression data, taken from 12 independent studies in blood and brain tissues, by Ch'ng et al. conclude that constructing a somewhat consistent transcriptome signature might be possible in the studies using a small number of brain samples. By contrast, the outcomes of the studies using blood cells are highly heterogeneous and rather inconsistent [5]. As pointed out by the investigators, part of the inconsistency in these studies could be due to the variation in their inclusion and exclusion criteria, which include variations in the scope of the ASD patients studied, differences in gender and age groups, and differences in sampling and experimental procedures. A review of the information presented on Table 1 supports the notion of such variations in different ASD studies. Another important factor to note, however, is the inconsistency in the use of reference genes in different studies, even in cases where the type of tissue/cells used for transcriptome analysis were the same or very similar.

Selection of appropriate reference gene(s) plays an essential part in proper normalization of RT-qPCR assays and comparison of gene expression profiles between different samples and clinical groups. It is also essential that validity and stability of expression for the candidate or intended internal control HKG/s is experimentally examined for particular source/s of RNA, disease status, and experimental design prior to the start of each experiment [10,40,41]. Surprisingly, a careful examination of the ASD gene expression studies listed on Table 1, however, reveals that the HKGs used as internal controls were not systematically evaluated for their stability of expression for the particular tissue/cell type, and biological and experimental conditions. Perhaps, the only one exception on that list is the case report study by Griesi-Oliveira et al. using dental pulp stem cells for their main RNA source. Aside from the fact that the particular female patient in this study suffered from a craniofacial dysmorphism in addition to ASD phenotype, it should be noted that because of the very small and restricted sample size (only one patient and two controls from the same family), validation of the reference genes in this study has a very low power. It is also interesting to note that even with such a small and restricted sample size, when the investigators used the geNorm applet for selection of the reference genes, they ended up with a set of four HKGs in order to generate a normalization factor [30]. The study by Nardone et al., using postmortem brain tissues, used a set of four HKGs based on a geNorm evaluation of candidate reference genes by a separate group of investigators on suicide subjects [34,45]. Finally, the study by Garbett et al., using a small set (six; four male and two female subjects) of postmortem brain tissue samples, selected only one HKG, *ACTB*, for validation of their microarray results based on the previous works by the same lab [18] on small numbers of postmortem brain samples from schizophrenic and epileptic patients [46,47].

An ideal reference gene should maintain a stable mRNA level in all sample groups under different experimental conditions. It might not be possible to find a "universal" reference gene or set of genes in different tissues for various biological and experimental conditions. However, it is quite feasible to find the most appropriate HKGs for normalization of gene expression profiling if one limits the type and number of tissues tested under a well-defined experimental setting [40,41]. As mentioned several times already, ASD encompass a heterogeneous and complex set of neurodevelopmental disorders. In the present study, in an effort to limit the number of confounders and heterogeneity, we confined the scope of the ASD subjects to drug naïve non-syndromic autistic male children and age-, and sex-matched healthy children picked from the same neighborhoods as the patients (average ages: 47.6 ± 21.9 vs. 41.2 ± 26.7 months, respectively). Considering the severity of childhood autism and also the high ratio of male children affected, the autistic patients used in this study represent a highly important yet defined subset of ASD patients. We also used saliva as an alternative "noninvasive" sampling source for RNA instead of the blood. As the most available and portable biofluid, saliva contains a wealth of information regarding the physiological states of the body and is a good indicator of the plasma levels of hormones, drugs, immune system, and neurological conditions [48,49]. In recent years, saliva has been used a valid source of biomarkers and transcriptome analysis for a number of systemic human diseases including sleep disorder [38] and breast cancer [50].

Saliva has also been used as a DNA source for epigenetic analysis in bipolar disorder and schizophrenia [51], for genetic analysis and investigation of the impact of nutritional intake and environmental toxins in ASD [52]. Most recently, Frank Middleton and colleagues used the salivary microRNA profiles for identification of children with ASD [53]. Here, we present the first systematic evaluation of HKGs in the salivary transcriptome to be used for normalization of RT-qPCR data in ASD research. Based on our analysis of gene expression stability using geNorm and NormFinder algorithms in parallel, *GAPDH* was determined as the most stable HKG to be used as an internal control for salivary transcriptome analysis and/or validation of microarray results by RT-qPCR in male childhood autism. By contrast, *ACTB* was evaluated as unsuitable to be used as a reference gene. It should be noted, however, that *GAPDH* does not appear to be stable enough to be used as a single reference gene for normalization of RT-qPCR data in this setting. Both geNorm and Normfinder analyses recommend combination of *GAPDH* and *YWHAZ* as the best option. However, the V value given by the geNorm algorithm in our second phase of study is above the ideal 0.15. A simple interpretation of the results from geNorm's point of view would entails using all four candidate genes as internal controls. However, considering the high variation of *ACTB* expression, and significantly low levels of *UBC* expression between the autistic and control samples (Figure S1 and Figure 4), it would not be advisable to add either of them to the *GAPDH* and *YWHAZ* combination.

The poor evaluation of *ACTB* as a reference gene in saliva samples, in a sharp contrast to *GAPDH*, initially came to us as a surprise. However, a careful review of the literature revealed this to be a well-supported outcome by various lines of evidence. While *ACTB* was traditionally used as a reference gene in saliva [38], even pioneer labs specializing in saliva work have recently switched to using *GAPDH* instead [50,54]. In contrast to this notion, in a recent report by Pandit and colleagues on a high-yield RNA-extraction protocol for saliva, the investigators used *ACTB* in combination with the saliva-specific histatin 3 gene (*HTN3*) for validation of the quality and quantity of their isolated RNA samples. They also used *ACTB* alone as their reference HKG for analysis of 2 cell lines and a cohort of cancer patients and controls [35]. However, a review of the *Cq* values listed for *ACTB* in their Table 1, shows a very high variation in the *Cq* values (18 Cq differences for all samples, and 13 Cq differences within the clinical samples only) for *ACTB*, making it unsuitable to be used as a reference gene. Furthermore, it should be kept in mind that the saliva samples taken in our study were obtained from young children (average age for both groups: 44.4 ± 23.9 months) that are going through a highly significant growth period. A key developmental and cytoskeletal protein coding gene like *ACTB* may not be suited as a reference gene for this age period. In support of this line of reasoning, a recent investigation of HKGs in leukocyte subpopulations from children by Yu and colleagues found that *GAPDH* had the most stable expression in children (five samples: 1, 3, 6, 9, and 12 years old). By contrast, the ACTB protein levels were inconsistent. The investigators reported that *ACTB* mRNA levels were not significantly different across their samples and propose a difference at the level of post-translational regulation. However, there is no mention of the *ACTB Cq* values/variation provided in the article [55].

In contrast to our findings indicating *ACTB* as an unsuitable internal control for RT-qPCR analysis in childhood autism, the study by Garbett and colleagues gives *ACTB* a high praise as a reference gene for transcriptome analysis in postmortem brain tissue samples from ASD patients [18]. Aside from the fact that we have used a different source for RNA, a close inspection of the report by Garbett et al. reveals some interesting points. The authors provide several reasons for why they chose *ACTB* as the reference gene for RT-qPCR verification of their microarray results, including that it had been previously established as a stable HKG in the literature (referring to a study by Chen et al. on the primary human skin fibroblasts [56]); and in two previous studies on human postmortem brain tissues by the same lab, one in subjects with schizophrenia [46] and one in epilepsy [47]. Aside from the fact that we have used a different source of RNA in the present study compared with the studies noted above, the reasoning outlined by Garbett et al. for selection of their internal control HKG is not convincing. The fact that *ACTB* has been previously used as an endogenous reference gene in primary human skin fibroblasts (a different tissue type), and that it has been used in the brain tissue samples in schizophrenia and epilepsy (different disease types), are not valid justifications for using *ACTB* as a reference gene in brain tissue samples for ASD studies. Two recent systematic evaluations of HKGs, with both studies including *ACTB* and *GAPDH*, for RT-qPCR in postmortem human brain tissues came up with entirely different sets of reference genes. While Silberberg and colleagues found *TFRC* and *RPLP0* as the most stable reference genes in schizophrenia and bipolar disorders [57], Penna and colleagues found CYC1 and EIF4A2 as the best reference genes in Alzheimer's disease [58]. Finally, it is interesting to note that a review of the reference genes used in ASD studies shows a noticeable shift from *ACTB* to *GAPDH* during the past 15 years (Table 1).

4. Materials and Methods

4.1. Subjects and Sampling Procedure

Participants recruited to this study included nine drug naïve non-syndromic male children diagnosed with autism (47.6 ± 21.9 months) and nine age-, gender-, and location-matched typically developing healthy controls (41.2 ± 26.7 months). Children with autism were diagnosed according to the Diagnostic and Statistical Manual of Mental Disorders fourth edition, Text Revised (DSM-IV-TR) criteria by two qualified clinicians, a child neurologist and a child and adolescent psychiatrist. The diagnosis of autism was confirmed by Autism Diagnostic Interview-Revised (ADI-R), which is a standardized semi-structured diagnostic algorithm for autism based on the definitions set by DSM-IV and International Statistical Classification of Diseases and Related Health Problems 10th Revision (ICD-10) [59,60]. Exclusion criteria for patients included any other medical disorder and/or diagnosis including significant neurological problems such as depression, epileptic seizures, and genetic syndromes such as tuberous sclerosis, Angelman, and Fragile-X. Sex-matched healthy control children were picked from the same neighborhood locations as the autistic subjects. All healthy controls were screened by the Strengths and Difficulties Questionnaire (SDQ) [61]. The study was conducted in accordance with the Declaration of Helsinki, and it had the approval of the ZUMS Ethics Committee (ZUMS.REC.1392 97; 13 October 2013). All subjects had signed informed consent, provided by their parents, for inclusion before participating in the study.

Two mL of whole saliva was collected from each child who was able to provide sputum into the Oragene RNA collection kit RE-100 (DNA Genotek Inc., Ottawa, ON, Canada). Saliva sampling was supervised and collected by trained personnel according to the instructions provided in the collection kit. In the case of children unable to spit voluntarily, sampling was done by a 2-mL syringe from under the tongues and gingival crevices, mainly with the help of the participating parents and/or caregivers. Briefly, children were recommended to refrain from eating and drinking for 1 h prior to sampling and also wash their mouths with drinking water at least 15 min before providing a sample. Once collected, the tube containing the sample was covered by placing the cap securely and inverting the container vigorously by hand vortexing for approximately 10 s, in order to allow the saliva to mix well with the Oragene RNA solution. Samples were then stored at −20 °C and subsequently transferred to the central laboratory at the Zanjan University of Medical Science (ZUMS) for further processing.

4.2. Total RNA Preparation and cDNA Synthesis

Total RNA was extracted from whole saliva samples using a combination of two protocols: Oragene RNA collection kit RE-100 (DNA Genotek Inc., Ottawa, ON, Canada) and RNX-Plus solution (SinaClone BioScience, Tehran, Iran) with some modifications to the manufacturers' instructions. Briefly, the saliva collected in the Oragene RNA collection kit was incubated in a water bath at 50 °C for 1 h. A 500-µL aliquot was then transferred into a 1.5-mL microcentrifuge tube and incubated in a water bath at 90 °C for 15 min. Twenty µL of the Neutralizer solution was added to the sample and vortexed for a few seconds, incubated on ice for 10 min, and centrifuged at 15,000× *g* for 3 min. The clear supernatant was then transferred into a new microcentrifuge tube, 2 volumes of cold 95% ethanol was added to the sample and mixed vigorously by hand. The sample was incubated at −20 °C for 30 min followed by centrifugation at 15,000× *g* for 3 min. The supernatant was discarded and the pellet was dissolved in 750 µL of RNX-Plus solution (SinaClone BioScience, Tehran, Iran) by vortexing, followed by incubation at room temperature for 5 min. A 200-µL volume of Chloroform was added to the solution and centrifuged for 15 min at 12,000× *g*. The upper phase was then transferred to a new microcentrifuge tube and an equal volume of isopropanol was added into the tube. The mixture was centrifuged for 15 min at 12,000× *g* and the resulting pellet was washed in 70% ethanol, air dried for 10 min, and dissolved in DEPC-treated ddH_2O. The quality and quantity of extracted RNA samples were analyzed by fiber optic spectrophotometry using a NanoDrop 2000c (Thermo Scientific, Waltham, MA, USA). While RNA quantity was measured using the A_{260} absorbance in DEPC-treated ddH_2O, the RNA purity was monitored by A_{260}/A_{280} absorbance ratios of sample dilutions in Tris pH 7.4. RNA samples with A_{260}/A_{280} ratios of 1.8–2.1 were used for cDNA in the study. The average concentration of the RNA samples used in the study was 220 ± 132 ng/µL. Potential residual genomic DNA was eliminated with RNase-free DNase I digestion (Thermo Scientific). Complementary DNA (cDNA) was synthesized from 500-ng total DNase I treated RNA per reaction using the PrimScriptTM Reagent Kit (Takara Inc., Shiga, Japan) following the manufacturer's instructions. Briefly, in a 10-µL reaction with 1× reaction buffer including $MgCl_2$ inside an RNase-free tube, the appropriate volume of RNA sample was first treated with 0.5 µL of DNase I (1 U/µL) by gently mixing the reaction and incubating it at 37 °C for 30 min, followed by inactivation of DNase I with addition of 1 µL of 50 mM

EDTA and incubation at 65 °C for 10 min. This DNase I treated RNA sample (11 μL) was then used for cDNA synthesis in a 20-μL reaction containing 4 μL of 5× PrimeScript™ buffer, 1 μL of PrimeScript™ RT Enzyme mix I, 1 μL of 50 μM Oligo dT primer, 1 μL of 100 μM Random 6 mers, and 2 μL of RNase-free ddH_2O. The RT reaction was mixed well and incubated at 37 °C for 15 min, followed by inactivation of the RT enzyme at 85 °C for 5 s. The cDNA samples were kept at −20 °C for further use.

4.3. Candidate Reference Gene Selection

A total of 8 commonly used housekeeping genes with a wide range of biological functions were used in this study (see Table 2 for details). Six of the eight genes were picked from the internal control panel of genes offered by PrimerDesign Ltd. (Southampton, UK) with the following "anchor nucleotide" and "context sequence length" [39] information for the primer sets: *18s rRNA* (235, 99 bp), *GAPDH* (1087, 142 bp), *RPL13A* (727, 223 bp), *SDHA* (1032, 154 bp), *UBC* (452, 192 bp), and *YWHAZ* (2585, 150 bp). The remaining two genes included *ACTB*, and *TFRC* with the following forward and reverse primer sequences: ACTB_F, 5′-CGAGCACAGAGCCTCGCCTTTGCC-3′, ACTB_R, 5′-TGTCGACGACGAGCGCGGCGATAT-3′; and TFRC_F, 5′-ACCGGCACCATCAAGCT-3′, TFRC_R, 5′-TGATCACGCCAGACTTTGC-3′.

4.4. Quantitative Real-Time PCR

The mRNA levels of the potential reference genes were quantified using Micro Amp Optical 8-Cap Strips (Life Technology, Pittsburgh, PA, USA) with an ABI 7300 Real-Time PCR System (Applied Biosystems, Foster City, CA, USA). Each 20-μL reaction contained 10 μL of RealQ Plus 2× PCR Master Mix Green, High ROX TM (Ampliqon Inc., Odense, Denmark), 25 ng of cDNA, and 300 nM of forward and reverse primers. PCR amplifications were performed in triplicates with an initial enzyme activation step at 95 °C for 10 min, followed by 40 cycles of 95 °C for 15 s (template denaturation), and 60 °C for 1 min (annealing and data collection). No-template controls (NTC) were included in each run. The inter-run technical variation was calculated as SD for three HKGs *Cq* values for a fixed repeated cDNA sample dilutions: *ACTB*, ±0.13; *GAPDH*, ±0.15; *YWHAZ*, ±0.14.

4.5. Gene Expression Stability Analysis

Analysis of expression stability for the candidate reference genes was initially carried out by using two commonly used statistical algorithms, geNorm (qbasePLUS software v2.2, Biogazelle) [40] and NormFinder (an Excel Add-in, provided by Molecular Diagnostic Labrotory, Dept. of Molecular Medicine, Aarhus University Hospital, Skejby Sygehus, Denmark) [41], both of which are Visual Basic Applications for Microsoft Excel, in parallel. The raw *Cq* values in an Excel spread sheet were also fed into the BestKeeper applet (verison 1, http://www.gene-quantification.com/bestkeeper.html) [44] for additional analysis.

5. Conclusions

To our knowledge, the present study is the first systematic evaluation of candidate HKGs as internal controls for normalization of gene expression profiles in autistic children. Based on the analysis of eight commonly used HKGs by geNorm and NormFinder algorithms in parallel, a combination of the top two most stable candidate reference genes, *GAPDH* and *YWHAZ*, could be recommended for normalization of RT-qPCR analysis of salivary transcriptome in drug naïve non-syndromic autistic male children. We hope that the information presented here paves the way for: (1) systematic evaluation of reference genes in ASD studies under different experimental settings; and (2) using saliva as an alternative source of RNA, instead of the brain and blood, for transcriptome analysis in ASD research. As a readily-available and resourceful biofluid, saliva could open a noninvasive window to the complex molecular world of autism not only for diagnosis but also for surveillance of disease status and treatment.

Acknowledgments: This work was supported in part by Zanjan University of Medical Sciences (ZUMS) grant number A-12-534-1/-6-8. We would like to thank Khadijeh Babaei from the High Institute for Research and Education in Transfusion Medicine, Blood Transfusion Center, Tehran, for the preliminary set up of total RNA extractions from saliva. We are also thankful to Hamid Pezeshk (Department of Mathematics, Statistics, and Computer Science, University of Tehran) and Mohammad H. Rahbar (Department of Internal Medicine, UT Health Science Center at Houston) for their helpful comments and suggestions.

Author Contributions: Mehrdad Pedram and Yasin Panahi designed the study, and Mehrdad Pedram supervised the project. Yasin Panahi carried out the RT-qPCR experiments and did the geNorm and NormFinder analysis. Reza Shervin Badv and Mohammad Reza Eskandari were involved in the discussion and design of the scope of ASD patients for the study, and they also took care of the clinical examination of the patients, diagnosis, and clinical follow-ups. Fahimeh Salasar Moghaddam, Zahra Ghasemi, and Mandana Hadi Jafari did the saliva sample collection and processing. Yasin Panahi and Mehrdad Pedram analyzed the data. Yasin Panahi, Fahimeh Salasar Moghaddam, and Mandana Hadi Jafari wrote the initial draft of the manuscript, and Zahra Ghasemi provided the first draft of Table 1. Mehrdad Pedram wrote and revised the full manuscript for submission. All authors read and approved the final manuscript.

Abbreviations

ACTB, β-actin protein; *ACTB*, β-actin gene; ASD, Autism spectrum disorders; Cq, Quantification Cycle; *GAPDH*, Glyceraldehyde-3-phosphate dehydrogenase gene; HKG, House Keeping Gene; MIQE, Minimum Information for Publication of Quantitative Real-Time PCR Experiments; RT-qPCR, Reverse Transcriptase Quantitative real-time PCR; *UBC*, Ubiquitin C gene; *YWHAZ*, Tyrosine 3 monooxygenase activation, zeta polypeptide gene.

References

1. Lai, M.C.; Lombardo, M.V.; Baron-Cohen, S. Autism. *Lancet* **2014**, *383*, 896–910. [CrossRef]
2. Lord, C.; Risi, S.; DiLavore, P.S.; Shulman, C.; Thurm, A.; Pickles, A. Autism from 2 to 9 years of age. *Arch. Gen. Psychiatry* **2006**, *63*, 694–701. [CrossRef] [PubMed]
3. Werling, D.M.; Geschwind, D.H. Sex differences in autism spectrum disorders. *Curr. Opin. Neurol.* **2013**, *26*, 146–161. [CrossRef] [PubMed]
4. Betancur, C.; Coleman, M. Etiological Heterogeneity in Autism Spectrum Disorders: Role of Rare Variants. In *The Neuroscience of Autism Spectrum Disorders*; Joseph, D., Buxbaum, P.R.H., Eds.; Academic Press: Waltham, MA, USA, 2013; pp. 113–144.
5. Ch'ng, C.; Kwok, W.; Rogic, S.; Pavlidis, P. Meta-analysis of gene expression in autism spectrum disorder. *Autism Res.* **2015**, *8*, 593–608. [CrossRef] [PubMed]
6. Berg, J.M.; Geschwind, D.H. Autism genetics: Searching for specificity and convergence. *Genome Biol.* **2012**, *13*, 247–263. [CrossRef] [PubMed]
7. Morey, J.S.; Ryan, J.C.; van Dolah, F.M. Microarray validation: Factors influencing correlation between oligonucleotide microarrays and real-time PCR. *Biol. Proced. Online* **2006**, *8*, 175–193. [CrossRef] [PubMed]
8. Nolan, T.; Hands, R.E.; Bustin, S.A. Quantification of mrna using real-time RT-PCR. *Nat. Protoc.* **2006**, *1*, 1559–1582. [CrossRef] [PubMed]
9. Huggett, J.; Dheda, K.; Bustin, S.; Zumla, A. Real-time RT-PCR normalisation; strategies and considerations. *Genes Immun.* **2005**, *6*, 279–284. [CrossRef] [PubMed]
10. Bustin, S.A.; Benes, V.; Garson, J.A.; Hellemans, J.; Huggett, J.; Kubista, M.; Mueller, R.; Nolan, T.; Pfaffl, M.W.; Shipley, G.L.; et al. The MIQE guidelines: Minimum information for publication of quantitative real-time PCR experiments. *Clin. Chem.* **2009**, *55*, 611–622. [CrossRef] [PubMed]
11. Li, R.; Shen, Y. An old method facing a new challenge: Re-visiting housekeeping proteins as internal reference control for neuroscience research. *Life Sci.* **2013**, *92*, 747–751. [CrossRef] [PubMed]
12. Purcell, A.E.; Jeon, O.H.; Zimmerman, A.W.; Blue, M.E.; Pevsner, J. Postmortem brain abnormalities of the glutamate neurotransmitter system in autism. *Neurology* **2001**, *57*, 1618–1628. [CrossRef] [PubMed]
13. Fatemi, S.H.; Stary, J.M.; Halt, A.R.; Realmuto, G.R. Dysregulation of reelin and Bcl-2 proteins in autistic cerebellum. *J. Autism Dev. Disord.* **2001**, *31*, 529–535. [CrossRef] [PubMed]
14. Araghi-Niknam, M.; Fatemi, S.H. Levels of Bcl-2 and p53 are altered in superior frontal and cerebellar cortices of autistic subjects. *Cell. Mol. Neurobiol.* **2003**, *23*, 945–952. [CrossRef] [PubMed]

15. Samaco, R.C.; Nagarajan, R.P.; Braunschweig, D.; LaSalle, J.M. Multiple pathways regulate MeCP2 expression in normal brain development and exhibit defects in autism-spectrum disorders. *Hum. Mol. Genet.* **2004**, *13*, 629–639. [CrossRef] [PubMed]
16. Hu, V.W.; Frank, B.C.; Heine, S.; Lee, N.H.; Quackenbush, J. Gene expression profiling of lymphoblastoid cell lines from monozygotic twins discordant in severity of autism reveals differential regulation of neurologically relevant genes. *BMC Genom.* **2006**, *7*, 118–136. [CrossRef] [PubMed]
17. Nishimura, Y.; Martin, C.L.; Vazquez-Lopez, A.; Spence, S.J.; Alvarez-Retuerto, A.I.; Sigman, M.; Steindler, C.; Pellegrini, S.; Schanen, N.C.; Warren, S.T. Genome-wide expression profiling of lymphoblastoid cell lines distinguishes different forms of autism and reveals shared pathways. *Hum. Mol. Genet.* **2007**, *16*, 1682–1698. [CrossRef] [PubMed]
18. Garbett, K.; Ebert, P.J.; Mitchell, A.; Lintas, C.; Manzi, B.; Mirnics, K.; Persico, A.M. Immune transcriptome alterations in the temporal cortex of subjects with autism. *Neurobiol. Dis.* **2008**, *30*, 303–311. [CrossRef] [PubMed]
19. Gregg, J.P.; Lit, L.; Baron, C.A.; Hertz-Picciotto, I.; Walker, W.; Davis, R.A.; Croen, L.A.; Ozonoff, S.; Hansen, R.; Pessah, I.N. Gene expression changes in children with autism. *Genomics* **2008**, *91*, 22–29. [CrossRef] [PubMed]
20. Enstrom, A.M.; Lit, L.; Onore, C.E.; Gregg, J.P.; Hansen, R.L.; Pessah, I.N.; Hertz-Picciotto, I.; van de Water, J.A.; Sharp, F.R.; Ashwood, P. Altered gene expression and function of peripheral blood natural killer cells in children with autism. *Brain Behav. Immun.* **2009**, *23*, 124–133. [CrossRef] [PubMed]
21. Hu, V.W.; Sarachana, T.; Kim, K.S.; Nguyen, A.; Kulkarni, S.; Steinberg, M.E.; Luu, T.; Lai, Y.; Lee, N.H. Gene expression profiling differentiates autism case–controls and phenotypic variants of autism spectrum disorders: Evidence for circadian rhythm dysfunction in severe autism. *Autism Res.* **2009**, *2*, 78–97. [CrossRef] [PubMed]
22. Hu, V.W.; Nguyen, A.; Kim, K.S.; Steinberg, M.E.; Sarachana, T.; Scully, M.A.; Soldin, S.J.; Luu, T.; Lee, N.H. Gene expression profiling of lymphoblasts from autistic and nonaffected sib pairs: Altered pathways in neuronal development and steroid biosynthesis. *PLoS ONE* **2009**, *4*, e5775. [CrossRef] [PubMed]
23. Sheikh, A.; Li, X.; Wen, G.; Tauqeer, Z.; Brown, W.; Malik, M. Cathepsin D and apoptosis related proteins are elevated in the brain of autistic subjects. *Neuroscience* **2010**, *165*, 363–370. [CrossRef] [PubMed]
24. Malik, M.; Sheikh, A.M.; Wen, G.; Spivack, W.; Brown, W.T.; Li, X. Expression of inflammatory cytokines, Bcl-2 and cathepsin D are altered in lymphoblasts of autistic subjects. *Immunobiology* **2011**, *216*, 80–85. [CrossRef] [PubMed]
25. Kuwano, Y.; Kamio, Y.; Kawai, T.; Katsuura, S.; Inada, N.; Takaki, A.; Rokutan, K. Autism-associated gene expression in peripheral leucocytes commonly observed between subjects with autism and healthy women having autistic children. *PLoS ONE* **2011**, *6*, e24723. [CrossRef] [PubMed]
26. Ghahramani Seno, M.M.; Hu, P.; Gwadry, F.G.; Pinto, D.; Marshall, C.R.; Casallo, G.; Scherer, S.W. Gene and miRNA expression profiles in autism spectrum disorders. *Brain Res.* **2011**, *1380*, 85–97. [CrossRef] [PubMed]
27. Luo, R.; Sanders, S.J.; Tian, Y.; Voineagu, I.; Huang, N.; Chu, S.H.; Klei, L.; Cai, C.; Ou, J.; Lowe, J.K. Genome-wide transcriptome profiling reveals the functional impact of rare de novo and recurrent CNVs in autism spectrum disorders. *Am. J. Hum. Genet.* **2012**, *91*, 38–55. [CrossRef] [PubMed]
28. Chow, M.L.; Pramparo, T.; Winn, M.E.; Barnes, C.C.; Li, H.-R.; Weiss, L.; Fan, J.-B.; Murray, S.; April, C.; Belinson, H. Age-dependent brain gene expression and copy number anomalies in autism suggest distinct pathological processes at young versus mature ages. *PLoS Genet.* **2012**, *8*, e1002592. [CrossRef] [PubMed]
29. Kong, S.W.; Collins, C.D.; Shimizu-Motohashi, Y.; Holm, I.A.; Campbell, M.G.; Lee, I.-H.; Brewster, S.J.; Hanson, E.; Harris, H.K.; Lowe, K.R. Characteristics and predictive value of blood transcriptome signature in males with autism spectrum disorders. *PLoS ONE* **2012**, *7*, e49475. [CrossRef] [PubMed]
30. Griesi-Oliveira, K.; Moreira Dde, P.; Davis-Wright, N.; Sanders, S.; Mason, C.; Orabona, G.M.; Vadasz, E.; Bertola, D.R.; State, M.W.; Passos-Bueno, M.R. A complex chromosomal rearrangement involving chromosomes 2, 5, and X in autism spectrum disorder. *Am. J. Med. Genet. B Neuropsychiatr. Genet.* **2012**, *159*, 529–536. [CrossRef] [PubMed]
31. Anitha, A.; Nakamura, K.; Thanseem, I.; Yamada, K.; Iwayama, Y.; Toyota, T.; Matsuzaki, H.; Miyachi, T.; Yamada, S.; Tsujii, M.; et al. Brain region-specific altered expression and association of mitochondria-related genes in autism. *Mol. Autism* **2012**, *3*, 12–24. [CrossRef] [PubMed]

32. Ginsberg, M.R.; Rubin, R.A.; Falcone, T.; Ting, A.H.; Natowicz, M.R. Brain transcriptional and epigenetic associations with autism. *PLoS ONE* **2012**, *7*, e44736. [CrossRef] [PubMed]
33. Choi, J.; Ababon, M.R.; Soliman, M.; Lin, Y.; Brzustowicz, L.M.; Matteson, P.G.; Millonig, J.H. Autism associated gene, engrailed2, and flanking gene levels are altered in post-mortem cerebellum. *PLoS ONE* **2014**, *9*, e87208. [CrossRef] [PubMed]
34. Nardone, S.; Sams, D.S.; Reuveni, E.; Getselter, D.; Oron, O.; Karpuj, M.; Elliott, E. DNA methylation analysis of the autistic brain reveals multiple dysregulated biological pathways. *Transl. Psychiatry* **2014**, *4*, e433. [CrossRef] [PubMed]
35. Pandit, P.; Cooper-White, J.; Punyadeera, C. High-yield RNA-extraction method for saliva. *Clin. Chem.* **2013**, *59*, 1118–1122. [CrossRef] [PubMed]
36. Lee, Y.H.; Zhou, H.; Reiss, J.K.; Yan, X.; Zhang, L.; Chia, D.; Wong, D.T. Direct saliva transcriptome analysis. *Clin. Chem.* **2011**, *57*, 1295–1302. [CrossRef] [PubMed]
37. Park, N.J.; Li, Y.; Yu, T.; Brinkman, B.M.; Wong, D.T. Characterization of RNA in saliva. *Clin. Chem.* **2006**, *52*, 988–994. [CrossRef] [PubMed]
38. Seugnet, L.; Boero, J.; Gottschalk, L.; Duntley, S.P.; Shaw, P.J. Identification of a biomarker for sleep drive in flies and humans. *Proc. Natl. Acad. Sci. USA* **2006**, *103*, 19913–19918. [CrossRef] [PubMed]
39. Bustin, S.A.; Benes, V.; Garson, J.A.; Hellemans, J.; Huggett, J.; Kubista, M.; Mueller, R.; Nolan, T.; Pfaffl, M.W.; Shipley, G.L. Primer sequence disclosure: A clarification of the MIQE guidelines. *Clin. Chem.* **2011**, *57*, 919–921. [CrossRef] [PubMed]
40. Vandesompele, J.; de Preter, K.; Pattyn, F.; Poppe, B.; van Roy, N.; de Paepe, A.; Speleman, F. Accurate normalization of real-time quantitative RT-PCR data by geometric averaging of multiple internal control genes. *Genome Biol.* **2002**, *3*, 1–12. [CrossRef]
41. Andersen, C.L.; Jensen, J.L.; Orntoft, T.F. Normalization of real-time quantitative reverse transcription-PCR data: A model-based variance estimation approach to identify genes suited for normalization, applied to bladder and colon cancer data sets. *Cancer Res.* **2004**, *64*, 5245–5250. [CrossRef] [PubMed]
42. Lallemant, B.; Evrard, A.; Combescure, C.; Chapuis, H.; Chambon, G.; Raynal, C.; Reynaud, C.; Sabra, O.; Joubert, D.; Hollande, F.; et al. Reference gene selection for head and neck squamous cell carcinoma gene expression studies. *BMC Mol. Biol.* **2009**, *10*, 78–88. [CrossRef] [PubMed]
43. Livak, K.J.; Schmittgen, T.D. Analysis of relative gene expression data using real-time quantitative PCR and the $2^{-\Delta\Delta Ct}$ method. *Methods* **2001**, *25*, 402–408. [CrossRef] [PubMed]
44. Pfaffl, M.W.; Tichopad, A.; Prgomet, C.; Neuvians, T.P. Determination of stable housekeeping genes, differentially regulated target genes and sample integrity: Bestkeeper—Excel-based tool using pair-wise correlations. *Biotechnol. Lett.* **2004**, *26*, 509–515. [CrossRef] [PubMed]
45. Keller, S.; Sarchiapone, M.; Zarrilli, F.; Videtic, A.; Ferraro, A.; Carli, V.; Sacchetti, S.; Lembo, F.; Angiolillo, A.; Jovanovic, N.; et al. Increased BDNF promoter methylation in the Wernicke area of suicide subjects. *Arch. Gen. Psychiatry* **2010**, *67*, 258–267. [CrossRef] [PubMed]
46. Arion, D.; Sabatini, M.; Unger, T.; Pastor, J.; Alonso-Nanclares, L.; Ballesteros-Yanez, I.; Garcia Sola, R.; Munoz, A.; Mirnics, K.; DeFelipe, J. Correlation of transcriptome profile with electrical activity in temporal lobe epilepsy. *Neurobiol. Dis.* **2006**, *22*, 374–387. [CrossRef] [PubMed]
47. Arion, D.; Unger, T.; Lewis, D.A.; Levitt, P.; Mirnics, K. Molecular evidence for increased expression of genes related to immune and chaperone function in the prefrontal cortex in schizophrenia. *Biol. Psychiatry* **2007**, *62*, 711–721. [CrossRef] [PubMed]
48. Zhang, L.; Xiao, H.; Wong, D.T. Salivary biomarkers for clinical applications. *Mol. Diagn. Ther.* **2009**, *13*, 245–259. [CrossRef] [PubMed]
49. Saxena, V.; Yadev, N.; Juneja, V.; Singh, A.; Tiwari, U.; Santha, B. Saliva: A miraculous biofluid for early detection of disease. *J. Oral Health Community Dent.* **2013**, *7*, 64–68.
50. Zhang, L.; Xiao, H.; Karlan, S.; Zhou, H.; Gross, J.; Elashoff, D.; Akin, D.; Yan, X.; Chia, D.; Karlan, B.; et al. Discovery and preclinical validation of salivary transcriptomic and proteomic biomarkers for the non-invasive detection of breast cancer. *PLoS ONE* **2010**, *5*, e15573. [CrossRef] [PubMed]
51. Nohesara, S.; Ghadirivasfi, M.; Mostafavi, S.; Eskandari, M.R.; Ahmadkhaniha, H.; Thiagalingam, S.; Abdolmaleky, H.M. DNA hypomethylation of MB-COMT promoter in the DNA derived from saliva in schizophrenia and bipolar disorder. *J. Psychiatr. Res.* **2011**, *45*, 1432–1438. [CrossRef] [PubMed]

52. Rahbar, M.H.; Samms-Vaughan, M.; Ma, J.; Bressler, J.; Dickerson, A.S.; Hessabi, M.; Loveland, K.A.; Grove, M.L.; Shakespeare-Pellington, S.; Beecher, C.; et al. Synergic effect of GSTP1 and blood manganese concentrations in autism spectrum disorder. *Res. Autism Spectr. Disord.* **2015**, *18*, 73–82. [CrossRef] [PubMed]
53. Hicks, S.D.; Ignacio, C.; Gentile, K.; Middleton, F.A. Salivary mirna profiles identify children with autism spectrum disorder, correlate with adaptive behavior, and implicate asd candidate genes involved in neurodevelopment. *BMC Pediatr.* **2016**, *16*, 1–11. [CrossRef] [PubMed]
54. Zhang, L.; Farrell, J.J.; Zhou, H.; Elashoff, D.; Akin, D.; Park, N.H.; Chia, D.; Wong, D.T. Salivary transcriptomic biomarkers for detection of resectable pancreatic cancer. *Gastroenterology* **2010**, *138*, 941–947. [CrossRef] [PubMed]
55. Yu, H.R.; Kuo, H.C.; Huang, H.C.; Huang, L.T.; Tain, Y.L.; Chen, C.C.; Liang, C.D.; Sheen, J.M.; Lin, I.C.; Wu, C.C.; et al. Glyceraldehyde-3-phosphate dehydrogenase is a reliable internal control in western blot analysis of leukocyte subpopulations from children. *Anal. Biochem.* **2011**, *413*, 24–29. [CrossRef] [PubMed]
56. Chen, J.; Sochivko, D.; Beck, H.; Marechal, D.; Wiestler, O.D.; Becker, A.J. Activity-induced expression of common reference genes in individual cns neurons. *Lab. Investig.* **2001**, *81*, 913–916. [CrossRef] [PubMed]
57. Silberberg, G.; Baruch, K.; Navon, R. Detection of stable reference genes for real-time PCR analysis in schizophrenia and bipolar disorder. *Anal. Biochem.* **2009**, *391*, 91–97. [CrossRef] [PubMed]
58. Penna, I.; Vella, S.; Gigoni, A.; Russo, C.; Cancedda, R.; Pagano, A. Selection of candidate housekeeping genes for normalization in human postmortem brain samples. *Int. J. Mol. Sci.* **2011**, *12*, 5461–5470. [CrossRef] [PubMed]
59. Steinhausen, H.C.; Erdin, A. Abnormal psychosocial situations and ICD-10 diagnoses in children and adolescents attending a psychiatric service. *J. Child Psychol. Psychiatry* **1992**, *33*, 731–740. [CrossRef] [PubMed]
60. Lord, C.; Pickles, A.; McLennan, J.; Rutter, M.; Bregman, J.; Folstein, S.; Fombonne, E.; Leboyer, M.; Minshew, N. Diagnosing autism: Analyses of data from the autism diagnostic interview. *J. Autism Dev. Disord.* **1997**, *27*, 501–517. [CrossRef] [PubMed]
61. Goodman, R. The strengths and difficulties questionnaire: A research note. *J. Child. Psychol. Psychiatry* **1997**, *38*, 581–586. [CrossRef] [PubMed]

8

GeneAnalytics Pathway Analysis and Genetic Overlap among Autism Spectrum Disorder, Bipolar Disorder and Schizophrenia

Naveen S. Khanzada [1], Merlin G. Butler [1,2] and Ann M. Manzardo [1,*]

1 Department of Psychiatry and Behavioral Sciences, University of Kansas Medical Center, Kansas City, KS 66160, USA; nkhanzada@kumc.edu (N.S.K.); mbutler4@kumc.edu (M.G.B.)
2 Department of Pediatrics, University of Kansas Medical Center, Kansas City, KS 66160, USA
* Correspondence: amanzardo@kumc.edu

Academic Editor: William Chi-shing Cho

Abstract: Bipolar disorder (BPD) and schizophrenia (SCH) show similar neuropsychiatric behavioral disturbances, including impaired social interaction and communication, seen in autism spectrum disorder (ASD) with multiple overlapping genetic and environmental influences implicated in risk and course of illness. GeneAnalytics software was used for pathway analysis and genetic profiling to characterize common susceptibility genes obtained from published lists for ASD (792 genes), BPD (290 genes) and SCH (560 genes). Rank scores were derived from the number and nature of overlapping genes, gene-disease association, tissue specificity and gene functions subdivided into categories (e.g., diseases, tissues or functional pathways). Twenty-three genes were common to all three disorders and mapped to nine biological Superpathways including Circadian entrainment (10 genes, score = 37.0), Amphetamine addiction (five genes, score = 24.2), and Sudden infant death syndrome (six genes, score = 24.1). Brain tissues included the medulla oblongata (11 genes, score = 2.1), thalamus (10 genes, score = 2.0) and hypothalamus (nine genes, score = 2.0) with six common genes (*BDNF*, *DRD2*, *CHRNA7*, *HTR2A*, *SLC6A3*, and *TPH2*). Overlapping genes impacted dopamine and serotonin homeostasis and signal transduction pathways, impacting mood, behavior and physical activity level. Converging effects on pathways governing circadian rhythms support a core etiological relationship between neuropsychiatric illnesses and sleep disruption with hypoxia and central brain stem dysfunction.

Keywords: mental illness; genetic profiling; GeneAnalytics molecular pathway analysis; circadian entrainment

1. Introduction

Severe neuropsychiatric disorders collectively present with similar behavioral, social, cognitive and perceptual disturbances including autism spectrum disorder (ASD). ASD includes classical autism, Asperger syndrome and pervasive developmental disorder with problems in social interaction and communication or repetitive behavior. Schizophrenia (SCH) presents with delusions, hallucinations, disorganized thinking and behavior with negative symptoms. Bipolar disorder (BPD) is considered a developmental disorder characterized by progressive cognitive impairment, residual symptoms, sleep disturbance, and emotional dysregulations with cycles of depression and mania. Schizophrenia and bipolar disorders share many common traits with ASD, including social and cognitive dysfunction and impaired ability to function, live and work independently [1]. Considerable overlap has been identified between the molecular mechanisms implicated in the etiology of schizophrenia, bipolar disorder, and autism, suggesting similar root causes [2]. Up to 30% of patients diagnosed with ASD during childhood will develop schizophrenia during adulthood [3]. Further, the presence of schizophrenia or bipolar disorder in first-degree relatives is a consistent and significant risk factor for ASD [4]. These three neuropsychiatric illnesses have complex inheritance patterns with >80% estimate for each disorder with multiple genetic and environmental factors influencing disease risk and course [2,4].

A recent large collaborative genetic study of families with schizophrenia and ASD showed significant overlap in candidate genes and susceptibility regions for both disorders using traditional karyotyping, genome-wide association studies (GWAS) and comparative genome hybridization (CGH) analyses by identifying chromosomal deletions and duplications in individuals with ASD [5–8]. ASD and SCH risk alleles appear to impact growth-signaling pathways with autism associated with loss of function in many genes [9–11], whereas schizophrenia tends to be associated with reduced function or activity of genes that up-regulate growth-related pathways [12–16].

Cytogenetic, linkage and association studies have identified common copy number variants (CNVs, deletions, duplications) between ASD and SCH which may produce dosage-dependent gain or loss of expression of genes contributing to phenotypic variation in presentation and course of illness. A large number of autism-specific CNVs have been found but with low recurrence (<1%) and they show a high level of genetic heterogeneity. For example, when the 15q11.2 BP1–BP2 region or 15q13.3 band contains a deletion or duplication in patients, then autism or a variety of neuropsychiatric traits including schizophrenia are identified [3,17–19]. Gene expression disturbances were found using postmortem cortical brain tissue from patients with autism, schizophrenia and bipolar disorder and they have shown a high correlation between the transcriptomes of ASD and schizophrenia, but not in BPD [5]. Hence, a large number of possible genetic and environmental factors do influence disease risk, expression and treatment.

Herein, we use the GeneAnalytics [20] program pathway analysis to further profile and characterize the underlying molecular architecture of clinically and etiologically relevant genes common to ASD [21], bipolar disorder [22] and schizophrenia [23] and associated diseases.

2. Results

The original gene lists reported in the literature included 792 genes for ASD [21], 290 genes for bipolar disorder [22] and 560 genes for schizophrenia [23], and of these, 23 genes were found in common in all three conditions (see Table 1). Functional analysis of the 23 genes identified from the submitted list of genes showed a high match for schizophrenia (17 genes, score = 15.1) with medium-match scores representing 25 other disorders including bipolar disorder (nine genes, score = 9.6) and autism spectrum disorder (10 genes, score = 9.1). Additional diseases identified were related to disorders of mental health including mood and personality disorders (see Table 2A). Tissues and cell types profiled for these 23 overlapping genes identified five common types of brain tissues which achieved high match scores (see Table 2B). These included the medulla oblongata (11 genes, score = 2.1), thalamus (10 genes, score = 2.0), hypothalamus (nine genes, score = 2.0), hippocampus (nine genes, score = 1.9) and cerebellum (eight genes, score = 1.9). Six (*BDNF*, *DRD2*, *CHRNA7*, *HTR2A*, *SLC6A3*, and *TPH2*) of the overlapping genes were matched to all five tissues types. Sixteen of the overlapping genes matched to a total of 36 Biological Superpathways with a total of nine Superpathways achieving significantly high match scores according to the GeneAnalytics pathway analysis and algorithm [20]. The Circadian entrainment pathway showed the highest match score involving 10 genes (score = 37.0), followed by Amphetamine addiction involving five genes (score = 24.3) and Sudden infant death syndrome (SIDS) susceptibility pathways (six genes, score = 24.1) (see Table 3).

Table 1. Twenty-three clinically relevant genes common to ASD, BPD and schizophrenia.

Gene Symbol	Gene Name	Chromosome Location
BDNF	Brain-derived neurotrophic factor	11p14.1
ANK3	Ankyrin 3	10q21.2
CACNA1C	Ca^2+ channel, voltage-dependent, L type, α1C subunit	12p13.33
CACNB2	Ca+ channel, voltage dependent, β2 subunit	10p12.33
CHRNA7	Cholinergic receptor, nicotinic, α7 (neuronal)	15q13.3
CNTNAP5	Contactin associated protein-like 5	2q14.3
CSMD1	CUB and sushi multiple domains 1	8p23.2
DISC1	Disruption in schizophrenia 1	1q42.2
DPP10	Dipeptidyl-peptidase 10 (non-functional)	2q14.1
DRD2	Dopamine receptor D2	11q23.2
FOXP2	Forkhead box P2	7q31.1
GSK3B	Glycogen synthase kinase 3β	3q13.33
HTR2A	5-Hydroxytryptamine (serotonin) receptor 2A, G-protein-coupled	13q14.2
MAOA	Monoamine oxidase A	Xp11.3
MTHFR	Methylenetetrahydrofolate reductase	1p36.22
NOS1AP	Nitric oxide synthase 1 (neuronal) adaptor protein	1q23.3
NRG1	Neuregulin 1	8p12
PDE4B	Phosphodiesterase 4B, CAMP-specific	1p31.3
SLC6A3	Solute carrier family 6 (neurotransmitter transporter, dopamine), member 3	5p15.33
SYN3	Synapsin III	22q12.3
TCF4	Transcription factor 4	18q21.1
TPH2	Tryptophan hydroxylase 2	12q21.1
ZNF804A	Zinc finger protein 804 A	2q32.1

Table 2. GeneAnalytics program mapping of diseases, tissues and cells that were significantly matched to 23 overlapping genes for autism spectrum disorder, bipolar disorder and schizophrenia.

A. Diseases	Genes Matched to Disease Type (Highmatch Score)	No. of Genes in Disease Type	Score
Schizophrenia	*ANK3, BDNF, CACNA1C, CHRNA7, DISC1, NRG1, DRD2, GSK3B, HTR2A, MAOA, MTHFR, NOS1AP, PDE4B, SLC6A3, SYN3, TPH2, ZNF804A*	249	15.1
	(Mediummatch scores > 6.0)		
Bipolar disorder	*BDNF, DISC1, DRD2, GSK3B, HTR2A, MAOA, NRG1, SLC6A3, ZNF804A*	39	9.6
Autism spectrum disorder	*BDNF, CHRNA7, DISC1, DRD2, FOXP2, HTR2A, MAOA, MTHFR, SLC6A3, TPH2*	103	9.1
Disease of mental health	*BDNF, DISC1, DRD2, HTR2A, MAOA, NRG1, SLC6A3, ZNF804A*	57	8.0
Attention deficit hyperactivity disorder	*BDNF, CHRNA7, DRD2, HTR2A, MAOA, SLC6A3, TPH2, ZNF804A*	63	7.8
Mood disorder	*BDNF, CACNA1C, DISC1, DRD2, HTR2A, MAOA, TPH2*	31	7.7
Psychotic disorder	*BDNF, CHRNA7, DISC1, DRD2, HTR2A, NRG1, SLC6A3*	37	7.5
Anxiety disorder	*BDNF, DRD2, HTR2A, MAOA, SLC6A3, TPH2*	21	7.1
Obsessive compulsive disorder	*BDNF, DRD2, HTR2A, MAOA, SLC6A3, TPH2*	29	6.8
Personality disorder	*DRD2, HTR2A, MAOA, SLC6A3, TPH2*	14	6.4
B. Tissues and Cells	**Genes Matched to Tissues and Cells**	**No. of Genes in Tissues And Cells**	**Score**
Medulla oblongata	*BDNF, CHRNA7, DRD2, FOXP2, HTR2A, MAOA, NRG1, PDE4B, SLC6A3, TCF4, TPH2*	2179	2.1
Thalamus	*BDNF, CHRNA7, DRD2, HTR2A, MTHFR, PDE4B, SLC6A3, TCF4, TPH2*	1736	2.0
Hypothalamus	*BDNF, CHRNA7, DRD2, FOXP2, HTR2A, MTHFR, PDE4B, SLC6A3, TCF4, TPH2*	1666	2.0
Hippocampus	*ANK3, BDNF, CHRNA7, DISC1, DRD2, FOXP2, HTR2A, SLC6A3, TPH2*	3335	1.9
Cerebellum	*ANK3, BDNF, CHRNA7, DRD2, FOXP2, HTR2A, SLC6A3, TPH2*	2609	1.9

Table 3. GeneAnalytics program mapping of superpathways with high match scores for 23 overlapping genes for autism spectrum disorder, bipolar disorder and schizophrenia.

Superpathways	Genes Matched to Superpathways	No. of Genes in Superpathways	Score
Circadian entrainment	*SLC6A3, GSK3B, HTR2A, MAOA, NOS1AP, PDE4B, TPH2, CACNA1C, CHRNA7, DRD2*	390	37.0
Amphetamine addiction	*SLC6A3, MAOA, BDNF, CACNA1C, DRD2*	87	24.3
SID susceptibility pathways	*HTR2A, MAOA, NOS1AP, TPH2, BDNF, CHRNA7*	185	24.1
Selective serotonin reuptake inhibitor pathways	*HTR2A, MAOA, TPH2*	29	17.5
Monoamine transport	*SLC6A3, MAOA, TPH2*	36	16.6
Transmission across chemical synapses	*SLC6A3, MAOA, SYN3, CACNB2, CHRNA7*	316	15.2
CREB pathways	*HTR2A, NRG1, BDNF, CACNA1C, CACNB2, CHRNA7*	562	14.9
Neurotransmitter clearance in the synaptic cleft	*SLC6A3, MAOA*	8	14.6
CAMP signaling pathways	*PDE4B, BDNF, CACNA1C, DRD2*	211	13.4

The remaining Superpathways identified did emphasize monoamine signaling and cellular re-uptake/transport. There was little intrinsic overlap between the 36 biological Superpathways with only one gene (*DRD2*) common to all nine Superpathways.

Examination of gene ontology pathways identified 17 genes that matched to a total of 32 GO-molecular functions but high match scores were found for only three molecular functions involving six genes: Serotonin binding with two genes (*HTR2, MAOA*) out of nine total pathway genes, score = 14.3; Dopamine binding with two genes (*SLC6A3, DRD2*) out of 10 total pathway genes, score = 14) and High Voltage-gated Calcium Channel Activity with two genes (*CACNA1C, CACNB2*) out of 10 total pathway genes, score = 14. The 23 overlapping genes mapped to a total of 55 GO-biological processes with high match scores identified for 16 biological processes involving 19 genes (see Table 4). These processes involved a variety of behavioral constructs including axon guidance, synaptic transmission, and particularly the activity of ion channels and dopamine homeostasis.

Table 4. GeneAnalytics program mapping of gene ontology (GO) biological processes with high match scores to 23 overlapping genes for autism spectrum disorder, bipolar disorder and schizophrenia.

GO-Biological Processes	Genes Matched to GO-Biological Processes	No. of Genes in GO-Biological Processes	Score
Startle response	*NRG1, CSMD1, DRD2*	20	19.1
Positive regulation of axon extension	*GSK3B, NRG1, DISC1*	30	17.4
Cellular calcium ion homeostasis	*HTR2A, CACNA1C, CHRNA7, DRD2*	107	17.2
Synaptic transmission	*SLC6A3, HTR2A, MAOA, CACNA1C, CACNB2, CHRNA7*	432	17.0
Dopamine catabolic process	*SLC6A3, MAOA*	5	16.0
Axon guidance	*GSK3B, NRG1, ANK3, BDNF, CACNA1C, CACNB2*	537	15.3
Synapse assembly	*NRG1, BDNF, DRD2*	52	15.0
Regulation of high voltage-gated calcium channel activity	*NOS1AP, PDE4B*	7	15.0
Regulation of potassium Ion transport	*ANK3, DRD2*	7	15.0
Response to hypoxia	*MTHFR, BDNF, CHRNA7, DRD2*	180	14.3
Negative regulation of synaptic transmission, glutamatergic	*HTR2A, DRD2*	9	14.3
Adenohypophysis development	*SLC6A3, DRD2*	9	14.3
Regulation of synaptic transmission, GABAergic	*SYN3, DRD2*	10	14.0
Behavioral response to ethanol	*CHRNA7, DRD2*	11	13.7
Regulation of dopamine secretion	*SLC6A3, CHRNA7*	11	13.7
Dopamine biosynthetic process	*HTR2A, DRD2*	12	13.4

A total of 106 phenotypes were mapped to the 23 overlapping genes with 36 phenotypes involving 18 genes having high match scores (see Table 5). The highest-matched phenotypes were behavioral despair (four genes, score = 24.8), hypoactivity (seven genes, score = 24.4), abnormal serotonin levels (four genes, score = 24.1) and abnormal response to novel objects (four genes, score = 22.2). Additionally, phenotypes impacted GABAergic neuron morphology, synaptic transmission and response to hypoxia and risk of death.

Table 5. GeneAnalytics profiling of high match score phenotypes to 23 overlapping genes for autism spectrum disorder, bipolar disorder and schizophrenia.

Phenotypes	Genes Matched to Phenotypes	No. of Genes	Score
Behavioral despair	*GSK3B, CACNA1C, CSMD1, DISC1*	28	24.8
Hypoactivity	*MAOA, FOXP2, ANK3, BDNF, CACNA1C, CHRNA7, DRD2*	314	24.4
Abnormal serotonin level	*MAOA, FOXP2, TPH2, BDNF*	32	24.1
Abnormal response to novel object	*SLC6A3, FOXP2, TPH2, DISC1*	44	22.2
Abnormal GABAergic neuron morphology	*BDNF, CHRNA7, DRD2*	11	21.7
Abnormal prepulse inhibition	*NRG1, DISC1, DRD2*	14	20.7
Abnormal social Investigation	*MAOA, SYN3, CACNA1C, DISC1*	14	20.7
Increase aggression towards males	*MAOA, TPH2, BDNF*	64	20.1
Small cerebellum	*MTHFR, FOXP2, ANK3, DISC1*	67	19.8
Decrease exploration in new environment	*GSK3B, FOXP2, BDNF, CACNA1C*	79	18.9
Abnormal CNS synaptic transmission	*SLC6A3, BDNF, CACNA1C, DRD2*	79	18.9
Premature death	*SLC6A3, MTHFR, FOXP2, ANK3, TPH2, BDNF, CACNA1C, DRD2*	830	18.6
Decrease startle reflex	*FOXP2, CSMD1, DISC1, DRD2*	84	18.6
Decrease anxiety-related response	*HTR2A, CHRNA7, DISC1, DRD2*	89	18.2
Increase dopamine level	*SLC6A3, MAOA, FOXP2*	31	17.2
Abnormal vocalization	*FOXP2, CACNA1C, DRD2*	37	16.5
Hyperactivity	*SLC6A3, NRG1, BDNF, CSMD1, DISC1*	272	16.3
Increased thigmotaxis	*SLC6A3, CACNA1C, CSMD1*	45	15.6
Abnormal serotonergic neuron morphology	*TPH2, BDNF*	6	15.4
Abnormal response to novel odor	*SLC6A3, DRD2*	6	15.4
Abnormal latent inhibition of conditioning	*DISC1, DRD2*	6	15.4
Impaired coordination	*SLC6A3, FOXP2, BDNF, CACNA1C, DRD2*	309	15.4
Abnormal learning/memory/conditioning	*GSK3B, CACNA1C, DISC1*	49	15.3
Limp posture	*NRG1, DRD2*	7	15.0
Decreased serotonin Level	*TPH2, DISC1*	7	15.0
Postnatal growth retardation	*SLC6A3, MTHFR, FOXP2, TPH2, BDNF, DRD2*	581	14.6
Abnormal pituitary gland physiology	*SLC6A3, DRD2*	8	14.6
Abnormal inhibitory postsynaptic currents	*SLC6A3, SYN3, BDNF*	60	14.4
Small nodose ganglion	*NRG1, BDNF*	9	14.3
Complete postnatal lethality	*FOXP2, ANK3, TCF4, BDNF, CACNA1C*	375	14.1
Small petrosal ganglion	*NRG1, BDNF*	10	14.0
Decreased somatotroph cell number	*SLC6A3, DRD2*	11	13.7
Abnormal grooming behavior	*SLC6A3, MAOA*	11	13.7
Abnormal excitatory postsynaptic currents	*NRG1, SYN3, DRD2*	72	13.6
Decreased left ventricle systolic pressure	*MAOA, NRG1*	12	13.4
Hunched posture	*MAOA, BDNF, DRD2*	78	13.3

3. Discussion

The molecular and genetic architecture of ASD, BPD and SCH with the identified 23 overlapping candidate susceptibility genes common to the three neuropsychiatric illnesses were analyzed to assess shared etiological factors and phenotypes to facilitate mechanistic understanding and potential development of new treatment approaches. Interestingly, the genetic architecture of the overlapping genes for the three disorders converged on brain structures (e.g., medulla oblongata, thalamus), neurotransmitter systems (e.g., dopamine, serotonin) and signal transduction pathways primarily involved in the regulation of circadian oscillations and sleep disturbances. GO-molecular processes were mapped to the neurotransmitter pathways (dopamine, andserotonin) and ion channels (high voltage–gated calcium channels) implicated in mood, addiction and psychotic disorders with regulatory function and expression in brain centers controlling Circadian entrainment.

The human thalamus, hypothalamus and hippocampus have been extensively targeted in relation to relaying and processing sensory and motor information, as well as regulating consciousness and sleep [24]. The central and peripheral circadian molecular clock is entrained through a complex and highly regulated molecular cascade in the suprachiasmatic nuclei (SCN) of the hypothalamus driven by the cyclical expression of *PER* and *CRY* [25–27]. The master lists of susceptibility genes for BPD and SCH contain *CLOCK*, an integral part of the Circadian entrainment pathway, and the identified ASD master gene list contains additional circadian-regulatory genes (e.g., *PER1*, *PER2*, *NPAS2*, *MTNR1A*, and *MTNR1B*). The master clock located in the suprachiasmatic nuclei of the hypothalamus synchronizes mainly by light signals, and releases glutamate and pituitary adenylate cyclase-activating polypeptide (PACAP) with the activation of signal transduction cascades, including nNOS activity, cAMP- and cGMP-dependent protein kinases. Additionally, multiple entrainment pathways converge to phosphorylate CREB and to activate *CLOCK* gene expression [25–27] (see Figure 1 for circadian pathways and related features).

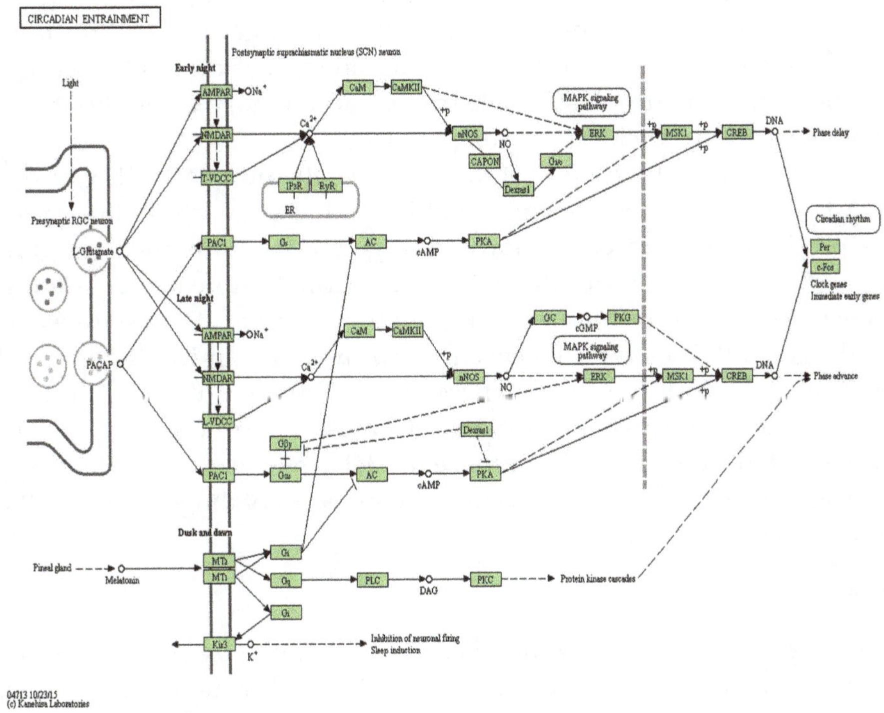

Figure 1. Circadian entrainment is an intrinsic, internal biological clock entrained by exogenous signals, such as endocrine and behavioral rhythms synchronized to environmental cues. The master clock located in the suprachiasmatic nuclei (SCN) of the hypothalamus synchronizes circadian oscillators in peripheral tissues. The main photic input to the suprachiasmatic nuclei comes from the retinal ganglion cells which use glutamate and PACAP, which leads to activation of AMPA and NMDA receptors. The release of glutamate and PACAP triggers the activation of signal transduction cascades including CamKII and nNOS activity, cAMP- and cGMP-dependent protein kinases and mitogen-activated protein kinase (MAPK). Also, melatonin affects non-photic entrainment by inhibiting light-induced phase shifts through inhibition of adenylate cyclase (AC). Additionally, multiple entrainment pathways converge to phosphorylate CREB and to activate *CLOCK* gene expression [28–31]. Solid and dotted lines indicate direct and indirect relationships, respectively.

Arousal and cortical responsiveness are modulated by a complex regulatory network including serotonergic feedback from the median raphe nuclei involved in the regulation of rapid eye movement (REM) sleep patterning [24]. Depletion of serotonin receptors and feedback are implicated in the pathology of Sudden infant death syndrome (SIDS), a secondary Superpathway identified in our study [32]. *BDNF*, a neurotrophic factor, and *CHRNA7* genes involved in the SIDS Superpathway were also implicated in the biological processes impacting the response to hypoxia and may reflect underlying vulnerability to neurological/physiological injury secondary to apnea, thereby influencing neurocognition and/or behavior. Mesencephalic dopaminergic neurons from the ventral tegmental area also project to the thalamic nuclei to directly modulate sleep induction and wakefulness through opposing effects of *DRD1* and *DRD2* receptors on adenylyl cyclase activity.

Neuronal activity and plasticity during brain development is sensitive to both neurotransmitter signaling of serotonin and dopamine and responsive to common genetic and environmental factors influencing brain maturation. Monoamine-sensitive periods also modulate select neurodevelopmental processes (e.g., neuron division, migration and dendritic connectivity) involved in the development of behavioral regulation and control as well as sleep patterns, which may reflect core etiological relationships linking neuropsychiatric illnesses to sleep disruption and hypoxia [28,33–38]. Additionally, the homeostatic value of sleep and circadian rhythmicity impact physiology and behavior in important ways, including the response to stress. Rhythmic circadian oscillations in glucocorticoid levels can modulate adult hippocampal growth and functioning through inhibitory effects of glucocorticoid hormones on neural stem cell and progenitor cell proliferation [39]. Thus, the disruption of circadian entrainment or loss of circadian regulation of glucocorticoid release could directly influence hippocampal neuroplasticity, learning and memory throughout life, which may play a role in psychopathology such as schizophrenia [40,41].

Our analyses are limited by the current status of research and availability of published literature reports on candidate genes as well as the reliability of the curated databases and integrated pathway analyses produced by the GeneAnalytics algorithms. Advances in genomic technology and bioinformatics will continue to identify and characterization new candidate genes, but not all identified genes will be equally important or certain to be causative. The relative contributions of any individual gene to the general disease prevalence must be assessed individually. Further, intrinsic bias in the curated literature may result from imbalances in the allocation of resources for study which may overemphasize some disease states or scientific disciplines over others (e.g., genetics of cancer over psychiatry). Nevertheless, the convergence of these model systems and overlaid genetic mechanisms provides relevant insight into the key macro systems involved in pathogenesis and the overlap of these three severe neuropsychiatric disorders.

4. Materials and Methods

We used recently published list of genes found to be clinically relevant and known to play a role in ASD [21], bipolar disorder [22] and schizophrenia [23] for molecular profiling and pathway analysis of genes common to all three neuropsychiatric conditions with similar features. GeneAnalytics (http://geneanalytics.genecards.org/ [20]) computer program and genomic databases are part of the GeneCards Suite developed by LifeMap Sciences (http://www.lifemapsc.com/products/genecards-suite-premium-tools/) and were used to map the resultant list of common genes to characterize molecular pathways, biological processes, molecular functions, phenotypes, tissues and cells, diseases and compounds affected by overlapping neuropsychiatric genes.

GeneAnalytics is powered by GeneCards, LifeMap Discovery, MalaCards and PathCards, which combine >100 archived data sources [20]. The databases contain gene lists for tissues and cells, diseases, phenotypes pathways and compounds curated from published literature reports to develop the best matched list of genes, scored and subdivided into their biological categories such as diseases or pathways. These applications are integrated with GeneCards human gene database, Malacards human disease database, PathCards, human biological pathways database, and LifeMap Discovery tissues and cells database in order to provide an extensive universe of data from human genes, proteins, cells, biological pathways, diseases and their relationships with integration valuable for research and discovery purposes.

Disease matching scores were derived based upon the number of overlapping genes found and the nature of the gene-disease associations. Tissues and cells were scored using a matching algorithm that weighs tissue specificity, abundance and function of the gene. Related pathways were then grouped into Superpathways to improve inferences and pathway enrichment, reduce redundancy and rank genes within a biological mechanism via the multiplicity of constituent pathways with the methodology and algorithm generated by the GeneAnalytics computer-based program. Superpathways were scored based upon transformation of the binomial p-value which was equivalent to a corrected p-value with significance defined at <0.0001.

5. Conclusions

Genetic overlap among autism spectrum disorder, bipolar disorder and schizophrenia was most strongly mapped to Superpathways and brain tissue types guiding Circadian entrainment. The results illustrate the converging effects of dopamine, serotonin and the signal transduction pathways involved in mood, behavior, cognition and impaired social functions; learning and memory are affected in these neuropsychiatric disorders which also guide brain development and sleep patterning disturbances. Thus, under-recognized sleep dysregulation as a common component of psychiatric illness appears to reflect the underlying molecular and genetic architecture of disease pathology in psychiatric illnesses. The convergence of pathways governing circadian rhythms supports the existence of a common core etiological relationship between neuropsychiatric illness and sleep disruption possibly related to central brain stem dysfunction impacting the presentation and underlying pathology and course of illness. This observation opens a new avenue to pursue for treatment modalities in order to change the clinical outcome and natural history of those affected with these relatively common mental health disorders in our current society.

Acknowledgments: We acknowledge support from the Consortium for Translational Research on Aggression and Drug Abuse and Dependence (ConTRADA) grant QB864900 from the University of Kansas and the National Institute of Child Health and Human Development (NICHD) grant HD02528. We thank Miwako Karikomi from Kanehisa Laboratories for granting the permission to publish the Kyoto Encyclopedia of Genes and Genomes (KEGG) pathways map image.

Author Contributions: Naveen Khanzada performed the literature review, compiled information for the GeneAnalytics analysis and primarily composed the manuscript. Merlin Butler contributed to the generation and interpretation of genetic data and the preparation of the manuscript. Ann Manzardo was responsible for the oversight of the study design, implementation, data analysis and interpretation, and manuscript preparation. All of the authors contributed to the final revision and accepted the manuscript.

Abbreviations

ASD	Autism spectrum disorder
BPD	Bipolar disorder
SCH	Schizophrenia
GWAS	Genome-wide association studies
CGH	Comparative genomic hybridization
CNV	Copy number variants
SIDS	Sudden infant death syndrome
SCN	Suprachiasmatic nuclei
PACAP	Pituitary adenylate cyclase-activating polypeptide
cAMP	Cyclic adenosine monophosphate
cGAMP	Cyclic guanosine monophosphate–adenosine monophosphate
nNOS	Nitric oxide synthase
CREB	cAMP response element-binding protein

References

1. American Psychiatric Association. *Diagnostic and Statistical Manual of Mental Disorders: DSMIV-TR*, 4th ed.; American Psychiatric Association: Washington, DC, USA, 2000.
2. Carroll, L.S.; Owen, M.J. Genetic overlap between autism, schizophrenia and bipolar disorder. *Genome Med.* **2009**, *1*, 102. [CrossRef] [PubMed]
3. Burbach, J.; Peter, H.; van der Zwaag, B. Contact in the genetics of autism and schizophrenia. *Trends Neurosci.* **2009**, *32*, 69–72. [CrossRef] [PubMed]
4. Sullivan, P.F.; Magnusson, C.; Reichenberg, A.; Boman, M.; Dalman, C.; Davidson, M.; Fruchter, E.; Hultman, C.M.; Lundberg, M.; Långström, N.; et al. Family history of schizophrenia and bipolar disorder as risk factors for autism. *Arch. Gen. Psychiatry* **2012**, *69*, 1099–1103. [CrossRef] [PubMed]
5. Sebat, J.; Lakshmi, B.; Malhotra, D.; Troge, J.; Lese-Martin, C.; Walsh, T.; Yamrom, B.; Yoon, S.; Krasnitz, A.; Kendall, J.; et al. Strong association of de novo copy number mutations with autism. *Science* **2007**, *316*, 445–449. [CrossRef] [PubMed]
6. Szatmari, P.; Paterson, A.D.; Zwaigenbaum, L.; Roberts, W.; Brian, J.; Liu, X.Q.; Vincent, J.B.; Skaug, J.L.; Thompson, A.P.; Senman, L.; et al. Autism Genome Project Consortium, Mapping autism risk loci using genetic linkage and chromosomal rearrangments. *Nat. Genet.* **2007**, *39*, 319–328. [CrossRef] [PubMed]
7. Marshall, C.R.; Noor, A.; Vincent, J.B.; Lionel, A.C.; Feuk, L.; Skaug, J.; Shago, M.; Moessner, R.; Pinto, D.; Ren, Y.; et al. Structural variation of chromosomes in autism spectrum disorder. *Am. J. Hum. Genet.* **2008**, *82*, 477–488. [CrossRef] [PubMed]
8. Kim, H.G.; Kishikawa, S.; Higgins, A.W.; Seong, I.S.; Donovan, D.J.; Shen, Y.; Lally, E.; Weiss, L.A.; Najm, J.; Kutsche, K.; et al. Disruption of neurexin 1 associated with autism spectrum disorder. *Am. J. Hum. Genet.* **2008**, *82*, 199–207. [CrossRef] [PubMed]
9. Belmonte, M.K.; Bourgeron, T. Fragile X syndrome and autism at the intersection of genetic and neural networks. *Nat. Neurosci.* **2006**, *9*, 1221–1225. [CrossRef] [PubMed]
10. Kwon, C.H.; Luikart, B.W.; Powell, C.M.; Zhou, J.; Matheny, S.A.; Zhang, W.; Li, Y.; Baker, S.J.; Parada, L.F. Pten regulates neuronal arborization and social interaction in mice. *Neuron* **2006**, *50*, 377–388. [CrossRef] [PubMed]
11. Hoeffer, C.A.; Tang, W.; Wong, H.; Santillan, A.; Patterson, R.J.; Martinez, L.A.; Tejada-Simon, M.V.; Paylor, R.; Hamilton, S.L.; Klann, E. Removal of FKBP12 enhances mTOR-Raptor interactions, LTP, memory, and perseverative/repetitive behavior. *Neuron* **2008**, *60*, 832–845. [CrossRef] [PubMed]
12. Cuscó, I.; Medrano, A.; Gener, B.; Vilardell, M.; Gallastegui, F.; Villa, O.; González, E.; Rodríguez-Santiago, B.; Vilella, E.; del Campo, M.; et al. Autism-specific copy number variants further implicate the phosphatidylinositol signaling pathway and the glutamatergic synapse in the etiology of the disorder. *Hum. Mol. Genet.* **2009**, *18*, 1795–1804. [CrossRef] [PubMed]
13. Emamian, E.S.; Hall, D.; Birnbaum, M.J.; Karayiorgou, M.; Gogos, J.A. Convergent evidence for impaired AKT1-GSK3β signaling in schizophrenia. *Nat. Genet.* **2004**, *36*, 131–137. [CrossRef] [PubMed]
14. Stopkova, P.; Saito, T.; Papolos, D.F.; Vevera, J.; Paclt, I.; Zukov, I.; Bersson, Y.B.; Margolis, B.A.; Strous, R.D.; Lachman, H.M. Identification of PIK3C3 promoter variant associated with bipolar disorder and schizophrenia. *Biol. Psychiatry* **2004**, *55*, 981–988. [CrossRef] [PubMed]
15. Kalkman, H.O. The role of the phosphatidylinositide 3-kinase-protein kinase B pathway in schizophrenia. *Pharmacol. Ther.* **2006**, *110*, 117–134. [CrossRef] [PubMed]
16. Krivosheya, D.; Tapia, L.; Levinson, J.N.; Huang, K.; Kang, Y.; Hines, R.; Ting, A.K.; Craig, A.M.; Mei, L.; Bamji, S.X.; et al. ErbB4-neuregulin signaling modulates synapse development and dendritic arborization through distinct mechanisms. *J. Biol. Chem.* **2008**, *283*, 32944–32956. [CrossRef] [PubMed]
17. Cox, D.M.; Butler, M.G. The 15q11.2 BP1–BP2 microdeletion syndrome: A review. *Int. J. Mol. Sci.* **2015**, *16*, 4068–4082. [CrossRef] [PubMed]
18. Burnside, R.D.; Pasion, R.; Mikhail, F.M.; Carroll, A.J.; Robin, N.H.; Youngs, E.L.; Gadi, I.K.; Keitges, E.; Jaswaney, V.L.; Papenhausen, P.R.; et al. Microdeletion/microduplication of proximal 15q11.2 between BP1 and BP2: A susceptibility region for neurological dysfunction including developmental and language delay. *Hum. Genet.* **2011**, *130*, 517–528. [CrossRef] [PubMed]

19. Ho, K.S.; Wassman, E.R.; Baxter, A.L.; Hensel, C.H.; Martin, M.M.; Prasad, A.; Twede, H.; Vanzo, R.J.; Butler, M.G. Chromosomal microarray analysis of consecutive individuals with autism spectrum disorders using an ultra-high resolution chromosomal microarray optimized for neurodevelopmental disorders. *Int. J. Mol. Sci.* **2016**, *17*, 2070. [CrossRef] [PubMed]
20. Ben-Ari, F.S.; Lieder, I.; Stelzer, G.; Mazor, Y.; Buzhor, E.; Kaplan, S.; Bogoch, Y.; Plaschkes, I.; Shitrit, A.; Rappaport, N.; et al. GeneAnalytics: An integrative gene set analysis tool for next generation sequencing, RNAseq and microarray data. *OMICS J. Integr. Biol.* **2016**, *20*, 139–151. [CrossRef] [PubMed]
21. Butler, M.G.; Rafi, S.K.; Manzardo, A.M. High-resolution chromosome ideogram representation of currently recognized genes for autism spectrum disorders. *Int. J. Mol. Sci.* **2015**, *16*, 6464–6495. [CrossRef] [PubMed]
22. Douglas, L.N.; McGuire, A.B.; Manzardo, A.M.; Butler, M.G. High-resolution chromosome ideogram representation of recognized genes for bipolar disorder. *Gene* **2016**, *586*, 136–147. [CrossRef] [PubMed]
23. Butler, M.G.; McGuire, A.B.; Masoud, H.; Manzardo, A.M. Currently recognized genes for schizophrenia: High-resolution chromosome ideogram representation. *Am. J. Med. Genet. B Neuropsychiatr. Genet. Part B* **2016**, *1B*, 181–202. [CrossRef] [PubMed]
24. Weber, F.; Chung, S.; Beier, K.T.; Xu, M.; Luo, L.; Dan, Y. Control of REM sleep by ventral medulla GABAergic neurons. *Nature* **2015**, *526*, 435–438. [CrossRef] [PubMed]
25. Reischl, S.; Kramer, A. Kinases and phosphatases in the mammalian circadian clock. *FEBS Lett.* **2011**, *585*, 1393–1399. [CrossRef] [PubMed]
26. Yin, L.; Wang, J.; Klein, P.S.; Lazar, M.A. Nuclear receptor Rev-Erbα is a critical lithium-sensitive component of the circadian clock. *Science* **2006**, *311*, 1002–1005. [CrossRef] [PubMed]
27. Zeidner, L.C.; Buescher, J.L.; Phiel, C.J. A novel interaction between Glycogen Synthase Kinase-3α (GSK-3α) and the scaffold protein receptor for activated C-Kinase 1 (RACK1) regulates the circadian clock. *Int. J. Biochem. Mol. Biol.* **2011**, *2*, 318–327. [PubMed]
28. Tarazi, F.I.; Tomasini, E.C.; Baldessarini, R.J. Postnatal development of dopamine D4-like receptors in rat forebrain regions: Comparison with D2-like receptors. *Brain Res. Dev. Brain Res.* **1998**, *110*, 227–233. [CrossRef]
29. Kanehisa, M.; Furumichi, M.; Tanabe, M.; Sato, Y.; Morishima, K. KEGG: New perspectives on genomes, pathways, diseases and drugs. *Nucleic Acids Res.* **2017**, *45*, D353–D361. [CrossRef] [PubMed]
30. Kanehisa, M.; Sato, Y.; Kawashima, M.; Furumichi, M.; Tanabe, M. KEGG as a reference resource for gene and protein annotation. *Nucleic Acids Res.* **2016**, *44*, D457–D462. [CrossRef] [PubMed]
31. Kanehisa, M.; Goto, S. KEGG: Kyoto Encyclopedia of Genes and Genomes. *Nucleic Acids Res.* **2000**, *28*, 27–30. [CrossRef] [PubMed]
32. Lavezzi, A.M.; Casale, V.; Oneda, R.; Weese-Mayer, D.E.; Matturri, L. Sudden infant death syndrome and sudden intrauterine unexplained death: Correlation between hypoplasia of raphé nuclei and serotonin transporter gene promoter polymorphism. *Pediatr. Res.* **2009**, *66*, 22–27. [CrossRef] [PubMed]
33. Severson, C.A.; Wang, W.; Pieribone, V.A.; Dohle, C.I.; Richerson, G.B. Midbrain serotoninergic neurons are central pH chemoreceptors. *Nat. Neurosci.* **2003**, *6*, 1139–1140. [CrossRef] [PubMed]
34. Gaspar, P.; Cases, O.; Maroteaux, L. The developmental role of serotonin: News from mouse molecular genetics. *Nat. Rev. Neurosci.* **2003**, *4*, 1002–1012. [CrossRef] [PubMed]
35. Haydon, P.G.; McCobb, D.P.; Kater, S.B. Serotonin selectively inhibits growth cone motility and synaptogenesis of specific identified neurons. *Science* **1984**, *226*, 561–564. [CrossRef] [PubMed]
36. Lauder, J.M. Ontogeny of the serotonergic system in the rat: Serotonin as a developmental signal. *Ann. N. Y. Acad. Sci.* **1990**, *600*, 297–313. [CrossRef] [PubMed]
37. McCarthy, D.; Lueras, P.; Bhide, P.G. Elevated dopamine levels during gestation produce region-specific decreases in neurogenesis and subtle deficits in neuronal numbers. *Brain Res.* **2007**, *1182*, 11–25. [CrossRef] [PubMed]
38. Popolo, M.; McCarthy, D.M.; Bhide, P. Influence of dopamine on precursor cell proliferation and differentiation in the embryonic mouse telencephalon. *Dev. Neurosci.* **2004**, *26*, 229–244. [CrossRef] [PubMed]
39. Fitzsimons, C.P.; Herbert, J.; Schouten, M.; Meijer, O.C.; Lucassen, P.J.; Lightman, S. Circadian and ultradian glucocorticoid rhythmicity: Implications for the effects of glucocorticoids on neural stem cells and adult hippocampal neurogenesis. *Front. Neuroendocrinol.* **2016**, *41*, 44–58. [CrossRef] [PubMed]

40. Tam, S.K.; Pritchett, D.; Brown, L.A.; Foster, R.G.; Bannerman, D.M.; Peirson, S.N. Sleep and circadian rhythm disruption and recognition memory in schizophrenia. *Methods Enzymol.* **2015**, *552*, 325–349. [PubMed]
41. Iyer, R.; Wang, T.A.; Gillette, M.U. Circadian gating of neuronal functionality: A basis for iterative metaplasticity. *Front. Syst. Neurosci.* **2014**, *8*, 164. [CrossRef] [PubMed]

9

Morphometric Analysis of Recognized Genes for Autism Spectrum Disorders and Obesity in Relationship to the Distribution of Protein-Coding Genes on Human Chromosomes

Austen B. McGuire †, Syed K. Rafi †, Ann M. Manzardo and Merlin G. Butler *

Departments of Psychiatry & Behavioral Sciences and Pediatrics, University of Kansas Medical Center, Kansas City, KS 66160, USA; austenmcguire@gmail.com (A.B.M.); rafigene@yahoo.com (S.K.R.); amanzardo@kumc.edu (A.M.M.)

* Correspondence: mbutler4@kumc.edu

† These authors contributed equally to this work.

Academic Editor: Nicholas Delihas

Abstract: Mammalian chromosomes are comprised of complex chromatin architecture with the specific assembly and configuration of each chromosome influencing gene expression and function in yet undefined ways by varying degrees of heterochromatinization that result in Giemsa (G) negative euchromatic (light) bands and G-positive heterochromatic (dark) bands. We carried out morphometric measurements of high-resolution chromosome ideograms for the first time to characterize the total euchromatic and heterochromatic chromosome band length, distribution and localization of 20,145 known protein-coding genes, 790 recognized autism spectrum disorder (ASD) genes and 365 obesity genes. The individual lengths of G-negative euchromatin and G-positive heterochromatin chromosome bands were measured in millimeters and recorded from scaled and stacked digital images of 850-band high-resolution ideograms supplied by the International Society of Chromosome Nomenclature (ISCN) 2013. Our overall measurements followed established banding patterns based on chromosome size. G-negative euchromatic band regions contained 60% of protein-coding genes while the remaining 40% were distributed across the four heterochromatic dark band sub-types. ASD genes were disproportionately overrepresented in the darker heterochromatic sub-bands, while the obesity gene distribution pattern did not significantly differ from protein-coding genes. Our study supports recent trends implicating genes located in heterochromatin regions playing a role in biological processes including neurodevelopment and function, specifically genes associated with ASD.

Keywords: G-negative euchromatin; G-positive heterochromatin; chromosome organization; high-resolution chromosome ideograms; protein-coding genes; obesity genes; autism spectrum disorder (ASD) genes

1. Introduction

Over the course of evolution, the architecture of chromosome structure has become substantially complex with the specific assembly and configuration of each chromosome influencing gene expression and function [1]. There is a need within the field of genetics to better understand chromosome structure and organization, including factors that influence chromosome function and gene location [2]. One aspect of chromosomal organizational research has sought to understand chromatin architecture, the combination of DNA and proteins within a nucleosome with condensation of the expansively long strands of DNA to help store and maintain DNA, the building blocks of genes (e.g., [3,4]).

The chromatin of eukaryotic chromosomes is divided into two main categories: euchromatin and heterochromatin. These regions in each chromosome contain different histone modifications that impact gene expression and DNA packaging styles [5].

Euchromatin chromosome regions tend to be less compact than the more tightly packed heterochromatin regions [5]. At most times during the cell cycle, the euchromatin region decondenses during interphase [6], and the less condensed packaging style is associated with greater gene transcription and activity with early replication [7,8]. Unlike euchromatin, heterochromatin regions are thought to contain less transcription and gene activity with later replication. Heterochromatin is further divided into two subtypes with distinct gene activity (expression) profiles: constitutive and facultative [9–11]. Constitutive heterochromatin is thought to be inactive (not expressed) while facultative heterochromatin may be either active or inactive [12] and less studied compared to the euchromatin regions in the genome [5,13,14]. The remodeling of facultative heterochromatin is known to silence euchromatin-based functional genes due to the gradual gain of lysine methylation in heterochromatic regions, but DNA sequencing of the heterochromatin regions is challenging due to the length and repetitive nature of the code [14]. Recent evidence suggests that heterochromatin may play an important role in development [13,15,16], such as the role of facultative heterochromatin in transcription-associated chromatin remodeling complexes. Heterochromatin regions were once thought to be largely inactive and only important in gene-expression silencing, but facultative heterochromatin is known to change and decondense, thereby allowing for transcription [10,17]. Chromatin remodeling is therefore reversible and dynamic but required for timely activation of functional genes during development [13]. More research is needed to better understand and elucidate differences and similarities between euchromatin and heterochromatin regions and their influence on gene position and activity.

Chromosome-banding methods have been used to visually delineate euchromatin from heterochromatin regions in the study of human chromosomes for more than 45 years. Chromosome banding is applied in the clinical setting for identification of structural and numerical anomalies with an average band accounting for about five megabases of DNA. Chromosome-banding techniques assimilate the DNA nucleotide sequence, associated proteins and functional organization of the chromosome through the use of DNA-staining procedures, most commonly Giesma stain. Giemsa preferentially stains transcriptionally less active, AT-nucleotide-rich sequences associated with heterochromatin regions, referred to as G-dark or Giemsa-positive, while the relatively active GC-nucleotide-rich euchromatin regions stain less intensely, leading these locations to be referred to as G-light or Giemsa-negative [18]. Earlier studies report that GC-nucleotide-poor regions constitute 63% of the human genome, whereas GC-nucleotide-rich regions make up 37% [19].

Protein-coding genes are responsible for the production of proteins to support cellular growth and functioning. The number of protein-coding genes has been estimated at 21,000 (e.g., [14]) and are distributed unevenly among the 24 different chromosomes as represented on high-resolution Ensembl ideograms (Ensembl, available at: http://uswest.ensembl.org/Homo_sapiens/Location/Genome?redirect=no) [20]. The greatest number of protein-coding genes are located on chromosomes 1, 19, 11, and 17, respectively, with the least number of protein-coding genes located on chromosomes Y, 21, 13, and 18 [21], not reflecting the size of the chromosome. However, chromosome 1 is considered the largest chromosome, and chromosome 19 is one of the smallest [21]. The distribution of genome-wide protein-coding genes among the chromosomes is reported by numerous credited sources, such as Ensembl [21] and the Genetics Home Reference provided through the National Institutes of Health (available at: http://ghr.nlm.nih.gov/chromosomes); however, less is known about the distribution of protein-coding genes among euchromatin and heterochromatin regions of the chromosomes. Distribution patterns associated with chromosome banding and proximity to fragile sites (regions susceptible to changes, disturbances and instability) could affect gene function or their location in relationship to subsets of protein-coding genes impacting different organ systems' development and function.

The current study was set forth to descriptively characterize and advance knowledge on the distribution of known genome-wide protein-coding genes in relationship to the G-negative euchromatin, G-positive heterochromatin banding regions and fragile sites, chromosome band locations and chromosome size and disease states for genes recognized in autism spectrum disorders (ASD) and obesity [22,23]. Analyzing the distribution and relationship of genome-wide protein-coding genes in comparison with clinically relevant and associated genes for neurodevelopment and brain function (e.g., ASD) and those involved in the peripheral system (e.g., obesity) could increase our understanding of gene location and function influenced by chromosomal euchromatin and heterochromatin regions in development and disease. Genome-wide protein-coding genes associated with these two gene disorder groups will encompass the full range of the human genome with a large number of genes distributed across the 24 chromosomes. ASD is a spectrum of neurological disorders with known genetic influences and estimated heritability as high as 90% [24], while obesity is a systemic-based energy imbalanced disorder with an average heritability of approximately 50% [25]. The number of recognized genes and their location in both disease state gene sets have recently been summarized [26,27]. The functional status of known and candidate ASD and obesity genes could be implied by their locations within the predominately active G-negative euchromatin or inactive G-positive heterochromatin bands on high-resolution chromosome ideograms. Hence, the purpose of the current study is to compile and examine the distribution of all known genome-wide protein-coding genes from published ideograms among the individual human chromosomes and their location in euchromatin and heterochromatin regions at each band level. Additionally, we will compare for the first time the distribution of protein-coding genes with clinically relevant and known ASD and obesity disease-causing genes to characterize and compare their relationship at the chromosome level and to recognize any deviation from the total protein-coding gene distribution patterns.

2. Results and Discussion

We conducted a morphometric analysis of published high-resolution chromosome ideograms to descriptively characterize the distribution and location of currently recognized relevant candidate or known genes for ASD, obesity and the total number of genome-wide protein-coding genes (see Figure 1). We measured and recorded the physical size (length in millimeters) of each chromosome as rendered ideogram representation of metaphase chromosomes along with their gene group status (*i.e.*, protein-coding [20], ASD [27], or obesity [26]). The location for each gene and distribution were determined from data collected from authoritative websites or published peer-reviewed sources. We then determined the location of these genes either on G-negative euchromatin bands or G-positive heterochromatin bands (and sub-bands) across each chromosome-based ideogram (see Figure 2). We determined their regional and chromosomal distribution patterns, and studied their position in relation to the physical size of the G-negative and G-positive chromatin as seen at the 850 high-resolution band level on the ISCN (2013) chromosome ideograms developed and scaled from cytological data [18] which are mostly equivalent to the high-resolution Ensembl ideograms, or in relation to the known genome-wide protein-coding, ASD, and obesity gene locations across the chromosomes. The Ensembl ideograms are based on chromosomes in the uncondensed state and may not necessarily reflect differential chromatin condensation in the structure of a metaphase chromosome whereby the heterochromatin may occupy different linear space than the euchromatin. However, a large positive correlation was found between the number of protein-coding and ASD genes (r = 0.65) per chromosome and between protein-coding and obesity genes (r = 0.85) per chromosome.

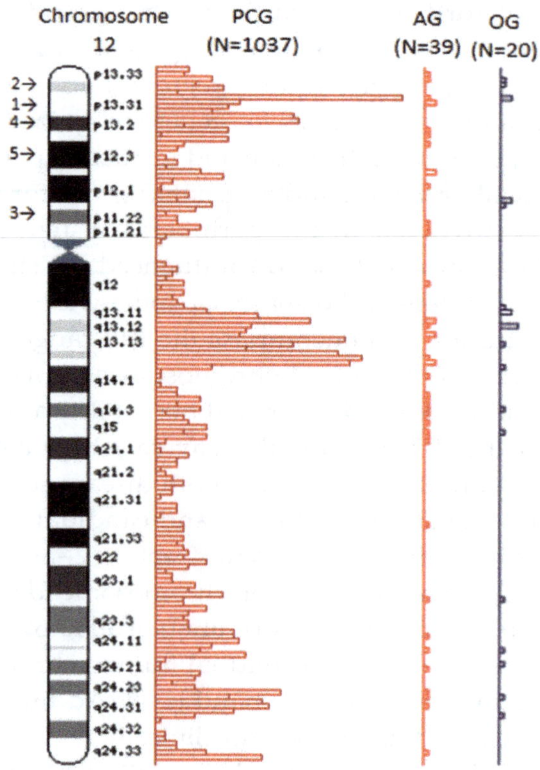

Figure 1. Sample chromosome ideogram with protein-coding, autism and obesity gene frequency distributions by Giemsa band. Ideogram representation of chromosome 12 taken from Genome Reference Consortium Ensembl website (http://uswest.ensembl.org/Homo_sapiens/Location/Genome) [21]. PCG = Protein-coding gene distribution, AG = Autism gene distribution, OG = Obesity gene distribution. 1 = Example of color 1 (euchromatin), 2 = Example of color 2 (heterochromatin), 3 = Example of color 3 (heterochromatin), 4 = Example of color 4 (heterochromatin), 5 = Example of color 5 (heterochromatin).

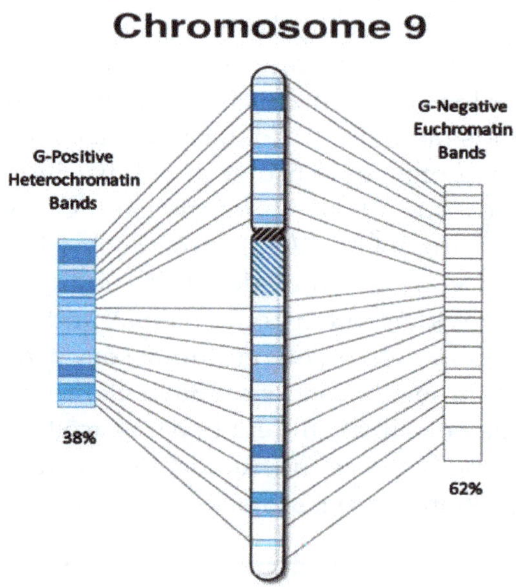

Figure 2. Sample stacked chromosome ideogram.

2.1. Gene Distributions

Our overall measurements followed known and established banding patterns based upon chromosome size (see Table 1 and Figure 3). Chromosomes were arranged in size from number 1 to chromosome Y, except for the X chromosome and when the removal of the qh, centromeric, and acrocentric chromosome p arm regions altered this pattern. For example, chromosome 1 is the longest chromosome, but after removal of the qh region, it became shorter in size than chromosome 2. Altogether, G-negative euchromatin regions encompassed 56.4% of the genome (see Table 1), which contrasts earlier reports of GC-nucleotide-rich regions which only constitute approximately 37% of the human genome [19]. Each chromosome appears to follow this same distribution of approximately 60% for G-negative euchromatin DNA and 40% for G-positive heterochromatin DNA. However, chromosomes 16, 17 and 22 deviated from this pattern with >70% G-negative euchromatin DNA. These chromosomes had at least a threefold difference in euchromatin *vs.* heterochromatin DNA with chromosome 22 having the highest G-negative euchromatin/G-positive heterochromatin ratio of 4.28. This observation deviated considerably from G-negative euchromatin/G-positive heterochromatin expected ratios based on similarly sized chromosomes (*i.e.*, chromosome 21 (1.80 ratio) and chromosome Y (2.03 ratio)).

Protein-coding, ASD, and obesity genes followed a similar distributional pattern across the genome (all 24 chromosomes) based upon the relative length of the individual chromosome (see Table 2) with the number of genes located on a chromosome proportional to the length of the chromosome. As chromosome size decreases, the percentage of total genes per chromosome also decreases. For example, chromosome 1 is the largest chromosome, prior to removal of the qh region, and harbors one of the greatest numbers of protein-coding, ASD, and obesity genes, whereas chromosome 22 is one of the smallest chromosomes and contains one of the smallest numbers of protein-coding, ASD, and obesity genes. Deviations from normal patterns were found, e.g., for chromosome 19 which encompassed 2.3% of the total genome size but contained 7.2% of the total number of protein-coding genes. Chromosome 11 makes up 4.6% of the genome length but possessed 7.4% of obesity genes. Chromosome X makes up 5.6% of the genome length but contained 9.1% of the ASD genes reflecting the established gender disparity with male preponderance seen in ASD (4:1 male:female) [28]. The influence of the observed deviations relative to the typical distribution pattern is unclear and will require further research.

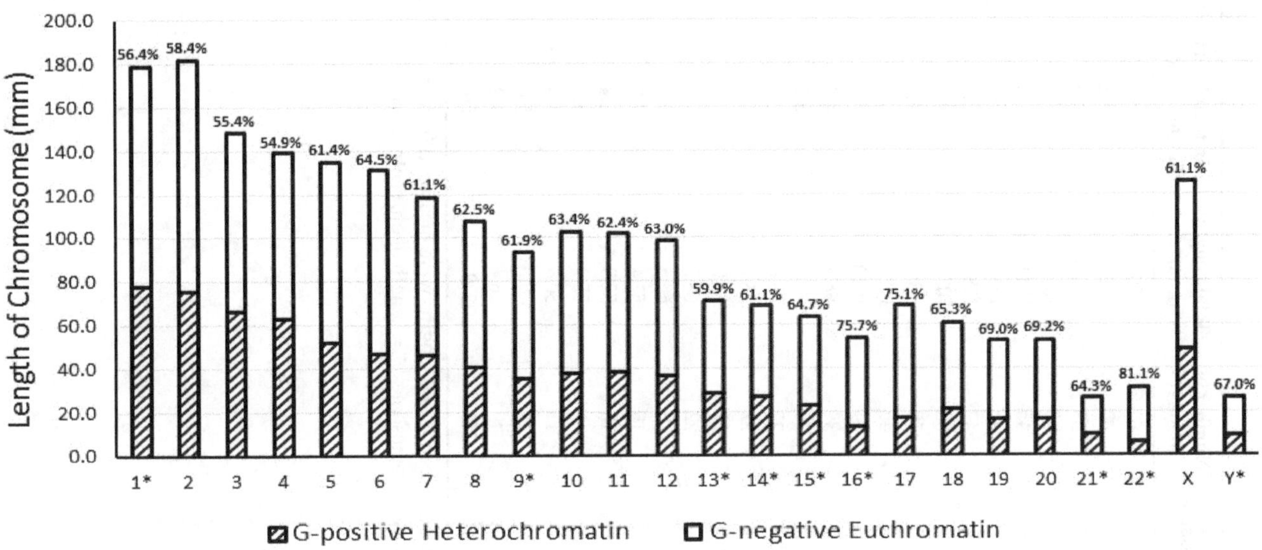

Figure 3. Giemsa band distributions as a proportion of chromosome length. * = Length of qh, centromeric and/or acrocentric chromosome p arm regions were excluded. Percentage above bar for each chromosome represents the proportion of G-negative euchromatin per chromosome.

Table 1. High-resolution chromosome ideogram measurements and Giemsa banding patterns.

Chromosome	Number of Bands	Total Length (mm)	% of Total Length of all Chromosomes	Total Euchromatin Length (mm)	% Euchromatin	Total Heterochromatin Length (mm)	% Heterochromatin	Ratio of Euchromatin/Heterochromatin
1 *	62	178.9	8.0	101.0	56.4	78.0	43.6	1.30
2	62	182.0	8.1	106.3	58.4	75.7	41.6	1.40
3	59	148.8	6.6	82.4	55.4	66.4	44.6	1.24
4	45	139.5	6.2	76.5	54.9	62.9	45.1	1.22
5	45	134.9	6.0	82.8	61.4	52.1	38.6	1.59
6	48	131.2	5.9	84.6	64.5	46.6	35.5	1.81
7	42	118.9	5.3	72.6	61.1	46.2	38.9	1.57
8	38	107.9	4.8	67.5	62.5	40.4	37.5	1.67
9 *	38	93.6	4.2	58.0	61.9	35.6	38.1	1.63
10	40	102.9	4.6	65.2	63.4	37.7	36.6	1.73
11	34	102.1	4.6	63.7	62.4	38.4	37.6	1.66
12	39	98.8	4.4	62.3	63.0	36.6	37.0	1.70
13 *	31	71.1	3.2	42.6	59.9	28.6	40.1	1.49
14 *	27	68.6	3.1	41.9	61.1	26.7	38.9	1.57
15 *	27	63.7	2.8	41.2	64.7	22.5	35.3	1.83
16 *	22	54.0	2.4	40.9	75.7	13.1	24.3	3.11
17	22	68.7	3.1	51.6	75.1	17.1	24.9	3.02
18	18	60.5	2.7	39.5	65.3	21.0	34.7	1.88
19	15	52.4	2.3	36.2	69.0	16.3	31.1	2.22
20	18	52.8	2.4	36.6	69.2	16.3	30.8	2.25
21 *	9	25.9	1.2	16.7	64.3	9.3	35.7	1.80
22 *	11	30.8	1.4	25.0	81.1	5.8	18.9	4.28
X	38	125.3	5.6	76.6	61.1	48.7	38.9	1.57
Y *	8	26.4	1.2	17.7	67.0	8.7	33.0	2.03
Total/Average	798	2239.7	100.0	1389.1	56.4	850.7	43.6	1.63

Chromosome bands and lengths were measured from ISCN (2013) high-resolution ideograms magnified ×125%. Measurements do not reflect the actual size of human mitotic metaphase chromosomes. * = Length of qh, centromeric and/or acrocentric chromosome p arm regions were excluded.

Table 2. Protein coding gene distribution among G-negative euchromatin and G-positive heterochromatin chromosome regions and relationship to autism and obesity genes.

Chromosome	PCG Sum	% of Total PCG	PCG in Eu	% of PCG in Eu	PCG in Het	% of PCG in Het	AG Sum	% of Total AG	AG in Eu	% of AG in Eu	AG in Het	% of AG in Het	OG Sum	% of Total OG	OG in Eu	% of OG in Eu	OG in Het	% of OG in Het
1 *	2056	10.1	1259	61.2	797	38.8	[illegible]	8.5	32	47.8	35	52.2	36	9.9	19	52.8	17	47.2
2	1255	6.3	867	69.1	388	30.9	[illegible]	8.6	40	58.8	28	41.2	31	8.5	19	61.3	12	38.7
3	1069	5.3	623	58.3	446	41.7	[illegible]	7.1	28	50.9	27	49.1	18	4.9	11	61.1	7	38.9
4	763	3.8	467	61.2	296	38.8	[illegible]	2.9	16	69.6	7	30.4	18	4.9	12	66.7	6	33.3
5	864	4.3	513	59.4	351	40.6	[illegible]	5.6	29	65.9	15	34.1	16	4.4	12	75.0	4	25.0
6	1041	5.1	520	50.0	521	50.0	[illegible]	4.7	13	36.1	23	63.9	25	6.8	13	52.0	12	48.0
7	962	4.7	655	68.1	307	31.9	[illegible]	6.6	27	51.9	25	48.1	17	4.7	10	58.8	7	41.2
8	662	3.3	409	61.8	253	38.2	[illegible]	3.2	17	68.0	8	32.0	14	3.8	7	50.0	7	50.0
9 *	769	3.8	529	68.8	240	31.2	[illegible]	3.2	17	68.0	8	32.0	7	1.9	5	71.4	2	28.6
10	737	3.6	401	54.4	336	45.6	[illegible]	4.2	15	45.5	18	54.5	12	3.3	5	41.7	7	58.3
11	1284	6.4	590	46.0	694	54.0	[illegible]	4.9	24	61.5	15	38.5	27	7.4	16	59.3	11	40.7
12	1037	5.1	610	58.8	427	41.2	[illegible]	4.9	25	64.1	14	35.9	20	5.5	14	70.0	6	30.0
13 *	311	1.5	181	58.2	130	41.8	[illegible]	1.5	6	50.0	6	50.0	6	1.6	2	33.3	4	66.7
14 *	807	4.0	550	68.2	257	31.8	[illegible]	2.2	8	47.1	9	52.9	6	1.6	4	66.7	2	33.3
15 *	604	3.0	340	56.3	264	43.7	[illegible]	4.4	20	57.1	15	42.9	18	4.9	12	66.7	6	33.3
16 *	852	4.2	622	73.0	230	27.0	[illegible]	4.3	23	67.6	11	32.4	22	6.0	12	54.5	10	45.5
17	1176	5.8	696	59.2	480	40.8	[illegible]	4.3	26	76.5	8	23.5	15	4.1	13	86.7	2	13.3
18	278	1.4	170	61.2	108	38.8	[illegible]	1.8	9	64.3	5	35.7	5	1.4	4	80.0	1	20.0
19	1422	7.2	708	49.8	714	50.2	[illegible]	2.5	10	50.0	10	50.0	17	4.7	6	35.3	11	64.7
20	539	2.7	337	62.5	202	37.5	[illegible]	1.5	6	50.0	6	50.0	9	2.5	5	55.6	4	44.4
21 *	221	1.2	157	71.0	64	29.0	[illegible]	1.1	5	55.6	4	44.4	0	0.0	0	0.0	0	0.0
22 *	487	2.5	301	61.8	186	38.2	[illegible]	2.8	17	77.3	5	22.7	7	1.9	2	28.6	5	71.4
X	811	4.0	503	62.0	308	38.0	[illegible]	9.1	40	55.6	32	44.4	19	5.2	8	42.1	11	57.9
Y *	138	0.7	75	54.3	63	45.7	[illegible]	0.4	2	66.7	1	33.3	0	0.0	0	0.0	0	0.0
Total/Average	20,145	100.0	12,083	60.0	8062	40.0	[illegible]	100.0	455	57.6	335	42.4	365	100.0	211	57.8	154	42.2

* = Length and genes of qh, centromeric and/or acrocentric chromosome p arm regions were excluded. PCG = Protein Coding Genes, AG = Autism Genes, OG = Obesity Genes, Eu = Euchromatin, Het = Heterochromatin.

This review of morphometric and Giemsa banding chromosome characteristics with respect to the distribution of selected gene groups per length of chromosome did find that many chromosomes possessed a higher proportion of protein-coding genes (e.g., 11, 14, 16, 17 and 22), ASD genes (e.g., 15, 16, 17 and 22), and/or obesity genes (e.g., 11, 15, 16, 17 and 22) than predicted based on their chromosome length. However, eight chromosomes (4, 5, 8, 9, 10, 13, 18 and Y) contained proportionally fewer genes representing the three gene groups than expected based upon their size. In addition, 13 chromosomes (2, 3, 4, 5, 6, 7, 8, 9, 10, 13, 18, X and Y) contained fewer protein-coding genes, 11 chromosomes (4, 5, 6, 8, 9, 10, 13, 14, 18, 20 and Y) had fewer ASD genes, and 10 chromosomes (3, 4, 5, 7, 8, 9, 10, 13, 14 and 18) had fewer obesity genes than expected based on size. The X chromosome had the greatest proportion of ASD genes above the expected level, chromosome 19 had the greatest proportion of protein-coding genes above expected, and chromosome 16 had the greatest proportion of obesity genes, again above expected based upon the length of the chromosome.

2.2. *Chromatin Subtyping by Giemsa Band Intensity and Fragile Sites*

2.2.1. Chromatin Subtyping

Analysis of chromatin subtype considered both genome-wide and chromosome-level gene distributions, and, as may be anticipated, the greatest number of genome-wide protein-coding (60%), ASD (57.6%) and obesity (57.8%) genes were located in the G-negative euchromatin band type (see Table 3). No significant differences were found between the proportion of ASD, obesity or protein-coding genes for euchromatin *vs.* overall heterochromatin regions ($\chi^2 = 2.4$, df = 2, $p = 0.29$). However, an asymmetric distribution pattern of ASD, obesity and protein-coding genes over the range of G-band intensity levels was observed across the genome. Figure 4 shows the proportion of genes per group by chromatin G-band intensity with light to dark banding scaled numerically by color from 1 to 5. As shown, the proportion of protein-coding genes progressively decreased from 12.6% to 6.8% as the banding color intensity increased (became darker representing colors 2 through 5) for the heterochromatin regions. However, the ASD and obesity genes appear to cluster more in the G-positive heterochromatin (colors 2–5) bands, particularly in medium grey (color 3) and dark grey (colors 4 and 5) as compared to light grey (color 2) and G-negative euchromatin (white, color 1) bands. The lowest number of ASD genes (*i.e.*, 69) were found in the G-positive heterochromatin band color 2 and the lowest number of obesity genes were found in the G-positive heterochromatin band color 5 (see Table 3). This overall difference was statistically significant ($\chi^2 = 31.6$, df = 8, $p < 0.0001$). Examination of standard residuals for ASD genes showed z = +2.21 (G-positive band color 4) and z = +3.14 (G-positive band color 5) relative to obesity and protein-coding genes and z = −2.97 for G-band color 2 (Table 4).

Table 3. Summary data of chromosome bands and genes by group for each chromatin type.

Chromatin Type	Number of Bands	PCG Sum	% of Total PCG	AG Sum	% of Total AG	OG Sum	% of Total OG
G-negative Euchromatin (Color 1)	417	12,083	60.0	455	57.6	211	57.8
G-positive Heterochromatin (Colors 2–5)	381	8062	40.0	335	42.4	154	42.2
Heterochromatin-Color 2	*89*	*2547*	*12.6*	*69*	*8.7*	*40*	*11.0*
Heterochromatin-Color 3	*123*	*2499*	*12.4*	*105*	*13.3*	*57*	*15.6*
Heterochromatin-Color 4	*88*	*1638*	*8.1*	*83*	*10.5*	*36*	*9.9*
Heterochromatin-Color 5	*81*	*1378*	*6.8*	*78*	*9.9*	*21*	*5.8*
Total	798	20,145	100.0	790	100.0	365	100.0

PCG = Protein-coding Genes, AG = Autism Genes, OG = Obesity Genes. Number of bands and genes were calculated after removal of qh, centromeric and acrocentric chromosome p arm regions.

Table 4. Summary of the percentage deviation with standardized residuals (z-scores) for chromosome bands and genes by group and chromatin type.

Group	G-Negative Euchromatin Band		G-Positive Heterochromatin Bands							
	Color 1		Color 2		Color 3		Color 4		Color 5	
	Number of Genes	*Percentage (z-Score)*	*Number of Genes*	*Percentage (z-Score)*	*Number of Genes*	*Percentage (z-Score)*	*Number of Genes*	*Percentage (z-Score)*	*Number of Genes*	*Percentage (z-Score)*
ASD	455	−3.8 (−0.82)	69	−30 (−2.97) *	105	+6.4 (+0.63)	83	+27.4 (+2.21) *	78	+42.4 (+3.14) *
Obesity	211	−3.4 (−0.51)	40	−12.1 (−0.82)	57	+25 (+1.69)	36	+19.6 (+1.07)	21	−17 (−0.86)
PCG	12,083	+0.2 (+0.23)	2547	+1.4 (+0.7)	2499	−0.7 (−0.35)	1638	−1.4 (−0.58)	1378	−1.4 (−0.51)

Chi-Square test percentage deviation and standardized residuals for each cell. ASD = Autism spectrum disorder, N = 790 genes; Obesity, N = 365 genes; PCG = Protein-coding genes, N = 20,145 genes. * Greater than or less than 2 standard deviational z-scores.

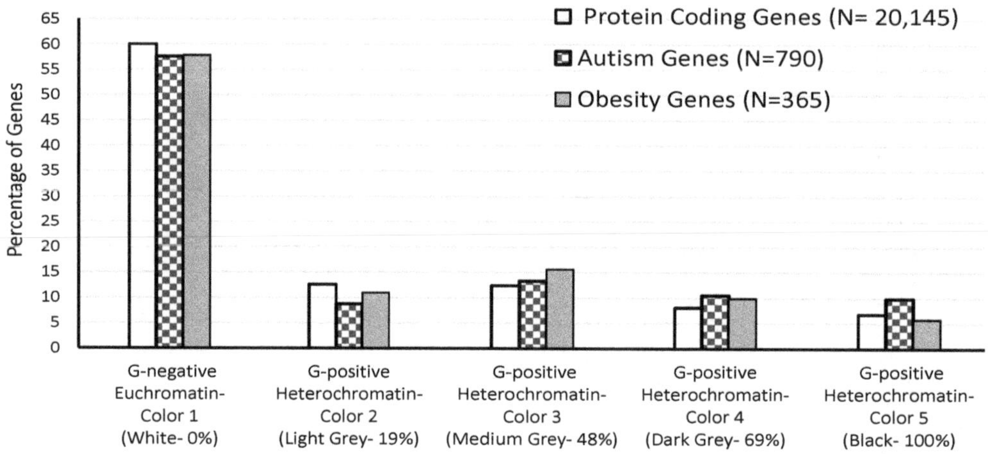

Figure 4. Genome-wide distribution of protein-coding, autism and obesity genes by Giemsa band intensity rating. Calculations excluded genes located in the qh, centromeric and acrocentric chromosome p arm regions.

Further analysis at the chromosome level (see Figure 5) showed that the X chromosome harbored a 2.28-fold higher proportion of ASD genes in relation to protein-coding genes, followed by chromosome 15 with a 1.5-fold higher portion of ASD genes; chromosome 7 (1.4-fold); chromosomes 2 (1.4-fold); chromosome 3 (1.3-fold); and chromosome 5 (1.3-fold). Examination of gene distributions for ASD, obesity and protein-coding genes on the X chromosome did not achieve statistical significance ($\chi^2 = 4.1$, df $= 2$, $p = 0.13$). The chromosomes with the highest proportion of ASD genes also had known ASD gene hotspots, such as: 15q11-q13, 15q13.3, 7q11.23, 7q32.2, Xq28, 22q13 [29], indicating these gene hotspots are dispersed throughout the genome. Chromosome 19 contained the lowest portion of ASD genes in relation to the number of protein-coding genes (0.4-fold differences). Unlike the X chromosome with the highest proportion of ASD genes (*i.e.*, 2.3-fold) in relation to protein-coding genes, the Y chromosome contained nearly four-fold fewer ASD genes (*i.e.*, 0.6-fold) in relation to protein-coding genes. Chromosome 15 had the greatest disparity between protein-coding and obesity genes (2.5-fold) followed by chromosome 9 with a twofold difference and chromosome 19 with 1.53-fold. The least difference in the proportion of obesity genes relative to protein-coding genes was seen for chromosome 15 (0.6-fold), while excluding chromosome 21 and Y as they did not contain recognized obesity genes.

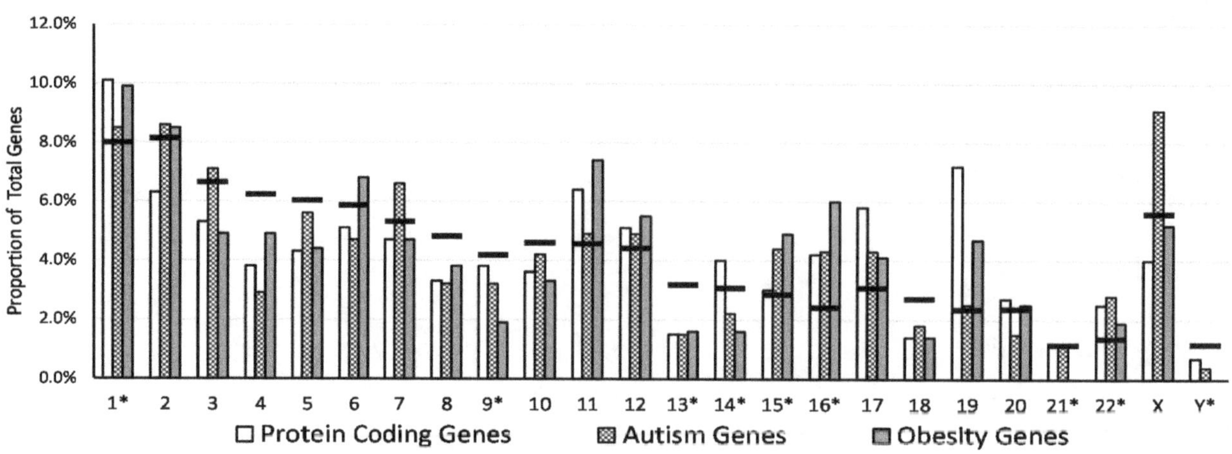

Figure 5. Distribution and proportion of protein-coding, autism and obesity genes by chromosome. * = Length and genes of qh, centromeric and/or acrocentric chromosome p arm regions were excluded. Horizontal black line (—) for each chromosome represents the expected proportion of genes based on chromosome size relative to the total length of all chromosomes summed together.

To further understand and conceptualize the different gene group distributions across chromosomes, chromosomes were ranked based on length, number of protein-coding, ASD, and obesity genes from the longest length or with the most number of genes to the shortest length or with the least number of genes per each gene group (see Table 5). As previously described, the gene number is generally positively correlated with the chromosome length which is reflected in the rank designation for the different gene groups. Deviations from this pattern were found for chromosome 4 with a low ranking for the number of protein-coding and autism genes compared with a relatively high rank based on length.

Table 5. Chromosome rank order by length and gene frequency distribution for protein coding, autism and obesity genes.

Chromosome	Length Rank	Ratio of Euchromatin/ Heterochromatin	PCG Number Rank	AG Number Rank	OG Number Rank
1 *	2	1.30	1	3	1
2	1	1.40	4	2	2
3	3	1.24	6	4	8
4	4	1.22	15	16	9
5	5	1.59	10	6	13
6	6	1.81	7	9	4
7	8	1.57	9	5	11
8	9	1.67	12	14	15
9 *	13	1.63	14	15	18
10	10	1.73	16	13	16
11	11	1.66	3	7	3
12	12	1.70	8	8	6
13 *	14	1.49	21	21	20
14 *	15	1.57	13	19	21
15 *	17	1.83	18	10	10
16 *	19	3.11	11	11	5
17	16	3.02	5	12	14
18	18	1.88	22	20	22
19	21	2.22	2	18	12
20	20	2.25	19	22	17
21 *	23	1.80	23	23	23
22 *	22	4.28	20	17	19
X	7	1.57	12	1	7
Y *	24	[illegible]	24	21	24

Chromosomes were ranked from 1 (greatest) to 24 (least) based on either length or number of genes per chromosome. PCG = Protein Coding Genes, AG = Autism Genes, OG = Obesity Genes. * = Length and genes of qh, centromeric and/or acrocentric chromosome p arm regions were excluded.

Heterochromatin regions are historically associated with gene silencing or inactivity and areas of less genomic activity [16], but the distribution of euchromatin and heterochromatin regions is not uniform across the chromosomes. We found that heterochromatin DNA regions did contribute genetically with 42.4% of the ASD genes and 42.2% of obesity genes located within the G-positive heterochromatin regions (colors 2–5). This observation was similar to the distribution patterns seen in genome-wide protein-coding genes. Furthermore, our results when analyzing the distribution of genes among G-negative euchromatin and G-positive heterochromatin bands at the chromosomal level supported that heterochromatin regions are also places of active gene expression and not silenced, with an average distribution of the three gene groups across each chromosome with 60% for euchromatin bands and 40% for heterochromatin bands (see Table 2). However, the majority of genes were located within the heterochromatin DNA regions in several select chromosomes with chromosomes 6, 11 and 19 containing ⩾50% of the protein-coding genes as opposed to euchromatin DNA regions. Similarly, chromosomes 1, 6, 10 and 14 contained ⩾50% of the recognized ASD genes in the heterochromatin *vs.* euchromatin regions while chromosomes 8, 10, 13, 19, 22 and X contained ⩾50% of the recognized obesity genes in the heterochromatin *vs.* euchromatin regions.

The G-negative *vs.* G-positive chromosome banding is based on Giemsa staining patterns. Giemsa binds to phosphate groups along the chromosome and perhaps more intensely to those phosphate groups at regions of DNA where there are high amounts of adenine-thymine bonding and that are relatively gene poor. In contrast, less condensed chromatin which tends to be rich in guanine and cytosine (GC-rich) and more transcriptionally active incorporates less Giemsa stain. These regions appear as light bands of varying intensities depending on the degree of AT/GC distribution pattern and transcriptional activity within the light banded regions [30–32]. The Giesma banding and splitting of bands are evident when reviewing the ISCN (2013) ideograms in progression from the 300, 400, 550, 700, and 850-band levels [18]. Giemsa negative and light band(s) appear *de novo* within Giemsa-positive (dark), and rarely, Giemsa-positive (dark) finer bands have been depicted as appearing from larger Giemsa-negative band regions [33]. Hence, the heterochromatic G-positive bands have been shown to contain long stretches of euchromatin DNA which may become G-negative upon extension of the chromosome length, as observed in prometaphase or late prophase banding patterns which far exceed the high-resolution 850-band level [34]. Conversely, as chromosomes condense during early mitosis, their sub-bands fuse in a highly coordinated fashion [35]. Sub-band fusion occurs when two large sub-bands flanking one minor sub-band come together to form one band, which takes on the cytological characteristics of the original flanking sub-bands, when studied from prophase (>1250 bands per haploid set) to late metaphase (~300 bands). Transcriptionally active autism or obesity-susceptibility genes located within the dark Giemsa bands at the 850-band level may be explained if the chromatin is stretched farther (e.g., >2000 band level at the early prophase stage) as narrow, unrecognized G-negative euchromatin regions are embedded within the larger heterochromatin DNA region [36,37]. Overrepresentation of ASD genes in darker heterochromatin bands may reflect the sequestration of transcriptionally active neurodevelopmental genes to inactive chromosome regions following their phase of functional developmental activity.

2.2.2. Fragile Sites

Chromosome fragile sites are also of interest when examining the location or distribution of protein-coding or disease-causing genes located on chromosome bands within the genome. Fragile sites are highly susceptible to changes, disturbances, and instability and thus might select against the location of important protein-coding genes. Analysis of chromosomal fragile sites, specifically aphidicolin-induced CFSs (aCFSs), has revealed that chromatin band-type coverage was the greatest predictor of genome-wide chromosomal fragility and that the majority of aCFSs were within euchromatin regions [38]. Furthermore, Butler [39] also reported on folate-sensitive fragile sites or lesions located at the 350 (mid-metaphase) chromosome band level from peripheral blood cells in a cohort of 117 males with intellectual disability. All but three chromosomes (*i.e.*, 19, 21 and Y) contained fragile sites in cells grown in folate deficient-culture conditions in Medium 199 [39]. Although chromosome 19 did not show fragile sites, it contained the second highest number of protein-coding genes in our morphometric study. Recent studies have reported fragile sites on chromosome 19, but at a lower number in relationship to other chromosomes with a high number of protein-coding genes [40]. One could speculate that a selection against fragile sites on chromosome 19 could exist and is less likely to be susceptible to chromosome breakage or damage resulting from fragile sites due to the quality and/or quantity of specific genes (e.g., housekeeping) that are important for survival. Links have also been reported between autism and fragile sites (e.g., fragile X syndrome) with fragile site stability involving autism-susceptibility genes impacted by folate levels and metabolism [41]. Folate has a key role in the synthesis of DNA and control of DNA methylation [42].

Additionally, the study by Butler [39] reported that spontaneous fragile sites were more concentrated within G-positive heterochromatin bands as compared to G-negative euchromatin bands (e.g., 157 fragile sites distributed over 171 G-negative euchromatin bands *vs.* 144 fragile sites distributed over 127 G-positive heterochromatin bands excluding centromeric, qh and acrocentric chromosome p arm regions) from 6009 cells grown in folate deficient-culture conditions using Medium 199. There was a lower ratio for the number of euchromatin fragile sites and chromosome bands (*i.e.*, 0.92) as compared to the number of heterochromatin fragile sites and chromosome bands (*i.e.*, 1.13). This difference may suggest that fragile sites tend to appear in areas that are less gene-rich and thus less likely to impact genomic function. The ratio of 1.1 was lower for G-negative euchromatin fragile sites ($N = 157$) and G-positive heterochromatin fragile sites ($N = 144$) compared with the ratio of protein-coding genes at 1.5, ASD genes at 1.4 and obesity genes at 1.4 for G-negative euchromatin and G-positive heterochromatin bands reported in our morphometric study. A better understanding of the effects of autism and obesity-susceptibility genes in relation to location of chromatin type and fragile sites could help researchers in understanding the etiology of autism and obesity, and future studies could analyze the connection between fragile site and gene location and chromatin type for specific gene disorder groups beyond autism and obesity. Furthermore, one could determine if chromatin type has an effect on cancer-susceptibility genes and fragile site location, given the well-documented connection between cancer and fragile sites [43].

The molecular mechanism initiated to silence or activate heterochromatic genes appears to result from a balance between negative factors that promote formation of condensed higher-order chromatin structure and positively acting transcription factors that bind to regulatory sequences which activate gene expression [44]. In general, the acetylation of histones is linked to transcriptional activation with histone acetylation decreasing inter-nucleosome interaction, thereby allowing greater accessibility for gene regulation. Histone methylation of both histones and the DNA molecule further directs gene control implicated in disease which underscores the importance of the functional relationships between histone and DNA methylation in maintaining epigenetic traits. Those ASD and obesity genes that are found to be present in the Giemsa-positive dark regions that are of various shades at the 850-band level are expected to be relatively GC-rich regions in defined euchromatin regions embedded within the current dark Giemsa bands, and transcriptionally active with H3K79me1-active histone modifications, and perhaps, acetylation with H3K27ac [45]. At the fiber FISH chromatin level which is greater than 15-fold magnifications to 850-band ideograms, the so-called heterochromatic—dark band domains contain approximately 17% of active gene expression [37]. Even during the cell division at the metaphase stage, one can expect them to contain brief H3K79me1-rich stretches of nucleosomes/chromatin fiber. Additionally, there are at least 39 histone modifications that are classified into active histone modifications and repressive histone modifications for use in chromatin domain prediction. Active modifications are positively correlated with gene expression levels and are known to mark euchromatin genomic regions, whereas repressive modifications are negatively correlated with expression levels and marking heterochromatic domains. Given the fact that the functionality of protein-coding genes is dynamic (euchromatin to facultative heterochromatin status), and the fact that ASD and obesity-causing genes code for functional proteins—either structural or regulatory proteins—their apparent cytogenetic location at the Giemsa-facultative heterochromatic-dark banded regions of varying intensities, cannot necessarily be construed as entirely indicative of their functional inactivation. Hence, the importance of studying histone modifications is emphasized, as mutations in this process may affect most gene structure and biological processes [46,47].

The current study at the 850-band level shows a threefold decrease in the number of protein-coding genes as well as the ASD and obesity genes with an overrepresentation of ASD genes in the facultative G-positive heterochromatic dark band regions. Our examination of the distribution of the protein-coding genes, autism and obesity genes per chromosome and assessment of the disease gene frequency in relation to the chromosome length and G-band characterization was undertaken to examine for bias or skewness in the distribution of disease genes. It is established that a subset of current human chromosome arms or segments were derived from acrocentric chromosomes of ancestral origin including chromosomes 2 and 4 (with relatively recent changes) [48,49]. In addition, the Y chromosome was recently derived or evolved from the X chromosome through shedding of duplicated genes and by retaining and amplifying male-specific genes to compensate for the loss of recombination in order to maintain the integrity of those genes in the absence of recombination with the X chromosome [50].

3. Experimental Section

The individual length of each G-negative euchromatin and G-positive heterochromatin chromosome bands was measured in millimeters and recorded from the 850-band high-resolution ideograms supplied by the International Society of Chromosome Nomenclature (ISCN) 2013 based on scaled cytological data [18] then utilized to calculate the ratio of the two band types per chromosome and chromosome arm. Digital representations were prepared for each chromosome with scaled and stacked images that summarized euchromatin and heterochromatin band distributions over the length of each chromosome (see Figure 2). The images were devoid of centromeric regions, constitutive heterochromatic regions at 1qh, 9qh, 16qh, and Yqh, and acrocentric short (p) arms for chromosomes 13, 14, 15, 21 and 22. To increase size and improve resolution for measurement purposes, each ideogram was uniformly magnified (×125%) from the original source [18]. Each scaled image of the summarized euchromatin and heterochromatin chromosome regions was carefully measured using a battery-operated Pittsburgh 6-inch digital caliper (Harbor Freight Tools, Camarillo, CA, USA) and recorded to the one-hundredth of a millimeter. In addition, the total length of G-negative euchromatin and G-positive heterochromatin bands was measured and recorded for each individual chromosome and summarized over the entire genome. The total length of euchromatin and heterochromatin regions per chromosome was then used to calculate the percent length for each band type by dividing the length of each chromatin region for a given chromosome by the overall length of the whole genome.

The location of known genome-wide protein-coding genes was displayed on electronic high-resolution chromosome ideograms supplied by the Genome Reference Consortium at the public access authoritative Ensembl website (available at: http://uswest.ensembl.org/ Homo_sapiens/ Location/Genome) via whole-genome location-based displays [21]. The ideograms were last accessed from the website on 7 December 2014 and updated in August of 2014 using Gencode version GENCODE 21. The total number of genome-wide protein-coding genes for each band was estimated based upon the length in millimeters of each histogram bar illustrating the location of protein-coding genes on the images and arranged perpendicularly to the axis of the high-resolution G-banded represented chromosome ideograms [21]. Figure 1 provides an example of the images used and protein-coding gene distribution, along with the distributions and numbers of recognized ASD and obesity gene sets at the chromosome band level. The total length of the measured histogram bars representing the number of protein-coding genes was then summarized for each chromosome. This sum was divided by the number of protein-coding genes for that specific chromosome. The resulting quotient was used to derive the number of protein-coding genes in each individual histogram bar unit representing these genes in humans. Protein-coding genes were then counted by rounding to the nearest number representing a gene. Each horizontal bar was matched with its respective specific band on the chromosome, showing the distribution and location of the genes. If a band had multiple protein-coding gene histogram bars, the sum of all the bars for that band was then calculated to identify the number of genes per high-resolution chromosome band. Because we focused on euchromatin and heterochromatin chromosome regions, the negligible number of protein-coding genes located at the centromeric, qh and acrocentric chromosome short (p) arm regions were excluded from data analysis. The total number of genome-wide protein-coding genes calculated equaled 20,145, in agreement with the total gene count information from the Ensembl website.

The Ensembl 2014 chromosome ideograms matched the ISCN 2013 chromosome ideograms [18,21], except for seven locations. In each of these instances, the Ensembl ideogram did not contain sub-bands as noted in the ISCN ideograms (e.g., the Ensembl 2014 ideogram showed one band at 1q32.1, whereas the ISCN 2013 ideogram showed three sub-bands at 1q32.11, 1q32.12, and 1q32.13). In these instances, the total number of protein-coding genes for the band on the Ensembl 2014 ideogram was divided by three and evenly distributed across the three more specific sub-bands found in the ISCN 2013 ideogram. The fractional number of genes were rounded to the nearest whole number.

The comparison of protein-coding genes was undertaken in the current study with the 792 neurodevelopmental or functional genes currently recognized as playing a role in ASD and their known chromosome locations [27]. Two ASD genes were excluded from analysis because of their location in a qh, centromeric, or acrocentric chromosome p arm region. Locations for the remaining 790 genes were further refined based on their promotor-molecular locations on the chromosome using website sources such as the Online Inheritance of Man (OMIM) (available at: www.omim.org) and GeneCards (available at: https://www.genecards.org). Additionally, the recognized genes for ASD were then identified as either located on the G-negative (light) euchromatin or G-positive (dark) heterochromatin bands represented in the 850-band chromosome ideograms supplied by ISCN. The distribution of genes from a second gene group representing the obesity-related genes with metabolic or systemic function were also evaluated in a similar manner. A list of 365 clinically relevant and candidate genes for obesity were analyzed (five genes were excluded from the master list of 370 reported obesity genes [26]) based on their location in the qh, centromeric, or acrocentric chromosome p arm regions, and their locations were further refined as stated above before being placed on G-negative euchromatin or G-positive heterochromatin bands on each chromosome.

We further investigated differences among the varying levels of G-positive banding intensity (coloring) within specific chromosome regions compared with the single level (white color) for G-negative bands. Adobe Photoshop (2015) (Adobe Systems Incorporated, San Jose, CA, USA) was used to determine the levels of the G-positive band shading intensity (scaled numerically from 2 to 5 for lightest to darkest color) patterns within the heterochromatin regions on the high-resolution Ensembl chromosome ideograms. Each distinct band on the chromosome was scanned and examined using the Color Picker Tool in Adobe Photoshop to determine the degree of color intensity or darkness. Briefly, the tool pointer was hovered over the band and the color recorded using a greyscale format from 0% (white) to 100% (black). There were a total of five different greyscale grades, one for G-negative and four for G-positive bands. White (color 1) represented the G-negative euchromatin band regions, while 19% were light grey (color 2), 48% medium grey (color 3), 69% dark grey (color 4), or 100% black (color 5) representing the G-positive heterochromatin band regions. The short (p) arm of the acrocentric chromosomes (*i.e.*, 13, 14, 15, 21, and 22) and qh regions (*i.e.*, 1, 9, 16, and Y) which lack protein-coding genes were excluded from the analysis. The Chi-Square test was used to compare the distribution of ASD, obesity and protein-coding genes among euchromatin *vs.* heterochromatin regions genome-wide. Due to the known male prevalence of ASD, *ad hoc* analyses also considered the relative distribution of ASD, obesity and protein-coding genes for euchromatin *vs.* heterochromatin regions of the X chromosome alone.

In review of the literature and our research to address gene-chromosome band relationships (location and type), we reviewed published resources pertaining to the chromosome distribution and signal patterns associated with DNA methylation. We previously reported global DNA promoter methylation patterns from the frontal cortex of alcoholics and controls and found the methylation density patterns targeting CpG islands of the promoters of genes correlated with recognized chromosome banding patterns [51]. Higher CpG methylation peaks or intensity readings at genes were found in G-negative (more genes) chromosome bands and decreased size of peaks in the G-positive (fewer genes) bands in alcoholic and control subjects. For example, we found that 16 of the 20 highest methylation peaks representing CpG islands at gene promoters on chromosome 6 were located on G-negative bands when superimposed over the human chromosome 6 ideogram (data not shown). Thus, the results of our methylation signal data based on global DNA promoter methylation found in high-resolution methylation-specific microarrays and characterization in alcoholics were similar to the visual chromosome G-positive and G-negative bands associated with the distribution of protein-coding genes in ideograms.

4. Conclusions

Our study supports recent trends implicating genes located in heterochromatin regions as playing a role in biological processes including neurodevelopment and function, specifically genes associated with autism spectrum disorder (ASD). For example, almost one-half of the genome-wide protein-coding genes and genes associated with ASD and obesity were located in the G-positive heterochromatin regions. We found a significant overrepresentation of genes contributing to neurological function or development (*i.e.*, ASD) in darker G-positive heterochromatin bands relative to protein-coding genes and those with a systemic basis of function or disease (*i.e.*, obesity). Some genes were overly represented in specific chromosomes (e.g., X chromosome and ASD genes). One could propose analyzing these cytogenetic regions (individually and collectively) in the future by examining the ratios between the protein-coding and ASD genes to further identify ASD gene congregation (if any) in these known ASD-critical regions (e.g., 15q11-q13, 7q11.23, *etc.*) in the chromosomes represented in ideograms, and to simultaneously check for protein-coding gene status at possibly unstable and highly recombinant chromatin locations. Similar questions could be raised regarding the obesity-related genes and they could be examined for obesity gene congregation on chromosome ideograms. Our observations may stimulate future research to analyze the distribution of other gene groups in relationship to chromatin regions and bands including the examination of epigenetically and bioinformatically defined methylation domains in chromatin from different tissues (e.g., Schroeder *et al.*, 2011 [52]). In addition, of interest to genetic researchers would be to investigate genes found in different cell sources with distinct functions, such as ASD genes expressed in neuron cells and obesity genes in hepatic cells, and their relationship, if any, between the location and position of genes having different functions (*i.e.*, ASD genes on behavior/cognition expressed in the central system or brain and obesity-related genes expressed systemically or in peripheral systems). The study of specific G-band (positive or negative) patterns and respective histone maps may correlate with different genome-wide expression, and accessibility could utilize the data from the recently published Epigenome Roadmaps project (available at: http://www.roadmapepigenomics.org/) and yield new information about clustering of specific groups of genes at the tissue or organ (brain, liver, blood, adipose) level or disease (ASD, obesity) state [53]. The above in-depth analysis is beyond the scope of our descriptive approach of examining the location and interaction of protein-coding, ASD and obesity genes at the chromosome or chromosome ideogram or band level. Our study may help researchers gain a better understanding of the foundation of gene clustering and distributions in relationship to chromosome size and proportion of chromosome banding type, as well as specific gene group distribution with similar or dissimilar function as a hierarchical arrangement of gene function and dynamics.

Acknowledgments: We thank Lorie Gavulic for excellent artistic design and preparation of chromosome ideograms and support from the National Institute of Child Health and Human Development (NICHD) grant HD02528.

Author Contributions: Austen B. McGuire, Syed K. Rafi, Merlin G. Butler, and Ann M. Manzardo conceived and designed the experiments; Austen B. McGuire and Syed K. Rafi performed the experiments; Austen B. McGuire, Syed K. Rafi, Ann M. Manzardo, and Merlin G. Butler analyzed the data; Merlin G. Butler contributed reagents/materials/analysis tools; Austen B. McGuire, Syed K. Rafi, Ann M. Manzardo, and Merlin G. Butler wrote the paper.

Abbreviations

ASD	Autism Spectrum Disorder
AT	Adenine-Thymine
CFS	Chromosome Fragile Sites
df	Degrees of Freedom
DNA	Deoxyribonucleic Acid
GC	Guanine-Cytosine
ISCN	International Society of Chromosome Nomenclature
OMIM	Online Inheritance of Man

References

1. Oberdoerffer, P.; Sinclair, D.A. The role of nuclear architecture in genomic instability and ageing. *Nat. Rev. Mol. Cell Biol.* **2007**, *8*, 692–702. [CrossRef] [PubMed]
2. Zhang, Y.; Máté, G.; Müller, P.; Hillebrandt, S.; Krufczik, M.; Bach, M.; Kaufmann, R.; Hausmann, M.; Heermann, D.W. Radiation induced chromatin conformation changes analysed by fluorescent localization microscopy, statistical physics, and graph theory. *PLoS ONE* **2015**, *10*, e0128555. [CrossRef] [PubMed]

3. Annunziato, A. DNA packaging: Nucleosomes and chromatin. *Nat. Educ.* **2008**, *1*, 26.
4. Mello, M.L.S. Cytochemical properties of euchromatin and heterochromatin. *Histochem. J.* **1983**, *15*, 739–751. [CrossRef] [PubMed]
5. Murakami, Y. Heterochromatin and Euchromatin. In *Encyclopedia of Systems Biology*; Dubitzky, W., Wolkenhauer, O., Yokota, H., Cho, K., Yokota, H., Eds.; Springer: New York, NY, USA, 2013; pp. 881–884.
6. Hsieh, T.; Fischer, R.L. Biology of chromatin dynamics. *Annu. Rev. Plant Biol.* **2005**, *56*, 327–351. [CrossRef] [PubMed]
7. Clamp, M.; Fry, B.; Kamal, M.; Xie, X.; Cuff, J.; Lin, M.F.; Kellis, M.; Lindblad-Toh, K.; Lander, E.S. Distinguishing protein-coding and noncoding genes in the human genome. *Proc. Natl. Acad. Sci. USA* **2007**, *104*, 19428–19433. [CrossRef] [PubMed]
8. Harrow, J.; Nagy, A.; Reymond, A.; Alioto, T.; Patthy, L.; Antonarakis, S.E.; Guigó, R. Identifying protein-coding genes in genomic sequences. *Genome Biol.* **2009**, *10*. [CrossRef] [PubMed]
9. Brown, T.; Robertson, F.W.; Dawson, B.M.; Hanlin, S.J.; Page, B.M. Individual variation of centric heterochromatin in man. *Hum. Genet.* **1980**, *55*, 367–373. [CrossRef] [PubMed]
10. Kwon, S.H.; Workman, J.L. The changing faces of HP1: From heterochromatin formation and gene silencing to euchromatic gene expression. *Bioessays* **2011**, *33*, 280–289. [CrossRef] [PubMed]
11. Belmont, A.S.; Dietzel, S.; Nye, A.C.; Strukov, Y.G.; Tumbar, T. Large scale chromatin structure and function. *Curr. Opin. Cell Biol.* **1999**, *11*, 307–311. [CrossRef]
12. Fraser, F.C.; Nora, J. *Genetics of Man*; Lea and Febiger: Philadelphia, PA, USA, 1986.
13. Dimitri, P.; Caizzi, R.; Giordano, E.; Carmela Accardo, M.; Lattanzi, G.; Biamonti, G. Constitutive heterochromatin: A surprising variety of expressed sequences. *Chromosoma* **2009**, *118*, 419–435. [CrossRef] [PubMed]
14. Strachan, T.; Read, A. Human Molecular Genetics. Organization of the Human Genome. In *Human Molecular Genetics*, 4th ed.; Owen, E., Ed.; Garland Science: New York, NY, USA, 2010; pp. 255–295.
15. Grewal, S.; Jia, S. Heterochromatin revisited. *Nat. Rev. Genet.* **2007**, *8*, 35–46. [CrossRef] [PubMed]
16. Yasuhara, J.C.; Wakimoto, B.T. Oxymoron no more: The expanding world of heterochromatic genes. *Trends Genet.* **2006**, *22*, 330–338. [CrossRef] [PubMed]
17. Trojer, P.; Reinberg, D. Facultative heterochromatin: Is there a distinctive molecular signature? *Mol. Cell* **2007**, *28*, 1–13. [CrossRef] [PubMed]
18. Shaffer, L.G.; McGowan-Jordan, J.; Schmid, M. *ISCN (2013): An International System for Human Cytogenetic Nomenclature*; S Karger: Basel, Switzerland, 2013.
19. Saccone, S.; Federico, C.; Solovei, I.; Croquette, M.F.; della Valle, G.; Bernardi, G. Identification of the gene-richest bands in human prometaphase chromosomes. *Chromosome Res.* **1999**, *7*, 379–386. [CrossRef] [PubMed]
20. Whole Genome. Ensembl. Available online: http://uswest.ensembl.org/Homo_sapiens/Location/Genome?redirect=no (accessed on 20 December 2014).
21. Flicek, P.; Amode, M.R.; Barrell, D.; Beal, K.; Billis, K.; Brent, S.; Carvalho-Silva, D.; Clapham, P.; Coates, G.; Fitzgerald, S.; *et al.* Ensembl 2014. *Nucleic Acids Res.* **2014**, *42*, D749–D755. [CrossRef] [PubMed]
22. Ogden, C.L.; Carroll, M.D.; Curtin, L.R.; McDowell, M.A.; Tabak, C.J.; Flegal, K.M. Prevalence of overweight and obesity in the United States, 1999–2004. *JAMA* **2006**, *295*, 1549–1555. [CrossRef] [PubMed]
23. Wingate, M.; Kirby, R.S.; Pettygrove, S.; Cunniff, C.; Schulz, E.; Ghosh, T.; Yeargin-Allsopp, M. Prevalence of autism spectrum disorder among children aged 8 years-autism and developmental disabilities monitoring network, 11 sites, United States, 2010. *MMWR Surveill. Summ.* **2014**, *63*, 1–21.
24. Herman, G.E.; Henninger, N.; Ratliff-Schaub, K.; Pastore, M.; Fitzgerald, S.; McBride, K.L. Genetic testing in autism: How much is enough? *Genet. Med.* **2007**, *9*, 268–274. [CrossRef] [PubMed]
25. Fagnani, C.; Silventoinen, K.; McGue, M.; Korkeila, M.; Christensen, K.; Rissanen, A.; Kaprio, J. Genetic influences on growth traits of BMI: A longitudinal study of adult twins. *Obesity* **2008**, *16*, 847–852.
26. Butler, M.G.; McGuire, A.M.; Manzardo, A.M. Clinically relevant known and candidate genes for obesity and their overlap with human infertility and reproduction. *J. Assist. Reprod. Genet.* **2015**, *32*, 495–508. [CrossRef] [PubMed]
27. Butler, M.G.; Rafi, S.K.; Manzardo, A.M. High-resolution chromosome ideogram representation of currently recognized genes for autism spectrum disorders. *Int. J. Mol. Sci.* **2015**, *16*, 6464–6495. [CrossRef] [PubMed]
28. Rice, C. Prevalence of autism spectrum disorders-autism and developmental disabilities monitoring network, United States, 2006. *MMWR Surveill. Summ.* **2009**, *58*, 3–8.

29. Marshall, C.R.; Noor, A.; Vincent, J.B.; Lionel, A.C.; Feuk, L.; Skaug, J.; Shago, M.; Moessner, R.; Pinto, D.; Ren, Y.; *et al.* Structural variation of chromosomes in autism spectrum disorder. *Am. J. Hum. Genet.* **2008**, *82*, 477–488. [CrossRef] [PubMed]
30. Comings, D.E. Mechanism of chromosome banding and implications for chromosome structure. *Annu. Rev. Genet.* **1978**, *12*, 25–46. [CrossRef] [PubMed]
31. Sumner, A.T. The nature and mechanisms of chromosome-banding. *Cancer Genet. Cytogenet.* **1982**, *6*, 59–87. [CrossRef]
32. Wittekind, D.H.; Gehring, T. On the nature of Romanowsky-Giemsa staining and the Romanowsky-Giemsa effect. I. Model experiments on the specificity of Azure B-Eosin Y stain as compared with other thiazine dye-Eosin Y combinations. *Histochem. J.* **1985**, *17*, 263–289. [CrossRef] [PubMed]
33. Bickmore, W.A. Karyotype Analysis and chromosome banding. *eLS* **2001**. [CrossRef]
34. Holmquist, G.P. Chromosome bands, their chromatin flavors, and their functional features. *Am. J. Hum. Genet.* **1992**, *51*, 17–37. [PubMed]
35. Drouin, R.; Lemieux, N.; Richer, C.L. Chromosome condensation from prophase to late metaphase: Relationship to chromosome bands and their replication time. *Cytogenet. Cell Genet.* **1991**, *57*, 91–99. [CrossRef] [PubMed]
36. Kosyakova, N.; Wiese, A.; Mrasek, K.; Claussen, U.; Leihr, T.; Nelle, H. The hierarchically organized splitting of chromosomal bands for all human chromosomes. *Mol. Cytogenet.* **2009**, *2*. [CrossRef] [PubMed]
37. Wang, J.; Lunyak, V.V.; Jordan, I.K. Genome-wide prediction and analysis of human chromatin boundary elements. *Nucleic Acid Res.* **2012**, *40*, 511–529. [CrossRef] [PubMed]
38. Fungtammasan, A.; Walsh, E.; Chiaromonte, F.; Eckert, K.A.; Makova, K.D. A genome-wide analysis of common fragile sites: What features determine chromosomal instability in the human genome? *Genome Res.* **2012**, *22*, 993–1005. [CrossRef] [PubMed]
39. Butler, M.G. Frequency and distribution of chromosome fragile sites or lesions in males with mental retardation: A descriptive study. *J. Tenn. Acad. Sci.* **1998**, *73*, 87–99.
40. Mrasek, K.; Schoder, C.; Teichmann, A.C.; Behr, K.; Franze, B.; Wilhelm, K.; Blaurock, N.; Claussen, U.; Liehr, T.; Weise, A. Global screening and extended nomenclature for 230 aphidicolin-inducible fragile sites, including 61 yet unreported ones. *Int. J. Oncol.* **2010**, *36*, 929–940. [PubMed]
41. Smith, C.L.; Bolton, A.; Nguyen, G. Genomic and epigenomic instability, fragile sites, schizophrenia and autism. *Curr. Genom.* **2010**, *11*, 447–469. [CrossRef] [PubMed]
42. Nazki, F.H.; Sameer, A.S.; Ganaie, B.A. Folate: Metabolism, genes, polymorphisms and the associated diseases. *Gene* **2014**, *533*, 11–20. [CrossRef] [PubMed]
43. Thys, R.G.; Lehman, C.E.; Pierce, L.C.; Wang, Y.H. DNA secondary structure at chromosomal fragile sites in human disease. *Curr. Genom.* **2015**, *16*, 60–70. [CrossRef] [PubMed]
44. Dillon, N.; Festenstein, R. Unravelling heterochromatin: Competition between positive and negative factors regulates accessibility. *Trends Genet.* **2002**, *18*, 252–258. [CrossRef]
45. Rougeulle, C.; Chaumeil, J.; Sarma, K.; Allis, C.D.; Reinberg, D.; Avner, P.; Heard, E. Differential histone H3 lys-9 and lys-27 methylation profiles on the X chromosome. *Mol. Cell. Biol.* **2004**, *24*, 5475–5484. [CrossRef] [PubMed]
46. Lan, L.; Nakajima, S.; Wei, L.; Sun, L.; Hsieh, C.L.; Sobol, R.W.; Bruchez, M.; van Houten, B.; Yasui, A.; Levine, A.S. Novel method for site-specific induction of oxidative DNA damage reveals differences in recruitment of repair proteins to heterochromatin and euchromatin. *Nucleic Acids Res.* **2013**, *42*, 2330–2345. [CrossRef] [PubMed]
47. Sims, R.J.; Nishioka, K.; Reinberg, D. Histone lysine methylation: A signature for chromatin function. *Trends Genet.* **2003**, *19*, 629–639. [CrossRef] [PubMed]
48. Ijdo, J.W.; Baldini, A.; Ward, D.C.; Reeders, S.T.; Wells, R.A. Origin of human chromosome 2: An ancestral telomere-telomere fusion. *Proc. Natl. Acad. Sci. USA* **1991**, *88*, 9051–9055. [CrossRef] [PubMed]
49. Yunis, J.J.; Prakash, O. The origin of man: A chromosomal pictorial legacy. *Science* **1982**, *215*, 1525–1530. [CrossRef] [PubMed]
50. Skawiński, W.; Parcheta, B. Polymorphism of the human Y chromosome: The evaluation of the correlation between the DNA content and the size of the heterochromatin and euchromatin. *Clin. Genet.* **1984**, *25*, 125–130. [CrossRef] [PubMed]

51. Manzardo, A.M.; Henkhaus, R.S.; Butler, M.G. Global DNA promoter methylation in frontal cortex of alcoholics and controls. *Gene* **2012**, *498*, 5–12. [CrossRef] [PubMed]
52. Schroeder, D.I.; Lott, P.; Korf, I.; LaSalle, J.M. Large-scale methylation domains mark a functional subset of neuronally expressed genes. *Genome Res.* **2011**, *21*, 1583–1591. [CrossRef] [PubMed]
53. Roadmap Epigenomics Consortium. Integrative analysis of 111 reference human epigenomes. *Nature* **2015**, *518*, 317–330.

10

Human Figure Drawings in Children with Autism Spectrum Disorders: A Possible Window on the Inner or the Outer World

Pamela Papangelo [1], Martina Pinzino [1], Susanna Pelagatti [2], Maddalena Fabbri-Destro [1,†,*] and Antonio Narzisi [3,†]

1 Institute of Neuroscience, National Research Council (CNR), Via Volturno 39/E, 43125 Parma, Italy; pamela.papangelo@gmail.com (P.P.); martinapinzino@outlook.it (M.P.)
2 Department of Informatics, University of Pisa, 56126 Pisa, Italy; susanna.pelagatti@gmail.com
3 IRCCS Stella Maris Foundation, 56126 Pisa, Italy; antonio.narzisi@fsm.unipi.it
* Correspondence: maddalena.fabbridestro@gmail.com
† Both authors contributed equally to this work.

Abstract: Background: Tests based on human figure drawings (HFD) have captured the attention of clinicians and psychologists for a long time. The aim of the present study was to evaluate the performance of HFD of children with autism spectrum disorders (ASDs) relative to typically developing (TD) controls. Methods: All children were asked to draw three human figures (man, woman, self-portrait) and were evaluated with a neuropsychological battery. HFD were scored according to the Maturity Scale, and correlative approaches testing maturity against neuropsychological scores were applied. Results: ASDs presented marked deficits in maturity. No significant correlation emerged for both groups between maturity and the theory of mind test. On the contrary, positive and significant correlations between maturity and the affect recognition test (AR) were found, with group-specific patterns. In TD, this result regarded drawings of others, but not self-portraits, while an opposite pattern emerged for ASD, whose sole maturity in self-portraits significantly correlated with the AR scores. Conclusion: These findings suggest that the use of HFD tests with individuals with autism may not be used in clinical practices. However, in basic research, HFDs could be used to highlight dependencies between drawing performance and neuropsychological features, thus possibly providing hints on the functioning of autism.

Keywords: human figure drawings; Draw-a-Man; drawings maturity; autism spectrum disorders; social perception

1. Introduction

Children have been using drawings to express themselves since ancient times and this topic has captured the interest of scientists since the late 19th century. Indeed, by analyzing the presence/absence of graphical aspects like details, colors, proportions, and shapes, it is possible to trace a developmental maturation trajectory based on children's drawings [1]. Historically, the Draw-a-Man test (DAMT) developed by Goodenough [2] represents the first systematic scoring system for children's drawings, devised with the intent to provide a surrogate measure of children's intelligence. Scores were initially based on the number of details and the accuracy of placement of each body part. DAMT was later revised by Harris [3], who proposed that children should be asked to draw not just one but three human figures: a generic man, a generic woman, and a self-portrait. The scoring system for the maturity estimation was updated, accounting also for the precision of details, and proportions.

Since these initial pioneering studies, several revisions and applications have been conducted to enhance the utility of DAMT, and more generally of human figure drawing (HFD) tests, in virtue of their versatility and usability also with children with limited attention span and language difficulties. There is no exception for the use of the HFD in the field of autism.

As far as autism spectrum disorders (ASDs) drawings are concerned, children with autism were reported to have an unusual drawing ability, far beyond their general intelligence level [4–6], and drawing skills not impaired relative to age-matched typical peers [7,8]. However, Lee and Hobson [9] reported slightly lower global scores in HFD for children with ASD relative to children with learning difficulties, whereas the same pattern did not emerge across groups in drawings of houses. Similarly, Lim and Slaughter [10] indicated that in HFD, children with autism are generally less sophisticated and detailed than children without autism. Given this controversial pattern of results, whether children with autism differ from age-matched TD peers is still a matter of debate, leaving open the question whether human figure drawings could be useful in the clinical practice of autism. Indeed, while international guidelines [11] excluded tests based on drawings from the batteries used for the diagnosis of ASDs, it is possible that the maturity score covaries in association with other neuropsychological indices not easily obtainable in children with ASDs.

Autism spectrum disorders (ASDs) are a severe multifactorial disorder characterized by an umbrella of peculiarities in the areas of social communication, restricted interests, and repetitive behaviors [12]. The incidence of ASDs is worldwide and recent epidemiological data estimated it to be higher than 1/100 [13]. ASDs vary greatly in the severity of their socio-communicative impairments [14] as well as in cognitive and language development.

Many of the social interpersonal difficulties in ASD derive to some extent from weaknesses in the children's social perception, which in turn relies on both cognitive [15] and motor processes [16]. Social perception refers to children's ability to represent and understand others, their mental states, emotions, and beliefs. Concerning theory of mind (ToM), several studies demonstrated that individuals with ASDs have performance lower than individuals with typical development [17]. These deficits are reported using different versions of ToM tasks, including those examining false beliefs [18], cartoon animations [19], or inferences of mental states from photographs [20].

A key aspect of social perception in ASDs pertains to emotion and affect recognition, yet inconsistent findings have been reported so far. Indeed, while Kuusikko et al. [21] and Krebs et al. [22] pointed to an impairment of children with ASDs in emotion recognition, other studies [23–25] failed to report such a deficit. To date, no evidence has been provided about the possible relationship between social perception scores and performance in human figure drawing tests.

Starting from these premises, in the present study we evaluated the performance of the Draw-a-Man test in a group of children with ASDs, and compared them against a group of age-matched typically developing controls. In particular, we tested two hypotheses: (1) ASDs have lower maturity scores in DAMT, and (2) performance at DAMT differs according to the subjects to-be-depicted (self vs. representation of others). The value of such an investigation is that if a difference is highlighted (i.e., ASDs present lower scores relative to TD), tests based on human figure drawings should not be considered in ASDs as indexing maturity, unless a proper normative ASD population is acquired. In addition to factorial contrasts, the clinical value of the HFD test could be further characterized by correlative approaches testing maturity against neuropsychological scores most common in the clinical practice of autism.

2. Materials and Methods

2.1. *Participants*

Twenty-one typically developing boys (TD, age M = 8.7, SD = 1.8) and 22 boys with autism spectrum disorders (ASDs, age M = 9.2, SD = 1.7) were included in the study. Groups resulted matched for chronological age ($p = 0.30$) and nonverbal IQ assessed by Raven's Colored Progressive Matrices [26] ($p = 0.72$).

Concerning the ASD group, inclusion criteria were: (a) diagnosis of autism spectrum disorder according to DSM-V/ICD-10 criteria and certified by the Italian Mental Health System (acknowledgement of handicap through Italian law n. 104/1992); (b) age 6–12 years; (c) non-verbal intelligence quotient within the 90–130 range; (d) capacity to adhere to experimental procedures; and (e) lack of comorbidities according to their medical records. Exclusion criteria consisted of (a) presence or history of any other axis I mental disorder; or (b) history of traumatic brain injury or any other neurological disorder as by their medical record. Participants with ASDs were all children with high functioning autism and were recruited via the parents' association "Autismo Pisa APS" sited in Pisa. TD were recruited in primary schools in Parma as children matching the same age criterion used for the ASDs group. Children with a history of neurological or psychiatric disorders were not enrolled, as well as those whose parents or teachers expressed concerns about their development.

Informed written consent was obtained from the parents of all participants, and oral consent from each child. This study was approved by the Local Ethical Committee (Comitato Etico Area Vasta Emilia Nord, prot.n.13051) and was conducted according to the Helsinki Declaration.

2.2. *Procedures*

2.2.1. Neuropsychological Evaluation

All children were evaluated with a neuropsychological battery including social perception and visuo-spatial domains. Both of them were indexed by subscales of the NEPSY-II test [27].

2.2.2. Social Perception

Social perception domain is evaluated by two different subtests of NEPSY-II [27]: theory of mind and affect recognition. Each subtest is designed to measure a different set of skills necessary for understanding the feelings, perceptions, and intentions of others.

Theory of mind (ToM) includes two tasks. In the verbal task, scenarios or pictures are shown to the child, who has later to answer questions that require knowledge of another individual's perspective. In the contextual task, the child is shown a picture depicting a social situation in which the face of the target individual is not shown. The child is then asked to select one out of four photographs, as the one depicting the most appropriate affect for the target individual in the picture. Overall, theory of mind evaluates the ability to comprehend others' perspectives, intentions, and beliefs.

The affect recognition (AR) test assesses the ability to recognize affects (happiness, sadness, anger, fear, disgust, and neutral) from photographs of children's faces in different tasks like same–different, on-line, and delayed similarity recognition.

2.2.3. Visuo-Spatial Processing

The evaluation of the visuo-spatial domain was limited to the design copying (DC) test from NEPSY-II [27], aimed at assessing motor and visual-perceptual skills associated with the ability to copy two-dimensional geometric figures. It returns a global score (general score), as well as sub-scores measuring the degree of motor abilities, global attributes of the design, and local elements or details of the design. Taken together, these latter three sub-scores form the so-called design copying process score.

2.2.4. Human Figure Drawing (HFD) Test

At the end of the neuropsychological evaluation, each participant was tested with the human figure drawing test, according to the procedures proposed by Royer [28]. HFD allows to explore the child's level of intellectual maturity.

Each participant was given seven colored crayons (blue, green, red, yellow, purple, brown, and black), one pencil, one eraser, and 3 sheets of paper (21 × 29.5 cm) placed vertically. He was requested to draw, on the first sheet, a person. Upon completion of the first drawing, the participant was asked to indicate its gender, and the drawing was removed. Of note, most participants (36 out of 43) started from a male drawing. On the second sheet, the participant was then asked to draw a person of the opposite gender. Upon completion of the second human figure, the drawing was removed and a third sheet provided on which the child was invited to "draw a self-portrait". Children were left free to choose the size and position in the sheet of their drawings. No time limit was imposed.

2.2.5. Non-Human Figure Drawings

Subsequently, children were asked to accomplish a similar task, but depicting three houses (one house, another house, and their own one) rather than human figures. In this way, we obtained a second set of drawings allowing to test two interconnected hypotheses: first, whether children with ASD have peculiar features relative to TD, in particular in terms of similarity among drawings; second, whether such features are specific for human figures, or generalizable also to other subjects.

2.3. *Coding of Drawings*

The human figure drawings were scored according to the Maturity Scale [28]. This scale accounts for the presence of evolutionary details of the drawing, further grouped in the evaluation of head (23 items), body (32 items) and clothing (14 items), and color use. No Maturity Scale has been validated to date for houses, thus we limited its use to HFD.

To evaluate the differences among the human figure drawings, a similarity score was calculated [29]. The judgement of similarity was evaluated in parallel for three aspects, i.e., dimensions (height and width), body (shapes and colors), and attributes (shapes and colors of clothes and accessories). For each aspect, a score from zero (marked difference) to two (maximum similarity) was assigned. Such a score was evaluated among the three drawings, coupled two-by-two, thus obtaining 3 different scores. The similarity score was also calculated for the house drawings by adapting the scale of similarity used for the human figure drawings, and still comparing the houses to each other, two-by-two. Three different subscales (dimensions, attributes, and accessories) were considered.

We also calculated for the human figure drawings the value score [29]. This evaluates the presence of biases in the representational appearance between two drawings; for example, in the case of a colorful and richly decorated suit versus a monochromatic suit, the value score is greater for the former. The value score was evaluated in parallel for four aspects, i.e., the space occupied by each figure, the articulation of the body, the number of attributes, and the number of colors. These subscales were used to establish whether two figures were equally valued. For each subscale, scores from zero (equality) to two (marked or very marked difference) were assigned.

Two experimenters evaluated the drawings following strictly the guidelines indicated in Royer [28] for the maturity score, and in Bombi and Pinto [29] for the similarity and value scores. In the case of agreement between the two judgments, the agreed score was noted. Conversely, in the case of disagreement between the two experimenters, the final score was obtained after a joint evaluation among the two scorers and the senior author.

2.4. *Statistical Analysis*

All collected variables (see Table 1) underwent the Shapiro–Wilk's W-test for verifying the assumption of normality. Parametric (one-way ANOVA, Bonferroni post-hoc) or non-parametric tests (Kruskal–Wallis, Mann–Whitney post-hoc) were applied accordingly. Eta-squared (η^2) was calculated as a measure of effect size.

The factorial analysis was intended at verifying the homogeneity among groups in terms of age and non-verbal IQ. The same analysis on the neuropsychological scores and Maturity Scale aimed at evaluating the differences between groups.

Table 1. Main scores for each test and group. Each cell contains the average score (M) and its standard deviation (SD).

	Non-Verbal IQ	Theory of Mind (ToM)	Affect Recognition (AR)	Design Coping (General- DCG)	Design Copying Process (DCP) Motor Ability (DCP-M)	Global Attributes (DCP-Glob)	Local Elements (DCP-Loc)
TD	M = 113.3 SD = 13.2	M = 12.7 SD = 2.9	M = 9.4 SD = 3.3	M = 9.4 SD = 2.4	M = 33.4 SD = 4.4	M = 29.4 SD = 5.1	M = 20.3 SD = 4.5
ASD	M = 112.3 SD = 11.1	M = 6.5 SD = 3.9	M = 7.8 SD = 4.3	M = 5.8 SD = 3.3	M = 28.5 SD = 7.1	M = 25.1 SD = 8.2	M = 16.2 SD = 6.6

Similarity and value scores spanned over a discrete and very narrow range (0, 1, 2), so a factorial analysis was not applicable. To evaluate comparatively these scores between groups, we then carried out a chi-squared tests inserting the count of each score for both ASD and TD, and evaluating whether their distribution varied across groups. In the case of a significant chi test, individual chi values were calculated to highlight which elements carried most of this disproportion.

Finally, we carried out correlation analyses testing the link between the Maturity Scale on one side, and indices of the social perception domain on the other. As we had no assumption on the linearity of such a relationship, we opted for using a Spearman rank correlation. In addition, the analysis was conducted separately for each group so to test the within-group dependency and not just a macroscopic between-group co-difference.

3. Results

Figure 1 reports the drawings from the HFDs of four participants, spanning over age (two 8 years old, two 11 years old) and groups (two TD and two ASDs).

We evaluated on the Maturity Scale and non-verbal IQ the presence of outliers as those subjects exceeding ±2 standard deviations of the sample's mean. Two ASDs and one TD children were outliers for the human figure drawings Maturity Scale, while two children with ASDs were outliers for the non-verbal IQ scores. Then, the final sample consisted of 21 TD and 22 ASD children. Table 1 recaps the average scores for each test and group.

The matching between populations was witnessed by the lack of significant difference between groups, as returned by the Mann–Whitney test, in terms of age (U(22, 21) = 188, Z = 1.04, $p = 0.30$) and non-verbal IQ (U(22, 21) = 216.5, Z = −0.36, $p = 0.72$).

The Maturity Scale resulted as highly significant between groups, as by the one-way ANOVA, for each HDF (HDF-1, F(1, 41) = 12.67, $p < 0.001$, $\eta^2 = 0.23$; HFD-2, F(1, 41) = 15.86, $p < 0.001$, $\eta^2 = 0.38$; HFD-self, F(1, 41) = 11.73, $p = 0.001$, $\eta^2 = 0.22$) (see Figure 2).

The same analysis returned a significant difference for ToM (F(1, 41) = 34.68, $p < 0.001$) indicating a marked difference between groups in the ability to comprehend others perspectives, intentions, and beliefs, with TD scores double relative to the ASD ones (TD M = 12.7, ASD M = 6.5). Similar results were obtained for the design copying general (DCG) score (F(1, 41) = 16.53, $p < 0.001$). When focusing on the subscale composing the design copy process (DCP), no difference between groups was found neither for DCP-global (TD M = 29.4, ASD M = 25.0) nor for DCP-local (TD M = 20.3, ASD M = 16.2). However, the motor subscale of copy design resulted to be significantly different between the two groups (DCP-motor: U(22, 21) = 127, Z = −2.51, $p = 0.01$) indicating that most of the difference in the DC performance between TD and ASDs relies on a poorer set of motor abilities of the latter group (TD M = 33.4, ASD M = 28.5). No difference emerges for scores at the AR test (U(22, 21) = 177, Z = −1.3, $p = 0.19$).

Figure 1. Examples of HFDs by ASD and TD children matched for age. Upper strips (black frame) relate to young children (8 years old), lower strips (grey frame) relate to older children in our range (11 years old). The triplets of maturity scores for the four subjects are (136.9, 125.0, 136.9), (72.4, 71.2, 76.2), (102.3, 112.1, 102.3), and (52.9, 50.1, 49.2), respectively.

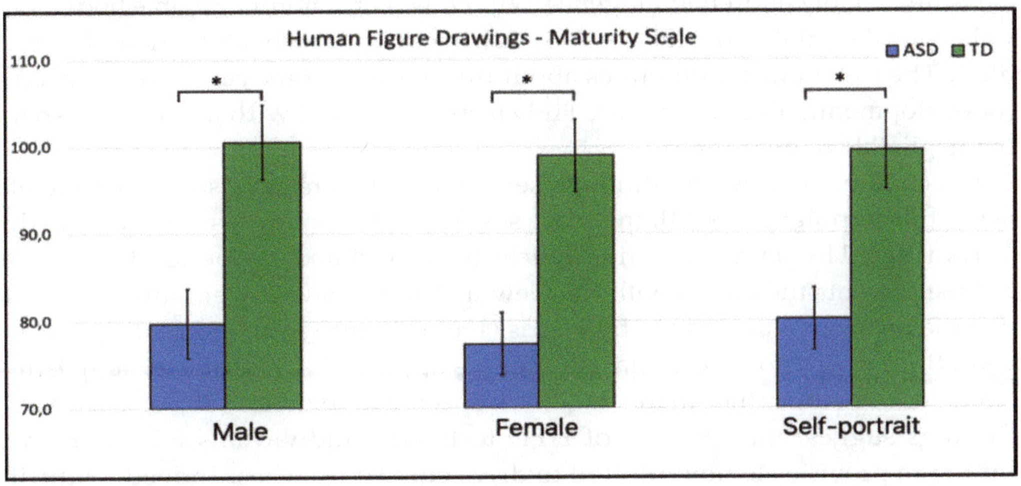

Figure 2. Maturity scale in the three drawings across ASDs and TD children. Bars indicate standard errors; asterisks a p-value < 0.01.

Concerning similarity, a chi-square test was applied to the three possible couples of human figure drawings (HFD-male vs. HFD-self, HFD-female vs. HFD-self, HFD-male vs. HFD-female). A significant difference emerged only in similarity between HFD-male and HFD-female (χ^2 (2, N = 43) = 7.39, p = 0.02). Examining individual chi values, this significance appears mostly due to an over-presence of score 2 (maximum similarity) in ASDs (26 vs. 19.4 expected, χ^2 = 2.2), while TD presented a lower rate of such a score (12 vs. 18.6 expected, χ^2 = 2.3). No other HFD comparison turned out significant. The same procedure was applied to the similarity scores obtained for the houses, so to evaluate whether the tendency to hyper-similarity was specific for human figures, or generalizable also to other subjects. Of note, none of the three house comparisons returned significant results (all $p > 0.4$).

Despite the correlation analysis between the maturity at HFD and ToM scores resulted as not significant for both groups in all the three drawings, a different pattern emerged between TD and ASDs. Indeed, while TD showed a tendency towards significance in all drawings (all p around 0.08) and r coefficients around 0.4, ASDs fell apart from significance, with r values around 0.

Concerning the correlation between maturity and affect recognition, TD exhibited significant and positive findings for HFD-male and HFD-female, while no link was found for HDF-self. Of note, this pattern was fully reversed examining children with ASDs, who exhibited a significant correlation in HFD-self vs. AR, while non-significant results for HFD-male and HFD-female were found. The results of the correlation analysis are reported in Table 2.

Table 2. Spearman correlation analysis between maturity and affect recognition scores, reporting (*r*) and *p*-values in the TD and ASD groups. Significant correlations ($p < 0.05$) are highlighted in grey.

Group	HFD	*r* (Spearman)	*p*-Value
TD	Male	0.53	0.015
	Female	0.53	0.012
	Self	0.33	0.14
ASD	Male	0.20	0.36
	Female	0.32	0.13
	Self	0.45	0.03

4. Discussion

Tests based on human figure drawings have captured the attention of clinicians and psychologists for a long time, likely due to the easiness and ecologicity of their administration, with the aim to achieve a surrogate measurement of children intelligence [30]. However, a non-negligible body of literature has repeatedly challenged the validity of HFD tests [31,32], in particular when non-neurotypical individuals are investigated. The lack of firm guidelines about this matter, moreover, leads to inconsistencies in clinical neurodevelopmental practice, where HFD tests are treated with a relevance spanning over a spectrum from negligible to over-rated.

Pertaining to children with ASDs, although several researchers have suggested the utility of HFD tests in assessing this population [9,33], there are several well-known case studies in which children with autism accompanied by severe cognitive deficits have exhibited a superior drawing ability [34,35]. The findings of the present study align with the view that ASDs have lower maturity in drawings than TD. In line with the revision of the DAMT by Harris (1963) [3], we requested participants to draw three different human figures, yet no substantial differences appeared across these, suggesting a globally lower functioning in drawing rather than a hallmark specific for a given subject (see for example [36]).

These findings suggest that the use of HFD tests with individuals with autism may be not warranted, failing to provide elements suited to drive clinical routines. Indeed, maturity scores are obtained via a normalization against a TD normative population which has—on average—higher scores. To be usable and informative at the individual level, data from a normative population including only children with ASDs should be collected, or at least reference values should be provided to clinicians about the range of maturity scores specific for autistic individuals.

Once ascertained that to date maturity cannot inform about an individual child with ASDs, it is still possible that scores at HFD correlate with the functioning of specific domains. This is why we tested in the same participants the construct of social perception that reflects a variety of psychological processes, mostly involved in ASD symptomatology, i.e., ToM and AR. ToM is defined as the cognitive ability leading to the awareness that others have minds with mental states, information, and motivations that may differ from one's own, allowing an individual to cognitively explain others behaviors [37]. In our study, coherently with previous literature [see 17], ToM scores resulted as highly segregated between ASDs and TD, yet no correlation emerged within both groups with HFD performance. This suggests a certain independency between performance in HFD and ToM tests, in turn reflecting a segregation between the underlying functions.

Concerning affective recognition, a completely different pattern was highlighted. Indeed, no difference appeared at the factorial analysis, suggesting a globally preserved (or restored via a rehabilitation intervention) ability of children with ASDs to explicitly recognize emotional expressions relative to control peers. Our results are in line with Narzisi et al., [38] who found that children with ASDs performed equally well as TD children in the affect recognition test (see also [39]), and with Tracy et al., [40], in which participants with ASDs succeeded in deciding whether an emotional photograph matched a target emotion. However, there is some evidence of atypical face perception processes in individuals with ASDs [41,42]. Indeed, while a deficit in face processing is not pathognomonic (meaning that it is not a definitive diagnostic sign), many children show a significant impairment in encoding facial features. In addition, Kuusikko et al. [21] indicated that despite that emotion recognition may improve with age in children with ASDs, it never completely achieves the level of typically developing individuals. Difficulties with social cognition do not always emerge in structured test situations, especially in high-functioning individuals with ASDs, and this may explain these inconsistent results. According to Harms et al., [43], some individuals with ASDs may utilize compensatory mechanisms (such as explicit cognitive processes) making the performance on facial emotion recognition tasks adequate in test situations, while atypical processing of stimuli is shown in neuroimaging studies [44] and difficulties in emotion recognition in real-life situations [45] are well-known.

Beyond the factorial analysis, we conducted a correlation analysis between scores obtained in HFD in the Maturity Scale and those obtained in the affective recognition test for both groups in order to get insights on the possible link between emotion recognition and drawing performance across multiple to-be-drawn subjects. Our results indicated not only the presence of positive and significant correlations, but also that they largely differed between groups. TD children showed a maturity score significantly associated with affect recognition in drawing other individuals, but not in self-portraits. An opposite pattern emerged for children with ASDs, whose sole maturity in self-portraits significantly correlated with the affective recognition scores.

Such a result could be interpreted in a very fascinating manner: in TD children, the capability to recognize others' emotions could underlie the competence to graphically represent others. In turns, in children with ASDs, emotion recognition is not associated with maturity in the representation of others, but rather it correlates only with maturity in the self-representation. In other words, affective recognition skills might be used by TD to decode the outer social world, but by ASD only to express/represent themselves.

One could speculate that this selective link reflects a lack of experience of the social world in ASD [10], due to their socio-communicative atypicalities and relational poverty further impacting on their cognitive style [46]. The link between maturity and social communicative skills is very interdependent in children with ASDs and it has been the subject of extensive theoretical and empirical investigations [47]. In children with TD, the goodness of early social experiences has been linked to later maturity outcomes [48,49]. As reported by Vivanti (2016) [47], on the contrary, it is plausible that an altered sociability during early development may uniquely impact social dimensions of learning, including de facto the ingredients underlying affective recognition.

Despite only partially covering the abilities underlying the human figure drawing test, we evaluated the design copying test from NEPSY-II [27] to collect an index of an overall drawing performance, comparative between the two groups. The factorial analysis showed a significant difference between children with ASDs and TD children with a difficulty in the global ability to copy two-dimensional geometric figures for the first group, suggesting a weakness in visuomotor integration. The global ability to copy is generally associated with preserved visual-perceptual skills, and our findings are consistent with the validation study of the NEPSY-II by Korkman et al. [27] and with the more recent study by Narzisi et al. [38]. A similar difference was found for the design copy process, and this effect resulted mainly due to one of its subscales, namely the motor subtest. Further, in this case, the group with ASD presented difficulties in fine motor control, in line with a large body of literature pointing at motor disorganization as one of the determinant features in autism [50].

5. Conclusions

In conclusion, our study indicates that children with ASDs have a marked deficit in the human figure drawing test. The lack of a global consensus in the interpretation of HFD results, as well as of normative data peculiar for autism, advocate for an effort, joint by developmental psychology and neuropsychiatry, to achieve a reliable framework for the assessment of individuals with ASDs.

However, out of the clinical practice, tests based on HFD could be considered in basic research for revealing dependencies between drawing performance and neuropsychological features, thus possibly providing hints on the functioning of autism. We hereby showed the existence of a link between maturity in HFD and affect recognition, but the specificity of this result for autism across neurodevelopmental disorders as well as the neural mechanisms at the basis of this alteration have yet to be ascertained. To answer these points, future studies might consider to test additional groups of patients, possibly involving affective disturbances, and accompanying HFD with neurophysiological recordings.

Author Contributions: P.P., M.F.-D. designed the experiment. P.P., M.P., S.P. and A.N. collected data, P.P., M.P. and M.F.-D. analyzed data. M.F.-D. and A.N. wrote the paper. All authors have contributed to, seen and approved the manuscript. All authors have read and agreed to the published version of the manuscript.

Acknowledgments: P.P. was financially supported by "Soremartec Italia Srl" (Alba, Cuneo, Italy). We wish to thank Pietro Avanzini for his statistical help and comments to the manuscript. Last but not least we wish to thank the families of the children participating to the study for their passionate and active participation.

References

1. Wittmann, B. A Neolitich childwood: Children's drawings as prehistoric sources. *Res. Anthropol. Aesthet.* **2013**, *63/64*, 125–142. [CrossRef]
2. Goodenough, F.L. *Measurement of Intelligence by Drawings*; World Book: New York, NY, USA, 1926.
3. Harris, E.B. *Children's Drawings as Measures of Intellectual Maturity: A Revision of the Goodenough Draw-a-Man Test*; Harcourt, Brace & World: New York, NY, USA, 1963.
4. O'Connor, N.; Hermelin, B. Low intelligence and special abilities. *Child Psychol. Psychiatry Allied Discip.* **1988**, *29*, 391–396. [CrossRef] [PubMed]
5. Sacks, O. *An Anthropoligist on Mars*; Knopf: New York, NY, USA, 1995.
6. Selfe, L. *Nadia: A Case of Extraordinary Drawing Ability in an Autistic Child*; Academic Press: New York, NY, USA, 1977.
7. Charman, T.; Baron-Cohen, S. Drawing development in autism: The intellectual to visual realism shift. *Br. J. Dev. Psychol.* **1993**, *11*, 171–185. [CrossRef]
8. Eames, K.; Cox, M.V. Visual realism in the drawings of autistic, Down's syndrome and normal children. *Br. J. Dev. Psychol.* **1994**, *12*, 235–239. [CrossRef]
9. Lee, A.; Hobson, P.R. Drawing self and others: How do children with autism differ from those with learning difficulties? *Br. J. Dev. Psychol.* **2006**, *24*, 547–565. [CrossRef]
10. Lim, H.K.; Slaughter, V. Brief report: Human figure drawings by children with Asperger's syndrome. *J. Autism Dev. Disord.* **2008**, *38*, 988–994. [CrossRef] [PubMed]

11. Volkmar, F.; Siegel, M.; Woodbury-Smith, M.; King, B.; McCracken, J. State M, American Academy of Child and Adolescent Psychiatry (AACAP). Practice parameter for the assessment and treatment of children and adolescents with autism spectrum disorder. *J. Am. Acad. Child Adolesc. Psychiatry* **2014**, *53*, 237–257. [CrossRef] [PubMed]
12. American Psychiatric Association. *Diagnostic and Statistical Manual of Mental Disorders*, 5th ed.; American Psychiatric Pub: Washington, DC, USA, 2013.
13. Maenner, M.J.; Shaw, K.A.; Baio, J. Prevalence of Autism Spectrum Disorder Among Children Aged 8 Years—Autism and Developmental Disabilities Monitoring Network, 11 Sites, United States, 2016. *MMWR Surveill. Summ.* **2020**, *69*, 1. [CrossRef]
14. Lord, C.; Petkova, E.; Hus, V.; Gan, W.; Lu, F.; Martin, D.M.; Ousley, O.; Guy, L.; Bernier, R.; Gerdts, J.; et al. A multisite study of the clinical diagnosis of different autism spectrum disorders. *Arch. Gen. Psychiatry* **2012**, *69*, 306–313. [CrossRef]
15. Baron-Cohen, S.; Leslie, A.M.; Frith, U. Does the autistic child have a "theory of mind". *Cognition* **1985**, *21*, 37–46. [CrossRef]
16. Rizzolatti, G.; Fabbri-Destro, M.; Cattaneo, L. Mirror neurons and their clinical relevance. *Nat. Clin. Pr. Neurol.* **2009**, *5*, 24–34. [CrossRef] [PubMed]
17. Kimhi, Y. Theory of mind abilities and deficits in autism spectrum disorders. *Top. Lang. Disord.* **2014**, *34*, 329–343. [CrossRef]
18. Kimhi, Y.; Shoam-Kugelmas, D.; Ben-Artzi, G.A.; Ben-Moshe, I.; Bauminger-Zviely, N. Theory of mind and executive function in preschoolers with typical development versus intellectually able preschoolers with autism spectrum disorder. *J. Autism Dev. Disord.* **2014**, *44*, 2341–2354. [CrossRef]
19. Salter, G.; Seigal, A.; Claxton, M.; Lawrence, K.; Skuse, D. Can autistic children read the mindof an animated triangle? *Autism* **2008**, *12*, 349–371. [CrossRef] [PubMed]
20. Rosset, D.B.; Rondan, C.; Da Fonseca, D.; Santos, A.; Assouline, B.; Deruelle, C. Typical emotion processing for cartoon but not for real faces in children with autistic spectrum disorders. *J. Autism Dev. Disord.* **2008**, *38*, 919–925. [CrossRef]
21. Kuusikko, S.; Haapsamo, H.; Jansson-Verkasalo, E.; Hurtig, T.; Mattila, M.-L.; Ebeling, H.; Jussila, K.; Bölte, S.; Moilanen, I.; Miettunen, H. Emotion recognition in children and adolescents with autism spectrum disorders. *J. Autism Dev. Disord.* **2009**, *39*, 938–945. [CrossRef]
22. Krebs, J.F.; Biswas, A.; Pascalis, O.; Kamp-Becker, I.; Remschmidt, H.; Schwarzer, G. Face processing in children with autism spectrum disorder: Independent or interactive processing of facial identity and facial expression? *J. Autism Dev. Disord.* **2011**, *41*, 796–804. [CrossRef]
23. Grossman, J.B.; Klin, A.; Carter, A.S.; Volkmar, F.R. Verbal bias in recognition of facial emotions in children with Asperger syndrome. *J. Child Psychol. Psychiatry Allied Discip.* **2000**, *41*, 369–379. [CrossRef]
24. Braverman, M.; Fein, D.; Lucci, D.; Waterhouse, L. Affect comprehension in children with pervasive developmental disorders. *J. Autism Dev. Disord.* **1989**, *19*, 301–315. [CrossRef]
25. Boucher, J.; Lewis, V. Unfamiliar face recognition in relatively able autistic children. *J. Child Psychol. Psychiatry* **1992**, *33*, 843–859. [CrossRef]
26. Raven, J.C. *CPM (Coloured Progressive Matrices)*; Giunti O.S.: Firenze, Italy, 1984.
27. Korkman, M.; Kirk, U.; Kemp, S. *NEPSY-II*; Giunti O.S. Psycometrics: Firenze, Italy, 2011.
28. Royer, J. *La Personnalité de L'enfant à Travers le Dessin du Bonhomme*; Editest: Bruxelles, Belgium, 1977.
29. Bombi, A.S.; Pinto, G. *I Colori Dell'amicizia. Studi Sulle Rappresentazioni Pittoriche Dell'amicizia tra Bambini*; Il Mulino: Bologna, Italy, 1993.
30. Abell, S.C.; Wood, W.; Liebman, S.J. Children's Human Figure Drawings as Measures of Intelligence: The Comparative Validity of Three Scoring Systems. *J. Psychoeduc. Assess.* **2001**, *19*, 204–215. [CrossRef]
31. Camara, W.J.; Nathan, J.S.; Puente, A.E. Psychological test usage: Implications in professional psychology. *Prof. Psychol. Res. Pract.* **2000**, *31*, 141–154. [CrossRef]
32. Cashel, M.L. Child and adolescent psychological assessment: Current clinical practices and the impact of managed care. *Prof. Psychol. Res. Pract.* **2002**, *33*, 446–453. [CrossRef]
33. Reynolds, C.R.; Hickman, J.A. *Draw-A-Person Intellectual Ability Test for Children, Adolescents, and Adults Examiner's Manual*; Pro-ed: Austin, TX, USA, 2004.
34. Mottron, L.; Belleville, S. Perspective production in a savant autistic draughtsman. *Psychol. Med.* **1995**, *25*, 639–648. [CrossRef] [PubMed]

35. O'Connor, N.; Hermelin, B. Visual and graphic abilities of the idiot savant artist. *Psychol. Med.* **1987**, *17*, 79–90. [CrossRef]
36. Nuara, A.; Papangelo, P.; Avanzini, P.; Fabbri-Destro, M. Body representation in children with unilateral cerebral palsy. *Front. Psychol.* **2019**, *10*, 354. [CrossRef]
37. Korkmaz, B. Theory of mind and neurodevelopmental disorders of childhood. *Pediatric Res.* **2011**, *69*, 101–108. [CrossRef]
38. Narzisi, A.; Muratori, F.; Calderoni, S.; Fabbro, F.; Urgesi, C. Neuropsychological profile in high functioning autism spectrum disorders. *J. Autism Dev. Disord.* **2013**, *43*, 1895–1909. [CrossRef]
39. Barron-Linnankoski, S.; Reinvall, O.; Lahervuori, A.; Voutilainen, A.; Lahti-Nuuttila, P.; Korkman, M. Neurocognitive performance of children with higher functioning autism spectrum disorders on the NEPSY-II. *Child Neuropsychol.* **2015**, *21*, 55–77. [CrossRef]
40. Tracy, J.L.; Robins, R.W.; Schriber, R.A.; Solomon, M. Is emotion recognition impaired in individuals with autism spectrum disorders? *J. Autism Dev. Disord.* **2011**, *41*, 102–109. [CrossRef]
41. Jemel, B.; Mottron, L.; Dawson, M. Impaired face processing in autism: Fact or artifact? *J. Autism Dev. Disord.* **2006**, *36*, 91–106. [CrossRef] [PubMed]
42. Adolphs, R.; Sears, L.; Piven, J. Abnormal processing of social information from faces in autism. *J. Cogn. Neuro Sci.* **2001**, *13*, 232–240. [CrossRef] [PubMed]
43. Harms, M.B.; Martin, A.; Wallace, G.L. Facial emotion recognition in autism spectrum disorders: A review of behavioral and neuroimaging studies. *Neuropsychol. Rev.* **2010**, *20*, 290–322. [CrossRef] [PubMed]
44. Nomi, J.S.; Uddin, L.Q. Face processing in autism spectrum disorders: From brain regions to brain networks. *Neuropsychologia* **2015**, *71*, 201–216. [CrossRef]
45. Constantino, J.N.; Gruber, C.P. *The Social Responsiveness Scale Manual*; Psychological Services: Los Angeles, CA, USA, 2005.
46. Happé, F. Autism: Cognitive deficit or cognitive style? *Trends Cogn. Sci.* **1999**, *3*, 216–222. [CrossRef]
47. Vivanti, G.; Hocking, D.R.; Fanning, P.; Dissanayake, C. Social affiliation motives modulate spontaneous learning in Williams syndrome but not in autism. *Mol. Autism* **2016**, *7*, 40. [CrossRef]
48. Bornstein, M.H.; Hahn, C.S.; Suwalsky, J.T. Physically developed and exploratory young infants contribute to their own long-term academic achievement. *Psychol. Sci.* **2013**, *24*, 1906–1917. [CrossRef]
49. Walker-Andrews, A.; Krogh-Jespersen, S.; Mayhew, E.; Coffield, C. The situated infant. In *Infant Mind: Origins of the Social Brain*; Legerstee, M., Haley, D., Bornstein, M., Eds.; Guilford Press: New York, NY, USA, 2013.
50. Fabbri-Destro, M.; Gizzonio, V.; Avanzini, P. Autism, motor dysfunctions and mirror mechanism. *Clin. Neuropsychiatry* **2013**, *10*, 177–187.

11

Behavioral and Autonomic Responses in Treating Children with High-Functioning Autism Spectrum Disorder: Clinical and Phenomenological Insights from Two Case Reports

Lucia Billeci [1], Ettore Caterino [2], Alessandro Tonacci [1,*] and Maria Luisa Gava [3]

1 Institute of Clinical Physiology, National Research Council of Italy, 56124 Pisa, Italy; lucia.billeci@ifc.cnr.it
2 Azienda USL Sudest Toscana, Centro Autismo UFSMIA di Grosseto, Ospedale di Castel del Piano, 58033 Grosseto, Italy; ettore.caterino@uslsudest.toscana.it
3 Associazione Nazionale Famiglie di Persone con Disabilità Intellettiva e/o Relazionale (ANFFAS), 18100 Imperia, Italy; marialuisa.gava@gmail.com
* Correspondence: atonacci@ifc.cnr.it

Abstract: In this study, we aimed to evaluate the process applied in subjects with Autism Spectrum Disorder (ASD) to elaborate and communicate their experiences of daily life activities, as well as to assess the autonomic nervous system response that subtend such a process. This procedure was evaluated for the first time in two eight-year-old girls with high-functioning ASDs. The subjects performed six months of training, based on the cognitive–motivational–individualized (c.m.i.®) approach, which mainly consisted in building domestic procedures and re-elaborating acquired experiences through drawing or the use of icons made by the children. Together with behavioral observations, the response of the autonomic nervous system during such re-elaboration was recorded. A change in communicative and interactive competences was observed, moving from a condition of spontaneity to one in which the girls were engaged in relating their experiences to a parent. Autonomic response highlighted how, in communicating their own experiences, they achieved a state of cognitive activation, which enabled a greater communicative and emotional connection with the interlocutor. This is a proof-of-concept study on the application of the c.m.i.®, which needs to be extensively validated in the clinical setting.

Keywords: high-functioning autism; language; experience; communication; autonomic nervous system; wearable technologies

1. Introduction

In the field of Autism Spectrum Disorders (ASD), several studies showed the importance of structuring a space, a time and a specific visual support as part of the related clinical intervention [1]. Many behavioral approaches provide a visual target to a child with ASD in order to implement the acquisition of a skill (i.e., washing the hands), assuming that the child would be more sensitized and would have a greater level of attention and orientation if induced to the object or action by an iconic structure.

However, according to our previous research study [2], our idea is that a child with ASD, somewhat similar to a typical developing child, should learn a procedure in a natural context (i.e., in their own environment) and then, eventually, use icons or visual references to recall the acquired skills. In this way, the child will be able to understand the real meaning of the visual reference used with respect to what the children have acquired during their own experience. In this way, the icons will only represent the starting point for recalling the actions the subject has previously learned (i.e., washing, dressing, cooking, etc.). Notably, this process requires the subject to be able to manipulate the experience acquired with a higher level of awareness and participation and then to verbalize and recall their own experiences. To recognize their experience, they should mentally manipulate the acquired contents (i.e., who, what, where and when) and the connections made among the motor actions performed. This is often difficult in children with high-functioning ASD due to the presence of deficits in executive functions [3,4], in social perception [5] and in narrative and pragmatic skills.

In this framework, the cognitive–motivational–individualized (c.m.i.®) approach is aimed at supporting an orientation and awareness process of personal reality and knowledge in subjects with verbal and/or cognitive and/or relational disabilities, so that they can organize and express their thoughts in a more understandable and orderly way. This approach, initially set up to facilitate work with augmentative and alternative communication (AAC) [6], represents a learning process since, through a specific reconstruction of daily life activities and work, the subject is helped to acquire these experiences in a more conscious and autonomous way. Specifically, to facilitate this process, a figurative reworking is proposed in order to make the experience concrete, visible and manually usable. From this perspective, the subject must retrace the practical process of the experience both on a symbolic plane and on a motor level, manipulating the components (i.e., what, where, who) and their connections or semantic constraints (i.e., what/where, who/what) in a praxis narrative form that refers to the experiential action. This would enable an understand of the process within which the subject retains the elements that are significant for them in reality (what he/she knows, what he/she does, what he/she likes, where the experiences take place and with whom they do these experiences) and how performing motor actions (acting on the images, the icons drawn from his/her everyday experience) re-elaborates his/her knowledge. The overall aim is to facilitate the integration between the experiential and phenomenal meaning performed with the body and language (lexical semantics) to avoid—as often happens in children with ASD—that, during the narration, the subject is only using the lexical meaning without the emotional content, which defines intentionality in the communication, the participation and, therefore, the intersubjective sense of language [7–9].

Together with behavioral observation, the assessment of physiological parameters during the task of reproducing the acquired experience in ASD subjects could help the clinician to understand the way the subjects are processing these experiences. In particular, several studies suggest that Autonomic Nervous System (ANS) activity is linked to social functioning in individuals with ASD [10–14]. Both the sympathetic (SNS) and parasympathetic (PNS) branches of the ANS contribute to social functioning and communication [15,16], with SNS activation reflecting a threat-oriented response, and PNS dominance easing adaptive social engagement [17]. More specifically, the PNS plays an important role in social functioning by innervating several organs in the face and in the neck and affecting various functions, including cardiac activity, which are related to social behavior and communication [18]. Thus, in a social setting, an increase in the PNS activity is related to an adaptive social behavior [13]. The SNS also plays an important role in social functioning, increasing heart rate (HR), sweating and alert state, mainly through acting on the so-called "fight or flight" mechanism [19,20].

Wearable technologies can be particularly relevant in the assessment of ANS in ASD due to their low obtrusiveness. In particular, the recording of the electrocardiogram (ECG) signal allows us to evaluate the activation of both the PNS and SNS by studying heart rate variability (HRV) [10]. On the other hand, the assessment of the galvanic skin response (GSR) is mainly related to the SNS, with a reduction in the signal associated with decreased SNS influence [21], whereas an increase in skin conductance during specific social tasks subtends higher SNS activation [22].

In this study, we aim to highlight how, in subjects with high-functioning ASD, it is a priority to enhance the mechanisms of self-awareness related to their experiences and knowledge rather than immediately using linguistic codes, icons or scripts or giving heuristic value to a phenomenological approach. More specifically, the objectives of the present study include: (i) to evaluate the behavior and communication of two subjects with ASD during the elaboration of an experiential content (procedural actions of shared daily life with the parent); (ii) to assess the ANS responses that underlie the subjects' behavior during such elaboration.

2. Materials and Methods

2.1. Participants

The subjects were two eight-year-old girls, with diagnoses of ASD, attending the "Autism service of the public health of the city of Grosseto". The protocol was approved by the Institutional Ethical Clearance board of the National Research Council (0087922/2019).

2.1.1. Subject 1—J

At the age of 3, J. received a clinical diagnosis of Autism Spectrum Disorder (ASD) confirmed with the Autism Diagnostic Observation Schedule-Generic (ADOS-G) [23]. Her non-verbal cognitive level, measured through Leiter-R [24] and Color Progressive Matrices [25] was average. In her clinical history, motor and language delays were reported. At the age of 3, J. showed a severe psychomotor and language regression. In this period, J. also partially lost sphincter control, showing sialorrhoea and feeding disturbance. She was severely apathetic. Before enrollment in this study, she started a psychoeducational intervention including speech and psychomotor therapies. At the age of the enrollment (6 y), J. presented a normostructured language with flat prosody and a socio-pragmatic disorder. Regarding her motor skills, she presented hypotonia and coarse-motor impairment, while she had adequate fine motor praxes and graph-pictorial skills.

2.1.2. Subject 2—B

At the age of 5, B. received a clinical diagnosis of Autism Spectrum Disorder (ASD) confirmed with ADOS-G. Her cognitive level, measured through Wechsler Preschool and Primary Scale of Intelligence (WPPSI-III) [26], was average (Full Scale Intelligence Quotient, FSIQ = 107). In her clinical history, language delay, marked issues in emotional dysregulation and Attention Deficit Hyperactivity Disorder (ADHD) were reported. Before enrollment in the study, she started a psychoeducational intervention. At the age of enrollment (6 y), B. was an hyperverbal child with high functioning ASD in comorbidity with ADHD and emotional dysregulation (i.e., meltdown). She used reinforcement strategies for performing school—and daily life—activities (i.e., planned and structured environments and activities, visual aids).

2.2. The c.m.i.® Approach

The c.m.i.® approach adopts a naturalistic and developmental approach (NBDI) [27]. It targets social, interactive and communication impairments in autism. The rationale is that children with autism would respond with enhanced communicative and social development to a style of parent communication adapted to their impairments [28]. The intervention is aimed to enhance the link between neuropsychological and relational skills. The rationale of c.m.i.® is the application of embodied cognition in the intervention for ASD. Inspired by Johnson-Glenberg and Megowan-Romanowicz [29], the three degrees of embodiment are considered: (a) sensorimotor experience; (b) link between body language and feelings; (c) emotional immersion experienced by the user.

The c.m.i.® methodology is aimed at supporting an orientation process and awareness of one's reality and knowledge in subjects with verbal, cognitive and relational disabilities so that they can organize and express their thoughts in a more comprehensible and orderly way. This experience is made explicit initially using the body—doing and perceiving also represent a form of non-verbal communication which subsequently and progressively evolves into language. The intervention allows a progressive maturation of orientation abilities in reality that affects the following dimensions: (i) spatial: where are things, people, objects; (ii) temporal: when events occur; (iii) instrumental: objects in the environment, their nature, their functions; (iv) relational: people around the subject.

2.3. Training According to the Cognitive Motivational Intervention (c.m.i.®)

The training of the two subjects according to the c.m.i.® approach was performed at home and involved the parents. It consisted of the following phases:

- Interview with the parents: During the interview, the parents were informed about the aims and modalities of the training approach and their involvement in the process. In addition, informed consent was obtained from the parents of the two girls enrolled, after receiving an exhaustive explanation of the study. Such explanation included: (a) the description of the theory of the cognitive motivational intervention; (b) the rationale of physiological signal acquisition and the procedures for data collection; (c) detailed description of home procedures; (d) the description of the re-elaboration of acquired experiences through drawing; (e) the modalities of using icons by the children.
- Observation of the two girls: This aimed at identifying the individual characteristics of the two girls. J. loves drawing and adds plenty of particulars in her drawings, although images look quite static. Conversely, B. is constantly in motion and uses continuous, redundant, sophisticated and dyspragmatic language. She does not like drawing, but rather prefers moving and talking. She has difficulties in maintaining task concentration. In order to manage individual differences among the subjects, meetings with parents were organized in order to explain to them the individual phenotypic profile of their child and how to manage the emotional experience of the child as well as their own. Specifically, therapists contacted the parents four times a month after the initial meeting.
- Training to realize the procedures: The parents were instructed how to guide the two girls in the acquisition of specific procedures, which consisted in cooking the girls' favorite foods (spaghetti for J. and biscuits for B.). Then, the girls were helped in acquiring information about the environments in which they were supposed to cook (which objects to use and where they are located). Once a week, the two girls were involved in making up their favorite food.

2.4. Evaluation of the Acquired Procedure

The evaluation of the acquired procedure was performed in a laboratory setting and was aimed at recalling the procedures acquired at home to allow the transition from praxis to a symbolic action when the girls reached a certain degree of autonomy. The session was guided by the experimenter who developed the c.m.i.® approach (M.L.G.).

The first phase of the evaluation (after six months) consisted in performing a graphical trace, which represented a symbolic reconstruction of the kitchen and objects used at home. Each girl was seated next to the experimenter at a table on which some papers and markers were positioned. First, the girl was guided in recovering the experience learned at home on the verbal level and subsequently in the drawing of the objects and the ingredients she used at home for cooking the selected food.

The second phase of the evaluation (after 10 months) consisted in the action on the represented, which dealt with the description of the experience acquired at home through the use of mobile icons to reproduce the motor action performed in the real scenario.

2.5. Physiological Signal Acquisition

During the evaluation procedure, the two subjects were equipped with two minimally obtrusive, wireless, wearable sensors for the monitoring of the electrocardiogram (ECG) and galvanic skin response (GSR). The ECG signal was acquired through the Shimmer ECG sensor (Shimmer Sensing, Dublin, Ireland) with a sampling frequency of 500 Hz, whereas the GSR signal was captured by the Shimmer3 GSR+ sensor (Shimmer Sensing, Dublin, Ireland) with a sampling frequency of 51.2 Hz. The Shimmer ECG acquired the relevant signal attached to a fitness-like chest strap manufactured by Polar Electro Oy (Kempele, Finland), whereas the Shimmer3 GSR+ captured the galvanic skin response by adhering to two nearby fingers of the subject's non-dominant hand through comfortable rings. The signals were acquired while the subject was seated on a chair at a table during the following phases:

- Baseline (3′): Basal measurement. Here, the subject was asked to stay as still as possible.
- Task (15′): Signal acquisition during the proposed tasks.
- Recovery (3′): Post-task basal measurement. The subject was required to stay as still as possible, similar to baseline.

2.6. Physiological Signal Analysis

The acquired physiological signals were processed using Matlab (Mathworks, Natick, MA, USA). In particular, the ECG signal was analyzed using home-made scripts for the calculation of the tachogram (RR series; i.e., the time elapsed between two successive R-waves) according to the Pan–Tompkins algorithm [30] and to extract both time and frequency domain features characterizing the ANS for each of the different phases.

The features extracted included:

- Heart rate (HR): the number of contractions of the heart occurring per time unit, expressed in bpm;
- Standard deviation of normal to normal RR intervals (SDNN): measure of heart rate variability (HRV), expressed in ms;
- Normalized component of the power spectral density of the ECG signal at low frequency (0.04–0.15 Hz) (nLF), which is related both to the sympathetic and parasympathetic response;
- Normalized component of the power spectral density of the ECG spectrum at high frequency (0.15–0.4 Hz) (nHF), which is mainly related to the parasympathetic response;
- Low versus high frequency components of the power spectral density of the ECG spectrum (LF/HF Ratio), which expresses the balance between the sympathetic and parasympathetic nervous system branches.

GSR signal was analyzed using Ledalab V3.4.9 (General Public License (GNU)), a Matlab-based tool enabling the user to extract typical features of the GSR signal, notably its tonic and phasic components [31]. Specifically—albeit both of the abovementioned components were extracted for this work only the tonic phase was analyzed, since the rationale of the study aimed at comparing the signal in the different phases rather than evaluating the response to a given single stimulation.

Additional details about the analysis procedure can be found in previous studies [32,33].

3. Results

To assess the effects of treatment for every child and, keeping in line with the case series design, data were examined on an individual participant basis. Individual changes in social communication, adaptive behavior and neural response to social stimuli are discussed below.

3.1. Behavioral Observations

After a six month period (follow-up) of behavioral observations of the two subjects included in the present work, a critical evaluation was conducted concerning the experience carried out at home.

J. loved drawing. Compared to her previous drawings that were very static, she added an increasing number of dynamic characteristics in her storytelling and her drawings (i.e., climbing stairs, drying clothes). She was very precise and participated in the reconstruction of the objects, using language, eye contact and checking whether the therapist or the adult was able to listen to her and whether her work was being appreciated, as shown in Figure 1a.

(a) (b)

Figure 1. The first evaluation consisting in the graphical trace. (**a**) The drawing by J., (**b**) B. watches the experimenter drawing while she verbalizes.

B. reported difficulties in terms of the graphical realization of the tasks demanded. She preferred to use her voice to describe the steps of the recipe learned at home, while the experimenter realized the drawing, as shown in Figure 1b. She displayed quite rich and cogent language, albeit not always adherent to reality. The deposition of her mother was particularly interesting, as she reported significantly less automated language and an optimal self-care when physically engaged in actions.

After 10 months (second follow-up), the re-evaluation consisted in the action of the represented task, aimed at representing actions developed at home within the praxis procedure using mobile icons on a re-constructed background. The adult helped the child in re-constructing the kitchen on a paper sheet, positioning fixed objects (including furniture), whereas mobile ones were manipulated to narrate the procedure of cooked food.

J. verbalized the different phases, being very careful in adding elements related to the procedure, as shown in Figure 2a.

(a) (b)

Figure 2. The second evaluation consisting in the action on the represented task. (**a**) The cooking of the biscuits realized with the icons by J., (**b**) B. reconstructing the procedure of cooking spaghetti.

B. often used mobile elements with good motor and language competence. Compared to the graphical trace evaluation, she expressed more self-control, as shown in Figure 2b.

Importantly, both girls' parents seemed to participate in their daughters' work. They highlighted with surprise and continuous discovery some characteristics of their daughters and they were more attentive about the movements of their children in the environment and about the way actions were followed (e.g., preparing "green" spaghetti and "white and black" biscuits, etc., spontaneously and with personal semantic links between objects and actions).

3.2. Autonomic Nervous System Response—Graphical Trace

With J., the task highlighted the presence of verbalization with and without ocular contact. When the drawing was similar to the experienced reality, the subject increased ocular contact with respect to the therapist, whereas a stereotyped drawing drove her to hypo-regulation and relational disinvestment.

According to behavioral observations, for J. the physiological signals were segmented in three different sub-phases during the execution of the task: verbalization with eye-contact, verbalization without eye-contact, and no response (during which she was concentrated on drawing and did not reply to the experimenter).

Concerning the ECG, an increased HR and a decreased HRV during verbalization with ocular contact was observed, as shown in Figure 3a,c. Conversely, during verbalization without eye contact, as well as during non-response phases and less cognitively-demanding tasks, the HRV was significantly increased, as shown in Figure 3c. Focusing on the SNS/PNS activation, it is worth noting that the SNS activity increased during the task, with somewhat of a SNS withdrawal during the verbalization with eye contact, probably due to a decrease in the stress level of the subject when interacting with the therapist, as shown in Figure 3b,d.

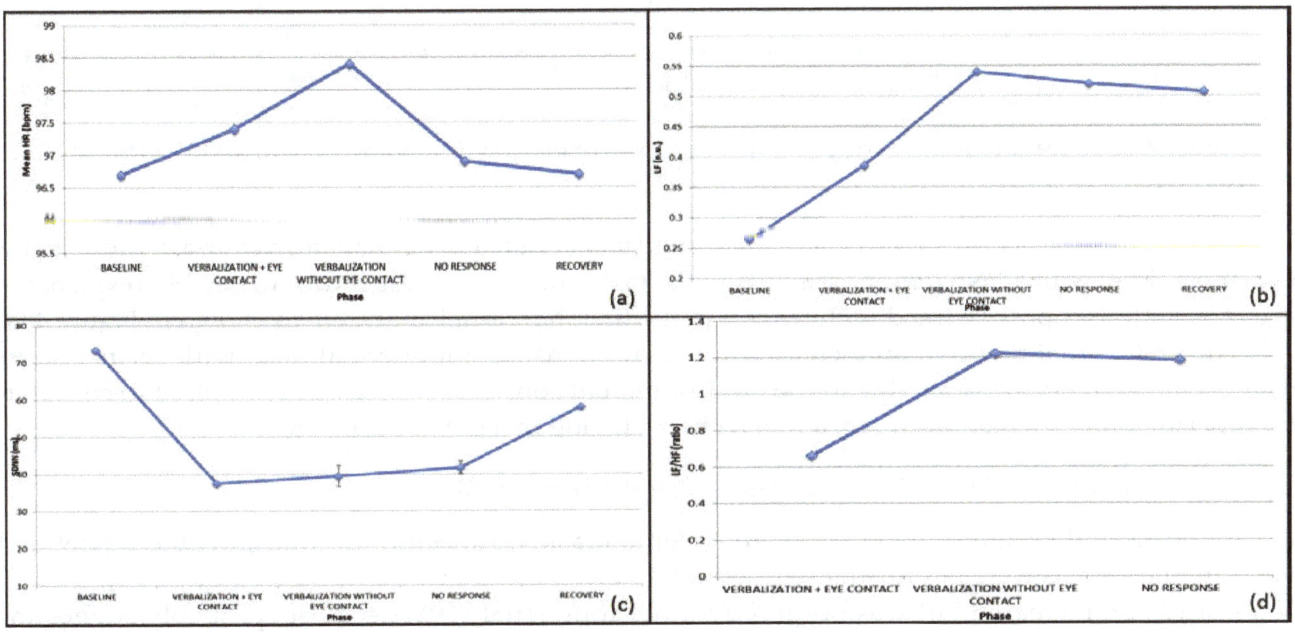

Figure 3. ECG features for J. during the various phases of the graphical trace: (**a**) HR, (**b**) LF, (**c**) SDNN, (**d**) LF/HF.

With J., the GSR signal displayed an increased phasic component, related to the response to a given stimulation during the task, whereas the tonic component mainly increased at recovery, indicating that the stress response, activated by the task performed, remained active after the completion of the task.

B. verbalized both during the execution of the graphical trace by the therapist and without the drawing. According to this behavioral observation, for B. the physiological signals were segmented in two different sub-phases during the execution of the task: verbalization with the graphical trace and verbalization without the graphical trace.

Concerning the ECG signal, the HR was increased from baseline to task during both phases, probably suggesting a higher arousal level while performing the tasks, followed by a similar decrease during recovery. Similar to the first subject, the HRV decreased here during the task, particularly while verbalizing and performing graphical trace (i.e., during a higher emotionally-demanding task), as shown in Figure 4a,c.

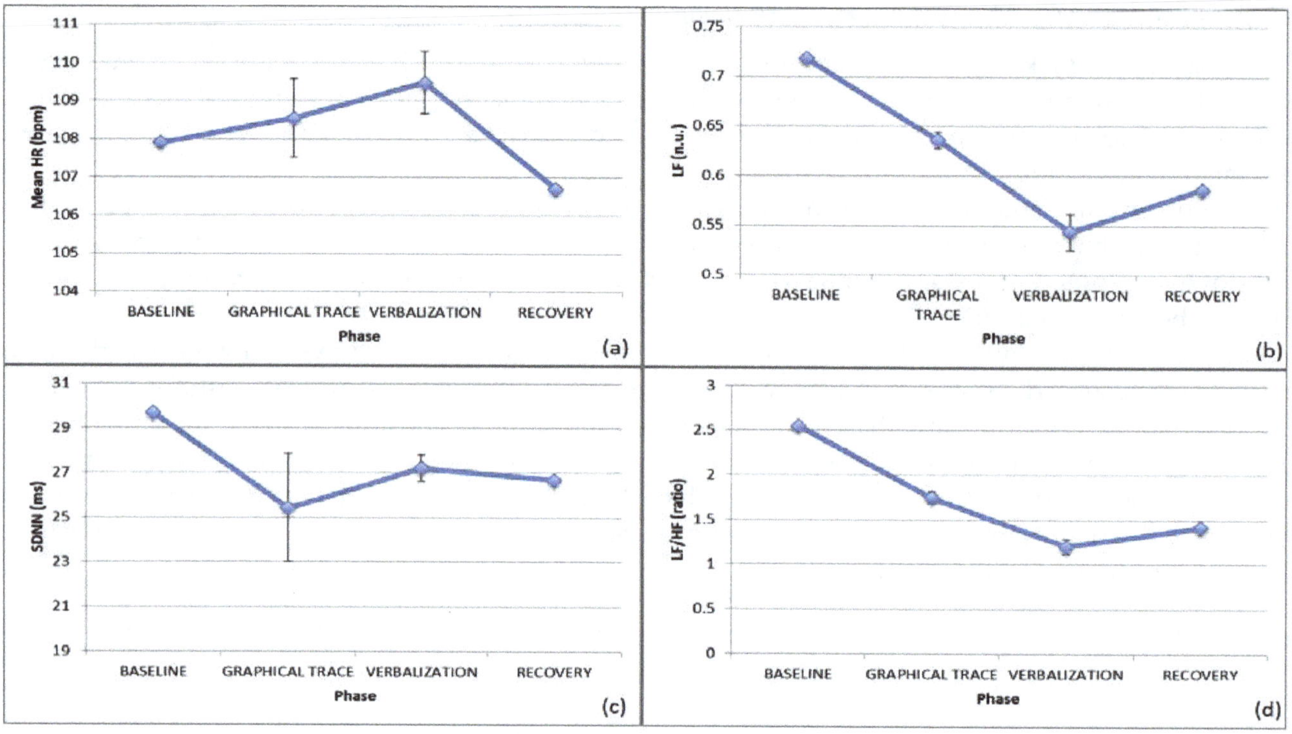

Figure 4. ECG features for B. during the various phases of the graphical trace: (**a**) HR, (**b**) LF, (**c**) SDNN, (**d**) LF/HF.

Focusing on the SNS/PNS activation, the second subject already displayed an over-activation of the SNS at baseline, with a PNS dominance during the task, ending with the return to a SNS prevalence at recovery, with the opposite trend with respect to the first individual analyzed, as shown in Figure 4b,d.

The GSR signal revealed an increased tonic and phasic component at task, with further stress evidence at recovery, possibly due to the environmental constraints necessarily applied to complete the experimental task (i.e., sitting on a given chair, staying in a given room, etc.).

3.3. *Autonomic Nervous System Response—Action on the Represented*

In the second task, the action on the represented task, no specific sub-phases could be defined, therefore the signals were not further segmented.

With J., an increased HR was observed with a contextual HRV decrease, probably suggesting significant cognitive involvement by the subject, as shown in Figure 5. Focusing on the SNS/PNS activation, the PNS component was dominating throughout the trial, with a slight increase in SNS activity at task.

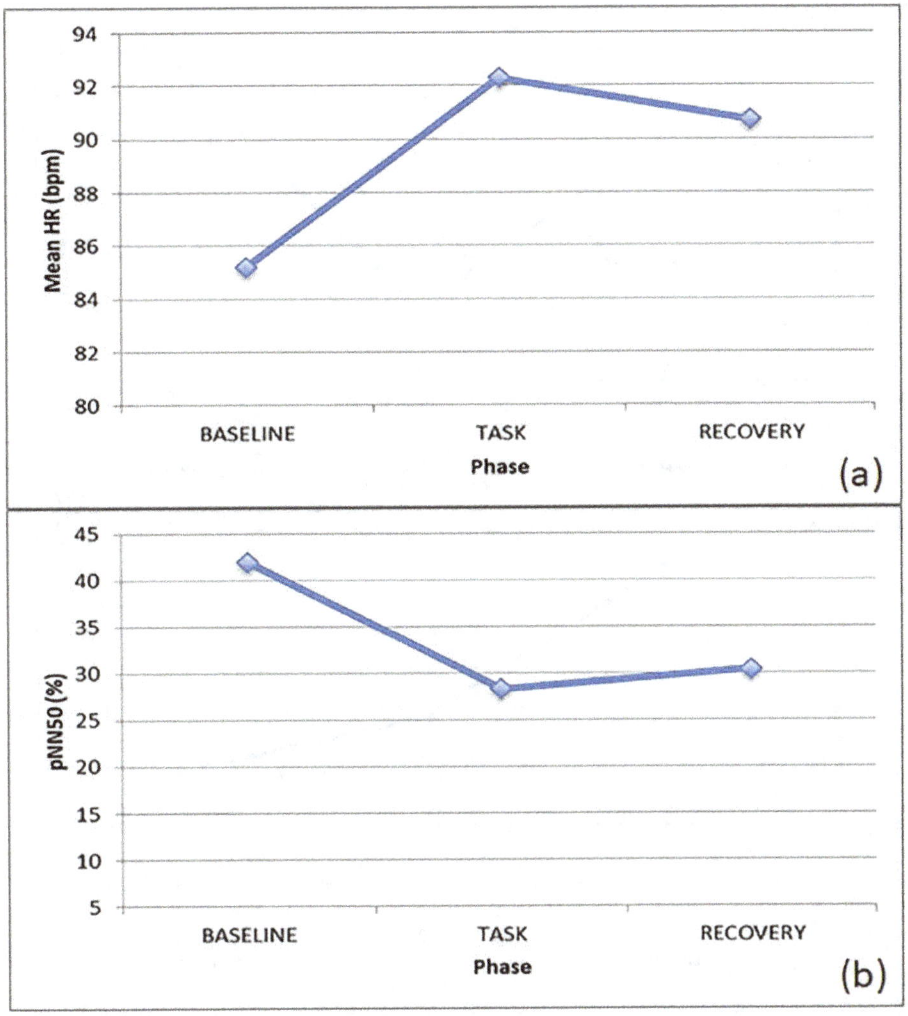

Figure 5. ECG features for J. during the various phases of the action on the represented: (**a**) HR, (**b**) pNN50.

The GSR signal showed an increased tonic component at task, probably suggesting an enhanced emotional involvement, whereas the phasic component appeared to be decreased, possibly because of the emotional involvement taking place for the engagement phase more than for the single tasks administered.

With B., a decreased HR and HRV at task was noticed, probably due to relaxation and enhanced task-demanded concentration, as shown in Figure 6.

The evaluation of SNS/PNS confirmed the tendency towards a SNS decrease at task, lasting up to the recovery phase, confirming the regulatory effect of the demanded task, considering the different basal involvement of the subject, who was more stressed at the beginning of the experimental protocol with respect to the previous individual.

Finally, as for the GSR signal, both the tonic and phasic components are higher as long as the test takes place, probably due to the abovementioned logistic constraints for the test administration for the previous subject tested.

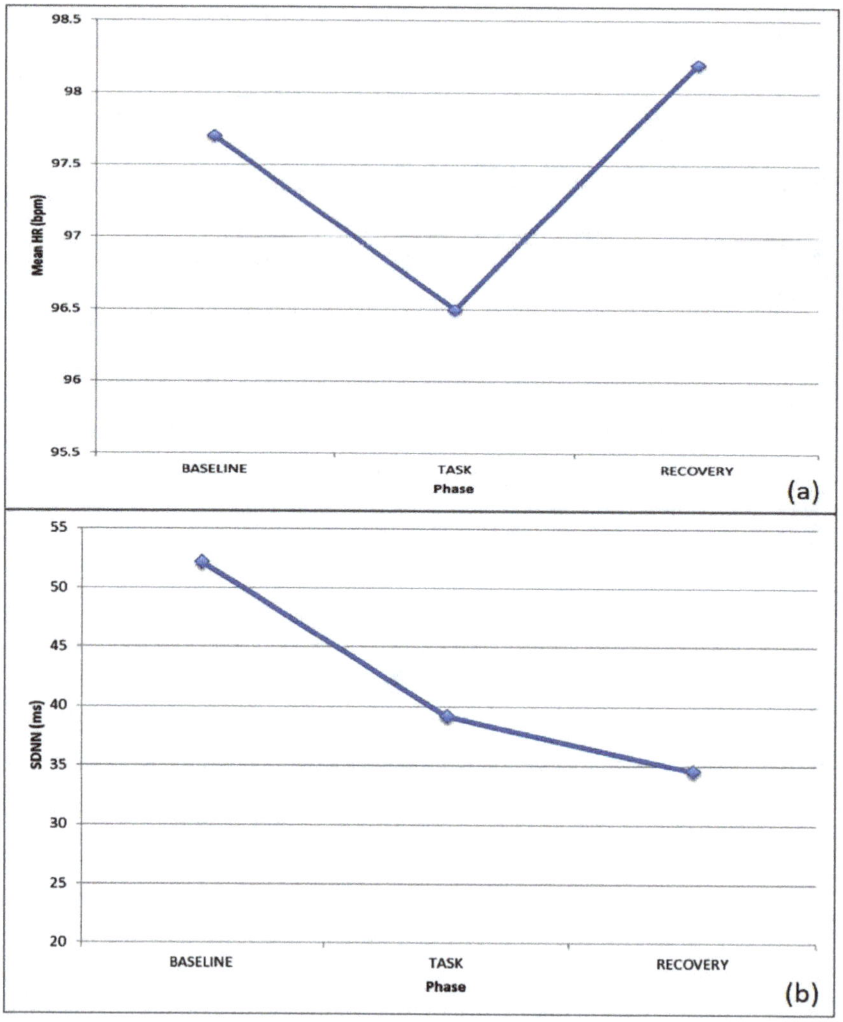

Figure 6. HR/HRV for B. during the various phases of the action on the represented: (**a**) HR, (**b**) SDNN.

4. Discussion

The most important lesson learned during the test administration and the discussion of the results of the present study protocol is the pivotal need for the personalization of the therapy that children with neurodevelopmental disorders should undergo. Indeed, despite the fact that the present study took into account just two subjects, with the same age and somewhat similar clinical characteristics, the personal attitudes, behaviors, and past histories surely played a significant role in their responses, with completely different neurophysiological adaptations to the tasks administered displayed by the two children. Indeed, different autonomic responses were seen between the two individuals, with different trends likely to be due to the personal attitudes of both subjects. With J., the clinical observation and the physiological parameters show how the girl, when left alone, tends towards a condition of hypo-regulation and relational closure. In this phase, she draws in a stereotyped way. When asked to design her own experiences, on the contrary, she expresses good communication skills, eye contact, and a greater adherence to the represented content. In this phase, the physiological parameters show that she is more engaged in the task and she has a good relationship with the examiner with the experiences she has learned in her own reality. With B.—who also has a hyper-regulated neurosensory profile at the baseline—progressive emotional regulation, emotional engagement and, therefore, good homeostasis, was obtained through cognitive reorganization (graphic trace, action on the represented task) and the narration of her experiences. Notably she remains regulated in the recovery phase after performing the drawing and the action on the represented task, as if, through this experience of reorganization, she could reach the regulation of her emotional components that usually tend to be dysregulated, impulsive and destabilizing.

These observations of individual characteristics and autonomic responses of the subjects, that happen quite often in presence of subjects with ASD, even with similar clinical characteristics, pave the way to a strongly personalized approach to the treatment.

To this extent, the proof of concept related to the importance of precision medicine in neurodevelopmental disorders has been already highlighted in past years, with interesting links postulated within the framework of genotype–phenotype relationships [34]. Indeed, treatment personalization might provide some benefit by addressing some of the deficits shown by children, even in the field of neurodevelopmental disorders [35].

The present work suggests that the cognitive–motivational–individualized (c.m.i.®) approach, the main focus of our investigation, sets its basis on this concept, completely relying on providing a complete overview of the individual aspects of a child and taking into account both cognitive and motivational dimensions to optimize the treatment outcome. In particular, the therapist administering the protocol should be able to empower the positive mindset of the individual treated. Indeed, ASD, even more than other neurodevelopmental disorders, presents individuals that are highly motivated to engage in their special interests, and are more motivated than non-ASD subjects (particularly typically developing controls) by intrinsic motivational factors, some of which are associated with positive effects [36]. Additionally, cognitive level should be taken into account in ASD, as demonstrated by the positive cognitive gains that behavioral and cognitive therapy has on individuals with ASD during adolescence (see [37] for an example) and even during adulthood [38].

Such positive preliminary impressions, albeit necessitating the confirmation on large-scale studies brought forward by the first results of this investigation, should be carefully considered, even in light of some acknowledged limitations. At first, the enrollment of just two subjects does not allow us to draw conclusions applicable to the general ASD population, or even to its subgroups (i.e., High-Functioning ASD); however, it gives us room for further investigation, applying c.m.i.® to larger cohorts likely to confirm an extreme heterogeneity of the treatment response. Notably, this study represents a proof-of-concept for the application of the c.m.i.® approach, which is based on a theoretical framework, and on the assessment of the physiological response of subjects with ASD during such treatment.

Second, the application, in this protocol, of c.m.i.® to only female subjects could reveal cognitive, behavioral and motivational characteristics that are specifically gender-biased, thus not reflecting the reality possibly observed among males, which represent the vast majority of ASD individuals (see [39] for some estimates).

Third, the fact that the two subjects enrolled belonged to an age group between 6 and 10 years, together with the absence of a control group, made it difficult to ascertain the likely positive effect due to c.m.i.® with respect to a general positive effect due to age. Therefore, future studies should include a control group to effectively discriminate further the contribution of c.m.i.® to the personal cognitive growth of ASD children.

Fourth, the use of wearables, even if recently more frequent in the scientific literature dealing with ASD (see, for example, [40,41]), should take advantage of a wider, better grounded amount of data, which will be possible step-by-step in next few years when such methodologies, still relatively new in the neurophysiological monitoring of ASD, will fully enter scientific society.

Under such premises, still taking into full consideration the abovementioned limitations, and if confirmed on large-scale studies, the proposed approach could flank traditional therapies, possibly improving the patients' outcomes based on their own specificities, paving the way for precision medicine in ASD and neurodevelopmental disorders. Further studies are needed to extensively apply and validate the proposed approach in a clinical setting.

5. Conclusions

The pilot study described here presented a novel approach for improving cognitive features of children and adolescents with ASD, leaning on personal motivations and own interests. Despite presenting some benefits for the patients included in the present study, the beneficial effects of this approach should be confirmed on larger cohorts, also taking advantage of the enrollment of control groups, lacking in our protocol. Eventual, likely positive results would further enable the large-scale application of the c.m.i. approach flanking traditional cognitive and behavioral therapies.

Author Contributions: Conceptualization, L.B., E.C. and M.L.G.; Data curation, L.B., A.T. and M.L.G.; Formal analysis, L.B. and A.T.; Funding acquisition, E.C. and M.L.G.; Investigation, L.B., E.C., A.T. and M.L.G.; Methodology, L.B., E.C. and M.L.G.; Project administration, L.B., E.C., A.T. and M.L.G.; Resources, E.C. and M.L.G.; Software, L.B. and A.T.; Supervision, E.C. and M.L.G.; Validation, L.B., E.C., A.T. and M.L.G.; Writing—original draft, L.B., E.C., A.T. and M.L.G.; Writing—review and editing, L.B., A.T. and M.L.G. All authors have read and agreed to the published version of the manuscript.

References

1. Beadle-Brown, J.; Wilkinson, D.; Richardson, L.; Shaughnessy, N.; Trimingham, M.; Leigh, J.; Whelton, B.; Himmerich, J. Imagining Autism: Feasibility of a drama-based intervention on the social, communicative and imaginative behaviour of children with autism. *Autism* **2018**, *22*, 915–927. [CrossRef]
2. Gava, M.L.; Caterino, E. Autismo: Pensiero, azione, comunicazione. L'applicazione del metodo c.m.i.® (cognitivo-motivazionale-individualizzato) a soggetti con autismo a basso funzionamento. *Autismo Disturbi Dello Svilupp.* **2014**, *12*, 249–271.
3. Pennington, B.F.; Rogers, S.J.; Bennetto, L.; Griffith, E.M.; Reed, D.T.; Shyu, V. Validity tests of the executive dysfunction hypothesis of autism. In *Autism as an Executive Disorder*; Russell, J., Ed.; Oxford University Press (OUP): Oxford, UK, 1997; pp. 143–178.
4. Peristeri, E.; Baldimtsi, E.; Andreou, M.; Tsimpli, I.M. The impact of bilingualism on the narrative ability and the executive functions of children with autism spectrum disorders. *J. Commun. Disord.* **2020**, *85*, 105999. [CrossRef]
5. Narzisi, A.; Muratori, F.; Calderoni, S.; Fabbro, F.; Urgesi, C. Neuropsychological Profile in High Functioning Autism Spectrum Disorders. *J. Autism Dev. Disord.* **2012**, *43*, 1895–1909. [CrossRef]
6. Gava, M.L. *La Comunicazione Aumentativa Alternativa tra Pensiero e Parola*; Franco Angeli: Milan, Italy, 2013.
7. King, D.; Dockrell, J.E.; Stuart, M. Event narratives in 11-14 year olds with autistic spectrum disorder. *Int. J. Lang. Commun. Disord.* **2013**, *48*, 522–533. [CrossRef] [PubMed]
8. Losh, M.; Capps, L. Narrative ability in high-functioning children with autism or Asperger's syndrome. *J. Autism Dev. Disord.* **2003**, *33*, 239–251. [CrossRef] [PubMed]
9. Peristeri, E.; Andreou, M.; Tsimpli, I.M. Syntactic and Story Structure Complexity in the Narratives of High- and Low-Language Ability Children with Autism Spectrum Disorder. *Front. Psychol.* **2017**, *8*, 2027. [CrossRef]
10. Dawson, G.; Finley, C.; Phillips, S.; Lewy, A. A comparison of hemispheric asymmetries in speech-related brain potentials of autistic and dysphasic children. *Brain Lang.* **1989**, *37*, 26–41. [CrossRef]
11. Romanczyk, R.; Gillis, J.M.; Baron, M.G.; Groden, J.; Groden, G.; Lipsitt, L.P. Autism and the Physiology of Stress and Anxiety. In *Stress and Coping in Autism*; Baron, M.G., Groden, J., Groden, G., Lipsitt, L., Eds.; Oxford University Press (OUP): Oxford, UK, 2006; pp. 183–204.
12. Faja, S.; Murias, M.; Beauchaine, T.P.; Dawson, G. Reward-based decision making and electrodermal responding by young children with autism spectrum disorders during a gambling task. *Autism Res.* **2013**, *6*, 494–505. [CrossRef] [PubMed]
13. Sheinkopf, S.J.; Neal-Beevers, A.R.; Levine, T.P.; Miller-Loncar, C.; Lester, B. Parasympathetic Response Profiles Related to Social Functioning in Young Children with Autistic Disorder. *Autism Res. Treat.* **2013**, *2013*, 868396. [CrossRef] [PubMed]
14. Neuhaus, E.; Bernier, R.; Beauchaine, T.P. Brief Report: Social Skills, Internalizing and Externalizing Symptoms, and Respiratory Sinus Arrhythmia in Autism. *J. Autism Dev. Disord.* **2013**, *44*, 730–737. [CrossRef]

15. Porges, S.W. The polyvagal theory: Phylogenetic substrates of a social nervous system. *Int. J. Psychophysiol.* **2001**, *42*, 123–146. [CrossRef]
16. Porges, S.W. The Polyvagal Theory: Phylogenetic contributions to social behavior. *Physiol. Behav.* **2003**, *79*, 503–513. [CrossRef]
17. Bal, E.; Harden, E.; Lamb, D.; Van Hecke, A.V.; Denver, J.W.; Porges, S.W. Emotion Recognition in Children with Autism Spectrum Disorders: Relations to Eye Gaze and Autonomic State. *J. Autism Dev. Disord.* **2010**, *40*, 358–370. [CrossRef] [PubMed]
18. Neuhaus, E.; Bernier, R.A.; Beauchaine, T.P. Children with Autism Show Altered Autonomic Adaptation to Novel and Familiar Social Partners. *Autism Res.* **2016**, *9*, 579–591. [CrossRef] [PubMed]
19. Stifter, C.A.; Dollar, J.M.; Cipriano, E.A. Temperament and emotion regulation: The role of autonomic nervous system reactivity. *Dev. Psychobiol.* **2011**, *53*, 266–279. [CrossRef] [PubMed]
20. Diamond, L.M.; Cribbet, M.R. Links between adolescent sympathetic and parasympathetic nervous system functioning and interpersonal behavior over time. *Int. J. Psychophysiol.* **2013**, *88*, 339–348. [CrossRef] [PubMed]
21. Hubert, B.; Wicker, B.; Monfardini, E.; Deruelle, C. Electrodermal reactivity to emotion processing in adults with autistic spectrum disorders. *Autism* **2009**, *13*, 9–19. [CrossRef]
22. Mathersul, D.C.; McDonald, S.; Rushby, J. Autonomic arousal explains social cognitive abilities in high-functioning adults with autism spectrum disorder. *Int. J. Psychophysiol.* **2013**, *89*, 475–482. [CrossRef]
23. Lord, C.; Risi, S.; Lambrecht, L., Jr.; Cook, E.H.; Leventhal, B.L.; DiLavore, P.C.; Pickles, A.; Rutter, M. The Autism Diagnostic Observation Schedule—Generic: A Standard Measure of Social and Communication Deficits Associated with the Spectrum of Autism. *J. Autism Dev. Disord.* **2000**, *30*, 205–223. [CrossRef] [PubMed]
24. Lewis, M.; Norbury, C.; Luyster, R.; Schmitt, L.; McDuffie, A.; Haebig, E.; Murray, D.S.; Timler, G.; Frazier, T.; Holmes, D.L.; et al. Leiter International Performance Scale-Revised (Leiter-R). In *Encyclopedia of Autism Spectrum Disorders*; Volkmar, F.R., Ed.; Springer: New York, NY, USA, 2013.
25. Villardita, C. Raven's colored Progressive Matrices and intellectual impairment in patients with focal brain damage. *Cortex* **1985**, *21*, 627–634. [CrossRef]
26. Wechsler, D. *WPPSI-III: Technical and Interpretative Manual*; The Psychological Corporation: San Antonio, TX, USA, 2002.
27. Schreibman, L.; Dawson, G.; Stahmer, A.C.; Landa, R.J.; Rogers, S.J.; McGee, G.G.; Kasari, C.; Ingersoll, B.; Kaiser, A.; Bruinsma, Y.; et al. Naturalistic Developmental Behavioral Interventions: Empirically Validated Treatments for Autism Spectrum Disorder. *J. Autism Dev. Disord.* **2015**, *45*, 2411–2428. [CrossRef] [PubMed]
28. Green, J.; Charman, T.; McConachie, H.; Aldred, C.; Slonims, V.; Howlin, P.; Le Couteur, A.; Leadbitter, K.; Hudry, K.; Byford, S.; et al. Parent-mediated communication-focused treatment in children with autism (PACT): A randomised controlled trial. *Lancet* **2010**, *375*, 2152–2160. [CrossRef]
29. Johnson-Glenberg, M.C.; Megowan-Romanowicz, C. Embodied science and mixed reality: How gesture and motion capture affect physics education. *Cogn. Res. Princ. Implic.* **2017**, *2*, 27. [CrossRef]
30. Pan, J.; Tompkins, W.J. A real-time QRS detection algorithm. *IEEE Trans. Biomed. Eng.* **1985**, *32*, 230–236. [CrossRef]
31. Benedek, M.; Kaernbach, C. A continuous measure of phasic electrodermal activity. *J. Neurosci. Methods* **2010**, *190*, 80–91. [CrossRef]
32. Billeci, L.; Tonacci, A.; Narzisi, A.; Manigrasso, Z.; Varanini, M.; Fulceri, F.; Lattarulo, C.; Calderoni, S.; Muratori, F. Heart Rate Variability During a Joint Attention Task in Toddlers With Autism Spectrum Disorders. *Front. Physiol.* **2018**, *9*, 467. [CrossRef]
33. Tonacci, A.; Di Monte, J.; Meucci, M.B.; Sansone, F.; Pala, A.P.; Billeci, L.; Conte, R. Wearable Sensors to Characterize the Autonomic Nervous System Correlates of Food-Like Odors Perception: A Pilot Study. *Electronics* **2019**, *8*, 1481. [CrossRef]
34. Sahin, M.; Sur, M. Genes, circuits, and precision therapies for autism and related neurodevelopmental disorders. *Science* **2015**, *350*, aab3897. [CrossRef]

35. Waschbusch, D.A.; Willoughby, M.T.; Haas, S.M.; Ridenour, T.; Helseth, S.; Crum, K.I.; Altszuler, A.R.; Ross, J.M.; Coles, E.K.; Pelham, W.E. Effects of Behavioral Treatment Modified to Fit Children with Conduct Problems and Callous-Unemotional (CU) Traits. *J. Clin. Child Adolesc. Psychol.* **2019**, 1–12. [CrossRef]
36. Grove, R.; Roth, I.; Hoekstra, R.A. The motivation for special interests in individuals with autism and controls: Development and validation of the special interest motivation scale. *Autism Res.* **2016**, *9*, 677–688. [CrossRef] [PubMed]
37. White, S.W.; Schry, A.R.; Miyazaki, Y.; Ollendick, T.H.; Scahill, L. Effects of Verbal Ability and Severity of Autism on Anxiety in Adolescents With ASD: One-Year Follow-Up After Cognitive Behavioral Therapy. *J. Clin. Child Adolesc. Psychol.* **2015**, *44*, 839–845. [CrossRef] [PubMed]
38. Hesselmark, E.; Plenty, S.; Bejerot, S. Group cognitive behavioural therapy and group recreational activity for adults with autism spectrum disorders: A preliminary randomized controlled trial. *Autism* **2014**, *18*, 672–683. [CrossRef] [PubMed]
39. Kirkovski, M.; Enticott, P.; Fitzgerald, P.B. A Review of the Role of Female Gender in Autism Spectrum Disorders. *J. Autism Dev. Disord.* **2013**, *43*, 2584–2603. [CrossRef]
40. Di Palma, S.; Tonacci, A.; Narzisi, A.; Domenici, C.; Pioggia, G.; Muratori, F.; Billeci, L. Monitoring of autonomic response to sociocognitive tasks during treatment in children with Autism Spectrum Disorders by wearable technologies: A feasibility study. *Comput. Biol. Med.* **2017**, *85*, 143–152. [CrossRef] [PubMed]
41. Billeci, L.; Tonacci, A.; Tartarisco, G.; Narzisi, A.; Di Palma, S.; Corda, D.; Baldus, G.; Cruciani, F.; Anzalone, S.M.; Calderoni, S.; et al. An Integrated Approach for the Monitoring of Brain and Autonomic Response of Children with Autism Spectrum Disorders during Treatment by Wearable Technologies. *Front. Mol. Neurosci.* **2016**, *10*, 799. [CrossRef]

12

"Mom Let's Go to the Dentist!" Preliminary Feasibility of a Tailored Dental Intervention for Children with Autism Spectrum Disorder in the Italian Public Health Service

Antonio Narzisi [1,†], Mariasole Bondioli [2,†], Francesca Pardossi [3,†], Lucia Billeci [4], Maria Claudia Buzzi [5], Marina Buzzi [5], Martina Pinzino [6], Caterina Senette [5], Valentina Semucci [7], Alessandro Tonacci [4], Fabio Uscidda [2], Benedetta Vagelli [8], Maria Rita Giuca [3,9] and Susanna Pelagatti [2,10,*]

1 IRCCS Stella Maris Foundation, 56018 Pisa (Calambrone), Italy; antonio.narzisi@fsm.unipi.it
2 Department of Informatics, University of Pisa, 56127 Pisa, Italy; mariasole.bondioli@gmail.com (M.B.); fabio.usc@gmail.com (F.U.)
3 Unit of Odontostomatology and Oral Surgery, University Hospital of Pisa, 56126 Pisa Italy; f.pardossi@yahoo.it (F.P.); mariarita.giuca@med.unipi.it (M.R.G.)
4 Institute of Clinical Physiology, National Research Council of Italy, (IFC-CNR), 56124 Pisa, Italy; lucia.billeci@ifc.cnr.it (L.B.); atonacci@ifc.cnr.it (A.T.)
5 Institute of Informatics and Telematics, National Research Council of Italy, (IIT-CNR), 56125 Pisa, Italy; claudia.buzzi@iit.cnr.it (M.C.B.); marina.buzzi@iit.cnr.it (M.B.); caterina.senette@iit.cnr.it (C.S.)
6 Institute of Neuroscience, National Research Council of Italy of Italy, (IN-CNR), 56125 Pisa, Italy; martinapinzino@outlook.it
7 UFSMIA, Zona Livorno, Azienda USL Toscana Nord Ovest, 57124 Livorno, Italy; valentina.semucci@uslnordovest.toscana.it
8 UFSMIA, Zona Pisana, Azienda USL Toscana Nord Ovest, 56121 Pisa, Italy; benedetta.vagelli@uslnordovest.toscana.it
9 Department of Surgical, Medical and Molecular Pathology and Critical Care Medicine, University of Pisa, 56126 Pisa, Italy
10 Autismo Pisa APS, Autism Parents Association, 56100 Pisa, Italy
* Correspondence: susanna.pelagatti@unipi.it
† These authors contributed equally to this work.

Abstract: Children with autism spectrum disorder (ASD) show worse oral health than their peers. Their access to health services is, at present, inadequate: few high-quality interventions have been designed and implemented to improve their care procedures so far. The purpose of this study is to describe an experience of dental care supported by Information and Communication Technologies (ICT), for children with ASD in a public health service. In our study, 59 children (mean age 9.9 years; SD = 5.43) participated in the MyDentist project. It integrates classic dental care techniques with new practices for desensitization and fear control, delivered through an enhanced customized ICT-based intervention aiming at familiarizing the child with ASD with the medical setting and procedures. Two questionnaires were filled out by parents to describe the acceptability of the MyDentist experience for their children. Significant results were shown from T0 (before initiating MyDentist) to T1 (after 6 months of the MyDentist experience) regarding improved oral hygiene and cooperation during dental treatments. Families positively assessed the use of ICT support. In conclusion, the project demonstrated acceptability by parents, suggesting that public health dental care and prevention can be successfully implemented without resorting to costly pharmacological interventions (with potential side effects), taking better care of children's health.

Keywords: autism; dental care; oral health; medical procedures; ICT; wearable sensors

1. Introduction

Autism spectrum disorder (ASD) is a severe multifactorial disorder characterized by an umbrella of specific symptoms in the areas of social communication, restricted interests, and repetitive behaviors [1]. The incidence of ASD is worldwide and recent epidemiological data estimated it to be 1/54 in United States and 1/87 in Italy [2,3]. ASD varies greatly in the severity of associated socio-communicative impairments and in the degree of cognitive and language development [4]. Although there is no specific relationship between ASD and oral disease, it is well-recognized that many individuals with ASD have much worse oral health than non-autistic people [5–10]. This may be related to barriers to dental services, sensory sensitivities and heightened levels of stress and anxiety during care; these factors may affect the level of cooperation of individuals with ASD in regard to daily hygiene routines, oral exams, and dental care [11–17]. The presence of comorbid self-injurious behaviors, poor oral care at home and specific dietary habits that can favor tooth decay should also be considered [17,18].

Sensory sensitivity is extremely heterogeneous in subjects with ASD [19,20]. It can include hyper-sensitivity to specific sensory input. Subjects with ASD can also experience sensory overload, becoming overwhelmed by incoming stimuli. In these situations, sights, sounds, smells, tastes, touch, balance and body awareness can feel like real physical pain [19,20].

These children can also present intellectual disabilities and significant behavioral issues [21].

These features make it difficult for dentists to assess and treat children with ASD; due to sensory sensitivity and/or intellectual disability, it may be necessary to resort to general anesthesia or sedation (conscious or deep) for dental care or invasive treatment [22–24].

Unfortunately, the professional training offered by most university programs does not deal specifically with people with ASD, so it is necessary to teach dental professionals how to treat them correctly [22]. Children with ASD need to be supported and guided during the visit by an interdisciplinary plan of action that takes into account their specific needs in order to promote better dental health [22,25,26]. Therefore, to increase the probability of successful dental treatment for patients with ASD, dentists should have an in-depth interdisciplinary understanding of ASD in terms of symptomatology and functional profiles [27,28]. However, as highlighted by the World Health Organization (WHO) and American Academy of Pediatric Dentistry, access to services and support for people with ASD is presently inadequate [29,30].

In order improve cooperation of patients with ASD in a dental setting, a link between the behavioral approach and the personalized use of information and communication technologies (ICT) could be efficacious. According to previous studies conducted on children with ASD, it is possible to achieve improved oral hygiene also with both Augmentative Alternative Communication (AAC) and online video modeling sessions [31,32]. The AAC encompasses the communication methods used to supplement speech for those with specific impairments in the production or comprehension of spoken language. Specifically, AAC technologies support children with ASD to (a) enhance language learning, (b) facilitate social interaction and (c) teach interaction strategies to communication partners [31]. Video modeling is a mode for teaching behaviors that uses video recording to provide a visual model of the targeted behavior or skill. Video modeling could include basic video modeling, video self-modeling, point-of-view video modeling, and video prompting [32].

This type of studies [31,32] provides preliminary support for the use of ICT-enhanced interventions to improve oral hygiene for children with autism [33,34]. Providing dental care to patients with ASD may require modifying the traditional treatment plans and settings [33,34], which include many sensory stimuli that may affect the way children behave. Therefore, it is extremely important to think about functional ways to reduce these users' anxiety and sensory hypersensitivity in order to increase their compliance with procedures and to carry out dental care as planned. Despite the high prevalence of issues in treating people with ASD, only few randomized controlled pilot studies have been designed and implemented to improve their dental care procedures so far [17,35–37]. The extreme importance of oral health in children with ASD is due to the potential beneficial effects on chewing/eating, language disorder and dental traumas [30].

The aim of this paper is to describe the first results of the project MyDentist, an in-the-field experience of dental care for children with ASD in an Italian public health service, with the support of a web application that includes various digital materials (video models, social stories, photos, and games), which can be personalized for each patient.

From a clinical point of view, the two specific aims of the MyDentist project were to provide adequate dental care for subjects with ASD and to support and motivate their maintaining acceptable oral health at home. The first aim focused on increasing the patient's collaboration when sitting in the dentist chair, considering the time needed by each specific patient when performing from the simplest to the most complex therapeutic treatment. In this way, it would be possible to reduce the use of general anesthesia, at least for those treatments that generally do not need it, thus lowering economic and psychological costs.

The second aim was choosing the most appropriate method to guide the patient during their oral hygiene routine at home. The selected strategies included teaching patients and parents and/or caregivers how to brush one's teeth, identifying the most suitable tool to reinforce motivation in taking care of oral health.

Confidence is achieved both during dental sessions at the clinic and at home, using games, videos and other digital activities personalized for each patient. Exploiting the combination of these techniques, we managed to first approach the simplest medical procedures (sitting in the dental chair, opening the mouth, having the oral cavity checked first only visually and then using tools such as mirror and explorer), and then to integrate increasingly complex instruments and methods.

At the same time, the project explored the use of wearable sensors to assess subjects' physiological response before and after the dental procedure by applying commercial devices and analyzing, ex-post, the modification of the Autonomic Nervous System activity via signal processing related to electrocardiogram (ECG) and Galvanic Skin Response (GSR), two significant, well-known physiological indicators of psychological stress, which will be better defined in Section 4.

2. Method

2.1. Sample

The total sample included 59 subjects (45 males; 14 females) aged between 4 and 16 years (mean age = 9.9 years; SD = 5.43) who were sequentially recruited at the Department of Pediatric Odontoiatry of Santa Chiara Hospital in Pisa during the period January 2019–October 2020. Inclusion criteria were a diagnosis of autism spectrum disorder (ASD) according to DSM-5 criteria [1] and pediatric age. The diagnosis was certified by the Italian Mental Health System. All subjects with ASD were native Italian speakers (Table 1).

The study was approved by the local Ethics Committee (Prot. N. 10–06/05/2019 AOUP, Pisa, Italy,) and was in accordance both with the ethical standards of the 1964 Declaration of Helsinki and the Italian Association of Psychology (AIP). The protocol for data acquisition with wearable sensors was approved by the Institutional Ethical Clearance board of CNR.

Table 1. Socio-demographic characteristics and functional profile of the sample.

Age	(in Years)
Mean	9.9
SD	5.43
Gender	*n*
Males	45
Females	14
DSM-5–ASD Severity Levels	
Level 1	5
Level 2	37
Level 3	17
Cognitive Functioning	
Normal range	5
Mild	4
Moderate	28
Severe	19
Language	
No words	29
2–3 words	14
Fluent	16

2.2. *Intervention*

2.2.1. MyDentist

MyDentist was developed as a multidisciplinary experimental approach to dental care and prevention for subjects with ASD, combining ICT, behavioral techniques and a specific clinical protocol designed for ASD. The protocol definition came from the combination of a special dentistry foundation, knowledge and previous experience on assistive technologies for people with ASD, and the crucial support from psychologists and speech therapists offering expert advice in the field of diagnosis of and intervention in ASD. The choice of a multidisciplinary approach derived from previous studies in the literature [24,29] and from a pilot study performed in 2017 [27].

The concepts on which MyDentist has been developed are the following: (i) the high frequency of use of general anesthesia; (ii) the difficulty to face a lack of collaboration when working with ASD patients; (iii) manifestations of anxiety in reaction to the context of the visit; (iv) the need to keep consistency between home oral hygiene and oral care at the clinic. Luckily, some recent experiences in this field have led to the development of new forms of intervention, constantly evolving and mainly focused on psychological approaches where dentists explore the use of different communication channels to enhance collaboration and interaction with children (reinforcement, costumes, play activities) [31,32].

For all these reasons, MyDentist builds on this preliminary literature to explore new forms of patient interaction with the clinical environment and with the medical staff. We propose digital activities to reduce anxiety during the visit, to teach medical procedures and familiarize the patient with the environment. Accessible training is delivered through multimodal activities and games based on AAC, exploiting the visual channel, usually the most effective sense in people with ASD [31]. ICT can facilitate the implementation of AAC, making it easy and comfortable to communicate anyplace, anytime through a mobile device (tablet, smartphone). Moreover, digital AAC (delivered via app) is highly scalable (vast amount of items vs. the paper/plastic version) and customizable, allowing one to add new (personalized) items.

A key feature of the MyDentist approach is the complete personalization of the medical protocol in order to adapt it to the particular needs of each ASD patient, to favor a relationship of trust between the patient and the health professional, and to positively exploit the digital activities.

2.2.2. The MyDentist Web Application

Several studies underline the positive effect of daily use of ICT tools with people with ASD, in both learning contexts and social situations [38–41]. As reported in these studies, people with ASD seem to like innovative educational approaches enhanced by ICT tools mainly because when using technology, they can avoid typical issues involved in human interaction, such as impatience, feelings of inadequacy, unpredictability of people's behavior, and poor recognition of emotions, irony, and figurative language.

The use of ICT to facilitate dental care delivered to patients with ASD is a relatively unexplored field. Isong et al. [35] and Barry et al. [42] both investigated the power of visual stimuli on achieving ASD patients 'cooperation during medical procedures. However, in both these studies ICT tools were not personalized and the children were passive users of digital content. Instead, during the MyDentist experience we tried to offer a personalization of the medical protocol in order to adapt it to the particular needs of each ASD patient, thus making it possible to favor a relationship of trust and to best take advantage of the digital activities proposed directly involving the patient, who become an active actor in the care protocol.

MyDentist delivers a large amount of digital material personalized for each patient: social stories and video models describing all the procedures, the behaviors at the dental clinic and the correct dental care at home, videos and photos taken during dental sessions, and serious games. Managing all this material is very complex and error prone, so MyDentist supports data management with a web application, accessible from any browser on both PCs and tablets. The application helps dentists to build personalized virtual paths following the intervention protocol of a single patient and to provide each patient with all the material needed to boost self-confidence, for instance the photos taken during previous sessions, homework to prepare for the next session and other relaxing and motivating material. The app can be used in many different ways:

- Digital Copybook mode (for all patients): during visits to collect photos and videos (selfies and not) that the child can review and show to family members once at home;
- Mirror mode: during the visits used in camera-selfie mode to allow the child to see himself during dental practices;
- Distractor mode: during the visit to distract or to relax with favorite videos/pictures;
- Reinforcement mode: at the end of the session to perform entertainment and play activities that work both as reinforcement and as consolidation of the activities carried out during the visit;
- Familiarization/learning mode: at home to recall previous visits, to prepare for the next one and to perform digital activities assigned by the dentist (playing games, watching videos, practicing social stories, etc.).

The Web Application (Figure 1) consists of two areas:

- Dentist Area: where the dentist creates the personalized profile of each patient, in order to schedule a visit, build a personalized clinical path, collect multimedia materials of visits, create personalized clinical programs by customizing games, share resources and assign home tasks.
- Patient Area: where each patient can access his/her personalized path. This includes games showing dental procedures in an amusing way (e.g., sequences, puzzles, memories); video models for dental procedures (for instance showing how to use a toothbrush), interactive PDF files to get used to dental clinic sounds, social stories that introduce the dental environment, procedures and/or objects and photos/videos collected during visits.

Figure 1. The MyDentist User Interfaces: the dentist's section (**A**) and the patient's section (**B**).

2.2.3. The MyDentist Intervention Protocol

In MyDentist each child follows a personalized path, which starts with one or more familiarization sessions, which goal is to make the child used to the people and the environment. After that, we applied one of three dental procedures. First, prophylaxis with either manual or ultrasonic instruments, which can be challenging for patients with ASD due to the sound of ultrasonic scalers, or noxious tasting prophylaxis paste with manual instruments. Second, fissure and pit sealing, which requires a degree of cooperation, are usually difficult for ASD people. This procedure, despite being a completely atraumatic and not painful, cannot be interrupted, and the patient must always keep their mouth open from beginning to end. In addition, the various materials used have a pronounced taste that may not be easily tolerated.

Third, dental treatment of deciduous and permanent elements is carried out using rotating instruments such as a dental drill and a micromotor. The use of instruments with diamond burrs is reserved for ASD patients with high collaboration skills, since these instruments could damage oral tissues in case of abrupt movements by the patient. In addition, these procedures are often preceded by injection of local anesthesia to cancel painful stimuli. Finally, restoration must be carried out using adhesive materials that require a dry oral setting and therefore a maximum control of salivation.

3. Procedure

3.1. MyDentist Intervention Path

All patients shared a basic path: a preliminary interview with parents, a first visit, some familiarization sessions via a psychological approach, and some operative sessions. A global vision of the MyDentist intervention, common to all the patients, is shown in Figure 2. However, for each step, a personalization of the path of prevention and treatment was defined, according to (1) the specific dental needs (urgent interventions/no urgency, need to improve and increase the norms of oral hygiene at home, need to familiarize the child with the dental clinic in order to be able to carry out preventive interventions); (2) the patient's needs (especially in relation to the educational/therapeutic paths that he/she was already following), also analyzing any manifestation of the spectrum in relation to the procedures carried out. The personalization path is created cooperating with parents and caregivers and based on observations during the sessions. Visits are basically setting adaptation sessions in which everyone arrives at a state of trust by progressively introducing him/her to the dental team, the clinical environment, the tools used, and the procedures to be implemented. It is fundamental not to force the subject to carry out certain actions but to perform them in their own time and way; it is also important to inform the parents/caregivers so that they also respect the chosen timing to proceed through the path.

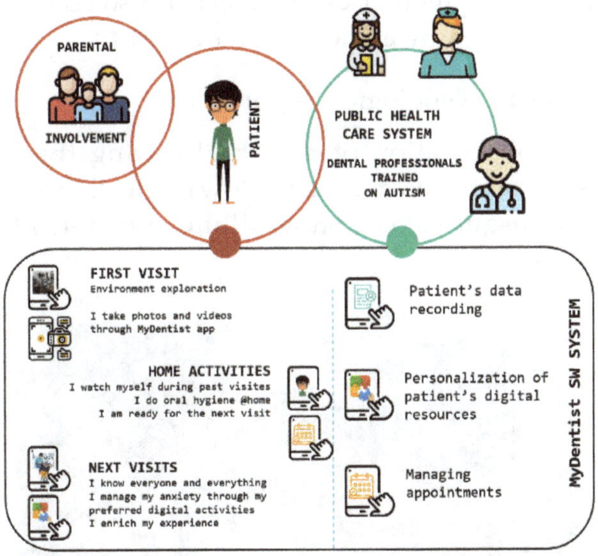

Figure 2. MyDentist global view.

3.1.1. Preliminary Interview with Parents

The interview with the parents takes place in the absence of the patient in order to collect as much information as possible about the child. During the interview, the patient's medical records are filled in with medical, family, and dental history data, which are essential in order to obtain the most complete patient profile. Eating habits (frequency and type of meals and snacks) including the use of sweetened drinks or soft drinks, are also noted. Moreover, oral hygiene habits at home are recorded: type of toothbrush and toothpaste, whether the patient is able to rinse, how many times a day the child brushes his/her teeth, whether alone or with the help of an adult, whether other aids are used (floss, mouthwash, etc.). We also record information about the neuropsychiatric assessment of the child: the diagnosis of ASD (when and by whom it was made, whether there are comorbidities) and the characteristics of the patient's communication (verbal or non-verbal subject, and if verbal whether structured or not), understanding, use of non-verbal language (e.g., pointing), presence of hyper-sensitivity. Next, we evaluate the potential use of images as communication support (what kind, in what way, with whom they are used), the use of ICT supports, the positive stimuli (e.g., music, cartoons) that can be used, and sports or hobbies if any. Finally, we collect information related to the child's present and past therapies (when, for how long).

The interview allows us to collect information about how to plan interventions and helps us to better identify the objectives to pursue, which must be tailored to fit the patient's needs. Finally, we explain to the parents what to do with their children (not to force children to do things they do not want to do during the initial meetings, prepare them with the material needed, communicate with the team periodically in order to record every change); we also instruct the parents on the correct habits to maintain for good oral health.

3.1.2. First Visit

The first visit helped the dentist to get to know each child and to test its reactions to simple requests such as to sit down on the dental chair or to open his/her mouth. During the visit, thanks to the parents' cooperation, we offered a kit of digital tools to the child to help him/her become familiar with the dentist and the clinical environment, before carrying out the medical intervention. The dentist (helped by the ICT mediator) personalized the kit's components in all the intervention phases depending on the child's needs. According to the indications of the parents and therapists, each visit (the first and the other ones) includes the possibility of familiarization at home with the dental activities to be performed in the following sessions through the use of ICT tools such as video modeling, social stories and cognitive learning games (puzzles, memories, sequences), also referring to photos and videos from previous sessions, with the aim of keeping anxiety under control.

3.1.3. Familiarization Session via a Psychological Approach

In order to facilitate the collaboration of the child during the visits we exploit the use of technological devices such as the tablet (as detailed below) as well the use of playful-communicative supports such as costumes and disguises (i.e., Snow White, Joy of Inside Out, Alice in Wonderland) and thematic songs (Figure 3).

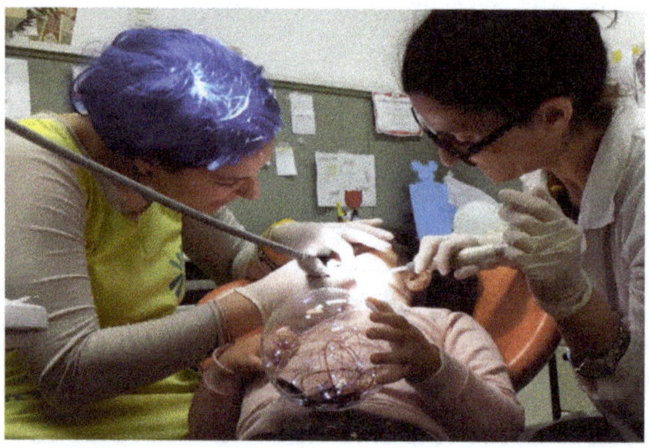

Figure 3. Dental room and the involved staff.

All the procedures, from the waiting room to the final greetings to the team, are carried out by having the child participate and making him/her aware of what the dentist is doing. This is done by communicating the steps of the operative phase. Usually, we adopted multiple strategies based on the child's skills: (a) supporting the verbal instructions with visual cues; (b) Augmentative and Alternative Communication (AAC) and video-modeling.

It is also particularly important to use positive reinforcement after reaching a specific objective and at the end of each session.

3.1.4. Operative Sessions

In the case of a familiarization visit (first visit or other visits if needed) the activities are more flexible but aim to keep to basic objectives such as sitting, collaborating, opening one's mouth, etc. Conversely, in the case of an operative session, such as the treatment of cavities or sealing molars, actions are more focused on small measures that increase attention and reduce distractors.

Whatever the type of visit, the MyDentist approach is based on reshaping the objectives of the session according to the collaboration shown by the patient, even during the visit itself, calibrating compliance with the needs expressed (directly or indirectly) by the child, with the aim of pushing the patient beyond his/her limits. The tablet is considered an integral part of the interaction with the patient but is also an advantage for the staff when collecting material for social stories, cognitive learning games, audio, and video archives.

Only when goals or sub-goals (at least one for each session) are considered achieved, the planned protocol moves to the reinforcement/play phase. Taking care to separate clearly these two stages, especially in the patient's perception, this final phase is devoted to reward the child with a prize such as listening to his/her favorite songs or watching his/her preferred video, playing or drawing with the tablet. Leveraging on the habits of the patient, this moment represents a particularly important ritual for the success of the visit, facilitating the maintenance of concentration even in the most operational sessions.

4. Instruments

4.1. Questionnaires

The research team developed the questionnaires to use in this study. Both questionnaires were pre/pilot tested on a subset of 10 parents. Two experts examined the questionnaires for face and content validation. One of the experts has 15 years of experience in the field of Autism Spectrum Disorder. Both experts have a master's degree in psychology and one of them has a PhD in Developmental Neurosciences. They have been involved in several national and European research projects. For face validity, the experts were asked if all questions were clearly worded and would not be misinterpreted. For content validity, the experts evaluated the relevance of the questions using a scale of 1 to 3, where 1 = not relevant, 2 = relevant but not necessary, and 3 = absolutely necessary. The experts were also asked if other questions should be added to the questions. The remarks of the two experts were collected and discussed and were used to revise the questionnaires. The experts examined the revised questionnaire and declared agreement with its content and clarity.

Parents anonymously completed two questionnaires in order to describe their personal experience with MyDentist. Questionnaire A was aimed at evaluating the approach of children to the dental experience. It was filled out two times, at T0 and after 6 months, T1. It is an 18-item parent-report measure designed to record the behaviors of subjects. Each item describes a specific behavior and the parent is asked to rate its frequency on a four-point Likert scale (0, never; 1, sometimes; 2, often; 3, regularly).

After 6 months of the MyDentist experience, a second questionnaire (Questionnaire B) was sent to the parents of children who participated in the MyDentist project. The questionnaire included 16 items with a positive or negative orientation toward the multi-media support. The questions regarded the evaluation of tablet use and the improvement (if present) in the child's skills. The parents had to answer through a Likert scale from 0 to 3 (0 = no, 1 = little, 2 = quite, 3 = very).

4.2. Psychophysiological Assessment

As mentioned in the previous sections, aside from observing a positive effect of the MyDentist approach as indicated by the results of the questionnaires, we would like to answer the following question: Is it possible to have an "objective" measure that provides an indicator of the effect of MyDentist on stress?

To answer such questions, our idea is to assess the response of the Autonomic Nervous System (ANS) using wearable devices. The ANS measurement is a useful instrument for evaluating the subject's stress and emotional state in ASD. Indeed, when perceiving a stressor, self-regulating processes start by automatically activating the ANS, its sympathetic component [43,44]. The ANS can be monitored non-invasively and reliably by means of wearable sensors, shown to be effective and useful even in young children and in children with disabilities [45–47].

Therefore, in order to be able to objectively evaluate the influence of the practice proposed with the MyDentist approach in modulating the anxiety state of subjects with ASD who undergo dental treatment, we intend to use non-invasive devices for recording ANS activity. Specifically, the idea is to assess the ANS activity before and after each dental session and to longitudinally monitor each child for an observation period of approximately 4–6 months. With this strategy, it would be possible to observe whether the dental session-associated stress is reduced as time passes thanks to the MyDentist application.

To assess the feasibility of applying such approach, we evaluated the ANS activity using wearable devices before and after the first dental session with MyDentist, with one child participating in the study (5-year-old child with ASD level 2 according to DSM-V criteria and an IQ in the "mild" range).

The child was equipped with two wearable sensors, the first of which for monitoring an electrocardiogram (ECG) and the other one devoted to galvanic skin response (GSR). The ECG signal was acquired through the Shimmer ECG sensor, v.2 (Shimmer Sensing, Dublin, Ireland) attached to a fitness-like chest strap manufactured by Polar Electro Oy (Kempele, Finland), in turn interfaced with the human body through two dry electrodes. The sampling frequency was set to 500 Hz. The GSR signal was captured by the Shimmer3 GSR+ sensor (Shimmer) by adhering to two neighboring fingers of the subject's non-dominant hand via comfortable rings embedding dry electrodes, with optimal comfort for the subject tested. As for the GSR, the sampling frequency was selected from among the ones available from the sensor firmware, set to 51.2 Hz. The signals were acquired while the subject was seated comfortably on a chair at a table in a quiet room for 5 min both before and after the session.

The acquired physiological signals were processed using Matlab (Mathworks, Natick, MA, USA). The ECG signal was analyzed for the calculation of the tachogram (RR series, i.e., the time elapsed between two successive R-waves), taking advantage of the Pan-Tompkins algorithm [48] and to extract both time- and frequency-domain features, including:

- Heart rate (HR): the number of contractions of the heart occurring per time unit, expressed in bpm;
- Root mean square of successive differences (RMSSD): measure of heart rate variability (HRV), specifically related to parasympathetic activity, expressed in ms;
- Normalized component of the power spectral density of the ECG signal at low frequency (0.04–0.15 Hz) (nLF); it is related both to the sympathetic and parasympathetic response;
- Normalized component of the power spectral density of the ECG spectrum at high frequency (0.15–0.4 Hz) (nHF); it is mainly related to the parasympathetic response;
- Low- vs. high-frequency components of the power spectral density of the ECG spectrum (LF/HF Ratio): under controlled conditions, it expresses the balance between the sympathetic and parasympathetic nervous system branches [49].

GSR signal was analyzed using Ledalab V3.4.9 (General Public License (GNU), Graz, Austria), a Matlab-based tool. The signal was first filtered by a moving average filter (n = 8) for artifact removal, followed by a continuous decomposition analysis (CDA) via the dedicated Ledalab function, leading to the extraction of tonic (and phasic, not used here) components. Indeed, just the tonic phase of the GSR signal was extracted and analyzed, since the main goal of the analysis was related to the assessment of slow changes in the autonomic activity rather than to the response of a single, time-defined stimulation that would have affected the phasic component of the GSR, as well [50].

5. Descriptive Analysis

Given the exploratory nature of the present study, there was no assumption of the sample size. Categorical data were summarized into frequency counts, percentages, and contingency tables, which were analyzed using chi-square analysis for both questionnaires. Analyses were carried out using SPSS version 21.0 for Windows (SPSS Inc. Chicago, IL, USA).

6. Results

6.1. Questionnaires

Significant results were shown from T0 (before initiating MyDentist) to T1 (after 6 months of MD experience) in 14 of the 18 questions to which the parent had replied (Table 2).

Table 2. Chi Square results between T0 and T1 at Questionnaire A.

	Never (0)		Sometimes (1)		Often (2)		Regularly (3)		Chi Square
	t0 n	t1 n	t0 n	t1 n	t0 n	t1 n	t0 n	t1 n	χ^2; p
Q.1 Does your child like to brush his teeth?	12	8	33	27	9	12	5	11	4.07; ns
Q.2 Is it possible to teach oral hygiene?	9	8	34	8	11	34	5	8	28.59; <0.001
Q.3 Is your child able to follow the rules for proper dental hygiene?	15	1	28	8	6	26	10	25	42.28; <0.001
Q.4 Is your child capable of using a toothbrush?	27	8	20	34	5	8	3	8	16.84; 0.001
Q.5 Is your child capable of putting toothpaste on the toothbrush?	32	17	16	8	6	17	5	17	19.06; <0.001
Q.6 Does the child use dental floss?	55	55	2	2	1	1	1	1	0; ns
Q.7 Does the child brush his teeth independently?	32	8	19	25	6	24	2	1	26.34; <0.001
Q.8 Is your child able to brush his teeth independently?	8	1	1	8	8	39	38	8	50.89; <0.001
Q.9 Is your child capable of brushing his teeth properly?	13	8	21	17	12	8	13	25	6.19; ns
Q.10 Is your child able to brush his teeth twice a day after meals?	13	25	26	8	11	24	9	1	24.54; <0.001
Q.11 Does the child brush his teeth after meals?	23	8	15	17	9	8	12	25	12; 0.007
Q.12 Does the child experience hypersensitivity (i.e., toothbrush)?	25	42	20	12	8	3	6	2	10.58; 0.014
Q.13 Has the child ever had dental treatment?	48	29	1	17	6	2	4	10	23.47; <0.001
Q.14 Has it ever been necessary to resort to general sedation?	29	1	9	1	5	1	15	56	58.87; <0.001
Q.15 Does the child have a dental visit at least once a year?	24	55	15	2	9	1	10	1	35.86; <0.001
Q.16 Does your child become upset when he has to go to the dentist?	30	1	20	7	7	25	2	25	63.10; <0.001
Q.17 Is your child collaborative during dental visits?	17	17	13	25	17	8	12	8	7.82; 0.049
Q.18 Does he have difficulty remaining seated for the duration of the visit?	12	9	33	29	9	11	5	9	2.02; ns

The result was significant at $p < 0.05$.

Families have positively assessed the use of multi-media support in MyDentist. Parents acknowledged that the multi-media supports were appropriately customized, facilitated a good compliance of the child with the dental setting and reduced the child's stress during the dental examination. According to parents' answers, the use of multi-media supports made children more familiar with dental hygiene, more adapted to and cooperative with the dental setting. Moreover, sensory issues and problematic behaviors appeared more manageable for the children. The multi-media supports helped children in translating acquired skills also out of the dental clinic and in learning the autonomous use of tools for dental hygiene. Parents evaluated the MyDentist project as useful, considered the advice received during the MyDentist experience to be applicable at home and recommended MyDentist to other parents of children with ASD. For only 1/3 of parents the multi-media support was considered hyper-stimulating (Table 3).

Table 3. Percentage of parents' answers to Questionnaire B.

	Questions	No	Little	Quite	Very
		%	%	%	%
Q.1	Was the multimedia support used in MyDentist (MD) useful?	0	0	40	60
Q.2	Was the multimedia support appropriately customized?	0	0	37.9	62.1
Q.3	Was the experience of MD appreciated by your child?	0	0	33.3	66.7
Q.4	Do you think that the tablet was hyper-stimulating for your child?	38.7	19.4	9.7	32.3
Q.5	Did the use of the tablet facilitate good compliance of the child with the dental setting?	0	0	35.5	64.6
Q.6	Did the use of the tablet reduce the child's stress during the dental examination?	14.2	0	42.9	42.9
Q.7	Did the child also use the tablet to become familiar with dental hygiene?	3.2	22.6	51.6	22.6
Q.8	Have you found the child to be better adapted to the dental setting?	0	0	71	29
Q.9	Is the child more cooperative during the dental examination?	0	6.2	25	68.8
Q.10	Is the child more able to control sensory issues during the dental examination?	0	0	48.9	51.6
Q.11	If present, have problematic behaviors during the dental examination decreased?	7.7	13.3	36.7	43.3
Q.12	Is the child more collaborative in performing home hygiene?	0	11.7	50	38.3
Q.13	Is the child more autonomous in the use of the suggested tools for dental hygiene?	9.4	15.6	46.9	28.1
Q.14	Was the MD project useful?	0	0	10.3	89.7
Q.15	Can you apply at home any advice received during the MD experience?	0	0	69	31
Q.16	Would you recommend MD to parents of children with autism?	0	0	0	100

6.2. Psychophysiological Assessment

Concerning the assessment through wearable sensors, in Figure 4 it can be observed that after the dental session, the parasympathetic contribution increased, as suggested by the rise in RMSSD, nHF and by the decrease of LF/HF. Accordingly, the tonic component of the GSR signal decreased with respect to the baseline pre-session after the dental session, as observed in Figure 5.

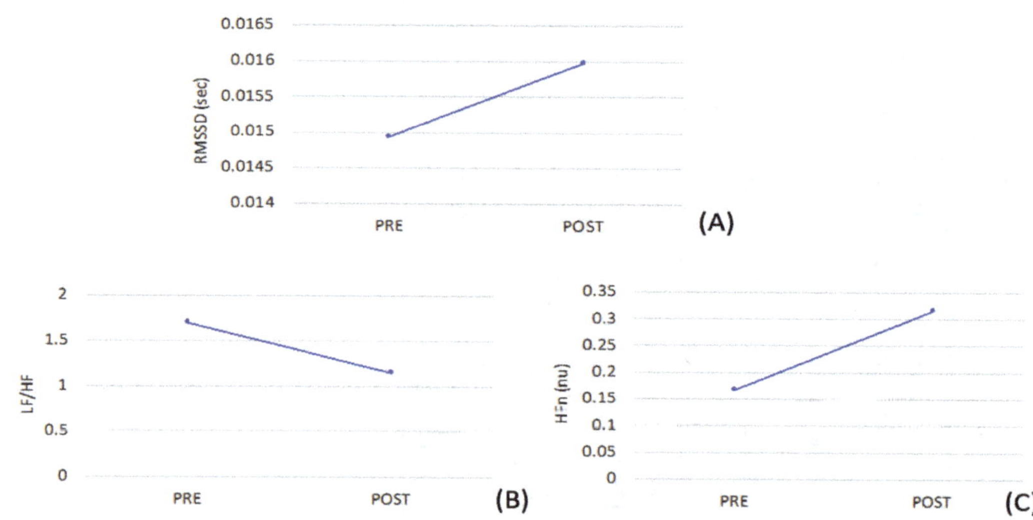

Figure 4. Trend of the features extracted from the R-R series: (**A**) Root Mean Square of the Successive Differences of the R-R signal (RMSSD), (**B**) LF/HF ratio, (**C**) normalized High Frequency component of the ECG signal.

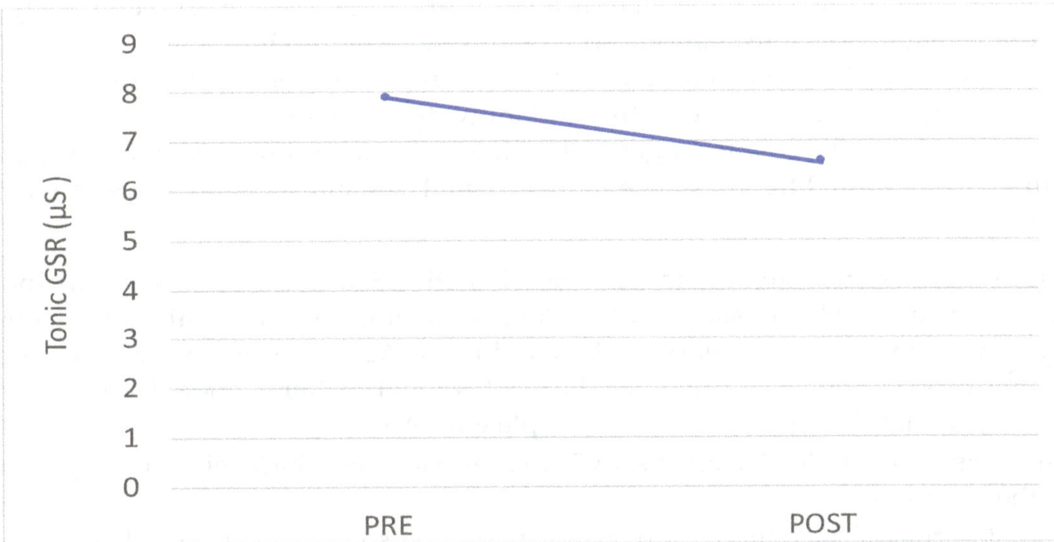

Figure 5. Trend of the tonic component of the Galvanic Skin Response (GSR) signal.

7. Discussion

Children with ASD have poor oral health and they present high care demands, which requires much time, effort, and patience [8,51]. Findings of this study suggest the feasibility of the MyDentist approach and the positive role of technology support [52]. Most of the families of the children involved in this study showed a positive level of involvement (there were no dropouts). Our descriptive data suggest that the children learned the basis of adequate oral care following the rules for proper dental hygiene, using a toothbrush and brushing teeth after meals. Moreover, they showed progressive compliance with the dental visits remaining in a seated position and managing their sensory issues better. Parents and caregivers alike manifested satisfaction for the MyDentist protocol and they strongly recommended it to parents of children with ASD. The ICT use in the MyDentist protocol was positively accepted by the families involved. They considered that the multimedia supports were appropriately customized to meet the child's needs; it facilitated good compliance of the child with the dental setting and reduced the child's stress during the dental examination. ICT has the potential to offer ASD users increased rehabilitation and support to empower their abilities, anytime, anyplace, and on any device (https://iite.unesco.org). Repetitive and predictable answers could help these patients control anxiety and accept new medical practices. Thus, to increase positive results, personalization becomes crucial for making the surrounding environment comfortable and user-friendly.

Our findings also underlined the importance of ICT as an important tool for teaching children with ASD better cooperative behaviors aiding them in the familiarization process with rules and techniques of appropriate oral hygiene. It is well-recognized that children with ASD experience challenges with communication which can negatively interfere with professional oral care [52]. However, most children with ASD tend to process visual information more efficiently than auditory information [53]. For these reasons, in our study AAC and video-modeling as teaching supports were used. Another key finding of the application of the MyDentist protocol is the improved collaborative behavior of the child in home oral hygiene practices. This suggests the potential translational effect of the MyDentist experience.

In addition, the preliminary investigation in a single subject regarding the use of wearable sensors to assess autonomic nervous system response suggested the feasibility of using this approach to evaluate the child's physiological response, thus confirming our previous studies [41–43]. This approach allows us to obtain useful information about the anxious response to a potentially stressful event [36]. In this specific child and for this specific session, it seemed that the child was more comfortable and relaxed after the session, expressing an increase in parasympathetic activity. It would be interesting to observe whether after using the MyDentist approach regularly, the child is more relaxed also before the session. In the near future, we intend to include a fairly large group of subjects compatibly with their profile in order provide more information about the response of the child than that merely obtained from behavioral observation. This would be extremely important for objectivizing the effect of the intervention and implementing more effective and individualized approaches.

In order to evaluate the cost for a generalization in other settings, we need to highlight that the MyDentist intervention differs from the regular dental care intervention for people with ASD in these aspects:

1. Professionals are trained in how to treat people with ASD. As mentioned in the Introduction, to increase the probability of successful dental treatment for patients with ASD, dentists should have an in-depth interdisciplinary understanding of ASD in terms of symptomatology and functional profiles, but unfortunately the professional training offered by most university programs does not deal specifically with people with ASD.
2. Professionals are also trained to use the MyDentist application, which helps to set up a personalized use of the ICT tools
3. In the first period of the intervention, an additional person acting as an ICT-mediator for both professionals and patients/caregivers joined the dental clinic staff.

Indeed, the cost of the MyDentist intervention can be estimated in:

- Cost for the design and development of the MyDentist application;
- Cost of the cloud-storage service;
- Cost of a tablet for the dental clinic;
- A 2-year employment contract for an ICT mediator.

Considering our experience, the professionals were already trained in how to interact with people with ASD and how to use the MyDentist application, since they participated in its design. Patients at home used their own mobile devices.

The estimated cost for replicating the MyDentist intervention in other settings should consider:

- For professionals:
  - Training regarding people with ASD and the most appropriate way to interact with them;
  - Training to use the MyDentist application: to this aim, we are finalizing all the documentation such as user manual, tutorials and demo, which will be freely available.
- For the clinic:
  - A 6- or 12-month employment contract for an ICT mediator.

The MyDentist application will be available for free, at no cost.

Regarding the training of dental staff, it depends on several factors such as the type of course, the duration and the organization that provides the course. However, in order to indicate in more detail what the cost may be, we believe it may be sufficient a brief training course with an ASD expert (e.g., psychologist, neuropsychologist or speech therapist). Furthermore, dental staff will also need an additional day for autonomously training on the MyDentist application reading the documentation and trying the app.

The ICT mediator is a person with skills on the use of digital tools in order to support the work of the dental staff showing how and when to use the application and the tablet. This does not require a very high technical ICT skills so a graduate person may be sufficient. However, the ICT mediator must also have ASD training, together with the dental staff, in order to know how to approach and interact with people with ASD.

In some cases, the treatment path may be longer than estimated, but there are benefits for both the patient, who could be treated while safely avoiding sedation for minor interventions, and presumably for the health system, due to the increase in successful interventions and the decrease in missed appointments or incomplete treatments caused by a lack of patient collaboration (increasing efficiency and reducing unnecessary costs).

8. Limits of the Study

In this preliminary study, some limitations must be acknowledged. The most relevant is undoubtedly the constrained dataset that strongly limits wide-ranging conclusions. In order to overcome the limits of our study, future investigations should consider: (1) a more systematic data about functional profiles of each experimental participant (ADOS/IQ scores; and robust characterization of the sample in terms of sensory sensitivity and co-morbid conditions; (2) the inclusion of a control group with ASD (e.g., assignment to routine/usual treatment) with a randomized assignment to conditions or, possibly, the adoption of a crossover strategy over the entire population of volunteers; (3) to collect pre- and post-intervention data on parents stress' degree; (4) the lack of a protocol or decision-making tree for the use of the MyDentist intervention.

Finally, a limit of our study was the evaluation of the autonomic nervous system response in only one child for a single session.

Thus, further research is needed to confirm our interesting preliminary (and descriptive) data to determine the effectiveness of the intervention. Moreover, in an upcoming study the enrollment of a larger number of subjects will be important in order to create subgroups of more homogeneous samples in terms of age range, IQ range and oral hygiene issues.

9. Future Direction

Given the overall encouraging results achieved by the exploratory study presented herein, we expect to extend the recording of physiological parameters to the visit phase, at least in a subgroup of individuals who might be more compliant with being equipped with wearables sensors, even during the visit, by the dentist. Such individuals, selected from among the subjects with high-functioning ASD, will compose the cohort for this further evaluation, and will be followed in the next study. This would enable comparing the compliance and the psychophysiological response, and therefore the overall benefit brought by the MyDentist App, with respect to the previous literature dealing with dental research, stress and ASD [54–57]. Finally, other parameters could be extracted from the physiological signals, including frequency of non-specific skin conductance responses (NS-SCRs) for the GSR.

10. Conclusions

Networking between families, caregivers and health providers should be activated with the aim of making everyone aware of the dental health problems that children with autism have to face [13,58,59].

It is essential to combine the efforts and professionalism of all the figures involved in helping a child with autism in order to draw up ad hoc guidelines for dental health in children with ASD.

In conclusion, these preliminary findings regarding the MyDentist project have shown the feasibility of dental care in children with ASD. Furthermore, the project showed the parents' acceptance of the MyDentist project and the feasibility of dental care in a public service without additional costs for families. In the first phase of the dental care program, an additional cost is required for dental clinics facilities to teach clinicians how to implement the intervention with persons with ASD, and to proficiently learn how to exploit the MyDentist program specificities. Moreover, an ICT mediator could be essential to provide the necessary technological support. However, also considering these constraints, we believe that the cost effectiveness is largely in favor of the intervention. Potential benefits for these special-needs patients are extremely important both in term of health (through prevention or treatment, if needed) and in terms of general wellbeing.

Author Contributions: Conceptualization, S.P., M.R.G.; Formal Analysis, A.N., L.B. A.T.; Data Curation, M.B., F.P., A.N., M.P.; Patient recruitment: M.B., F.P., B.V., V.S.; ICT developers: F.U., M.C.B., M.B., C.S.; Writing—Original Draft Preparation, A.N.; Writing—review and editing, A.N., L.B.; Supervision, S.P., M.R.G.; Project Writing, S.P., M.R.G. All authors have read and agreed to the published version of the manuscript.

Acknowledgments: The authors wish to thank all the participants, the children and their parents.

References

1. American Psychiatric Association (APA). *Diagnostic and Statistical Manual of Mental Disorders*, 5th ed.; American Psychiatric Association: Washington, DC, USA, 2013.
2. Maenner, M.J.; Shaw, K.A.; Baio, J.; Washington, A.; Patrick, M.; DiRienzo, M.; Christensen, D.L.; Wiggins, L.D.; Pettygrove, S.; Andrews, J.G.; et al. Prevalence of Autism spectrum disorder Among Children Aged 8 Years—Autism and Developmental Disabilities Monitoring Network, 11 Sites, United States, 2016. *Mmwr Surveill. Summ.* **2020**, *69*, 1–12. [CrossRef] [PubMed]
3. Narzisi, A.; Posada, M.; Barbieri, F.; Chericoni, N.; Ciu_olini, D.; Pinzino, M.; Romano, R.; Scattoni, M.L.; Tancredi, R.; Calderoni, S.; et al. Prevalence of Autism spectrum disorder in a large Italian catchment area, a school-based population study within the ASDEU project. *Epidemiol. Psychiatr. Sci.* **2018**, *29*, e5. [CrossRef] [PubMed]
4. Levy, S.E.; Mandell, D.S.; Schultz, R.T. Autism. *Lancet* **2009**, *7*, 162738. [CrossRef]
5. Delli, K.; Reichart, P.A.; Bornstein, M.; Livas, C. Management of children with autism spectrum disorder in the dental setting: Concerns, behavioural approaches and Recommenda-tions. *Med. Oral Patol. Oral Y Cir. Bucal* **2013**, *18*, e862–e868. [CrossRef]
6. Gandhi, R.P.; Klein, U. Autism spectrum disorders: An update on oral health management. *J. Evid. Based Dent. Pract.* **2014**, *14*, 115–126. [CrossRef]
7. Lu, J.; Sun, C.A. Evaluation of the effect of concentrated growth factor in oral rehabilitation. *Shanghai Kou Qiang Yi Xue* **2018**, *27*, 93–95. [PubMed]
8. Robertson, M.D.; Schwendicke, F.; de Araujo, M.P.; Radford, J.R.; Harris, J.C.; McGregor, S.; Innes, N.P.T. Dental caries experience, care index and restorative index in children with learning disabilities and children without learning disabilities; a systematic review and meta-analysis. *BMC Oral Health* **2019**, *19*, 146. [CrossRef]
9. Chandrashekhar, S.; Bommangoudar, J.S. Management of Autistic Patients in Dental Office: A Clinical Update. *Int. J. Clin. Pediatr Dent.* **2018**, *11*, 219–227. [CrossRef]
10. Du, R.Y.; Yiu, C.K.Y.; King, N.G. Oral Health Behaviours of Preschool Children with Autism Spectrum Disorders and Their Barriers to Dental Care. *J. Autism Dev. Disord.* **2019**, *49*, 453–459. [CrossRef]
11. Kuhaneck, H.M.; Chisholm, E.C. Improving Dental Visits for Individuals with Autism Spectrum Disorders Through an Understanding of Sensory Processing. *Spec. Care Dent.* **2012**, *32*, 229–233. [CrossRef]
12. Stein, L.I.; Polido, J.C.; Cermak, S.A. Oral care and sensory over-responsivity in children with autism spectrum disorders. *Pediatr Dent.* **2013**, *35*, 230–235. [PubMed]
13. Stein, L.I.; Lane, C.J.; Williams, M.E.; Dawson, M.E.; Polido, J.C.; Cermak, S.A. Physiological and behavioral stress and anxiety in children with autism spectrum disorders during routine oral care. *Biomed. Res. Int.* **2014**, *2014*, 694876. [CrossRef]
14. Khrautieo, T.; Srimaneekarn, N.; Rirattanapong, P.; Smutkeeree, A. Association of sensory sensitivities and toothbrushing cooperation in autism spectrum disorder. *Int. J. Paediatr Dent.* **2020**, *30*, 505–513. [CrossRef] [PubMed]
15. Bartolomé-Villar, B.; Mourelle-Martínez, M.R.; Diéguez-Pérez, M.; de Nova-García, M.J. Incidence of Oral Health in Paediatric Patients with Disabilities: Sensory Disorders and Autism Spectrum Disorder. Systematic Review II. *J. Clin. Exp. Dent.* **2016**, *8*, e344–e351. [CrossRef] [PubMed]
16. Neil, L.; Choque Olsson, N.; Pellicano, E. The Relationship between Intolerance of Uncertainty, Sensory Sensitivities, and Anxiety in Autistic and Typically Developing Children. *J. Autism Dev. Disord.* **2016**, *46*, 1962–1973. [CrossRef] [PubMed]
17. Cermak, S.A.; Stein Duker, L.I.; Williams, M.I.; Dawson, M.E.; Lane, C.J.; Polido, J.C. Sensory Adapted Dental Environments to Enhance Oral Care for Children with Autism Spectrum Disorders: A Randomized Controlled Pilot Study. *J. Autism Dev. Disord.* **2015**, *45*, 2876–2888. [CrossRef]

18. Duker, L.I.S.; Henwood, B.F.; Bluthenthal, R.N.; Juhlin, E.; Polido, J.C.; Cermak, S.A. Parents' perceptions of dental care challenges in male children with autism spectrum disorder: An initial qualitative exploration. *Res. Autism Spectr Disord.* **2017**, *39*, 63–67. [CrossRef]
19. Kilroy, E.; Aziz-Zadeh, L.; Cermak, S. Ayres Theories of Autism and Sensory Integration Revisited: What Contemporary Neuroscience Has to Say. *Brain Sci.* **2019**, *21*, 68. [CrossRef]
20. Robertson, C.E.; Baron-Cohen, S. Sensory perception in autism. *Nat. Rev. Neurosci.* **2017**, *18*, 671–684. [CrossRef]
21. Epitropakis, C.; DiPietro, E.A. Medication Compliance Protocol for Pediatric Patients with Severe Intellectual and Behavioral Disabilities. *J. Pediatr Nurs.* **2015**, *30*, 329–332. [CrossRef]
22. Rouches, A.; Lefer, G.; Dajean-Trutaud, S.; Lopez-Cazaux, S. Amélioration de la santé orale des enfants avec autisme: Les outils à notre disposition. *Arch. De Pédiatrie* **2018**, *25*, 145–149. [CrossRef] [PubMed]
23. Ferrazzano, G.F.; Salerno, C.; Bravaccio, C.; Ingenito, A.; Sangianantoni, G.; Cantile, T. Autism spectrum disorders and oral health status: Review of the literature. *Eur. J. Paediatr. Dent.* **2020**, *21*, 9–12. [PubMed]
24. Capp, P.L.; de Faria, M.E.; Siqueira, S.R.; Cillo, M.T.; Prado, E.G.; de Siqueira, J.T. Special care dentistry: Midazolam conscious sedation for patients with neurological diseases. *Eur J. Paediatr Dent.* **2010**, *11*, 162–164. [PubMed]
25. Summers, J.; Shahrami, A.; Cali, S.; D'Mello, C.; Kdako, M.; Palikucin-Reljin, A.; Lunsky, Y. Self-Injury in Autism spectrum disorder and intellectual disability: Exploring the role of reactivity to pain and sensory input. *Brain Sci.* **2017**, *7*, 140. [CrossRef]
26. Stiefel, D.J. Dental care considerations for disabled adults. Special care in dentistry. American Association of Hospital Dentists, the Academy of Dentistry for the Handicapped, and the American Society for Geriatric Dentistry. *Spec. Care Dent.* **2002**, *22* (Suppl. 3), 26S.
27. Bondioli, M.; Buzzi, M.C.; Buzzi, M.; Pelagatti, S.; Senette, C. ICT to aid dental care of children with autism. In Proceedings of the 19th International ACM SIGACCESS Conference on Computers and Accessibility, Baltimore, MD, USA, 30 October–1 November 2017.
28. da Silva, S.N.; Gimenez, T.; Souza, R.C.; Mello-Moura, A.C.V.; Raggio, D.P.; Morimoto, S.; Lara, J.S.; Soares, G.C.; Tedesco, T.K. Oral health status of children and young adults with autism spectrum disorders: Systematic review and meta-analysis. *Int. J. Paediatr. Dent.* **2017**, *27*, 388–398. [CrossRef]
29. WHO. *Sixty-Seventh World Health Assembly*; WHO: Geneva, Switzerland, 2014.
30. American Academy of Pediatric Dentistry. *Reference Manual 2010–2011*; American Academy of Pediatric Dentistry: Chicago, IL, USA, 2010.
31. Grewal, N.; Sethi, T.; Grewal, S. Widening horizons through alternative and augmentative communication systems for managing children with special health care needs in a pediatric dental setup. *Spec. Care Dent.* **2015**, *35*, 114–119. [CrossRef]
32. Popple, B.; Wall, C.; Flink, L.; Powell, K.; Discepolo, K.; Keck, D.; Mademtzi, M.; Volkmar, F.; Shic, F. Brief Report: Remotely Delivered Video Modeling for Improving Oral Hygiene in Children with ASD: A Pilot Study. *J. Autism Dev. Disord.* **2016**, *46*, 2791–2796. [CrossRef]
33. Bernard-Opitz, V.; Sriram, N.; Nakhoda-Sapuan, S. Enhancing social problem solving in children with autism and normal children through computer-assisted instruction. *J. Autism Dev. Disord.* **2001**, *31*, 377–384. [CrossRef]
34. Rank, R.C.I.C.; Vilela, J.E.R.; Rank, M.S.; Ogawa, W.N.; Imparato, J.C.P. Effect of awards after dental care in children's motivation. *Eur. Arch. Paediatr Dent.* **2019**, *20*, 85–93. [CrossRef]
35. Isong, I.A.; Rao, S.R.; Holifield, C.; Iannuzzi, D.; Hanson, E.; Ware, J.; Nelson, L.P. Addressing Dental Fear in Children With Autism Spectrum Disorders: A Randomized Controlled Pilot Study Using Electronic Screen Media. *Clin. Pediatr (Phila.)* **2014**, *53*, 230–237. [CrossRef]
36. Mah, J.W.; Tsang, P. Visual Schedule System in Dental Care for Patients with Autism: A Pilot Study. *J. Clin. Pediatr Dent.* **2016**, *40*, 393–399. [CrossRef] [PubMed]
37. Nilchian, F.; Shakibaei, F.; Jarah, Z.T. Evaluation of Visual Pedagogy in Dental Check-ups and Preventive Practices Among 6-12-Year-Old Children with Autism. *J. Autism Dev. Disord.* **2017**, *47*, 858–864. [CrossRef] [PubMed]

38. Prado, I.M.; Carcavalli, L.; Abreu, L.G.; Serra-Negra, J.M.; Paiva, S.M.; Martins, C.C. Use of distraction techniques for the management of anxiety and fear in paediatric dental practice: A systematic review of randomized controlled trials. *Int J. Paediatr Dent.* **2019**, *29*, 650–668. [CrossRef] [PubMed]
39. Charlop, M.H.; Milstein, J.P. Teaching autistic children conversational speech using video modeling. *J. Appl. Behav. Anal.* **1989**, *22*, 275–285. [CrossRef]
40. Da Silva, M.L.; Gonçalves, D.; Guerreiro, T.; Silva, H. A web-based application to address individual interests of children with autism spectrum disorders. *Procedia Comput. Sci.* **2012**, *14*, 20–27. [CrossRef]
41. Passerino, L.M.; Santarosa, L.M.C. Autism and digital learning environments: Processes of interaction and mediation. *Comput. Educ.* **2018**, *51*, 385–402. [CrossRef]
42. Barry, S.M. *Improving Access and Reducing Barriers to Dental Care for Children with Autism Spectrum Disorder*; University of Leeds: West Yorkshire, UK, 2012.
43. Porges, S.W. The polyvagal theory: Phylogenetic substrates of a social nervous system. *Int. J. Psychophysiol.* **2001**, *42*, 123–146. [CrossRef]
44. Porges, S.W. The Polyvagal Theory: Phylogenetic contributions to social behavior. *Physiol. Behav.* **2003**, *79*, 503–513. [CrossRef]
45. Billeci, L.; Tonacci, A.; Tartarisco, G.; Narzisi, A.; Di Palma, S.; Corda, D.; Baldus, G.; Cruciani, F.; Anzalone, S.M.; Calderoni, S.; et al. The MICHELANGELO Study Group. An Integrated Approach for the Monitoring of Brain and Autonomic Response of Children with Autism spectrum disorders during Treatment by Wearable Technologies. *Front. Neurosci.* **2016**, *10*, 276. [CrossRef]
46. Di Palma, S.; Tonacci, A.; Narzisi, A.; Domenici, C.; Pioggia, G.; Muratori, F.; Billeci, L. The MICHELANGELO Study Group. Monitoring of autonomic response to sociocognitive tasks during treatment in children with autism spectrum disorders by wearable technologies: A feasibility study. *Comp. Biol. Med.* **2017**, *85*, 143–152. [CrossRef] [PubMed]
47. Billeci, L.; Tonacci, A.; Narzisi, A.; Manigrasso, Z.; Varanini, M.; Fulceri, F.; Lattarulo, C.; Calderoni, S.; Muratori, F. Heart Rate Variability during a Joint Attention Task in Toddlers with Autism spectrum disorders. *Front. Physiol.* **2018**, *9*, 467. [CrossRef]
48. Pan, J.; Tompkins, W.J. A real-time QRS detection algorithm. *Ieee Trans. Biomed. Eng.* **1985**, *32*, 230–236. [CrossRef] [PubMed]
49. Shaffer, F.; Ginsberg, J.P. An Overview of Heart Rate Variability Metrics and Norms. *Front. Public Health* **2017**, *5*, 258. [CrossRef] [PubMed]
50. Boucsein, W. *Electrodermal Activity*; Springer Science & Business Media: Berlin, Germany, 2012.
51. Hoefman, R.; Payakachat, N.; van Exel, J.; Kuhlthau, K.; Kovacs, E.; Pyne, J.; Tilford, J.M. Caring for a Child with Autism spectrum disorder and Parents' Quality of Life: Application of the CarerQol. *J. Autism Dev. Disord.* **2014**, *44*, 1933–1945. [CrossRef]
52. Naidoo, M.; Singh, S. A Dental Communication Board as an Oral Care Tool for Children with Autism spectrum disorder. *J. Autism Dev. Disord.* **2020**, *5*, 1–13. [CrossRef]
53. Yamasaki, T.; Maekawa, T.; Takahashi, H.; Fujita, T.; Kamio, Y.; Tobimatsu, S. Electrophysiology of Visual and Auditory Perception in Autism Spectrum Disorders. *Compr. Guide Autism* **2014**, 791–808.
54. Fakhruddin, K.S.; El Batawi, H.Y. Effectiveness of audiovisual distraction in behavior modification during dental caries assessment and sealant placement in children with autism spectrum disorder. *Dent. Res. J.* **2017**, *14*, 177–182. [CrossRef]
55. Jaber, M.A. Dental caries experience, oral health status and treatment needs of dental pa-tients with autism. *J. Appl. Oral Sci.* **2011**, *19*, 212–217. [CrossRef]
56. Corridore, D.; Zumbo, G.; Corvino, I.; Guaragna, M.; Bossù, M.; Polimeni, A.; Vozza, I. Prevalence of oral disease and treatment types proposed to children affected by Autistic Spectrum Disorder in Pediatric Dentistry: A Systematic Review. *Clin. Ter.* **2020**, *171*, e275–e282.
57. Penmetsa, C.; Penmetcha, S.; Cheruku, S.R.; Mallineni, S.K.; Patil, A.K.; Namineni, S. Role of Dental Discomfort Questionnaire-Based Approach in Recognition of Symptomatic Expressions Due to Dental Pain in Children with Autism spectrum disorders. *Contemp Clin. Dent.* **2019**, *10*, 446–451. [PubMed]

58. Elmore, J.L.; Bruhn, A.M.; Bobzien, J.L. Interventions for the Reduction of Dental Anxiety and Corresponding Behavioral Deficits in Children with Autism Spectrum Disorder. *J. Dent. Hyg.* **2016**, *90*, 111–120. [PubMed]
59. Shah, A.; Singh, S.; Ajithkrishnan, C.G.; Bipinkumar Kariya, P.; Patel, H.; Ghosh, A. Caregiver's Sense of Coherence: A Predictor of Oral Health-Related Behaviors of Autistic Children in India. *Contemp. Clin. Dent.* **2019**, *10*, 197–202. [PubMed]

13

Autistic Traits Differently Account for Context-Based Predictions of Physical and Social Events

Valentina Bianco [1,†], Alessandra Finisguerra [2,†], Sonia Betti [1,3], Giulia D'Argenio [1,4] and Cosimo Urgesi [1,2,*]

1 Laboratory of Cognitive Neuroscience, Department of Languages and Literatures, Communication, Education and Society, University of Udine, 33100 Udine, Italy; valentina.bianco@uniud.it (V.B.); sonia.betti@studenti.unipd.it (S.B.); GIULIA.D'ARGENIO@phd.units.it (G.D.)
2 Scientific Institute, IRCCS E. Medea, Pasian di Prato, 33037 Udine, Italy; alessandra.finisguerra@lanostrafamiglia.it
3 Department of General Psychology, University of Padova, 35131 Padova, Italy
4 PhD Program in Neural and Cognitive Sciences, Department of Life Sciences, University of Trieste, 34128 Trieste, Italy
* Correspondence: cosimo.urgesi@uniud.it
† These authors contributed equally to this work.

Abstract: Autism is associated with difficulties in making predictions based on contextual cues. Here, we investigated whether the distribution of autistic traits in the general population, as measured through the Autistic Quotient (AQ), is associated with alterations of context-based predictions of social and non-social stimuli. Seventy-eight healthy participants performed a social task, requiring the prediction of the unfolding of an action as interpersonal (e.g., to give) or individual (e.g., to eat), and a non-social task, requiring the prediction of the appearance of a moving shape as a short (e.g., square) or a long (e.g., rectangle) figure. Both tasks consisted of (i) a familiarization phase, in which the association between each stimulus type and a contextual cue was manipulated with different probabilities of co-occurrence, and (ii) a testing phase, in which visual information was impoverished by early occlusion of video display, thus forcing participants to rely on previously learned context-based associations. Findings showed that the prediction of both social and non-social stimuli was facilitated when embedded in high-probability contexts. However, only the contextual modulation of non-social predictions was reduced in individuals with lower 'Attention switching' abilities. The results provide evidence for an association between weaker context-based expectations of non-social events and higher autistic traits.

Keywords: autistic traits; autism; action observation; action prediction; context; priors

1. Introduction

Autism spectrum disorder (ASD) consists of a range of neurodevelopment conditions characterized by deficits in reciprocal social behavior and communication, as well as by restrictive and repetitive behaviors and interests, which are present in the early developmental period [1]. Beside the other manifestations of this disorder, including social withdrawal and isolation [2], the presence of sensory abnormalities [3] and difficulties in mentalizing processes [4], it has been repeatedly shown that individuals with ASD struggle with making predictions or with deciding what to pay attention to on the basis of prior expectations about the sensory world [5]. The impairments in discerning the predictive relationships between events may not only compromise habituation processes [6], but they may also generate anxiety, resulting in the typical insistence of sameness usually observed in individuals with ASD [7].

This difficulty is further amplified when people are involved in social situations, where unpredictable interactions could take place. Indeed, dealing with social interactions in an effective way often requires the ability to anticipate others' behavior, predicting their intentions from observing their movements. Movement kinematic information, however, may be ambiguous in many (if not most) social situations [8,9]. Thus, a social observer needs to integrate this sensory evidence with knowledge of past experiences aiming at the same goal or with contextual cues facilitating action prediction [10–16].

According to predictive coding accounts [17], the brain works as a Bayesian inference machine, merging prior expectations with current evidence to assess the probability of future outcomes as a result of rule learning. For instance, in the visual domain, prior contextual information is responsible for the elementary regularities that bias our perception of shape and color [18] as well as for the effects of perceptual learning on the processing of visual objects [19]. Moving to the framework of social cognition, studies challenging the comprehension of social behavior showed that individuals with typical development strongly rely on prior knowledge regarding the context in which actions are usually observed in order to recognize action unfolding [13–16], especially when perceptual information is scarce [20]. The predictive coding account may explain the perceptual impairments of ASD individuals in both the social and non-social domains. Indeed, an impaired learning curve may generate deficits in picking up statistical constancies in the environment, favoring routine and attention to details at the price of the broad picture (see [21] for review). Accordingly, reduced reliance on prior expectations relative to sensory inputs has been shown to lead to a plethora of abnormalities consistently observed in ASD individuals [21,22]. In a similar vein, although the ability to read the goal of an action during action observation seems to be preserved in ASD ([23], but see also [24,25] for contrasting results), there is consistent evidence that, when the outcome of the action is ambiguous, individuals with ASD exhibit impairments in using contextual priors to predict action unfolding [20,26–28]. Collectively, these observations highlight the difficulties of ASD individuals in integrating the available sensory evidence with previous experience when dealing with the prediction of both physical and social stimuli.

ASD has been traditionally considered as a clinical condition distinct from typical-development functioning [29]; however, there is consistent consensus in considering the disorder as the upper extreme of a constellation of impairments that may be continuously distributed in nature [30–32]. Along this continuum, people can, indeed, be characterized to a different extent by the presence of subclinical autistic traits. These traits can be measured by a self-report questionnaire, the Autism-Spectrum Quotient (AQ, [30]), which is widely used in research and clinical practice to measure autistic traits in the general population (see [33] for a systematic review). The AQ describes the subclinical autistic impairments across different domains related to either social behavior (i.e., Social skills and Communication) or non-social aspects of cognition (i.e., Imagination, Attention to detail, and Attention Switching).

Previous studies measuring autistic traits in the general population showed that high autistic traits (i.e., AQ scores > 21, 1 standard deviation, s.d., above the group mean) are associated with altered perceptual adaptation for social objects [34]. Furthermore, either individuals with ASD or typical-development individuals high in autistic traits (i.e., AQ scores, Mean = 22.13, s.d. = 5.74) presented a reduced sensitivity to context-based integration of sensory feedback with prior expectation [35]. These observations supported the view of a greater reliance on new information relative to prior information in ASD and high-autistic–trait individuals. A recent study [15] extended these findings to action scenarios, by investigating the association between autistic traits and motor responses during the observation of others' actions embedded in contexts. Indeed, observing actions embedded in contexts that are congruent or incongruent with the unfolding kinematics, respectively, facilitated or inhibited discrimination performance and motor activation, as compared to observing actions embedded in an ambiguous context [14–16]. Notably, lower sensitivity to contextual information and higher reliance on the sensory evidence provided by kinematics were found in individuals with higher autistic traits [16], in particular in the domains of Social skills and Attention to details [16,36].

This points to an association between both social and non-social aspects of autistic traits and impairments in the integration of sensory evidence and contextual information.

Crucially, there is extensive evidence that the behavioral traits associated to social and non-social aspects of cognition may be independently distributed in the general population, pointing to different neurocognitive bases ([37] for review). However, it is still unclear how social and cognitive aspects of autistic traits might be related to the use of previous experience to predict social or non-social events. In the present study, we sought to investigate at what extent the presence of autistic traits might interfere with the ability to implicitly learn the associations between a contextual cue and a specific event (i.e., contextual priors), and to use this association in order to make predictions under perceptual uncertainty. The relation between the amount of social or cognitive autistic traits and context-based predictions were tested in a social domain pertaining the prediction of actions and in a non-social domain pertaining the anticipation of appearing objects. Specifically, concerning this latter domain, we used moving shapes as stimuli in order to manipulate arbitrary associations between a contextual cue and the moving shape, thus avoiding any previously-learned semantic associations that could affect context-based manipulations for everyday-life objects. It is noteworthy that moving shapes have been used as control stimulus for action observation in previous neuroimaging and brain stimulation studies. In particular, a study by Schubotz and co-workers [38] showed that sequential presentations of biological (i.e., action) and non-biological abstract stimuli (i.e., circles) share the recruitment of premotor regions, while triggering distinctive patterns of activations in other fronto-parietal areas. In a similar vein, a more recent study by Paracampo and co-workers [39] asked participants to predict the outcome of hand or shape movements and found that, in spite of comparable difficulty, only the first task was affected by interferential stimulation of the left primary motor cortex. In both of these studies, moving shapes were used as control stimuli for assessing the action-specific or the domain general brain involvement in predictive mechanisms. Capitalizing on these studies, here we adopted an action prediction and a shape prediction task to assess the use of prior information in driving prediction across the two domains.

In the present study, we hypothesized that, in both domains, participants should be biased towards the implicitly-learned contextual priors in order to compensate for perceptual uncertainty. Moreover, we hypothesized that the presence of autistic traits involving social aspects might relate to a reduced reliance on contextual priors to predict the unfolding of actions, while those involving non-social aspects of cognition, especially attention switching, might relate to a reduced reliance on contextual priors to predict the fate of physical events (i.e., object appearance).

2. Materials and Methods

2.1. Participants

Seventy-eight healthy young university students (49 Female, mean age = 24.12, s.d. = 6.06 years) participated in the study. We determined the sample size for testing the effects of a single predictor in the multiple regression design of our study (number of predictors = 5 AQ scales) through the G*POWER software [40]. Based on the results of a previous study on the predictive effects of the AQ subscales on action-context integration in adults with typical development [16], we estimated a medium effect size of $f^2 = 0.15$ [41] and set the significance level at $\alpha = 0.05$, and the desired power ($1 - \beta$) at 0.9. Participants were recruited at the University of Udine. All participants were right-handed [42] and had normal or corrected-to-normal vision. The study was approved by the local Ethics Committee (Prot. N. 47/2015/Sper, 26/05/2015 Comitato Etico Regionale Unico, Friuli Venezia Giulia, Italy) and was carried out in accordance with the ethical standards of the 1964 Declaration of Helsinki. All participants were naïve to the aims and hypothesis of the experiment and provided their written informed consent prior to the enrollment in the study. Only after the end of the whole experiment, participants were debriefed about the experimental hypothesis.

2.2. General Design

We used two separate prediction tasks, requiring participants to observe videos of social actions, in an action prediction task, or videos showing moving geometrical shapes, in a shape prediction task. In particular, we presented these videos in two different alternative force choice (2AFC) tasks in a paradigm including a probabilistic learning (familiarization) phase followed by a prediction (testing) phase and allowing the assessment of contextual prior in making predictions [20] when sensory evidence is scarce. Notably, the strength of priors in driving prediction is thought to be especially brought into play in 2AFC, given that top-down signals encoding conditional expectations might influence obliged decisions regarding the physical nature of sensory input [43].

A within-subject design was used. For each participant, the experiment consisted of two separate experimental sessions during which the action prediction task and the shape prediction task were administered, respectively. Each task session lasted around 20 min. The familiarization phase comprised a total of 160 trials equally divided into 4 identical familiarization blocks, while the testing phase was made of a total of 80 trials, presented in 2 identical testing blocks of 40 trials. Each testing block was administered after two familiarization blocks, allowing a few minutes' rest between blocks. The order of the two tasks was counterbalanced across participants. At the end of the two task sessions, participants' autistic traits were assessed by administering the AQ questionnaire (AQ, [30]).

2.3. Stimuli and Tasks

Action Prediction Task. For the action prediction task, the same videos and paradigm proposed by Amoruso et al. [20] were used. During this task, participants watched videos showing a male child (10 years old) who was sitting in front of a peer and was grasping with his right hand an object, an apple or a glass, to perform either an individual action (to eat, to drink) or an interpersonal one (to offer). Based on the kinematics of the hand approaching the object, two possible hints could be suggested: reaching for grasping the object from its side signaled the action of moving the object toward the mouth with the individual intention of eating or drinking, while reaching for grasping the object from its top prompted the interpersonal action of offering the object. Notably, each action was performed in the presence of specific contextual cues: for actions performed upon the apple, the two possible contextual cues were a violet or an orange dish; for the actions performed with the glass, the two possible cues were a white or a blue tablecloth. In this way, stimuli consisted of a total of 8 different videos (Figure 1a).

For both phases (familiarization and testing phase) of this task, participants were asked to watch the videos and to predict the action unfolding (eat/drink versus offer). However, videos of the familiarization and testing phase dramatically differed in their length and thus in the amount of visual information provided. Indeed, videos of the familiarization phase were interrupted after the hand pre-shaping and the reaching phase, two frames before the hand contact with the object, when the amount of visual information was sufficient to distinguish the individual from the interpersonal action (Figure 1b). Differently, videos of the testing phase were interrupted during the hand pre-shaping phase, thus when the movement kinematic was still ambiguous (Figure 1c). It is important to note that, even though participants watched only the initial part of the videos, when these were originally recorded, the child was asked to perform the complete action in order to provide reliable kinematics information. For further details on video recording, please refer to [19].

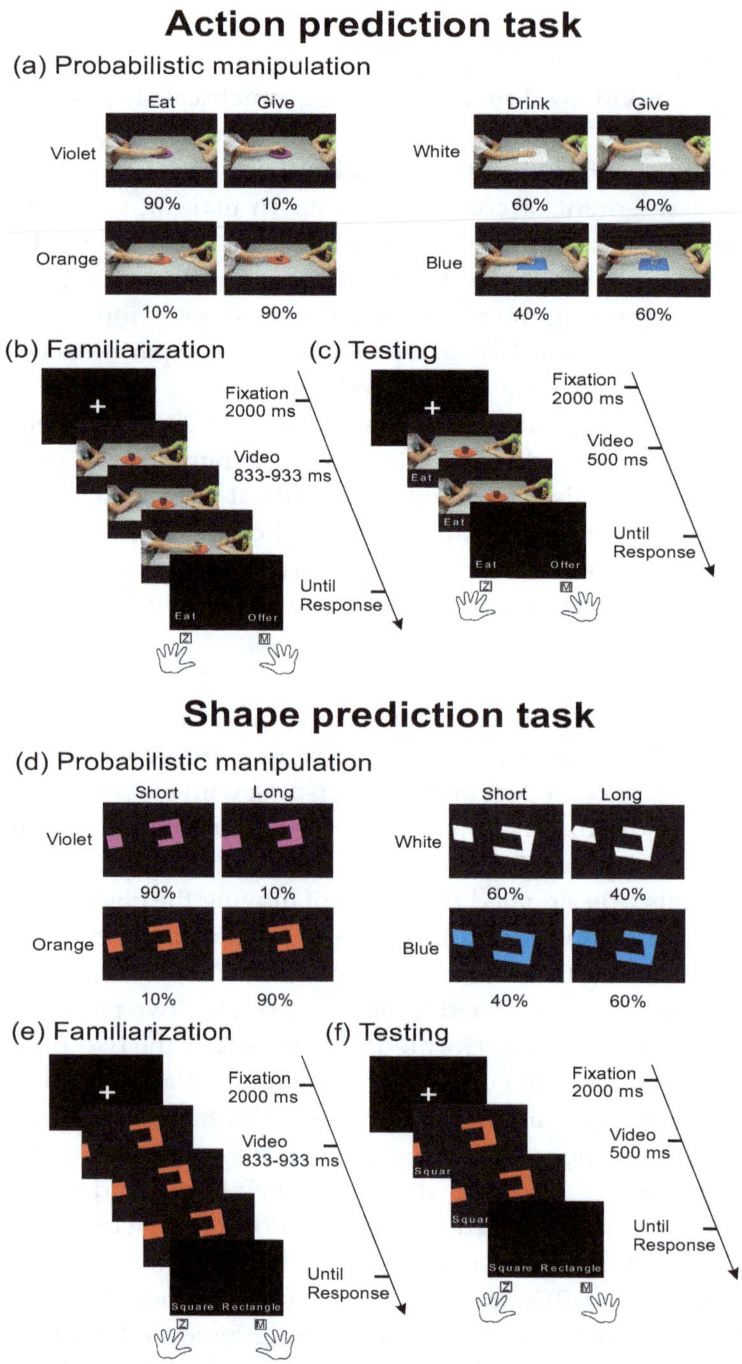

Figure 1. Stimuli and Experimental tasks. Action prediction task: (**a**) sketch of probabilities manipulation for the familiarization phase. Action-context associations were manipulated in terms of their probability of co-occurrence to 90%, 10%, 60%, and 40%; (**b**) familiarization phase showing videos of a child performing individual or interpersonal actions. Participants had to predict action unfolding; (**c**) testing phase showing the same videos during familiarization but of shortened duration. Participants had to predict action unfolding, as during the familiarization phase. Shape prediction task; (**d**) sketch of probabilities manipulation for the familiarization phase. Shapes-context associations were manipulated in terms of their probability of co-occurrence to 90%, 10%, 60% and 40%; (**e**) familiarization phase showing videos of moving shapes approaching the receptor shape. Participants had to predict shape identity; (**f**) testing phase showing the same videos during familiarization but of shortened duration. Participants had to predict shape identity, as during the familiarization phase.

Crucially, during the familiarization phase, we manipulated the probability of co-occurrence between each action and the contextual cues. More specifically, the probability of co-occurrence was set in order to have the 90%, 60%, 40% or 10% of trials representing an action-contextual cue association (namely, for 36, 24, 16, and 4 trials, respectively). For instance, an apple presented on a violet plate could be grasped 90% of the time to eat and 10% of the time to offer. In the same block, an apple presented on an orange plate could be grasped 90% of the time to offer and 10% of the time to eat. For the actions performed on the glass presented in the same block, a glass presented on a white tablecloth could be grasped 60% of the time to drink and 40% of the time to offer. Conversely, in the same block, a glass presented on a blue tablecloth was grasped 60% of the time to offer and 40% of the time to drink (Figure 1a). In this way, we sought to implicitly manipulate prior expectations regarding the action unfolding, based on the presence of these contextual cues. Importantly, the probabilistic manipulation was kept identical across the two repetitions of the familiarization phase within each participant, but we counterbalanced across participants the probability of associations between each action and a given contextual cue.

The same instructions were given during the familiarization and the testing phases. However, according to Amoruso et al. [20], in this last phase during which video duration was drastically reduced, given the perceptual uncertainty generated by the ambiguity of action kinematics, a response bias towards previously acquired contextual priors should occur. Notably, during this phase, all possible action-contextual cues associations were equally presented, thus 10 trials for each of the 8 action-contextual cue video associations were included in the whole testing phase. Before the beginning of the task, participants received information regarding the identity of the objects and demonstrations of the different possible ways of manipulating them. More specifically, we provided participants with specific examples with the original objects used in the videos (e.g., 'this is how we grasp an apple when we want to offer it'). However, explicit information about the associations between contextual cues and actions were not provided.

Shape Prediction Tasks

We developed this task to compare context-based predictions in social and non-social domains. To this aim, the same logic of the action prediction task was followed in designing the task.

Video frames were created in Power Point (Microsoft Corporation, Redmond, WA, USA). They depicted colored geometric shapes appearing from the left side of the screen and moving toward the right, where a still complementary receptor figure was presented. The moving geometric shapes could be a right-angle polygon (a square or a rectangle) or an acute-angle polygon (a parallelogram or a trapezoid). The shapes of each pair of polygons looked similar on their right side, which was immediately visible at the beginning of the movement. However, with the increased visibility of the horizontal segments during the movement, the identity of the specific polygon could be detected according to the ratio between the major and minor axis of the figure, thus according to whether the horizontal segment was longer than (i.e., rectangle or trapezoid) or equal to (i.e., square or parallelogram) the visible right vertical segment. The still receptor hosted, on its left side, a concavity that was suited for binding the moving shape (Figure 1d). As in the action prediction task, we manipulated specific contextual cues based on the color of the moving shape and receptor. In particular, the square and the rectangle could be colored either in orange or in violet, while the parallelogram and the trapezoid could be colored either in white or in blue. This way, 8 different videos were created (Figure 1d). The receptor always had the same color of the moving shape, thus facilitating the salience of the color cue since the very beginning of the video.

For both the familiarization and the testing phases of this task, participants were asked to observe the videos and to predict the moving shape. Importantly, during the familiarization phase, the shapes fully appeared on the screen and thus could be easily identified (Figure 1e). Conversely, during the testing phase, videos were interrupted just one frame after the halfway appearance of the horizontal segment, thus providing minimal information about the ratio of the major-minor axis of the shape and its identity (Figure 1f). In both phases, we varied, across participants, two different response modality versions of the same task. For a first response modality (position response), which was administered to 38 participants, the left side of each complementary receptor contained two concavities, respectively, in its lower and upper parts; each concavity could host only a specific moving shape. Participants were required to report the upper or lower position of the receptor that could host the moving shape. For the second response modality (naming response), which was administered to 40 participants, the receptor presented only one concavity that could bind both possible shapes in each pair (i.e., the square or the rectangle, for one receptor, and the parallelogram or the trapezoid for the other). Participants were required to report the polygon name of the moving shape (please refer to the *Procedure and trial structure* section for further details). This way, we manipulated the contribution of the spatial and verbal ability demands that could affect the difficulty of the shape prediction task and that could be differently loaded in the two tasks.

Crucially, during the familiarization phase, we manipulated the probability of co-occurrence between each polygon and its color, using the same probability settings of the action prediction task. For instance, a violet shape could end up appearing as a square 90% of the time and as a rectangle 10% of the time. Conversely, an orange shape could end up appearing as a rectangle 90% of the time and as a square the remaining 10% of the time. In the same block, a blue shape could be a trapezoid 60% of the time and a 40% of the time, while a white shape could be a parallelogram 60% of the time a trapezoid 40% of the time (Figure 1d).

The same instructions were given in both phases. However, as in the testing phase, video duration was drastically reduced and therefore the shape identity was more ambiguous; we expected participants' responses to be biased towards the contextual priors (i.e., shape–color associations) acquired during the familiarization phase. Notably, during this phase, all possible shape–color associations were equally presented, namely 10 trials for each of the 8 shape–color associations.

As in the action prediction task, the probabilistic manipulation was kept identical across the two repetitions of the familiarization phase within each participant, but we counterbalanced the probability of associations between each polygon and a given color across participants. Before performing the tasks, participants received information regarding the identity of all the possible geometric figures by using two-dimensional paper figures. More specifically, we provided participants with specific hints regarding the similarity of the right side but different major-minor axis ratio of the two shapes in each pair. The possible associations between color and shapes, however, were never explicitly acknowledged.

2.4. Procedure and Trial Structure

The same procedure and trial structure were used in the two tasks. Participants were seated in front of a computer screen at a distance of about 60 cm, with their arms positioned palm down on the keyboard. Stimuli were presented using the E-Prime software (version 2.0, Psychology Software Tools, Inc., Pittsburgh, PA, USA). Video resolution was set at 1280 × 768 pixels, with a refresh rate of 60 Hz. Trials started with the presentation of a central fixation cross (remaining on the screen for 2000 ms), which was followed by video presentation (Figure 1). Videos were presented frame-by frame at a rate of 30 Hz. In the familiarization phase, videos lasted 833–933 ms (25–28 frames), while in the testing phase videos were interrupted after 500 ms (i.e., after the initial 15 frames). For the familiarization phase, at the end of each video, a response prompt was presented at the bottom of the screen until participant's response. It showed, respectively, at the left and right of the screen, the verbal descriptors of the two possible actions (the Italian verbs "mangiare/bere" or "offrire"; in English "to eat/drink" or "to offer") or the position/name of the two possible concavities/polygons (the Italian adverbs "sopra" and "sotto", in English "up" and "down"; the Italian names "quadrato" and "rettangolo", or "trapezio" and "parallelogramma", in English "square" and "rectangle", or "trapezoid" and "parallelogram"). For the testing phase, the response prompt appeared at video onset and remained on the screen until the participant's response; this way, participants could provide their response as soon as they were able to guess the correct response. Participants were asked to respond with their index fingers using the left

(Z) or the right (M) keys corresponding to the left or right location of the descriptors. The position of the descriptors was counterbalanced between participants. An empty black screen was presented for 1000 ms between each consecutive trial.

2.5. Autistic Traits Measure

At the end of the two experimental sessions, participants completed the Italian version of the Autism-Spectrum Quotient (AQ, [30,44]), a self-report questionnaire measuring autistic traits in the general population that is widely used in research and clinical practice. The AQ consists of 50 items divided into five subscales. The Attention switching subscale measures deficits in control processes of cognition and measures the ability to switch rapidly between multiple tasks. This ability is crucial in real life scenarios, where we are challenged by a constantly changing environment and we have to adapt accordingly, frequently switching attention among multiple sources of salient events. This subscale includes items such as: "I prefer to do things the same way over and over again"; "If there is an interruption, I can switch back to what I was doing very quickly". The Attention to Detail subscale measures the tendency to focus more on individual pieces of information at the expense of perceiving the global picture. Typical items are: "I notice patterns in things all the time"; "I usually concentrate more on the whole picture, rather than on the small details". The Communication subscale measures deficits in the skill to properly provide and receive different kinds of information and includes items like: "I frequently find that I don't know how to keep a conversation going"; "I find it easy to read between the lines when someone is talking to me". The Imagination subscale covers deficits in the ability to form sensory images and experiences in the mind. Example items are: "If I try to imagine something, I find it very easy to create a picture in my mind"; "I find it difficult to imagine what it would be like to be someone else". Finally, the Social Skills subscale concerns deficits in knowing how to act in different types of social situations and is measured with items such as: "I prefer to do things with others rather than on my own"; "I find it difficult to work out people's intentions". For each item, participants are required to provide one of four responses: 'definitely agree', 'slightly agree', 'slightly disagree', and 'definitely disagree'. Answers are scored 1 or 0 indicating the presence or absence of autistic traits. Higher scores reflect higher autistic traits, thus greater impairment in attention switching, imagination, communication and social skills abilities, as well as a perceptual bias toward details in spite of a deficit in global processing for the Attention to Detail subscale. Individual AQ total scores range between 0 and 50, while subscale scores range between 0 and 10.

2.6. Data Handling

Individual AQ total and subscale scores were calculated according to standard procedures [30,44]. Independent sample *t*-test (two-tailed) was used to compare the score of male and female participants within our sample and with those reported in age-, education-, and gender-matched Italian samples reported a previous study [45].

Individual performance in the familiarization and prediction phase was expressed as d prime (d′), a bias corrected measure of sensitivity in discriminating between two categories, and as response criterion (c), which checks for the existence of a bias in providing a specific response (see [46]). For the action prediction task, individual actions identified as individual were considered 'hits', while interpersonal actions identified as individual were considered 'false alarms'. For both versions of the shape prediction task, short shapes identified as short were considered 'hits', while long shapes identified as short were considered 'false alarms'.

Individual d′ and c values for the familiarization phase were entered into separate 2×2 mixed repeated measure analysis of variance (RM-ANOVA), with Task (Action vs. Shape prediction) as within-subject variable and shape-prediction Response Modality (Position vs. Naming) as between-subject factor. For the familiarization phase, the d′ and c values were averaged across the four probability conditions due to their unequal number of trials generated by the probabilistic manipulation. For the testing phase, the d′ and c values were subjected to mixed 2X2X4 RM-ANOVAs with Task and Probability (10%, 40%, 60%, 90%) as within-subject variables and shape-prediction Response Modality as between-subject factor. Estimates of the effect size were obtained using the partial η squared ($\eta_p{}^2$, [41]). *Post-hoc* pairwise comparisons were carried out using the Newman–Keuls test.

Based on the results of the RM-ANOVA, we calculated, for the testing phase of each task, a facilitation index by subtracting, for each participant, the d′ value obtained in the condition of lowest probability (10%) from the average d′ values obtained in the other probabilities of association (40%, 60%, 90%). In this way, we obtained individual measures of the reliance in using contextual priors to predict the unfolding action or shape.

Then, standard multiple linear regression models were tested to assess whether the individual level of contextual modulation in the two tasks was predicted by autistic traits. Scores at the five AQ subscales (Attention switching, Attention to detail, Communication, Imagination, Social skills) were entered as independent variables, while the Action or Shape d′ Facilitation indexes were entered as dependent variables. The assumptions for multiple regression analysis were met, given the presence of linear relationships between the dependent and the independent variables, and all variables were also checked for homoscedasticity and collinearity.

All analyses were implemented in Statistica software (Version number 12, Statsoft, Tulsa, OK, USA). The alpha value for all statistical tests was set at 0.05.

3. Results

3.1. AQ Scores

Analysis of the distribution of the AQ total score revealed that it was normally distributed, with skewness of 0.41 (s.e. = 0.27) and kurtosis of −0.44 (s.e. = 0.53). The individual AQ total scores ranged between 3 and 36 (Mean = 16.4, s.d. = 7.5), spanning from low (i.e., < 13) to high (i.e., > 18) levels of autistic traits [30]. As expected [30], men (N = 30; Mean = 18.3, s.d. = 8.56) tended to have higher AQ scores than women (N = 48, Mean = 15.21, s.d. = 6.58), but the difference between the two gender groups did not reach significance ($t_{76} = 1.8$, $p = 0.076$). Importantly, a recent study [45] describing a sample of Italian University students of fact-based humanities, which best matched our sample for age, study-field, and gender, revealed comparable distributions of AQ scores for both men (N = 29; Mean = 17.9, s.d. = 6; t_{57} = -0.21, $p = 0.837$) and women (N = 30; Mean = 17.5, s.d. = 6.9; $t_{68} = 1.41$, $p = 0.163$). Table 1 describes the statistics for each AQ subscale.

Table 1. Distribution and collinearity indexes of the AQ subscale scores.

AQ Subscale	Mean	St. Dev.	Range	Skewness	Kurtosis	Tolerance
Attention Switching	4.3	2.2	0–9	−0.08	−0.75	0.507
Attention to detail	4.8	2.2	0–10	0.05	−0.45	0.847
Communication	2.0	2.0	0–8	0.87	−0.17	0.463
Imagination	2.7	1.8	0–7	0.35	−0.65	0.750
Social skills	2.3	2.2	0–9	1.03	0.30	0.413

3.2. Behavioral Results: ANOVA

For the familiarization phase, the RM-ANOVA on d′ values did not report any significant effects for Task ($F_{1,76} = 0.86$, $p = 0.355$), Response Modality ($F_{1,76} = 3.60$, $p = 0.061$) and their interaction ($F_{1,76} = 0.68$, $p = 0.411$). Similarly, the RM-ANOVA on c values did not report any significant effects for Task ($F_{1,76} = 2.12$, $p = 0.149$), Response Modality ($F_{1,76} = 0.89$, $p = 0.348$) and Interaction ($F_{1,76} = 1.87$, $p = 0.175$).

For the testing phase, the RM-ANOVA on d′ values yielded a main effect of Probability ($F_{3,228} = 12.28$, $p < 0.001$, $\eta_p{}^2 = 0.13$). Post-hoc comparisons revealed that d′ values were lower for the 10% (mean = 1.653; s.e. = 0.12) than the 40% (mean = 2.020; s.e. = 0.081), 60% (mean = 2.133; s.e. = 0.086) and 90% (mean = 2.242; s.e. = 0.076) conditions, thus suggesting a decreased sensitivity in target discrimination under low predictability based on the contextual cues. No significant differences were observed among the 40%, 60%, and 90% conditions (all *ps* > 0.07). Importantly, the main effect of Task ($F_{1,76} = 0.49$, $p = 0.484$) and the Task × Probability Interaction ($F_{3,228} = 1.03$, $p = 0.376$) were not significant, suggesting that the two tasks were matched for prediction difficulty and that no differences in prior modulation were present between the Action Prediction and the Shape Prediction tasks (see Figure 2). Regarding the Response Modality of the Shape Prediction Task, a main effect emerged ($F_{1,76} = 16.14$, $p < 0.001$, $\eta_p^2 = 0.17$), since we found that performing the prediction tasks was easier in Position Response (mean = 2.285; s.e. = 0.097) than in Naming Response (mean = 1.738; s.e. = 0.095). Importantly, no interaction between Response Modality and the other factors was found (Task × Response Modality: $F_{1,76} = 3.77$, $p = 0.056$, Probability × Response Modality: $F_{3,228} = 1.11$, $p = 0.342$, Task × Probability × Response Modality, $F_{3,228} = 0.07$ $p = 0.974$), thus ruling out a possible influence of relative difficulty of task performance due to response modality on context probability modulation.

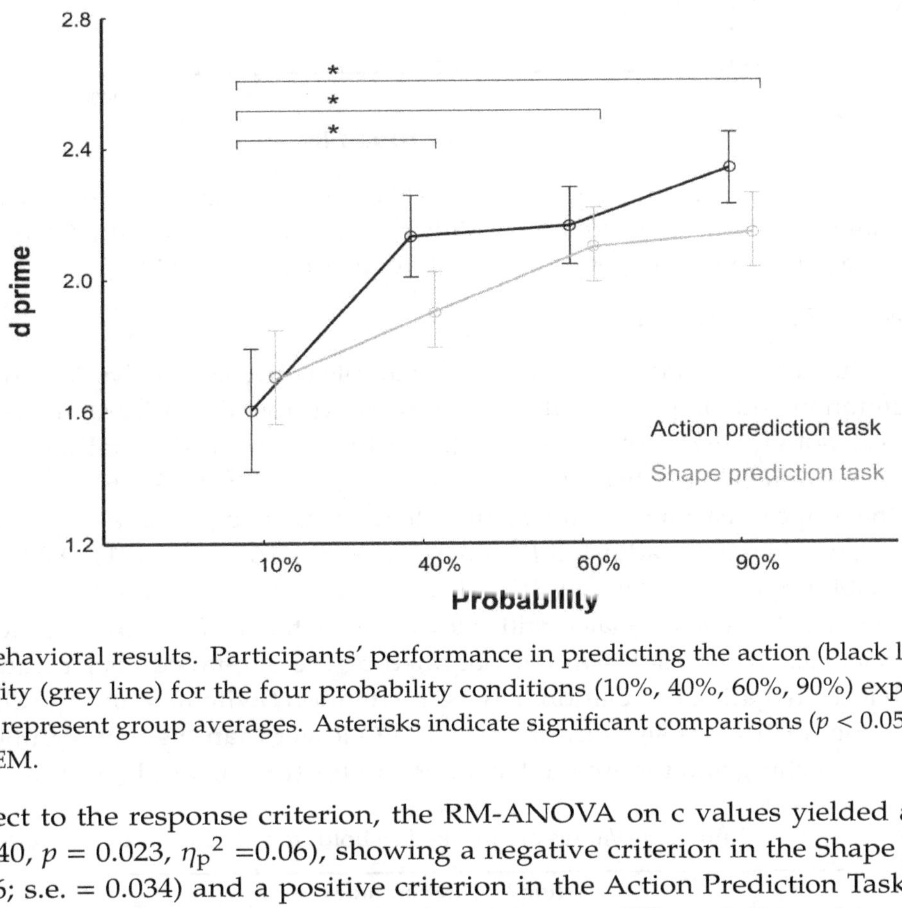

Figure 2. Behavioral results. Participants' performance in predicting the action (black line) and the shape identity (grey line) for the four probability conditions (10%, 40%, 60%, 90%) expressed as d'. Data points represent group averages. Asterisks indicate significant comparisons ($p < 0.05$). Error bars represent SEM.

With respect to the response criterion, the RM-ANOVA on c values yielded a main effect of Task ($F_{1,76} = 5.40$, $p = 0.023$, $\eta_p^2 = 0.06$), showing a negative criterion in the Shape Prediction Task (mean = −0.046; s.e. = 0.034) and a positive criterion in the Action Prediction Task (mean = 0.045; s.e. = 0.021, $p = 0.03$). This suggests that participants were differently biased in reporting one of the two outcomes in the two tasks. This, however, did not interact with Probability ($F_{3,228} = 0.29$, $p = 0.833$), nor was the main effect of Probability significant ($F_{3,228} = 0.34$, $p = 0.799$), ruling out a change in responses bias depending on the strength of the contextual prior (see Figure 3). We also found a main effect of Response Modality ($F_{1,76} = 12.83$, $p = 0.008$, $\eta_p^2 = 0.14$), further modulated by a significant Response Modality X Task Interaction ($F_{1,76} = 20.51$, $p < 0.001$ $\eta_p^2 = 0.21$). Post-hoc comparisons showed lower c values in Position Response (mean = −0.21; s.e. = 0.049) than Naming Response (mean = 0.117; s.e. = 0.047) for the Shape ($p < 0.001$), but not for the Action Prediction Task (Position response: mean = 0.062; s.e. = 0.031; Naming response: mean = 0.029; s.e. = 0.03, $p = 0.567$). This shows that the different response modalities of the two shape prediction versions led to a different bias in reporting the appearance of a long or a short shape. Importantly, no interaction with Probability was found ($F_{3,228} = 0.85$, $p = 0.470$), ruling out that the contextual modulation was affected by changes in responses bias across the two task versions.

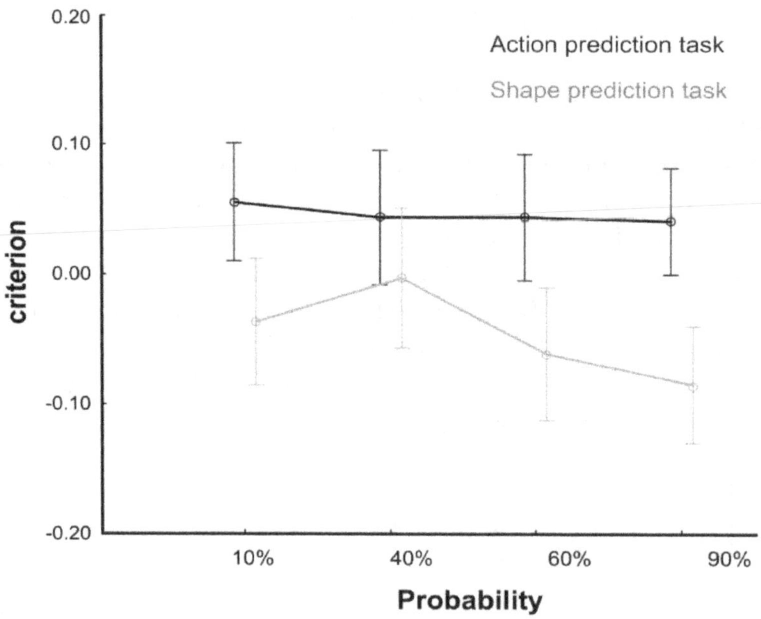

Figure 3. Behavioural results. Participants' response biases in predicting the action (black line) and the shape identity (grey line) for the four probability conditions (10%, 40%, 60%, 90%) expressed as criterion (c). Data points represent group averages. Error bars represent SEM.

3.3. Behavioral Results: Regression Analysis

Table 2 shows the summary statistics of standard multiple regression analyses conducted separately for Action d′ Facilitation and Shape d′ Facilitation indices. Multicollinearity statistics confirmed that the assumption was not violated (Tolerance > 0.4). For the Action d′ Facilitation index, none of the subscale scores was a significant predictor (whole model: adjusted $R^2 = -0.0461$; $F_{5,72} = 0.70$; $p = 0.628$). Interestingly, for the Shape d′ Facilitation index, the Attention switching subscale score was a significant predictor ($p = 0.019$; whole model: adjusted $R^2 = 0.035$; $F_{5,72} = 1.561$; $p = 0.181$). All the other subscale scores were not reliable predictors (all *ps* > 0.407). Thus, a higher level of cognitive autistic trait reflecting Attention Switching deficits were associated with a lower contextual prior modulation for the non-social, but not for the social task. This result was corroborated by the one-tailed Fisher transformation test, which showed that the negative correlation between Attention Switching and the Shape facilitation index (r = −0.270, Figure 4b) was significantly ($p = 0.046$) lower than the non-significant correlation between Attention Switching and the Action facilitation index (r = −0.007, Figure 4a).

Table 2. *p*-Values are marked as bold, for $p < 0.05$.

Action Facilitation Index			
Coefficients	**β**	**t**	***p*-Level**
Attention Switching	0.051	0.316	0.752
Attention to detail	−0.073	−0.589	0.557
Communication	−0.146	−0.864	0.390
Imagination	0.219	1.648	0.103
Social skills	−0.045	−0.251	0.802
Shape Facilitation Index			
Coefficients	**β**	**t**	***p*-Level**
Attention Switching	**−0.375**	**−2.392**	**0.019**
Attention to detail	0.022	0.185	0.853
Communication	0.143	0.875	0.384
Imagination	−0.077	−0.597	0.552
Social skills	0.081	0.469	0.639

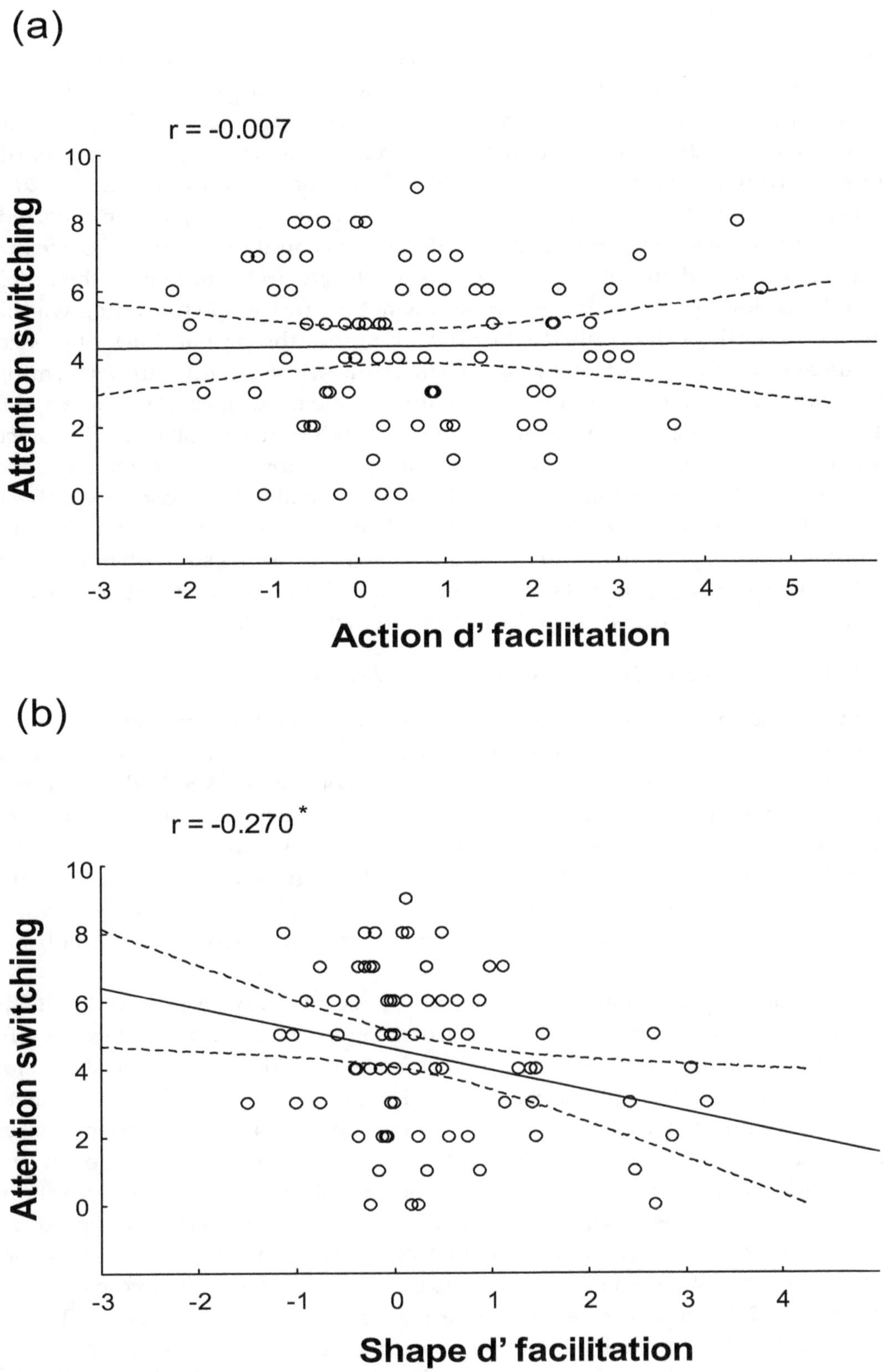

Figure 4. Correlational results. (**a**) lack of significant correlation between facilitation index for the action prediction task and attention switching scores; (**b**) significant negative correlation between facilitation index for the shape prediction task and attention switching scores.

4. Discussion

The present study tested to which extent the level of autistic traits in a general (i.e., non ASD) population could be associated with the ability to learn and use contextual priors to make predictions of social and non-social events. In line with the predictive coding account [17], we expected that contextual priors should modulate the precision of both action and shape predictions. Furthermore, in line with studies showing poor use of contextual priors for actions in ASD individuals [20] and poorer integration of action-context cues in individuals with higher autistic traits [16], we expected that social and cognitive aspects of the autistic traits should differently account for the use of contextual priors to predict the outcomes of social and physical events, respectively. In keeping with the first hypothesis, we showed that behavioral performance in predicting action and shape unfolding was significantly influenced by the strength of the contextual priors: the more the probabilities of co-occurrence of a contextual cue and a given event, the more participants were accurate in performing the tasks. This modulation was independent from the social nature of the task, since it was detected for both the action and shape prediction tasks. Moreover, it was independent from task difficulty, since we found comparable modulation for the two versions of the shape prediction task where the response modality was manipulated to load more spatial or verbal abilities. Crucially, the second hypothesis was only partially supported, since we found that cognitive (i.e., Attention Switching), but not social (i.e., Social Skills or Communication) aspects of the autistic traits accounted for the strength of contextual prior in the shape prediction task. However, we failed to find an association between either social or non-social autistic traits and use of contextual prior in the action prediction task.

4.1. Contextual Modulation of Social and Physical Event Prediction

The ideomotor theory [47] and forward models of action [48]) claim that the ability to predict action intention represents a crucial aspect of motor control and relies on previously learnt bidirectional associations between the motor act and its consequent sensory effects [49]). Action prediction mechanisms have been studies using different techniques. For instance, paradigms investigating the processing of anticipated action effects showed that self-generated stimuli are perceived as less intense than externally-triggered stimuli, resulting in sensory attenuation [50]. Other neurophysiological studies focused on the brain correlates of the anticipated action effects [51]. Here, we addressed action prediction from a Bayesian perspective related to the associations between action observation and contextual priors.

Using the same action prediction task of this study, a recent study [20] showed that children with typical development were able to use previously learned contextual information to successfully predict an ongoing action. In contrast, despite similar performance of children with typical development and children with ASD in discriminating fully observed actions, children with ASD did not leverage priors to predict action unfolding when visual information was ambiguous. The present study replicated the same pattern of findings in a large sample of young adult observers with typical development, thus providing evidence for consisting reliance on contextual priors in action perception across the lifespan. A recent study [52] also found that, in conditions of impoverished kinematic information available to an observer, explicit verbal information concerning the ongoing action strongly biased action prediction. In contrast, when kinematics was fully visible, the explicit verbal information had little, if no effect, with informative kinematics overriding the verbal information. The condition of fully visible kinematics was comparable to our familiarization condition, in which the unfolding action was clearly showed until one frame before the hand–object contact. Indeed, our participants could easily recognize the action outcome and used this experience in the testing phase, when kinematic information was reduced. Still, differently than in Koul et al. [52]'s study, some action-specific kinematic cues were still available during the testing phase and participants integrated this information with that provided by contextual priors, rather than overwriting kinematic evidence with the contextual prior. Thus, prediction performance was not completely biased to the contextual prior and even in the lowest probability condition participant's sensitivity was well above 0. Of note, given that sensitivity was defined based on kinematics and not on the context, this means that kinematics was correctly identified, but performance was modulated by contextual priors. In keeping with the predictive coding view of action processing [53,54], when observing someone performing an action, our brain generates top-down expectations to explain away the perceptual kinematics. In this recursive processing, incoming kinematic evidence is continuously matched with experiential or contextual priors in order to reduce the prediction error and reach a more precise model of the perceived action. Evidence for the integration of contextual prior and kinematic information has come from neuroimaging [13] and neurophysiological [12,14–16,54] investigations of modulation of motor activity according to the compatibility between the observed action and the embedding context.

The present study extended the same implicit learning of stimulus-context associations to a non-social domain, namely the prediction of an appearing object based on its color. Results provided evidence of prior-related perceptual advantages in the prediction of this physical event. In line with the predicting coding theory [17], it appeared that, when observing ambiguous moving geometric shapes, our brain generates predictions to guess in a proactive way the identity of the observed stimulus, leading to a modulation of perceptual areas according to the compatibility between the object identity and the embedding context (see [55]). In this sense, future studies are needed to clarify whether the context-based modulation of motor activity during action observation is specific for actions or rather reflects a general mapping of predictability [38].

4.2. Attention Switching Accounts for Context-Based Prediction of Physical Events

Several studies have provided evidence of altered perception of the world in individuals with autism [56–60] and in typically-developing individuals with high autistic traits [61–63].

Three main theories have been proposed to explain the abnormalities associated with atypical visual processing in autism. The Weak Central Coherence model [64] highlights the superior focus on the local aspects of a scene at the expense of the global "bigger picture". The Enhanced Perceptual Functioning model [65] emphasizes the enhancement in the detection of visual features. Interestingly, in a predictive coding account [65], these abnormalities may stem from an unbalance in the integration of top-down and bottom-up signals for the perception of the external world. Indeed, individuals with autism or high autistic traits may rely less on priors and more on sensorial evidence, showing a 'hypo-priors' mode of processing [66]. Empirical studies, however, have provided contrasting findings on whether the perceptual abnormalities of autism-like perception are due to weaker prior (e.g., [67,68]) or more precise sensorial information (e.g., [63,69]). Nevertheless, all these theories share the notion that individuals with autism-like perception do not integrate visual information in an optimal manner, thus perceiving an overwhelming sense of 'sensory overload' when dealing with the environment [70].

Using a task tapping the implicit learning of arbitrary shape–color associations, here we showed that high autistic traits accounted for a reduced ability to use the expectations arising from previous experience in order to discriminate among geometric shapes in situations of reduced visual information. In particular, individuals with less attention switching abilities tended not to take advantage of previously learned shape–color associations to disambiguate the appearing shape, pointing to a role of weak contextual priors in an autism-like perception of the world.

The role of a specific autistic trait linked to executive function deficits is consistent with a seminal work by Courchesne et al. [71] where authors showed an impaired ability of individuals with ASD to execute rapid attention switches during an attention shifting paradigm. Furthermore, as also demonstrated by a functional neuroimaging study using an adaptive version of the embedded figure test (EFT, [72]), participants with ASD are more dependent on perception, thus adopting a more local approach when faced with a task, compared to typically developing individuals. Notably, given the involvement of distinct cortical activations in individuals with ASD and individuals with typical development, the differences in behavioral performance seemed to be associated with different underlying neural systems, suggesting that individuals with and without autism use different cognitive strategies and engage different neural networks in performing the same task.

4.3. Autistic Traits Accounts for Context-Based Prediction of Actions

Several studies showed that, in individuals with ASD, although action understanding is preserved ([23] but see also [24,25] for contrasting results), impairments arise when the goal of the action has to be inferred on the basis of contextual cues [27,73], pointing to a reduced reliance on prior knowledge as the core of social interaction deficits in ASD. Therefore, we expected an association between the AQ measures of social behavior (i.e., communication, social skills) and the context-based predictions of social events. Contrary to these expectations, however, we did not find any correlation between any AQ subscales and the advantage provided by contextual cues during the performance of the action prediction task. The lack of significant results might also seem partially in contrast to previous study [16], where the authors found a negative correlation between the AQ subscales social skills and communication and neurophysiological correlates of the integration between top-down contextual expectations and movement kinematics. However, similar to the present study, the authors failed to find significant correlations between behavioral performance and AQ scores. In a similar vein, while a deficit in using contextual priors to predict action unfolding was observed in children with ASD as compared to those with typical development, the relative distribution of the deficit was not accounted for by their deficits in social perception abilities, but by their behavioral problems [20]. This might reflect that, while autistic traits may be associated with a different neural processing of social actions, this does not necessarily lead to an action prediction failure.

Otherwise, the lack of association between autistic traits and context-based predictions in individuals with either typical development or in ASD, despite the deficits shown by the last group as a whole, might reflect the dissociation between ASD and autistic traits. Consolidated views support the proposal of considering ASD as a dimensional rather than categorical disorder, with blurry and quantitative distinctions between subclinical autistic traits observed in the general population and individuals diagnosed as ASD [31,74]). Following this view, previous investigations have demonstrated the existence of a significant correlation between autistic traits and the sensory and perceptual alterations found in clinical autism [75]. Crucially, individuals with high autistic-trait scores showed similar perceptual difficulties in global processing often associated with clinical ASD than individuals with low-autistic trait scores [76]. Conversely, contrary evidence has been provided by Silverman et al. [77], who showed that autistic traits related to communication and social skills in ASD are not strongly correlated with the symptoms of stereotyped and repetitive behaviors. This is in line with the alternative view proposed by genetic studies (e.g., [78]) suggesting that ASD is best characterized as a category distinct from autistic traits [79]. Notably, to reconcile these two positions and explain contrasting findings, a categorical-dimensional hybrid model of ASD has been proposed [80,81]). This model, which has been also considered for defining the ASD diagnostic criteria in the fifth edition of the Diagnostic and Statistical Manual for Mental Disorder, has conceived the presence of either a categorical distinction between individuals with and without ASD or a dimensional representation of ASD symptoms. However, by assessing the associations between naturally varying levels of autistic traits on the ability to make experience-dependent predictions on upcoming events, without testing individuals with an ASD diagnosis, the present study does not allow establishing the extent at which clinical forms of ASD and autistic-like behaviors overlap.

5. Conclusions and Limitations

In conclusion, we showed that, while ASD has been associated to deficits linked to the context-based prediction of actions, the distribution of autistic traits in the general population is related to the strength of contextual priors only in the prediction of physical events. This conclusion, however, needs to be commensurate with the limitations of this study. First of all, while we powered our study to detect significant AQ prediction effects based on previous studies, it is possible that the relative uniformity of the sample, all young university students mainly enrolled in fact-based-humanities courses, might have shrunk the range of AQ variations, thus limiting predictive power. Furthermore, the unbalanced representations of male and female participants in our sample, partly related to the distribution of male and female students in the sampled university courses, might have also biased the distribution of AQ scores to lower levels of autistic traits, thus masking a possible association between action prediction and high autistic traits. Indeed, a recent study has documented an interactive effect of gender and study field on the AQ distribution in a large sample of university students [44]. In addition, using action videos depicting child models might have altered the type of action processing in our adult sample. Furthermore, we did not test here individuals with ASD and could not verify whether and how ASD and autistic traits are differently associated with context-based prediction of physical and social events. Finally, while the non-social task was designed to match the social one for difficulty and general procedure, it mapped less on everyday-life situations, thus lacking ecological validity as compared to the social task. Future studies are needed to couple the present behavioral data with neurophysiological measures and to include both behavioral and neural measures of individuals with ASD, in order to advance our understanding of the relation between object and action prediction, autistic traits, and ASD.

Author Contributions: Conceptualization, A.F. and C.U.; Methodology, A.F. and C.U.; Formal Analysis, V.B., A.F., and C.U.; Investigation, V.B., A.F., S.B., G.D., and C.U.; Data Curation, V.B.; Writing—Original Draft Preparation, V.B. and A.F.; Writing—Review and Editing, S.B., G.D., and C.U.; Supervision, C.U.; Funding Acquisition, C.U. and A.F. All authors have read and agree to the published version of the manuscript.

Acknowledgments: We thank Eva Francesca Sponton and Valentina Azzano Cantarutti for their contribution in data collection.

References

1. American Psychiatric Association. *Diagnostic and Statistical Manual of Mental Disorders*, 5th ed.; DSM-5; Psychiatric Association: Washington, DC, USA; Burbank, CA, USA, 2013.
2. Orsmond, G.I.; Shattuck, P.T.; Cooper, B.P.; Sterzing, P.R.; Anderson, K.A. Social participation among young adults with an autism spectrum disorder. *J. Autism Dev. Disord.* **2013**, *43*, 2710–2719. [CrossRef] [PubMed]
3. Leekam, S.R.; Nieto, C.; Libby, S.J.; Wing, L.; Gould, J. Describing the sensory abnormalities of children and adults with autism. *J. Autism Dev. Disord.* **2007**, *37*, 894–910. [CrossRef] [PubMed]
4. White, S.; Hill, E.; Happé, F.; Frith, U. Revisiting the strange stories: Revealing mentalizing impairments in autism. *Child Dev.* **2009**, *80*, 1097–1117. [CrossRef] [PubMed]
5. Sinha, P.; Kjelgaard, M.M., Gandhi, T.K., Tsourides, K.; Cardinaux, A.L.; Pantazis, D.; Diamond, S.P. Held RM. Autism as a disorder of prediction. *Proc. Natl. Acad. Sci. USA* **2014**, *111*, 15220–15225. [CrossRef] [PubMed]
6. Kleinhans, N.M.; Johnson, L.C.; Richards, T.; Mahurin, R.; Greenson, J.; Dawson, G.; Aylward, E. Reduced neural habituation in the amygdala and social impairments in autism spectrum disorders. *Am. J. Psychiatry* **2009**, *166*, 467–475. [CrossRef]
7. Gillott, A.; Furniss, F.; Walter, A. Anxiety in high-functioning children with autism. *Autism* **2001**, *5*, 277–286. [CrossRef]
8. Amoruso, L.; Finisguerra, A. Low or high-level motor coding? The role of stimulus complexity. *Front. Hum. Neurosci.* **2019**, *13*, 332. [CrossRef]
9. Finisguerra, A.; Amoruso, L.; Makris, S.; Urgesi, C. Dissociated representations of deceptive intentions and kinematic adaptations in the observer's motor system. *Cerebral Cortex* **2018**, *28*, 33–47. [CrossRef]
10. Iacoboni, M.; Molnar-Szakacs, I.; Gallese, V.; Buccino, G.; Mazziotta, J.C.; Rizzolatti, G. Grasping the intentions of others with one's own mirror neuron system. *PLoS Biol.* **2005**, *3*, e79. [CrossRef]
11. Ansuini, C.; Giosa, L.; Turella, L.; Altoè, G.; Castiello, U. An object for an action, the same object for other actions: Effects on hand shaping. *Exp. Brain Res.* **2008**, *185*, 111–119. [CrossRef]
12. Amoruso, L.; Finisguerra, A.; Urgesi, C. Contextualizing action observation in the predictive brain: Causal contributions of prefrontal and middle temporal areas. *NeuroImage* **2018**, *177*, 68–78. [CrossRef] [PubMed]
13. Wurm, M.F.; Schubotz, R.I. 2016 What's she doing in the kitchen? Context helps when actions are hard to recognize. *Psychon. Bull Rev.* **2016**, *24*, 503–509. [CrossRef] [PubMed]
14. Amoruso, L.; Urgesi, C. Contextual modulation of motor resonance during the observation of everyday actions. *NeuroImage* **2016**, *134*, 74–84. [CrossRef] [PubMed]
15. Amoruso, L.; Finisguerra, A.; Urgesi, C. Tracking the time course of top-down contextual effects on motor responses during action comprehension. *J. Neurosci.* **2016**, *36*, 11590–11600. [CrossRef] [PubMed]

16. Amoruso, L.; Finisguerra, A.; Urgesi, C. Autistic traits predict poor integration between top-down contextual expectations and movement kinematics during action observation. *Sci. Rep.* **2018**, *8*, 16208. [CrossRef] [PubMed]
17. Friston, K. The free-energy principle: A unified brain theory? *Nat. Rev. Neurosci.* **2010**, *11*, 127–138. [CrossRef] [PubMed]
18. Land, E.H. The retinex theory of color vision. *Sci. Am.* **1977**, *237*, 108–129. [CrossRef]
19. Gilbert, C.D.; Sigman, M.; Crist, R.E. The neural basis of perceptual learning. *Neuron* **2001**, *31*, 681–697. [CrossRef]
20. Amoruso, L.; Narzisi, A.; Pinzino, M.; Finisguerra, A.; Billeci, L.; Calderoni, S.; Urgesi, C. Contextual priors do not modulate action prediction in children with autism. *Proc. R. Soc. Lond.* **2019**, *286*, 20191319. [CrossRef]
21. Van de Cruys, S.; Evers, K.; Van der Hallen, R.; Van Eylen, L.; Boets, B.; de-Wit, L.; Wagemans, J. Precise minds in uncertain worlds: Predictive coding in autism. *Psychol. Rev.* **2014**, *121*, 649. [CrossRef]
22. Lawson, R.P.; Rees, G.; Friston, K.J. An aberrant precision account of autism. Front. Hum. *Neuroscience* **2014**, *8*, 302.
23. Hamilton, A.F.D.C. Research review: Goals, intentions and mental states: Challenges for theories of autism. *J. Child Psychol. Psychiatry* **2009**, *50*, 881–892. [CrossRef] [PubMed]
24. Iacoboni, M.; Dapretto, M. The mirror neuron system and the consequences of its dysfunction. *Nat. Rev. Neurosci.* **2006**, *7*, 942–951. [CrossRef] [PubMed]
25. Zalla, T.; Labruyere, N.; Georgieff, N. Goal-directed action representation in autism. *J. Autism Dev. Disord.* **2006**, *36*, 527–540. [CrossRef] [PubMed]
26. Cattaneo, L.; Fabbri-Destro, M.; Boria, S.; Pieraccini, C.; Monti, A.; Cossu, G.; Rizzolatti, G. Impairment of actions chains in autism and its possible role in intention understanding. *Proc. Natl. Acad. Sci. USA* **2007**, *104*, 17825–17830. [CrossRef]
27. Chambon, V.; Farrer, C.; Pacherie, E.; Jacquet, P.O.; Leboyer, M.; Zalla, T. Reduced sensitivity to social priors during action prediction in adults with autism spectrum disorders. *Cognition* **2017**, *160*, 17–26. [CrossRef]
28. Gomot, M.; Wicker, B. A challenging, unpredictable world for people with autism spectrum disorder. *Int. J. Psychophysiol.* **2012**, *83*, 240–247. [CrossRef]
29. Volkmar, F.R.; Cohen, D.J.; Paul, R. An evaluation of DSM-III criteria for infantile autism. *J. Am. Acad. Child Psy.* **1986**, *25*, 190–197. [CrossRef]
30. Baron-Cohen, S.; Wheelwright, S.; Skinner, R.; Martin, J.; Clubley, E. The autism-spectrum quotient (AQ): Evidence from Asperger syndrome/high-functioning autism, males and females, scientists and mathematicians. *J. Autism Dev. Disord.* **2001**, *31*, 5–17. [CrossRef]
31. Constantino, J.; Todd, R. Autistic traits in the general population—A twin study. *Arch. Gen. Psychiatry* **2003**, *60*, 524–530. [CrossRef]
32. Posserud, M.B.; Lundervold, A.J.; Gillberg, C. Autistic features in a total population of 7–9-year-old children assessed by the ASSQ (Autism Spectrum Screening Questionnaire). *J. Child Psychol. Psychiatry* **2006**, *47*, 167–175. [CrossRef] [PubMed]
33. Ruzich, E.; Allison, C.; Smith, P.; Watson, P.; Auyeung, B.; Ring, H.; Baron-Cohen, S. Measuring autistic traits in the general population: A systematic review of the Autism-Spectrum Quotient (AQ) in a nonclinical population sample of 6900 typical adult males and females. *Mol. Autism* **2015**, *6*, 2. [CrossRef] [PubMed]
34. Miu, A.C.; Pană, S.E.; Avram, J. Emotional face processing in neurotypicals with autistic traits: Implications for the broad autism phenotype. *Psychiatry Res.* **2012**, *198*, 489–494. [CrossRef] [PubMed]
35. Palmer, C.J.; Paton, B.; Kirkovski, M.; Enticott, P.G.; Hohwy, J. Context sensitivity in action decreases along the autism spectrum: A predictive processing perspective. *Proc. R. Soc. B-Biol. Sci.* **2015**, *282*, 20141557. [CrossRef]
36. Amoruso, L.; Finisguerra, A.; Urgesi, C. Spatial frequency tuning of motor responses reveals differential contribution of dorsal and ventral systems to action comprehension. *Proc. Natl. Acad. Sci. USA* **2020**, *117*, 13151–13161. [CrossRef]
37. Happé, F.; Ronald, A.; Plomin, R. Time to give up on a single explanation for autism. *Nat. Neurosci.* **2006**, *9*, 1218–1220. [CrossRef]
38. Schubotz, R.I.; Von Cramon, D.Y. Sequences of abstract nonbiological stimuli share ventral premotor cortex with action observation and imagery. *J. Neurosci.* **2004**, *24*, 5467–5474. [CrossRef]

39. Paracampo, R.; Montemurro, M.; de Vega, M.; Avenanti, A. Primary motor cortex crucial for action prediction: A. tDCS study. *Cortex* **2018**, *109*, 287–302. [CrossRef]
40. Faul, F.; Erdfelder, E.; Lang, A.G.; Buchner, A. G* Power 3: A flexible statistical power analysis program for the social, behavioral, and biomedical sciences. *Behav. Res. Methods* **2007**, *39*, 175–191. [CrossRef]
41. Cohen, J. The effect size. *Stat. Power Anal. Behav. Sci.* **1988**, *2*, 77–83.
42. Oldfield, R.C. The assessment and analysis of handedness: The Edinburgh inventory. *Neuropsychologia* **1971**, *9*, 97–113. [CrossRef]
43. Summerfield, C.; Koechlin, E. A neural representation of prior information during perceptual inference. *Neuron* **2008**, *59*, 336–347. [CrossRef] [PubMed]
44. Ruta, L.; Mazzone, D.; Mazzone, L.; Wheelwright, S.; Baron-Cohen, S. The Autism-Spectrum Quotient—Italian version: A cross-cultural confirmation of the broader autism phenotype. *J. Autism Dev. Disord.* **2012**, *42*, 625–633. [CrossRef] [PubMed]
45. Conson, M.; Senese, V.P.; Baiano, C.; Zappullo, I.; Warrier, V.; Salzano, S.; Baron-Cohen, S. The effects of autistic traits and academic degree on visuospatial abilities. *Cogn. Process.* **2020**, *21*, 127–140. [CrossRef] [PubMed]
46. Stanislaw, H.; Todorov, N. Calculation of signal detection theory measures. *Behav. Res. Methods* **1999**, *31*, 137–149. [CrossRef]
47. Shin, Y.K.; Proctor, R.W.; Capaldi, E.J. A review of contemporary ideomotor theory. *Psychol. Bull.* **2010**, *136*, 943. [CrossRef] [PubMed]
48. Pickering, M.J.; Clark, A. Getting ahead: Forward models and their place in cognitive architecture. *Trends Cogn. Sci.* **2014**, *18*, 451–456. [CrossRef]
49. Waszak, F.; Cardoso-Leite, P.; Hughes, G. Action effect anticipation: Neurophysiological basis and functional consequences. *Neurosc. Biobehav. Rev.* **2012**, *36*, 943–959. [CrossRef]
50. Cardoso-Leite, P.; Mamassian, P.; Schütz-Bosbach, S.; Waszak, F. A new look at sensory attenuation: Action-effect anticipation affects sensitivity, not response bias. *Psychol. Sci.* **2010**, *21*, 1740–1745. [CrossRef]
51. Blakemore, S.J.; Wolpert, D.M.; Frith, C.D. Central cancellation of self-produced tickle sensation. *Nat. Neurosci.* **1998**, *1*, 635–640. [CrossRef]
52. Koul, A.; Soriano, M.; Tversky, B.; Becchio, C.; Cavallo, A. The kinematics that you do not expect: Integrating prior information and kinematics to understand intentions. *Cognition* **2019**, *182*, 213–219. [CrossRef] [PubMed]
53. Kilner, J.M.; Friston, K.J.; Frith, C.D. Predictive coding: An account of the mirror neuron system. *Cogn. Process* **2007**, *8*, 159–166. [CrossRef] [PubMed]
54. Kilner, J.M. More than one pathway to action understanding. *Trends Cogn. Sci.* **2011**, *15*, 352–357. [CrossRef] [PubMed]
55. Bar, M. Visual objects in context. *Nat. Rev. Neurosci.* **2004**, *5*, 617–629. [CrossRef]
56. Ego, C.; Bonhomme, L.; de Xivry, J.J.O.; Da Fonseca, D.; Lefèvre, P.; Masson, G.S.; Deruelle, C. Behavioral characterization of prediction and internal models in adolescents with autistic spectrum disorders. *Neuropsychologia* **2016**, *91*, 335–345. [CrossRef]
57. Tewolde, F.G.; Bishop, D.V.; Manning, C. Visual motion prediction and verbal false memory performance in autistic children. *Autism Res.* **2018**, *11*, 509–518. [CrossRef]
58. Balsters, J.H.; Apps, M.A.; Bolis, D.; Lehner, R.; Gallagher, L.; Wenderoth, N. Disrupted prediction errors index social deficits in autism spectrum disorder. *Brain* **2017**, *140*, 235–246. [CrossRef]
59. Goris, J.; Braem, S.; Nijhof, A.D.; Rigoni, D.; Deschrijver, E.; Van de Cruys, S.; Wiersema, J.R.; Brass, M. Sensory prediction errors are less modulated by global context in autism spectrum disorder. *Biol. Psychiatry Cogn. Neurosci. Neuroimaging* **2018**, *3*, 667–674. [CrossRef]
60. Turi, M.; Burr, D.C.; Igliozzi, R.; Aagten-Murphy, D.; Muratori, F.; Pellicano, E. Children with autism spectrum disorder show reduced adaptation to number. *Proc. Natl. Acad. Sci. USA* **2015**, *112*, 7868–7872. [CrossRef]
61. Braukmann, R.; Ward, E.; Hessels, R.S.; Bekkering, H.; Buitelaar, J.K.; Hunnius, S. Action prediction in 10-month-old infants at high and low familial risk for Autism Spectrum Disorder. *Res. Autism Spectrum Disord.* **2018**, *49*, 34–46. [CrossRef]
62. Karvelis, P.; Seitz, A.R.; Lawrie, S.M.; Seriès, P. Autistic traits, but not schizotypy, predict increased weighting of sensory information in Bayesian visual integration. *ELife* **2018**, *7*, e34115. [CrossRef] [PubMed]

63. Skewes, J.C.; Jegindø, E.-M.; Gebauer, L. Perceptual inference and autistic traits. *Autism* **2015**, *19*, 301–307. [CrossRef] [PubMed]
64. Frith, U.; Happé, F. Autism: Beyond "theory of mind". *Cogn. Cogn.* **1995**, 13–30. [CrossRef]
65. Mottron, L.; Burack, J.A. Enhanced perceptual functioning in the development of autism. In *The Development of Autism: Perspectives from Theory and Research*; Lawrence Erlbaum Associates Publishers: Mahwah, NJ, USA, 2001; pp. 131–148.
66. Pellicano, E.; Burr, D.C. When the world becomes 'too real': A Bayesian explanation of autistic perception. *Trends Cogn. Sci.* **2012**, *16*, 504–510. [CrossRef] [PubMed]
67. Lawson, R.P.; Aylward, J.; White, S.; Rees, G. A striking reduction of simple loudness adaptation in autism. *Sci. Rep.* **2015**, *5*, 16157. [CrossRef] [PubMed]
68. Lawson, R.P.; Mathys, C.; Rees, G. Adults with autism overestimate the volatility of the sensory environment. *Nat. Neurosci.* **2017**, *20*, 1293–1299. [CrossRef]
69. Manning, C.; Kilner, J.M.; Neil, L.; Karaminis, T.; Pellicano, E. Children on the autism spectrum update their behaviour in response to a volatile environment. *Dev. Sci.* **2017**, *20*, e12435. [CrossRef]
70. Simmons, D.R.; Robertson, A.; McKay, L.S.; Toal, E.; McAleer, P.; Pollick, F.E. Vision in autism spectrum disorders. *Vis. Res.* **2009**, *49*, 2705–2739. [CrossRef]
71. Courchesne, E.; Townsend, J.; Akshoomoff, N.; Saitoh, O.; Yeung-Courchesne, R.; Lincoln, A.J.; James, H.E.; Haas, R.H.; Schreibman, L.; Lau, L. Impairment in shifting attention in Autistic and Cerebellar Patients'. *Behav. Neurosci.* **1994**, *108*, 848–865.
72. Ring, H.; Baron-Cohen, S.; Wheelwright, S.; Williams, S.C.; Brammer, M.; Andrew, C.; Bullmore, E.T. Cerebral correlates of preserved cognitive skills in autism: A functional MRI study of embedded figures task performance. *Brain* **1999**, *122*, 1305–1315. [CrossRef]
73. Schuwerk, T.; Sodian, B.; Paulus, M. Cognitive Mechanisms Underlying Action Prediction in Children and Adults with Autism Spectrum Condition. *J. Autism Dev. Disord.* **2016**, *46*, 3623–3639. [CrossRef]
74. Spiker, D.; Lotspeich, L.J.; DiMiceli, S.; Myers, R.M.; Risch, N. Behavioral phenotypic variation in autism multiplex families: Evidence for a continuous severity gradient. *Am. J. Med. Genet.* **2002**, *114*, 129–136. [CrossRef] [PubMed]
75. Robertson, A.; Simmons, D. The Relationship between Sensory Sensitivity and Autistic Traits in the General Population. *J. Autism Dev. Disord.* **2013**, *43*, 775–784. [CrossRef] [PubMed]
76. Grinter, E.J.; Maybery, M.; Van Beek, P.L.; Pellicano, E.; Badcock, J.C.; Badcock, D.R. Global Visual Processing and Self-Rated Autistic-like Traits. *J. Autism Dev. Disord.* **2009**, *39*, 1278–1290. [CrossRef] [PubMed]
77. Silverman, J.M.; Smith, C.J.; Schmeidler, J.; Hollander, E.; Lawlor, B.A.; Fitzgerald, M.; Buxbaum, J.D.; Delaney, K.; Galvin, P. the Autism Genetic Research Exchange Consortium Symptom domains in autism and related conditions: Evidence for familiality. *Am. J. Med. Genet.* **2002**, *114*, 64–73. [CrossRef] [PubMed]
78. Abrahams, B.S.; Geschwind, D.H. Advances in autism genetics: On the threshold of a new neurobiology. *Nat. Rev. Genet.* **2008**, *9*, 341–355. [CrossRef] [PubMed]
79. Frazier, T.W.; Youngstrom, E.A.; Sinclair, L.; Kubu, C.S.; Law, P.; Rezai, A.; Constantino, J.N.; Eng, C. Autism Spectrum Disorders as a Qualitatively Distinct Category From Typical Behavior in a Large, Clinically Ascertained Sample. *Assessment* **2010**, *17*, 308–320. [CrossRef]
80. Elton, A.; Di Martino, A.; Hazlett, H.C.; Gao, W. Neural Connectivity Evidence for a Categorical-Dimensional Hybrid Model of Autism Spectrum Disorder. *Boil. Psychiatry* **2016**, *80*, 120–128. [CrossRef]
81. Frazier, T.W.; Youngstrom, E.A.; Speer, L.; Embacher, R.; Law, P.; Constantino, J.; Findling, R.L.; Hardan, A.Y.; Eng, C. Validation of Proposed DSM-5 Criteria for Autism Spectrum Disorder. *J. Am. Acad. Child Adolesc. Psychiatry* **2012**, *51*, 28–40. [CrossRef]

Early Motor Development Predicts Clinical Outcomes of Siblings at High-Risk for Autism: Insight from an Innovative Motion-Tracking Technology

Angela Caruso [1], Letizia Gila [1], Francesca Fulceri [1], Tommaso Salvitti [1], Martina Micai [1], Walter Baccinelli [2], Maria Bulgheroni [2] and Maria Luisa Scattoni [1,*,†] on behalf of the NIDA Network Group

[1] Research Coordination and Support Service, Istituto Superiore di Sanità, Viale Regina Elena 299, 00161 Roma, Italy; angela.caruso@iss.it (A.C.); letizia.gila@iss.it (L.G.); francesca.fulceri@iss.it (F.F.); tommaso.salvitti@iss.it (T.S.); martina.micai@iss.it (M.M.)

[2] Ab.Acus srl, Milano, via F. Caracciolo 77, 20155 Milano, Italy; walterbaccinelli@ab-acus.eu (W.B.); mariabulgheroni@ab-acus.com (M.B.)

* Correspondence: marialuisa.scattoni@iss.it

† NIDA Network Group: Fabio Apicella, Andrea Guzzetta, Massimo Molteni, Giovanni Valeri, Stefano Vicari.

Abstract: Atypical motor patterns are potential early markers and predictors of later diagnosis of Autism Spectrum Disorder (ASD). This study aimed to investigate the early motor trajectories of infants at high-risk (HR) of ASD through MOVIDEA, a semi-automatic software developed to analyze 2D and 3D videos and provide objective kinematic features of their movements. MOVIDEA was developed within the Italian Network for early detection of Autism Spectrum Disorder (NIDA Network), which is currently coordinating the most extensive surveillance program for infants at risk for neurodevelopmental disorders (NDDs). MOVIDEA was applied to video recordings of 53 low-risk (LR; siblings of typically developing children) and 50 HR infants' spontaneous movements collected at 10 days and 6, 12, 18, and 24 weeks. Participants were grouped based on their clinical outcome (18 HR received an NDD diagnosis, 32 HR and 53 LR were typically developing). Results revealed that early developmental trajectories of specific motor parameters were different in HR infants later diagnosed with NDDs from those of infants developing typically. Since MOVIDEA was useful in the association of quantitative measures with specific early motor patterns, it should be applied to the early detection of ASD/NDD markers.

Keywords: neurodevelopmental disorders; autism spectrum disorder; high-risk infants; motor development; screening; technology

---

1. Introduction

Neurodevelopmental disorders (NDDs) are a group of conditions with onset in the developmental period characterized by impairments of personal, social, and academic functioning (Diagnostic and statistical manual of mental disorders, DSM-5, APA 2013). The global rate of NDDs from 2009–2011 to 2015–2017 increased from 16.2% to 17.8% (e.g., Autism Spectrum Disorder (ASD): 1.1–2.5%; Attention-Deficit/Hyperactivity Disorder: 8.5–9.5%) [1]. Given the importance of early detection and intervention programs in improving infants' and parents' outcomes, previous research focused on the identification of early biomarkers and behavioral measures to determine risk status even before the emergence of clear behavioral symptoms [2,3]. In this scientific framework, the Italian National of Health hosts the Network for early detection of Autism Spectrum Disorders (NIDA Network), including pediatric hospitals and clinical research centers of Italian territory with high expertise in early detection and intervention programs in ASD. The NIDA Network delivered new tools and standards for research and clinical development across the nation and is currently coordinating the most extensive surveillance program of development in infants at risk for NDDs in Italy. The aim of the NIDA Network is the early detection of behavioral markers of NDDs to provide intervention programs in a timely manner.

Several studies revealed that some early behavioral measures might be effective in predicting abnormal developmental trajectories [4–7]. Moreover, a growing body of literature pointed toward nonsocial behavioral measures, such as motor skills, restricted and repetitive interests, sensory and visual processing, and attention disengagement [8–11]. Significant findings emerged from studies focusing on early motor development of children later diagnosed with NDDs [10,11]. Indeed, both fine and gross motor impairments are associated with NDD occurrence in the general population [8] and high-risk infants (i.e., siblings of children with a diagnosis of ASD, preterm and low birth weight infants) [9,10,12,13]. Overall, the most frequently reported early motor signs of NDDs are abnormalities in fluency, complexity, and variability of spontaneous general movements, and delays in early gross motor milestones [14,15], motor maturity [8,16], and motor functioning [17,18]. Findings reflect the heterogeneity of clinical symptomatology of NDDs, and instruments adopted to evaluate infants' motor patterns are extremely variable, ranging from analysis of General Movements (GMs) based on the Prechtl method assessment to parental reports and specific clinical motor batteries [19–25].

The study of motor development at an early age may be crucial in ASD research fields [26,27]. Indeed, several studies showed that the motor patterns of infants later diagnosed with ASD appeared consistently less developed than in neurotypical peers (see review [28,29]) and that spontaneous motor activity was impaired already in the first months of life [25,30]. Moreover, some studies addressing differences in motor milestones documented the presence of early repetitive behaviors in infants with ASD compared to ones with typical development or developmental disabilities, starting from six months of age [31–33].

Relevant findings emerged from studies regarding the early motor development of siblings of children with ASD (high-risk (HR) infants) who present an increased risk (~20%) of developing ASD compared to the general population [34]. Mounting research highlights that their motor developmental trajectories differ from those at low risk (LR; siblings of children without a diagnosis of ASD/NDD) at a mere six months of age [22,24,35–40]. A recent systematic review showed that fine motor competencies at six months predicted the clinical outcome [9] and language skills of siblings of children with ASD [22]. Moreover, very early repetitive/stereotypical behaviors and atypical body movements (6–12 months [41], 12 months [42], and from 18 months [43]) were reported to be associated with ASD outcome in HR infants, in line with the acknowledgement of restricted and repetitive behaviors as a core symptom of ASD.

Although the use of innovative technological instruments has increased over recent decades, limited impacts were observed on early screening and detection of ASD/NDDs [44]. Given the importance of further exploring early motor trajectories, more research should be promoted to implement technological tools to obtain objective measures of motor patterns and describe quantitative and qualitative features of infant movements. Over the last few decades, a set of innovative technologies, including computer vision and motion sensor-based approaches, as well as machine learning approaches, were implemented with the aim to emulate GM analysis and pinpoint objective measures of kinematic analysis [45–52], but none were transferred to clinical practice.

Recently, the NIDA Network developed a motion-tracking technology named MOVIDEA [46]. The technology was developed under the arising need to identify an easy, cost-effective instrument to investigate early motor markers of NDDs. MOVIDEA is a noninvasive technology measuring quantitative motor patterns in infants through two- and three-dimensional kinematic analyses [46]. The current study describes the application of MOVIDEA on a large library of video recordings of spontaneous movements of LR and HR infants. Our aim was to detect early quantitative differences in the motor trajectories of HR infants who received a diagnosis of NDDs or who did not receive a diagnosis compared to LR age-matched peers. Due to the small sample size of HR infants who developed ASD (n = 3), we included them in the group of infants who developed NDDs (n = 15), resulting in a total sample size of 18 infants with NDDs.

Evaluation of kinematic parameters permitted the investigation motor differences as a function of age and outcome, with the aim to improve early discrimination and screening of infants at higher risk of developing NDDs.

2. Materials and Methods

2.1. Participants

The current study was performed within the NIDA Network, enrolling LR and HR infants with the aim of detecting early signs of ASD/NDD through the recording and analysis of infant cry and motor patterns at 10 days and 6, 12, 18, and 24 weeks of age. At 6, 12, 18, 24, and 36 months, each infant/toddler underwent a comprehensive clinical/diagnostic assessment using standardized tools/tests and structured interviews, with parents for checking the presence/absence of an ASD or NDD diagnosis. Infant recruitment and data collection are still ongoing. The present study was carried out according to the standards for good ethical practice and the guidelines of the Declaration of Helsinki. The study protocol was approved by the Ethics Committee of the Italian Institute of Health (Approval Number: Pre 469/2016). A written informed consent from a parent/guardian of each participant was obtained.

For the purposes of the current study, the sample included data from 103 infants (54 females and 49 males), of which 53 were LR (infants with a sibling without any clinical diagnosis and no family history of ASD) and 50 were HR (infants with an older sibling with a clinical diagnosis of ASD). The inclusion criteria for infants were: (1) gestational age ≥ 36 weeks; (2) birth weight ≥ 2500 g; (3) Apgar index > 7 at the 5th minute; (4) absence of known medical, genetic, or neurological conditions associated with ASD; (5) absence of major complications in pregnancy and/or delivery likely to affect brain development.

HR infants were subdivided into two groups based on their clinical outcome at 24 or 36 months (using the Autism Diagnostic Observational Scale [53] and the DSM-5 criteria), as confirmed by expert clinicians of the NIDA team blinded to experimental data, resulting in 18 HR infants diagnosed with NDDs (HR-NDD) and 32 who did not receive any diagnosis (HR-no diagnosis). Infants in the LR group did not receive any clinical diagnosis at 24 or 36 months.

Video recordings of spontaneous movements were performed at 10 days and 6, 12, 18, and 24 weeks of age at home while the infant was lying on the bed (either naked or in a bodysuit not covering the limbs). To acquire images of spontaneous movement of the full infant body, the camera was placed 50 cm above the child and at chest height. See Table 1 for the description of the participants' characteristics and age during assessment.

Table 1. Video recordings available at various ages of assessment.

Age of Assessment	LR (n = 53)		HR-No Diagnosis (n = 18)		HR-NDD (n = 32)	
	Female	Male	Female	Male	Female	Male
	n	n	n	n	n	n
10 days	16	31	7	15	5	7
6 weeks	21	43	12	21	4	12
12 weeks	24	46	15	24	5	13
18 weeks	16	36	15	23	5	8
24 weeks	12	28	8	13	7	14

LR: Low-risk infants with a typical development; HR-NDD: High-risk infants diagnosed with NDDs; HR-No diagnosis: High-risk infants who did not receive any diagnosis.

2.2. *Kinematic Analysis through MOVIDEA Software*

Before applying MOVIDEA to the video library, each video was assessed for its eligibility for analysis. Then, one author cut each video to ensure the same properties, i.e., 3 min length, infant in supine position, in a condition of a quite awake state, well-being, and spontaneous motor activity, without crying or fussing episodes. Video frames containing interferences caused by the operator or parents or accidental movements of the camera were excluded from the analysis. Videos were analyzed by two coders blinded to the infant's risk status (LR or HR). Prior to starting coding, coders were trained and reached an excellent degree of agreement.

The MOVIDEA software computed the motor features using two different approaches. First, the trajectories covered by the infant's limbs during the free movement were extracted using a semi-automatic limb-tracking procedure. Second, movement quantification was performed through image processing techniques applied to the video frames. The software was developed using MATLAB ver. R2017a and its standard tools.

We analyzed the following set of kinematic features considered to eb meaningful for the identification of pathological motion patterns [46,54]:

- Quantity of motion (Qmean), i.e., the mean number of pixels where movement occurred divided by the total number of pixels in the image (percentage);
- Centroid of motion (C), i.e., the central point (2D coordinates measured in pixels) of the infant's movement computed for each motion image extracted from the video recording (Figure 1), with analysis of standard deviation in the X (Cxsd) and Y directions (Cysd), velocity (Vcmean), and acceleration (Acmean);
- Periodicity for the left and right hands (H-periodicity) and for the left and right feet (F-periodicity), which were nondimensional parameters aimed at measuring the presence of repetitive movements in the motion of the limbs.

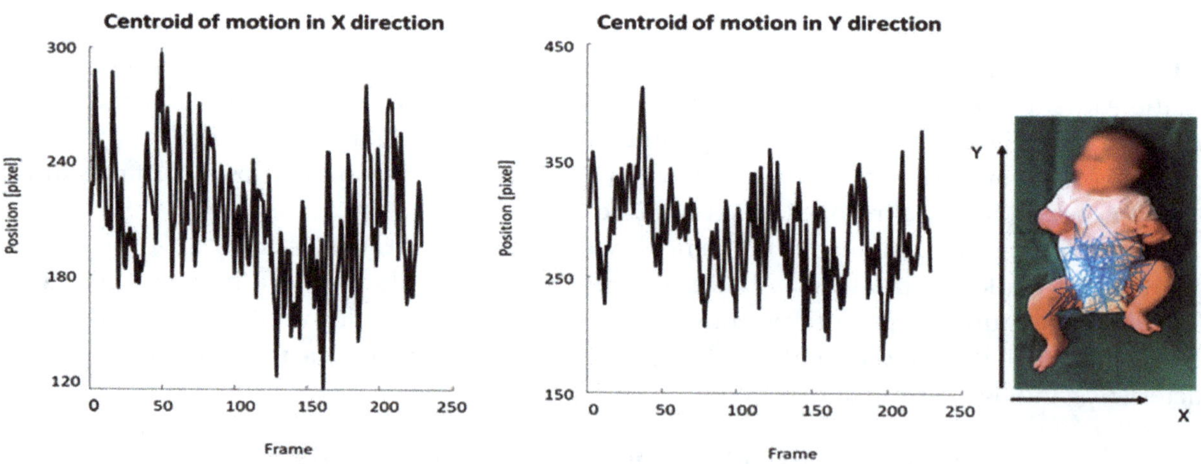

Figure 1. Graphic representation of the centroid of motion in the X and Y directions. The blue line depicts the trajectory of the centroid of motion of the infant's movement extracted from a video recording.

For details on the methods used to estimate measures as references and tracking methods, refer to Baccinelli and colleagues [46].

2.3. *Statistical Analysis*

An Analysis of Variance (ANOVA) with repeated measures was performed to analyze the kinematic parameters extracted by the MOVIDEA software (refer to Baccinelli and colleagues [46]), with the outcome (LR, HR-no diagnosis, and HR-NDD infants) as factor and age (10 days and 6, 12, 18, and 24 weeks) as the repeated measures. No significant sex differences were detected in the motor parameters analyzed. For this reason, data regarding sex were collapsed. Post-hoc comparisons were performed using Newman Keuls test. For all comparisons, significance was set at a p-value below 0.05. All statistical analyses were conducted using STATA 12.0 software (Stata Statistical Software: Release 12. College Station, TX, USA: StataCorp LP) [55,56].

3. Results

Using the MOVIDEA software, we evaluated specific kinematic parameters related to upper and lower limb movements in the space and using the head and the trunk as references (see Table 2).

Table 2. MOVIDEA kinematic parameters' means (SD) of the three groups of infants (LR, HR-no diagnosis, and HR-NDD).

Parameter	LR		HR-No Diagnosis		HR-NDD	
	n	Mean (SD)	*n*	Mean (SD)	*n*	Mean (SD)
Qmean						
10 days	31	0.008 (0.006)	15	0.008 (0.003)	7	0.006 (0.005)
6 weeks	43	0.012 (0.008)	21	0.014 (0.005)	12	0.016 (0.009)
12 weeks	46	0.011 (0.006)	24	0.015 (0.009)	13	0.019 (0.005)
18 weeks	36	0.010 (0.007)	23	0.018 (0.011)	8	0.012 (0.005)
24 weeks	28	0.011 (0.009)	13	0.016 (0.009)	14	0.017 (0.009)
Cxsd						
10 days	31	58.210 (21.422)	15	46.589 (13.116)	7	53.976 (13.967)
6 weeks	43	51.999 (13.722)	21	43.243 (10.278)	12	43.372 (9.371)
12 weeks	46	54.223 (14.314)	24	41.800 (10.001)	13	39.843 (9.384)
18 weeks	36	57.612 (16.725)	23	49.113 (23.310)	8	48.621 (15.325)
24 weeks	28	55.010 (15.419)	13	52.645 (19.299)	14	53.890 (16.267)
Cysd						
10 days	31	72.398 (31.810)	15	78.819 (34.812)	7	78.012 (23.567)
6 weeks	43	57.223 (19.110)	21	68.222 (23.111)	12	65.830 (21.765)
12 weeks	46	55.230 (20.111)	24	68.450 (20.701)	13	62.692 (18.991)
18 weeks	36	58.716 (25.416)	23	68.412 (24.411)	8	71.768 (26.802)
24 weeks	28	62.320 (18.799)	13	63.899 (23.789)	14	68.175 (16.267)
Acmean						
10 days	31	−0.015 (0.071)	15	0.017 (0.052)	7	0.161 (0.307)
6 weeks	43	−0.002 (0.024)	21	−0.002 (0.028)	12	−0.001 (0.043)
12 weeks	46	−0.004 (0.030)	24	0.001 (0.027)	13	0.005 (0.015)
18 weeks	36	0.016 (0.052)	23	−0.005 (0.033)	8	−0.011 (0.034)
24 weeks	28	−0.017 (0.139)	13	−0.002 (0.041)	14	−0.023 (0.030)
Vcmean						
10 days	31	26.835 (7.432)	15	23.040 (5.128)	7	24.640 (5.665)
6 weeks	43	28.396 (6.225)	21	24.624 (5.356)	12	24.250 (4.036)
12 weeks	46	31.726 (7.301)	24	26.374 (5.170)	13	24.194 (4.570)
18 weeks	36	32.792 (8.828)	23	27.730 (9.116)	8	28.687 (6.638)
24 weeks	28	28.652 (7.402)	13	27.884 (10.032)	14	27.466 (8.335)
H-periodicity						
10 days	31	0.034 (0.012)	15	0.035 (0.006)	7	0.030 (0.004)
6 weeks	43	0.041 (0.011)	21	0.040 (0.013)	12	0.046 (0.014)
12 weeks	46	0.041 (0.010)	24	0.044 (0.018)	13	0.049 (0.013)
18 weeks	36	0.039 (0.010)	23	0.042 (0.018)	8	0.038 (0.010)
24 weeks	28	0.043 (0.013)	13	0.049 (0.023)	14	0.043 (0.011)
F-periodicity						
10 days	31	0.032 (0.007)	15	0.035 (0.007)	7	0.031 (0.003)
6 weeks	43	0.043 (0.011)	21	0.045 (0.014)	12	0.052 (0.018)
12 weeks	46	0.047 (0.015)	24	0.053 (0.022)	13	0.052 (0.017)
18 weeks	36	0.042 (0.015)	23	0.047 (0.016)	8	0.037 (0.010)
24 weeks	28	0.044 (0.014)	13	0.042 (0.012)	14	0.043 (0.010)

LR: Low-risk infants with typical development; HR-no diagnosis: High-risk infants who did not receive any diagnosis; HR-NDD: High-risk infants diagnosed with NDDs. Qmean: Quantity of motion; Cxsd: Standard deviation in the X direction of centroid of motion; Cysd: Standard deviation in the Y direction of centroid of motion; Acmean: Mean acceleration of centroid of motion; Vcmean: Mean velocity of centroid of motion; H-periodicity: Periodicity for the left and right hands; F-periodicity: Periodicity for the left and right feet.

3.1. Quantity of Motion

Analysis revealed a main effect of the outcome (F(2,319) = 8.83; $p = 0.0002$) with HR-NDD and HR-no diagnosis infants moving more than LR infants ($p = 0.001$ and $p < 0.0001$, respectively) and a main effect of the age (F(4,319) = 7.16; $p < 0.0001$) with differences at 10 days compared to 6, 12, 18, and 24 weeks ($p < 0.0001$ for all comparisons) (Figure 2).

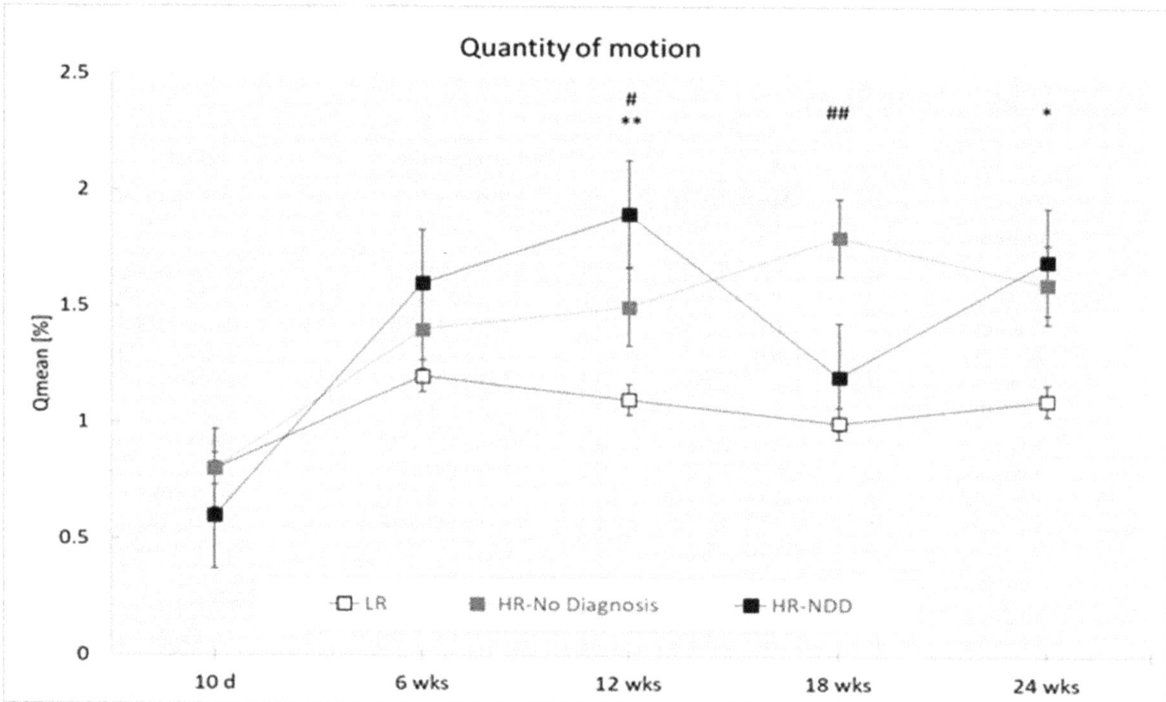

Figure 2. Quantity of motion in a 3-min session, measured at 10 days and 6, 12, 18, and 24 weeks in three groups of infants (LR, $n = 53$; HR-no diagnosis, $n = 32$; HR-NDD infants, $n = 18$). d = days; wks = weeks. Data are expressed as mean ± SEM. * $p < 0.05$ and ** $p < 0.01$ between HR-NDD and LR infants; # $p < 0.05$ and ## $p < 0.01$ between HR-no Diagnosis and LR infants.

Post-hoc comparisons performed on the two-way interaction outcome at x age (F(8,319) = 1.69; $p = 0.1003$) reported that HR-NDD and HR-no diagnosis infants moved more compared to LR infants at 12 weeks ($p = 0.001$ and $p = 0.023$, respectively). HR-no diagnosis infants moved more compared to LR infants at 18 weeks ($p < 0.0001$), and HR-NDD infants moved more compared to LR at 24 weeks ($p = 0.031$).

3.2. Centroid of Motion (Cxsd and Cysd)

Analysis revealed a main effect of the outcome (Cxsd: (F(2,319) = 10.76; $p < 0.0001$; Cysd (F(2,319) = 4.81; $p < 0.0088$. HR-NDD and HR-no diagnosis infants showed lower mean values of Cxsd compared to LR infants (respectively: $p = 0.001$; $p < 0.001$) (Figure 3) and a higher mean value of Cysd compared to LR infants (respectively: $p = 0.027$; $p = 0.003$) (Figure 4). Analysis revealed a main effect of age for Cxsd (F(4,319) = 3.50; $p = 0.0081$), with differences at 10 days compared to 6 weeks ($p = 0.025$) and 12 weeks ($p = 0.033$), at 6 weeks compared to 18 weeks ($p = 0.026$) and 24 weeks ($p = 0.026$), and at 12 weeks compared to 18 weeks ($p = 0.035$) and 24 weeks ($p = 0.034$). Analysis revealed a main effect of age for Cysd (F(4,319) = 2.39; $p = 0.0508$), with differences at 10 days compared to 6 weeks ($p = 0.002$), 12 weeks ($p < 0.0001$), 18 weeks ($p = 0.009$), and 24 weeks ($p = 0.013$).

Post-hoc comparisons performed on the two-way interaction outcome at x age (Cxsd: F(8,319) = 0.67; $p = 0.7198$; Cysd: F(8,319) = 0.25; $p = 0.9812$) revealed that HR-NDD infants showed a lower mean value of Cxsd in comparison to LR infants at 12 weeks ($p = 0.004$). HR-no diagnosis infants showed a lower mean value of Cxmean in comparison to LR infants at 10 days ($p = 0.019$), at 6 weeks ($p = 0.043$), at 12 weeks ($p = 0.002$), and at 18 weeks ($p = 0.046$). HR-No diagnosis infants showed a higher mean value of Cysd in comparison to LR infants at 18 weeks ($p = 0.027$).

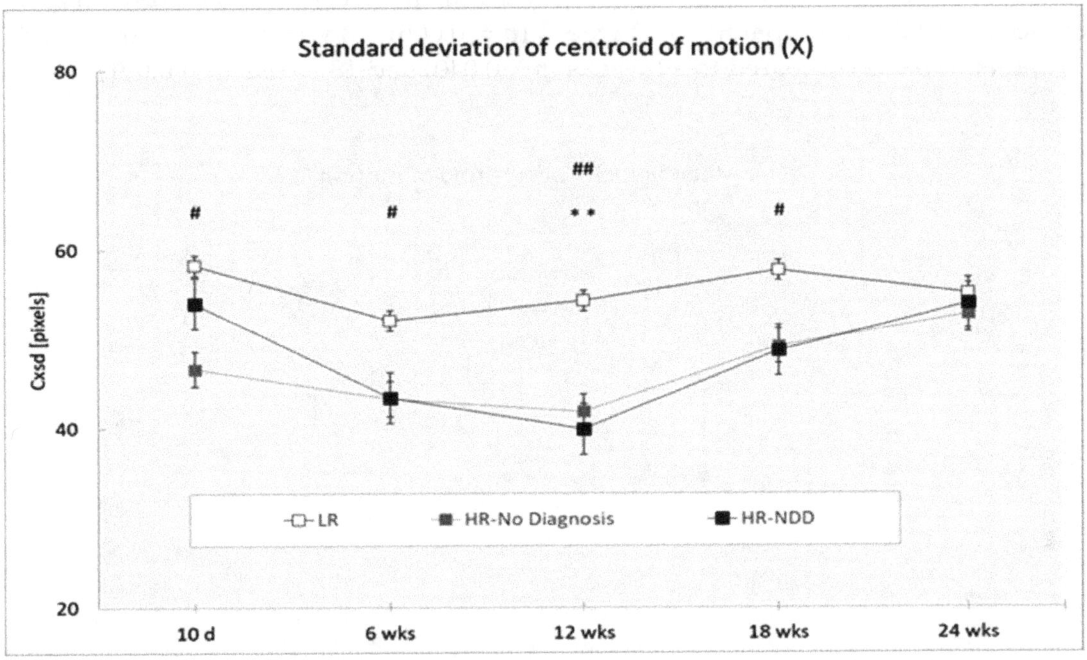

Figure 3. Standard deviation of centroid of motion in X direction (Cxsd) in a 3-min session, measured at 10 days and 6, 12, 18, and 24 weeks in three groups of infants (LR, $n = 53$; HR-no diagnosis, $n = 32$; HR-NDD infants, $n = 18$), d = days; wks = weeks. Data are expressed as mean ± SEM. ** $p < 0.01$ between HR-NDD and LR infants; # $p < 0.05$ and ## $p < 0.01$ between HR-no diagnosis and LR infants.

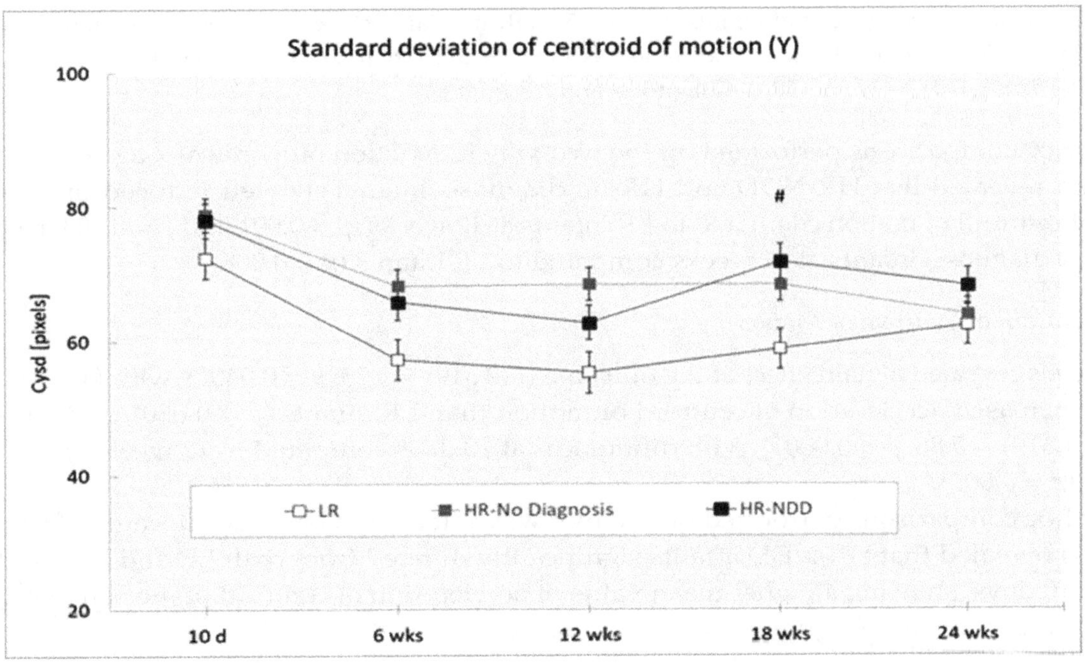

Figure 4. Standard deviation of centroid of motion in Y direction (Cxsd) in a 3-min session, measured at 10 days and 6, 12, 18, and 24 weeks in three groups of infants (LR, $n = 53$; HR-no diagnosis, $n = 32$; HR-NDD infants, $n = 18$). d = days; wks = weeks. Data are expressed as mean ± SEM. # $p < 0.05$ between HR-no diagnosis and LR infants.

3.3. *Velocity of Centroid of Motion*

Analysis revealed a main effect of the outcome ($F(2,319) = 10.96$; $p < 0.0001$), with HR-NDD and HR-no diagnosis infants showing reduced mean values of velocity of centroid of motion than LR infants ($p < 0.0001$ for both comparison groups) (Figure 5), and a main effect of age ($F(4,319) = 3.22$; $p = 0.0130$), with differences at 10 days compared to 12 weeks ($p = 0.005$), 18 weeks ($p < 0.0001$), and 24 weeks ($p = 0.041$), and at 6 weeks compared to 12 weeks ($p = 0.040$) and 18 weeks ($p = 0.001$).

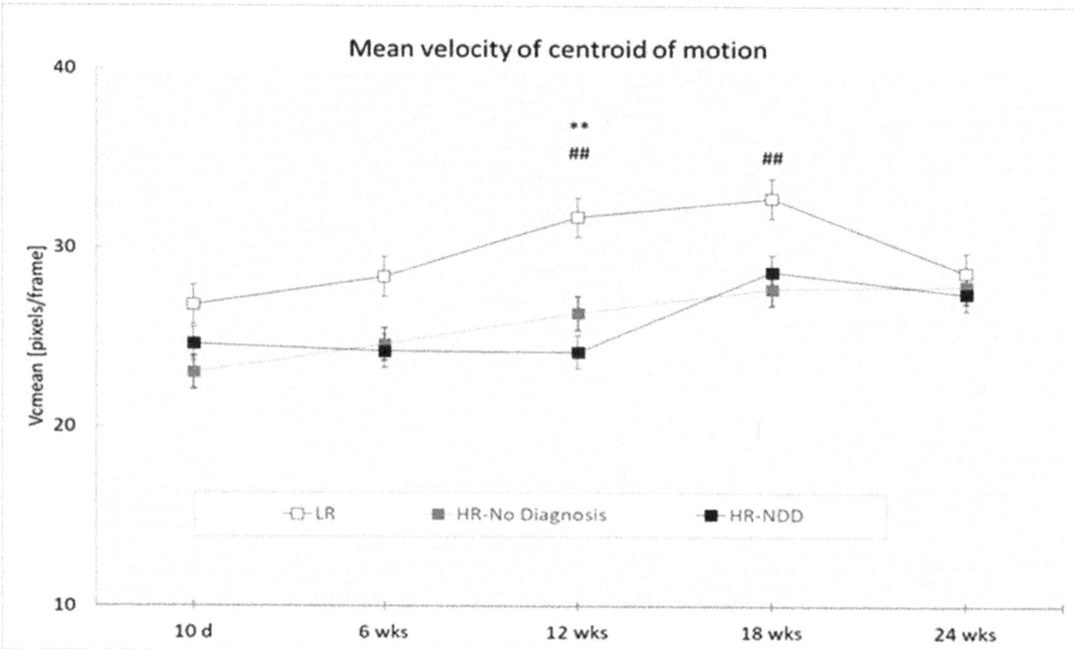

Figure 5. Mean velocity of centroid of motion in a 3-min session, measured at 10 days and 6, 12, 18, and 24 weeks in three groups of infants (LR, $n = 53$; HR-no diagnosis, $n = 32$; HR-NDD infants, $n = 18$). d = days; wks = weeks. Data are expressed as mean ± SEM. ** $p < 0.01$ between HR-NDD and LR infants; ## $p < 0.01$ between HR-no diagnosis and LR infants.

Post-hoc comparisons performed on the two-way interaction outcome at x age ($F(8,319) = 0.72$, $p = 0.6749$) revealed that HR-NDD and HR-no diagnosis infants showed reduced mean values of velocity of centroid of motion compared to LR infants at 12 weeks ($p = 0.001$ and $p = 0.003$, respectively) and HR-no diagnosis infants at 18 weeks compared to LR infants ($p = 0.008$).

3.4. *Acceleration of Centroid of Motion*

Analysis revealed a main effect of the outcome ($F(2,319) = 3.25$; $p = 0.0402$), with HR-NDD infants showing increased acceleration of centroid of motion than LR infants ($p = 0.050$), and a main effect of age ($F(4,319) = 5.88$; $p < 0.0001$), with differences at 10 days compared to 12 weeks ($p = 0.040$) and 24 weeks ($p = 0.009$).

Post-hoc comparisons performed on the two-way interaction outcome at x age ($F(8,218) = 4.55$; $p < 0.0001$) revealed that HR-NDD infants significantly differed from both LR and HR-no diagnosis infants at 10 days, showing a higher mean value of acceleration of centroid of motion ($p < 0.0001$ for both comparison groups) (Figure 6).

3.5. *Periodicity*

Analysis did not reveal a main effect of the outcome for either hand periodicity ($F(2,319) = 1.28$; $p = 0.2803$) or foot periodicity ($F(2,319) = 1.22$; $p = 0.2956$). Analysis revealed a main effect of age (hand periodicity: $F(4,319) = 6.39$; $p = 0.0001$; foot periodicity: $F(4,319 = 10.66$; $p < 0.0001$).

Hand periodicity was decreased at 10 days compared to 6, 12, 18, and 24 weeks ($p < 0.0001$) and at 18 compared to 24 weeks ($p = 0.041$) (Figure 7). Foot periodicity was decreased at 10 days compared to 6, 12, 18, and 24 weeks ($p < 0.0001$) and at 6 compared to 12 weeks ($p = 0.038$). By contrast, foot periodicity was increased at 12 weeks compared to 18 weeks ($p = 0.003$) and 24 weeks ($p = 0.011$) (Figure 8).

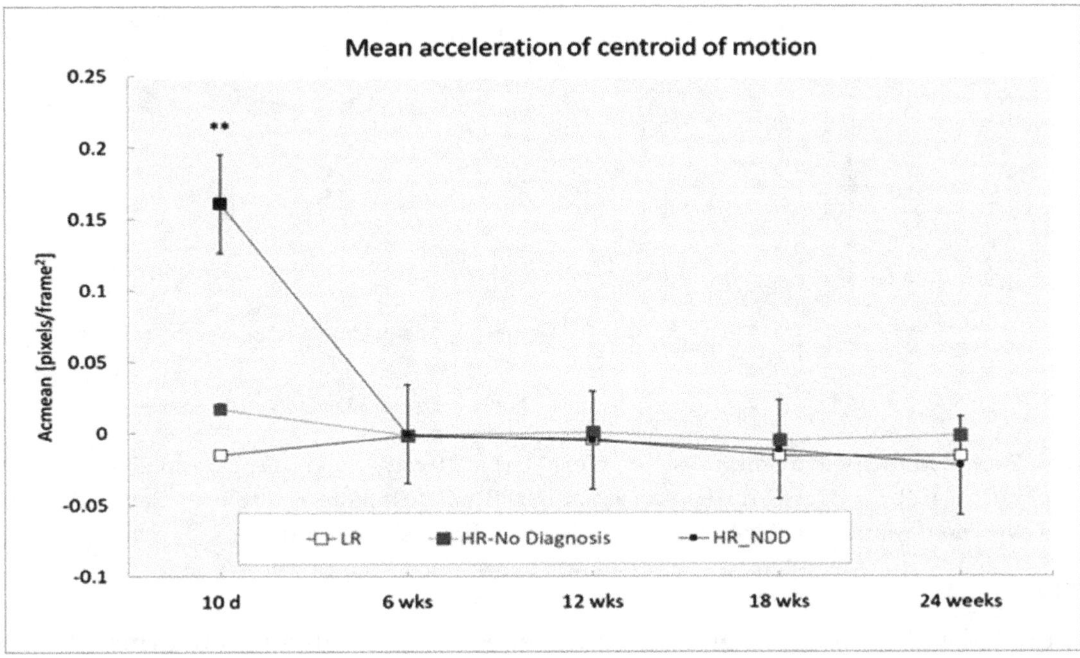

Figure 6. Mean acceleration of centroid of motion in a 3-min session, measured at 10 days and 6, 12, 18, and 24 weeks in three groups of infants (LR, $n = 53$; HR-no diagnosis, $n = 32$; HR-NDD infants, $n = 18$). d = days; wks = weeks. Data are expressed as mean ± SEM. ** $p < 0.01$ between HR-NDD and LR infants.

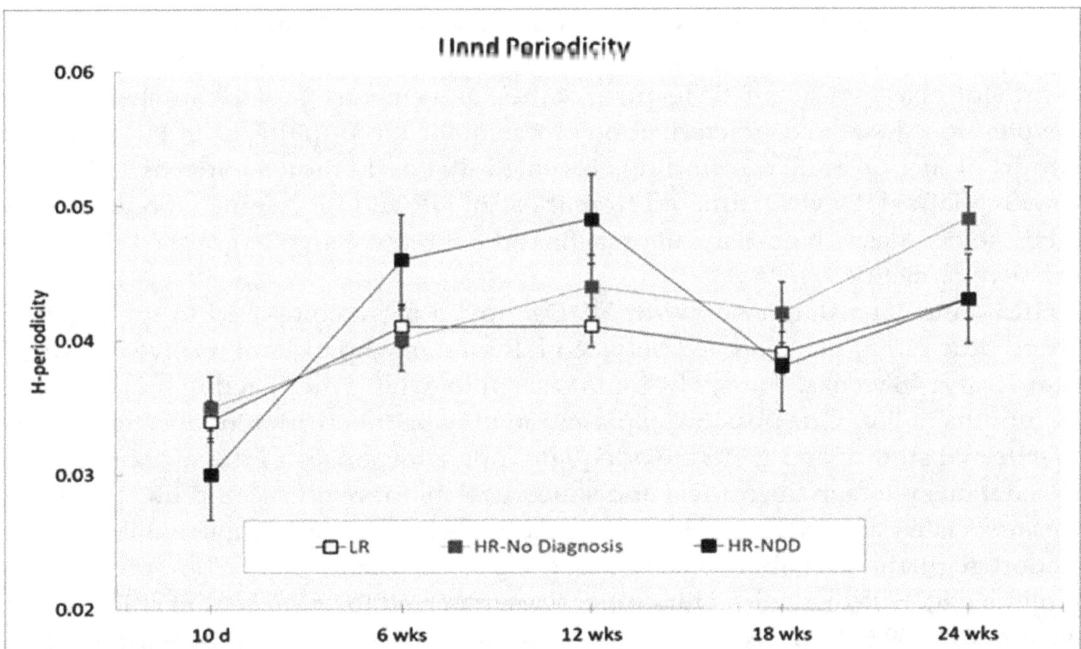

Figure 7. Hand periodicity in a 3-min session, measured at 10 days and 6, 12, 18, and 24 weeks in three groups of infants (LR, $n = 53$; HR-no diagnosis, $n = 32$; HR-NDD infants, $n = 18$). d = days; wks = weeks. Data are expressed as mean ± SEM. Periodicity is a nondimensional value.

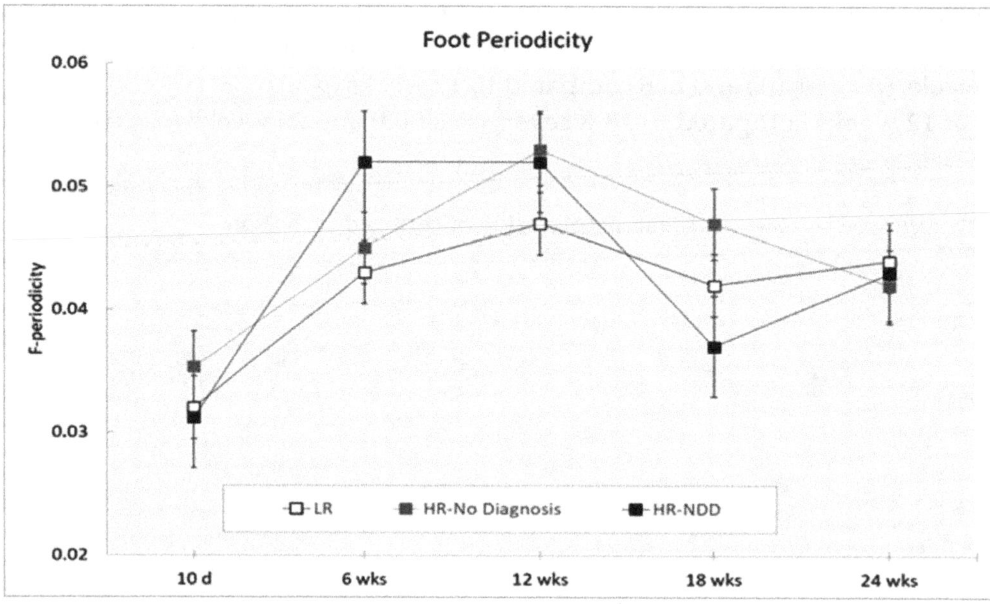

Figure 8. Foot periodicity in a 3-min session, measured at 10 days and 6, 12, 18, and 24 weeks in three groups of infants (LR, $n = 53$; HR-no diagnosis, $n = 32$; HR-NDD infants, $n = 18$). d = days; wks = weeks. Data are expressed as mean ± SEM. Periodicity is a nondimensional value.

4. Discussion

The study of early motor patterns might be effective in predicting abnormal developmental trajectories of infants at risk for developing ASD/NDD. Technological tools able to obtain objective measures of specific motor parameters might support the early detection of NDDs. To this aim, the Italian Network for early detection of Autism Spectrum Disorder (NIDA Network) developed a noninvasive motion-tracking technology, named MOVIDEA, to measure quantitative motor patterns in infants at risk for NDDs.

The main objective of this study was to investigate very early motor trajectories of infants at risk for developing ASD through MOVIDEA, a semi-automatic software able to analyze 2D and 3D videos and provide objective kinematic features of their movements. To our knowledge, this is the first research devoted to a detailed characterization of kinematic motor patterns in HR infants within the first six months of life. Overall, our findings revealed that early motor patterns of HR infants later diagnosed with NDDs (HR-NDD) differed from those of HR and LR infants who did not receive any diagnosis (HR-no diagnosis: high-risk infants who did not receive any diagnosis; LR: low-risk infants with typical development).

First, HR infants later diagnosed with NDDs moved more compared to typically developing LR infants and differences also emerged between HR infants who did not receive any diagnosis and LR infants at 12 and 18 weeks. Thus, HR infants seem to exhibit more active motor profiles during the first six months of life. One possible explanation may be their different abilities to perceive and respond to external stimuli and generate adequate motor responses to them. Abnormalities in the inhibition/excitation system in the cortical and subcortical motor regions could underlie general motor dysfunctions associated with NDDs [57]. Self-regulation behaviors (general irritability, range of states, state regulation, regulation capability) were described as predictors of psychomotor development at 4 and 12 months [58]. Self-regulation difficulties were reported to be present in children with ASD at only one year of age [59,60]. Moreover, neurobiological studies showed that self-regulation in ASD is related to dysfunction in certain brain circuits associated with social–emotional processing [59,61], suggesting the importance of assessing neonatal motor features during development [58].

Second, variability of the "centroid of motion" parameter was different between HR and LR infants. Since the centroid of motion is the central point of the infant's movement in a given motion image, its standard deviation in the X and Y directions throughout the video recording provide information regarding the variability of the location of the free movement's central point. On the other hand, the velocity and acceleration of the centroid of motion provide a measure regarding how fast the global movement changes over time and if significant jerks of movements are present. Our data reported that HR infants later diagnosed with NDDs moved in the X direction with reduced variability at 12 weeks of age at the same time point during which they expressed an increased quantity of motion compared to LR infants. Also, HR infants who did not receive any diagnosis moved in the X direction with reduced variability across several time points of development (from 10 days to 18 weeks of age), and increased variability of centroid of motion was measured in the vertical direction (Cysd) at 18 weeks of age. Differences also emerged in the acceleration and velocity of centroid of motion. HR infants later diagnosed with NDDs showed increased acceleration of centroid of motion at 10 days after birth, compared to HR and LR infants who did not receive any diagnosis. Also, HR infants later diagnosed with NDDs and HR who did not receive any diagnosis demonstrated decreased velocity of centroid of motion compared to LR infants at 12 weeks of age. Differences remained significant at 18 weeks for HR infants who did not receive any diagnosis. Even if MOVIDEA provided mixed findings, it seems that the movement of HR-NDD infants is characterized by reduced variability and velocity as well as increased acceleration. It is possible that abnormal patterns of centroid of motion in HR infants may reflect abnormal quality of movement, as already observed through the GM evaluation, and could be predictive of a later diagnosis of NDDs. Typical GMs are characterized by complexity and variation [62], supporting the hypothesis that motor variability and appropriate integration of sensorimotor information are expressions of typical motor development [63,64]. A lack of movement variability was mostly identified in infants who developed delays or disabilities [65–67] and abnormal GMs were reported in several infants with ASD and NDDs [25,30,68,69]. Moreover, a previous study measuring kinematic parameters using wearable sensors in 1–8-month-old infants detected different acceleration features between at-risk infants diagnosed with developmental delay or with no diagnosis and infants with typical development [70].

Finally, MOVIDEA detected changes across age of development in hand and foot periodic movements. Periodicity was described as the repetition of the same movement multiple times with high amplitude of the end effectors [54]. The presence of certain motor repetitive behaviors in early infancy is considered a necessary step for the development of voluntary purposeful movements and seems to have an adaptive role. Thus, these are considered to be indices of a typical psychomotor development [71]. However, increased frequency of repetitive movements was widely described in various NDDs [33,72], reflecting a continuum extending from typical to atypical development. We speculate that atypical periodicity, especially for the upper extremities, could interfere with later manual exploration or poor development of fine motor skills. During the fidgety period, the upper limb movement repertoire undergoes a maturational process, with the enrichment of motor patterns addressing the exploration of the body and environment, while the lower limb repertoire appears to be functionally limited [50].

In conclusion, our results revealed that HR infants who received a diagnosis of NDD showed an increased general motor activity associated with reduced variability and velocity, as well as increased acceleration of global movement in the space. Moreover, we reported patterns of increased periodicity of limbs, especially for the upper limbs, throughout the first 12 weeks of age. This developmental profile may reflect the motor difficulties of HR-NDD infants during the writhing and fidgety periods and provide a window into which it is possible to more deeply investigate the development of motor competences in high-risk infants.

The subtle motion analysis through MOVIDEA has several advantages and strengths. Nowadays, most movement assessment systems used for infants require external tracking equipment, i.e., special markers or wearable sensors to be located on the limbs, which are not easily adaptable to different recording settings [52]. Conversely, MOVIDEA gives the chance to obtain measurements via noninvasive assessment without any additional special devices that could interfere with spontaneous infant motor activity. It is important to consider that the use of noninvasive technology may well fit recordings in real-life settings and naturalistic neonatal environments (e.g., hospitals, pediatrician ambulatories, homes), thereby allowing detailed motion analysis. In particular, possible applications of the MOVIDEA tracking system may be on home-video segments, as well as on videos recorded in clinical settings to routinely monitor infants at neurodevelopmental risk. These videos may be recorded directly by parents/caregivers or professionals minimally trained to videotape infants, taking into account the experimental set-up described in the methodological section. Moreover, MOVIDEA collects measurable and quantifiable information not based on visual scoring of infant motor performances, completed by clinicians during well-child visits or trained operators. We believe that this computer-based analysis of infants' movements may support and integrate the analysis of motor patterns of infants at risk of NDDs in research settings [73,74]. Further studies could explore whether the features extracted by MOVIDEA software correlate with the qualitative and quantitative analysis performed by GM experts.

Some limitations of this study should be discussed. First, only a small sample size of HR-NDD infants was collected. Due to this limitation, it was not possible to carry out statistical analysis according to each separate NDD. Second, the accuracy of the extracted MOVIDEA features still need to be implemented and validated by experts in the field.

Overall, this experimental study identified potential early behavioral indexes that are related to later diagnosis of NDDs and may be precursors of altered movements during goal-directed behaviors. Moreover, the findings highlight the importance of a longitudinal assessment of motor development for LR and HR infants. Expanding knowledge regarding typical and atypical motor competencies is useful to detect a developmental motor trajectory as early as possible in the first weeks of life. Further video analyses should be carried out using the MOVIDEA software to increase the potential value of this objective, reliable, and quantifiable technology to identify early motor deficits in infants at risk for NDD.

Author Contributions: Conceptualization: M.L.S.; investigation: L.G., A.C., and NIDA Network group; formal analysis: T.S.; software: W.B. and M.B.; writing—original draft preparation: A.C., F.F., and M.M.; writing—review and editing: M.L.S and A.C.; funding acquisition: M.L.S. All authors have read and agreed to the published version of the manuscript.

References

1. Zablotsky, B.; Black, L.I.; Maenner, M.J.; Schieve, L.A.; Danielson, M.L.; Bitsko, R.H.; Blumberg, S.J.; Kogan, M.D.; Boyle, C.A. Prevalence and Trends of Developmental Disabilities among Children in the United States: 2009–2017. *Pediatrics* **2019**, *144*, e20190811. [CrossRef] [PubMed]
2. Karmel, B.Z.; Gardner, J.M.; Meade, L.S.; Cohen, I.L.; London, E.; Flory, M.J.; Lennon, E.M.; Miroshnichenko, I.; Rabinowitz, S.; Parab, S.; et al. Early medical and behavioral characteristics of NICU infants later classified with ASD. *Pediatrics* **2010**, *126*, 457–467. [CrossRef] [PubMed]
3. McPartland, J.C. Considerations in biomarker development for neurodevelopmental disorders. *Curr. Opin. Neurol.* **2016**, *29*, 118–122. [CrossRef] [PubMed]
4. Licari, M.K.; Alvares, G.A.; Varcin, K.; Evans, K.L.; Cleary, D.; Reid, S.L.; Glasson, E.J.; Bebbington, K.; Reynolds, J.E.; Wray, J.; et al. Prevalence of Motor Difficulties in Autism Spectrum Disorder: Analysis of a Population-Based Cohort. *Autism Res.* **2020**, *13*, 298–306. [CrossRef]
5. Miller, M.; Iosif, A.M.; Young, G.S.; Hill, M.M.; Ozonoff, S. Early Detection of ADHD: Insights from Infant Siblings of Children With Autism. *J. Clin. Child Adolesc. Psychol.* **2018**, *47*, 737–744. [CrossRef]
6. Sacrey, L.A.; Bennett, J.A.; Zwaigenbaum, L. Early Infant Development and Intervention for Autism Spectrum Disorder. *J. Child Neurol.* **2015**, *30*, 1921–1929. [CrossRef]
7. Zwaigenbaum, L. Advances in the early detection of autism. *Curr. Opin. Neurol.* **2010**, *23*, 97–102. [CrossRef]
8. Athanasiadou, A.; Buitelaar, J.K.; Brovedani, P.; Chorna, O.; Fulceri, F.; Guzzetta, A.; Scattoni, M.L. Early motor signs of attention-deficit hyperactivity disorder: A systematic review. *Eur. Child Adolesc. Psychiatry* **2019**. [CrossRef]

9. Canu, D.; Van der Paelt, S.; Canal-Bedia, R.; Posada, M.; Vanvuchelen, M.; Roeyers, H. Early non-social behavioural indicators of autism spectrum disorder (ASD) in siblings at elevated likelihood for ASD: A systematic review. *Eur. Child Adolesc. Psychiatry* **2020**. [CrossRef]
10. Garrido, D.; Petrova, D.; Watson, L.R.; Garcia-Retamero, R.; Carballo, G. Language and motor skills in siblings of children with autism spectrum disorder: A meta-analytic review. *Autism Res.* **2017**, *10*, 1737–1750. [CrossRef]
11. Micai, M.; Fulceri, F.; Caruso, A.; Guzzetta, A.; Gila, L.; Scattoni, M.L. Early behavioral markers for neurodevelopmental disorders in the first 3 years of life: An overview of systematic reviews. manuscript submitted for publication.
12. Fuentefria, R.D.N.; Silveira, R.C.; Procianoy, R.S. Motor development of preterm infants assessed by the Alberta Infant Motor Scale: Systematic review article. *J. Pediatr.* **2017**, *93*, 328–342. [CrossRef] [PubMed]
13. Palomo, R.; Belinchon, M.; Ozonoff, S. Autism and family home movies: A comprehensive review. *J. Dev. Behav. Pediatr.* **2006**, *27*, S59–S68. [CrossRef] [PubMed]
14. Gurevitz, M.; Geva, R.; Varon, M.; Leitner, Y. Early markers in infants and toddlers for development of ADHD. *J. Atten. Disord.* **2014**, *18*, 14–22. [CrossRef] [PubMed]
15. Jaspers, M.; de Winter, A.F.; Buitelaar, J.K.; Verhulst, F.C.; Reijneveld, S.A.; Hartman, C.A. Early childhood assessments of community pediatric professionals predict autism spectrum and attention deficit hyperactivity problems. *J. Abnorm. Child Psychol.* **2013**, *41*, 71–80. [CrossRef] [PubMed]
16. Jacobvitz, D.; Sroufe, L.A. The early caregiver-child relationship and attention-deficit disorder with hyperactivity in kindergarten: A prospective study. *Child Dev.* **1987**, *58*, 1496–1504. [CrossRef]
17. Achermann, S.; Nystrom, P.; Bolte, S.; Falck-Ytter, T. Motor atypicalities in infancy are associated with general developmental level at 2 years, but not autistic symptoms. *Autism* **2020**. [CrossRef]
18. Focaroli, V.; Taffoni, F.; Parsons, S.M.; Keller, F.; Iverson, J.M. Performance of Motor Sequences in Children at Heightened vs. Low Risk for ASD: A Longitudinal Study from 18 to 36 Months of Age. *Front. Psychol.* **2016**, *7*, 724. [CrossRef]
19. Jasmin, E.; Couture, M.; McKinley, P.; Reid, G.; Fombonne, E.; Gisel, E. Sensori-motor and daily living skills of preschool children with autism spectrum disorders. *J. Autism Dev. Disord.* **2009**, *39*, 231–241. [CrossRef]
20. Landa, R.; Garrett-Mayer, E. Development in infants with autism spectrum disorders: A prospective study. *J. Child Psychol. Psychiatry* **2006**, *47*, 629–638. [CrossRef]
21. Landa, R.J.; Gross, A.L.; Stuart, E.A.; Faherty, A. Developmental trajectories in children with and without autism spectrum disorders: The first 3 years. *Child Dev.* **2013**, *84*, 429–442. [CrossRef]
22. LeBarton, E.S.; Landa, R.J. Infant motor skill predicts later expressive language and autism spectrum disorder diagnosis. *Infant Behav. Dev.* **2019**, *54*, 37–47. [CrossRef] [PubMed]
23. Libertus, K.; Landa, R.J. The Early Motor Questionnaire (EMQ): A parental report measure of early motor development. *Infant Behav. Dev.* **2013**, *36*, 833–842. [CrossRef] [PubMed]
24. Libertus, K.; Sheperd, K.A.; Ross, S.W.; Landa, R.J. Limited fine motor and grasping skills in 6-month-old infants at high risk for autism. *Child Dev.* **2014**, *85*, 2218–2231. [CrossRef] [PubMed]
25. Phagava, H.; Muratori, F.; Einspieler, C.; Maestro, S.; Apicella, F.; Guzzetta, A.; Prechtl, H.F.; Cioni, G. General movements in infants with autism spectrum disorders. *Georgian Med. News* **2008**, *156*, 100–105.
26. Harris, S.R. Early motor delays as diagnostic clues in autism spectrum disorder. *Eur. J. Pediatr.* **2017**, *176*, 1259–1262. [CrossRef]
27. Iverson, J.M. Early Motor and Communicative Development in Infants With an Older Sibling With Autism Spectrum Disorder. *J. Speech Lang Hear. Res.* **2018**, *61*, 2673–2684. [CrossRef]
28. Moseley, R.L.; Pulvermuller, F. What can autism teach us about the role of sensorimotor systems in higher cognition? New clues from studies on language, action semantics, and abstract emotional concept processing. *Cortex* **2018**, *100*, 149–190. [CrossRef]
29. West, K.L. Infant Motor Development in Autism Spectrum Disorder: A Synthesis and Meta-analysis. *Child Dev.* **2019**, *90*, 2053–2070. [CrossRef]
30. Einspieler, C.; Sigafoos, J.; Bolte, S.; Bratl-Pokorny, K.D.; Landa, R.; Marschik, P.B. Highlighting the first 5 months of life: General movements in infants later diagnosed with autism spectrum disorder or Rett Syndrome. *Res. Autism Spectr. Disord.* **2014**, *8*, 286–291. [CrossRef]
31. Kim, S.H.; Lord, C. Restricted and repetitive behaviors in toddlers and preschoolers with autism spectrum disorders based on the Autism Diagnostic Observation Schedule (ADOS). *Autism Res.* **2010**, *3*, 162–173. [CrossRef]

32. Morgan, L.; Wetherby, A.M.; Barber, A. Repetitive and stereotyped movements in children with autism spectrum disorders late in the second year of life. *J. Child Psychol. Psychiatry* **2008**, *49*, 826–837. [CrossRef] [PubMed]
33. Purpura, G.; Costanzo, V.; Chericoni, N.; Puopolo, M.; Scattoni, M.L.; Muratori, F.; Apicella, F. Bilateral Patterns of Repetitive Movements in 6- to 12-Month-Old Infants with Autism Spectrum Disorders. *Front. Psychol.* **2017**, *8*, 1168. [CrossRef]
34. Ozonoff, S.; Young, G.S.; Carter, A.; Messinger, D.; Yirmiya, N.; Zwaigenbaum, L.; Bryson, S.; Carver, L.J.; Constantino, J.N.; Dobkins, K.; et al. Recurrence risk for autism spectrum disorders: A Baby Siblings Research Consortium study. *Pediatrics* **2011**, *128*, e488–e495. [CrossRef] [PubMed]
35. Bryson, S.E.; Zwaigenbaum, L.; Brian, J.; Roberts, W.; Szatmari, P.; Rombough, V.; McDermott, C. A prospective case series of high-risk infants who developed autism. *J. Autism Dev. Disord.* **2007**, *37*, 12–24. [CrossRef] [PubMed]
36. Estes, A.; Zwaigenbaum, L.; Gu, H.; St John, T.; Paterson, S.; Elison, J.T.; Hazlett, H.; Botteron, K.; Dager, S.R.; Schultz, R.T.; et al. Behavioral, cognitive, and adaptive development in infants with autism spectrum disorder in the first 2 years of life. *J. Neurodev. Disord.* **2015**, *7*, 24. [CrossRef]
37. Flanagan, J.E.; Landa, R.; Bhat, A.; Bauman, M. Head lag in infants at risk for autism: A preliminary study. *Am. J. Occup. Ther.* **2012**, *66*, 577–585. [CrossRef]
38. Iverson, J.M.; Wozniak, R.H. Variation in vocal-motor development in infant siblings of children with autism. *J. Autism Dev. Disord.* **2007**, *37*, 158–170. [CrossRef]
39. Iverson, J.M.; Shic, F.; Wall, C.A.; Chawarska, K.; Curtin, S.; Estes, A.; Gardner, J.M.; Hutman, T.; Landa, R.J.; Levin, A.R.; et al. Early motor abilities in infants at heightened versus low risk for ASD: A Baby Siblings Research Consortium (BSRC) study. *J. Abnorm. Psychol.* **2019**, *128*, 69–80. [CrossRef]
40. Nickel, L.R.; Thatcher, A.R.; Keller, F.; Wozniak, R.H.; Iverson, J.M. Posture Development in Infants at Heightened vs. Low Risk for Autism Spectrum Disorders. *Infancy* **2013**, *18*, 639–661. [CrossRef]
41. Brian, J.; Bryson, S.E.; Garon, N.; Roberts, W.; Smith, I.M.; Szatmari, P.; Zwaigenbaum, L. Clinical assessment of autism in high-risk 18-month-olds. *Autism* **2008**, *12*, 433–456. [CrossRef]
42. Elison, J.T.; Wolff, J.J.; Reznick, J.S.; Botteron, K.N.; Estes, A.M.; Gu, H.; Hazlett, H.C.; Meadows, A.J.; Paterson, S.J.; Zwaigenbaum, L.; et al. Repetitive behavior in 12-month-olds later classified with autism spectrum disorder. *J. Am. Acad. Child Adolesc. Psychiatry* **2014**, *53*, 1216–1224. [CrossRef] [PubMed]
43. Chawarska, K.; Shic, F.; Macari, S.; Campbell, D.J.; Brian, J.; Landa, R.; Hutman, T.; Nelson, C.A.; Ozonoff, S.; Tager-Flusberg, H.; et al. 18-month predictors of later outcomes in younger siblings of children with autism spectrum disorder: A baby siblings research consortium study. *J. Am. Acad. Child Adolesc. Psychiatry* **2014**, *53*, 1317–1327. [CrossRef] [PubMed]
44. Bolte, S.; Bartl-Pokorny, K.D.; Jonsson, U.; Berggren, S.; Zhang, D.; Kostrzewa, E.; Falck-Ytter, T.; Einspieler, C.; Pokorny, F.B.; Jones, E.J.; et al. How can clinicians detect and treat autism early? Methodological trends of technology use in research. *Acta Paediatr.* **2016**, *105*, 137–144. [CrossRef] [PubMed]
45. Adde, L.; Helbostad, J.L.; Jensenius, A.R.; Taraldsen, G.; Stoen, R. Using computer-based video analysis in the study of fidgety movements. *Early Hum. Dev.* **2009**, *85*, 541–547. [CrossRef]
46. Baccinelli, W.; Bulgheroni, M.; Simonetti, V.; Fulceri, F.; Caruso, A.; Gila, L.; Scattoni, M.L. Movidea: A Software Package for Automatic Video Analysis of Movements in Infants at Risk for Neurodevelopmental Disorders. *Brain Sci.* **2020**, *10*, 203. [CrossRef]
47. Karch, D.; Wochner, K.; Kim, K.; Philippi, H.; Hadders-Algra, M.; Pietz, J.; Dickhaus, H. Quantitative score for the evaluation of kinematic recordings in neuropediatric diagnostics. Detection of complex patterns in spontaneous limb movements. *Methods Inf. Med.* **2010**, *49*, 526–530. [CrossRef]
48. Marchi, V.; Hakala, A.; Knight, A.; D'Acunto, F.; Scattoni, M.L.; Guzzetta, A.; Vanhatalo, S. Automated pose estimation captures key aspects of General Movements at eight to 17 weeks from conventional videos. *Acta Paediatr.* **2019**, *108*, 1817–1824. [CrossRef]
49. Marcroft, C.; Khan, A.; Embleton, N.D.; Trenell, M.; Plotz, T. Movement recognition technology as a method of assessing spontaneous general movements in high risk infants. *Front. Neurol.* **2014**, *5*, 284. [CrossRef]
50. Marchi, V.; Belmonti, V.; Cecchi, F.; Coluccini, M.; Ghirri, P.; Grassi, A.; Sabatini, A.M.; Guzzetta, A. Movement analysis in early infancy: Towards a motion biomarker of age. *Early Hum. Dev.* **2020**, *142*, 104942. [CrossRef]
51. Marschik, P.B.; Pokorny, F.B.; Peharz, R.; Zhang, D.; O'Muircheartaigh, J.; Roeyers, H.; Bolte, S.; Spittle, A.J.; Urlesberger, B.; Schuller, B.; et al. A Novel Way to Measure and Predict Development: A Heuristic Approach to Facilitate the Early Detection of Neurodevelopmental Disorders. *Curr. Neurol. Neurosci. Rep.* **2017**, *17*, 43. [CrossRef]

52. Tsuji, T.; Nakashima, S.; Hayashi, H.; Soh, Z.; Furui, A.; Shibanoki, T.; Shima, K.; Shimatani, K. Markerless Measurement and Evaluation of General Movements in Infants. *Sci. Rep.* **2020**, *10*, 1422. [CrossRef] [PubMed]
53. Lord, C.; Rutter, M.; DiLavore, P.C.; Risi, S.; Gotham, K.; Bishop, S.L. *Autism Diagnostic Observation Schedule*, 2nd ed.; Western Psychological Services: Torrance, CA, USA, 2012.
54. Meinecke, L.; Breitbach-Faller, N.; Bartz, C.; Damen, R.; Rau, G.; Disselhorst-Klug, C. Movement analysis in the early detection of newborns at risk for developing spasticity due to infantile cerebral palsy. *Hum. Mov. Sci.* **2006**, *25*, 125–144. [CrossRef]
55. Hsu, J.C. *Multiple Comparisons: Theory and Methods*; Hardback Published by Chapman & Hall in February 1996; The Ohio State University: Columbus, OH, USA, 1996.
56. Maxwell, S.E.; Delaney, H.D.; Kelley, K. *Designing Experiments and Analyzing Data: A Model Comparison Perspective*, 3rd ed.; Routledge: New York, NY, USA, 2018.
57. Sohal, V.S.; Rubenstein, J.L.R. Excitation-inhibition balance as a framework for investigating mechanisms in neuropsychiatric disorders. *Mol. Psychiatry* **2019**, *24*, 1248–1257. [CrossRef] [PubMed]
58. Canals, J.; Hernandez-Martinez, C.; Esparo, G.; Fernandez-Ballart, J. Neonatal Behavioral Assessment Scale as a predictor of cognitive development and IQ in full-term infants: A 6-year longitudinal study. *Acta Paediatr.* **2011**, *100*, 1331–1337. [CrossRef] [PubMed]
59. Christiansen, H.; Hirsch, O.; Albrecht, B.; Chavanon, M.L. Attention-Deficit/Hyperactivity Disorder (ADHD) and Emotion Regulation Over the Life Span. *Curr. Psychiatry Rep.* **2019**, *21*, 17. [CrossRef] [PubMed]
60. Gomez, C.R.; Baird, S. Identifying Early Indicators for Autism in Self-Regulation Difficulties. *Focus Autism Dev. Disabil. J.* **2005**, *20*, 106–116. [CrossRef]
61. Bachevalier, J.; Loveland, K.A. The orbitofrontal-amygdala circuit and self-regulation of social-emotional behavior in autism. *Neurosci. Biobehav. Rev.* **2006**, *30*, 97–117. [CrossRef]
62. Hadders-Algra, M. Neural substrate and clinical significance of general movements: An update. *Dev. Med. Child Neurol.* **2018**, *60*, 39–46. [CrossRef]
63. Dusing, S.C.; Brown, S.E.; Van Drew, C.M.; Thacker, L.R.; Hendricks-Munoz, K.D. Supporting Play Exploration and Early Development Intervention From NICU to Home: A Feasibility Study. *Pediatr. Phys. Ther.* **2015**, *27*, 267–274. [CrossRef]
64. Dusing, S.C.; Harbourne, R.T. Variability in postural control during infancy: Implications for development, assessment, and intervention. *Phys. Ther.* **2010**, *90*, 1838–1849. [CrossRef]
65. Adde, L.; Yang, H.; Saether, R.; Jensenius, A.R.; Ihlen, E.; Cao, J.Y.; Stoen, R. Characteristics of general movements in preterm infants assessed by computer based video analysis. *Physiother. Theory Pract.* **2018**, *34*, 286–292. [CrossRef] [PubMed]
66. Hadders-Algra, M. Variation and variability: Key words in human motor development. *Phys. Ther.* **2010**, *90*, 1823–1837. [CrossRef] [PubMed]
67. Kyvelidou, A.; Harbourne, R.T.; Stergiou, N. Severity and characteristics of developmental delay can be assessed using variability measures of sitting posture. *Pediatr. Phys. Ther.* **2010**, *22*, 259–266. [CrossRef] [PubMed]
68. Hamer, E.G.; Bos, A.F.; Hadders-Algra, M. Specific characteristics of abnormal general movements are associated with functional outcome at school age. *Early Hum. Dev.* **2016**, *95*, 9–13. [CrossRef]
69. Zappella, M.; Einspieler, C.; Bartl-Pokorny, K.D.; Krieber, M.; Coleman, M.; Bolte, S.; Marschik, P.B. What do home videos tell us about early motor and socio-communicative behaviours in children with autistic features during the second year of life—An exploratory study. *Early Hum. Dev.* **2015**, *91*, 569–575. [CrossRef]
70. Abrishami, M.S.; Nocera, L.; Mert, M.; Trujillo-Priego, I.A.; Purushotham, S.; Shahabi, C.; Smith, B.A. Identification of Developmental Delay in Infants Using Wearable Sensors: Full-Day Leg Movement Statistical Feature Analysis. *IEEE J. Transl. Eng. Health Med.* **2019**, *7*, 2800207. [CrossRef]
71. Thelen, E. Rhythmical stereotypies in normal human infants. *Anim. Behav.* **1979**, *27*, 699–715. [CrossRef]
72. Leekam, S.; Tandos, J.; McConachie, H.; Meins, E.; Parkinson, K.; Wright, C.; Turner, M.; Arnott, B.; Vittorini, L.; Le Couteur, A. Repetitive behaviours in typically developing 2-year-olds. *J. Child Psychol. Psychiatry* **2007**, *48*, 1131–1138. [CrossRef]
73. Einspieler, C.; Prechtl, H.F. Prechtl's assessment of general movements: A diagnostic tool for the functional assessment of the young nervous system. *Ment. Retard. Dev. Disabil. Res. Rev.* **2005**, *11*, 61–67. [CrossRef]
74. Prechtl, H.F.; Einspieler, C.; Cioni, G.; Bos, A.F.; Ferrari, F.; Sontheimer, D. An early marker for neurological deficits after perinatal brain lesions. *Lancet* **1997**, *349*, 1361–1363. [CrossRef]

Chromosomal Microarray Analysis of Consecutive Individuals with Autism Spectrum Disorders Using an Ultra-High Resolution Chromosomal Microarray Optimized for Neurodevelopmental Disorders

Karen S. Ho [1,2,*], E. Robert Wassman [1], Adrianne L. Baxter [1], Charles H. Hensel [1], Megan M. Martin [1], Aparna Prasad [1], Hope Twede [1], Rena J. Vanzo [1] and Merlin G. Butler [3]

1 Lineagen, Inc., Salt Lake City, UT 84109, USA; bwassman@lineagen.com (E.R.W.); abaxter@lineagen.com (A.L.B.); chensel@lineagen.com (C.H.H.); mmartin@lineagen.com (M.M.M.); aprasad@lineagen.com (A.P.); htwede@lineagen.com (H.T.); rvanzo@lineagen.com (R.J.V.)

2 Department of Pediatrics, University of Utah, Salt Lake City, UT 84132, USA

3 Departments of Psychiatry, Behavioral Sciences and Pediatrics, University of Kansas Medical Center, Kansas City, UT 66160, USA; mbutler4@kumc.edu

* Correspondence: kho@lineagen.com

Academic Editor: Michele Fornaro

Abstract: Copy number variants (CNVs) detected by chromosomal microarray analysis (CMA) significantly contribute to understanding the etiology of autism spectrum disorder (ASD) and other related conditions. In recognition of the value of CMA testing and its impact on medical management, CMA is in medical guidelines as a first-tier test in the evaluation of children with these disorders. As CMA becomes adopted into routine care for these patients, it becomes increasingly important to report these clinical findings. This study summarizes the results of over 4 years of CMA testing by a CLIA-certified clinical testing laboratory. Using a 2.8 million probe microarray optimized for the detection of CNVs associated with neurodevelopmental disorders, we report an overall CNV detection rate of 28.1% in 10,351 consecutive patients, which rises to nearly 33% in cases without ASD, with only developmental delay/intellectual disability (DD/ID) and/or multiple congenital anomalies (MCA). The overall detection rate for individuals with ASD is also significant at 24.4%. The detection rate and pathogenic yield of CMA vary significantly with the indications for testing, age, and gender, as well as the specialty of the ordering doctor. We note discrete differences in the most common recurrent CNVs found in individuals with or without a diagnosis of ASD.

Keywords: chromosomal microarray; copy number variants; neurodevelopmental disorders; autism spectrum disorder; variants of unknown significance; FirstStepDx PLUS

1. Introduction

Neurodevelopmental disabilities, including developmental delay (DD), intellectual disability (ID), and autism spectrum disorder (ASD) affect up to 15% of children [1]. However, in the vast majority of cases, a child's clinical presentation does not allow for a definitive etiological diagnosis.

Autism spectrum disorder is characterized by impairment in three domains with onset of one or more of these before the age of 3 years: social interaction; communication skills; and restricted, repetitive, and stereotyped patterns of behavior, interests, and activities. About 40% of individuals with ASD also have a learning disability, and roughly 30% have other co-morbidities such as seizures [1–3].

The etiology of ASD is complex and prominently involves genetic factors, including single gene changes, large genomic structural changes (i.e., deletions or duplications) known as copy number variants (CNV), and other polygenic conditions often influenced by the environment and epigenetic changes [2,3]. Genetic testing to pinpoint the underlying cause of ASD is critical to an individual's clinical management. Further, chromosomal microarray analysis (CMA) has demonstrated the highest diagnostic yield for individuals with ASD as compared to other genetic tests. Therefore, along with previously recognized indications of DD, ID and multiple congenital anomalies (MCA), children and adults presenting with ASD should be offered CMA as a first tier genetic evaluation based on the clinical guidelines from multiple professional societies [2–10].

Microarrays that employ a variety of designs and range of coverage for certain genomic regions have been applied to the clinical testing of individuals with these conditions. Diagnostic yield has increased over time as such arrays have evolved to include better coverage [7–21]. In 2011 the ACMG issued a guideline regarding optimal microarray design and recommended inclusion of additional probe content in areas of known clinical relevance [22]. The following data summarizes our experience with real-world clinical CMA testing of individuals with a diagnosis of ASD in a CLIA-certified laboratory over a period of 4.2 years. The microarray platform utilized in this study was specifically designed to increase detection of CNVs in genomic regions of demonstrated relevance to DD/ID/ASD. We also compare our experience to a non-ASD population clinically tested in parallel in the same laboratory and on the same platform.

2. Results

A total of 10,351 custom, ultra-high resolution CMAs optimized for the detection of neurodevelopmental disorders (FirstStepDx PLUS® (FSDX PLUS®)) were performed over a period of four years. This testing population had a M:F ratio of 2.5:1 and a mean age of 7.0 years. Based on ICD-9 and ICD-10 codes at the time of referral, 55% of cases represented patients with a diagnosis of ASD with or without other features (ASD+ and ASD only, respectively). Tables 1 and 2 show summary data of our neurodevelopmental patient cohort.

Table 1. Summary data of our neurodevelopmental patient cohort.

Cohort Characteristics	Total
Number of Samples	10,351
Number of Males/Females (2.5:1)	7422/2929
Non-ASD *	4657
Any ASD †	5694
ASD+ ‡	2844 (27.4%)
ASD only §	2850 (27.5%)

* "Non-ASD" represents that portion of the cohort with no testing indication of ASD; † "Any ASD" refers to the portion of the cohort that has ASD as a sole testing indication, or in combination with any other testing indications, thus it represents both "ASD only" and "ASD+" cohorts combined; ‡ "ASD+" refers to the portion of the cohort with an indication of ASD as well as another testing indication, such as MCA, seizures, DD, and/or ID; § "ASD only" refers to the portion of the cohort with ASD as the only testing indication.

The mean age of testing was younger for the non-ASD group versus the ASD only group or the ASD+ group (Table 2). Overall, neurologists were the most common referring physicians (36%), followed by developmental pediatricians (31%), pediatricians (16%), and medical geneticists (14%). Although psychiatrists referred only 2% of total cases, they had the highest percentage of their referrals for an indication of ASD (72%) with or without other features, while only 29% of the cases referred by geneticists had an indication including ASD. Of the total caseload, 74% of the ASD cases were referred by pediatric neurologists and developmental/behavioral pediatricians.

Table 2. Mean age at chromosomal microarray analysis (CMA) testing, grouped by diagnostic referral codes.

Population	Mean Age at Testing (Years)	Standard Deviation (Years)
All	7.0	5.6
Non ASD *	6.5	6.0
ASD only †	7.3	5.0
ASD+ ‡	7.5	5.1

* Non-ASD" represents that portion of the cohort with no testing indication of ASD; † "ASD only" refers to the portion of the cohort with ASD as the only testing indication; ‡ "ASD+" refers to the portion of the cohort with an indication of ASD as well as another testing indication, such as MCA, seizures, DD, and/or ID.

Overall, we observe a 28.0% diagnostic yield for potentially abnormal CNVs (Table 3), with an average of 1.2 reportable CNVs detected per individual. Interestingly, the rate of pathogenic findings is significantly lower (4.4%) when the diagnostic indication is ASD only compared to diagnostic indication of DD/ID/MCA without a reported diagnosis of ASD (non-ASD cohort) (12.5%) ($p < 0.001$). The pathogenic rate is only slightly higher in the ASD+ group (6.7%). However, VOUS rates are similar across the ASD only, ASD+, and non-ASD cohorts. The observation of lower rates of reportable CNVs for the ASD only cohort as compared to the ASD+ cohort, and the non-ASD cohort is maintained when looking at the overall yields for each group.

Table 3. Diagnostic yields of genetic testing in 10,351 consecutive children with neurodevelopmental disorders by diagnostic referral codes.

Result	All	Non-ASD *	Any ASD †	ASD+ ‡	ASD Only §
Pathogenic	8.6%	12.5%	5.4%	6.5%	4.4%
VOUS	19.4%	20.1%	19.0%	19.4%	18.5%
Overall Yield	28.1%	32.6%	24.4%	25.9%	22.9%

* "Non-ASD" represents that portion of the cohort with no testing indication of ASD; † "Any ASD" refers to the portion of the cohort that has ASD as a sole testing indication, or in combination with any other testing indications, thus it represents both "ASD only" and "ASD +" cohorts combined; ‡ "ASD+" refers to the portion of the cohort with an indication of ASD as well as another testing indication, such as MCA, seizures, DD, and/or ID; § "ASD only" refers to the portion of the cohort with ASD as the only testing indication.

We stratified our cohort by age to determine whether there were differences in the rate of pathogenic findings when data were viewed this way, and found that rates were highest in the non-ASD cohort in the first year of life (18.9%), which then dropped to 10.7%–12.4% during childhood and adolescence (Table 4). In the ASD cohort, the overall pathogenic rate was slightly higher for individuals with ASD+ as compared to the overall pathogenic rate for individuals with ASD only. The pathogenic rate in the ASD+ cohort started at 4.1% in the youngest group and rose to 8.5% in the 5.5–10 years range (Table 5). The pathogenic rate in the ASD only cohort rose gradually with age from 3.4% in the youngest cohort (0–3.4 years) to a peak at 7.0% in adolescence (Table 6).

While largely targeting a pediatric population, a subset of 383 patients comprised adults over 18 years of age at the time of testing (parental and sibling studies excluded). Interestingly, in the non-ASD cohort the pathogenic rate in adults tested was 18.1%, the highest for any age cohort in this population after the first year of life (Table 4). While the percentage of pathogenic findings in adults with an indication of ASD (9.8% for ASD+; 5.6% for ASD only) was much lower than in the non-ASD population. It is worth noting that older age cohorts maintain high diagnostic yields with or without indications of ASD (Tables 4–6).

Table 4. Diagnostic yield by age in patients without autism spectrum disorder (ASD) (1750 (37.6%) females, 2907 (62.4%) males, Total n = 4657).

Age in Years	Number of Tests	Pathogenic (% Yield)	VOUS (% Yield)	Normal (% Yield)
0–1.0	439	83 (18.9%)	84 (19.1%)	272 (62.0%)
1.0–3.5	1407	151 (10.7%)	275 (19.5%)	981 (69.7%)
3.5–5.4	688	81 (11.8%)	147 (21.4%)	460 (66.8%)
5.5–10	1107	132 (11.9%)	244 (22.0%)	731 (66.1%)
10.1–18	834	103 (12.4%)	155 (18.6%)	576 (69.0%)
18+	182	33 (18.1%)	29 (15.9%)	120 (66.0%)
Total	4657	583 (12.5%)	934 (20.1%)	3140 (67.4%)

Table 5. Diagnostic yield by age in patients with ASD and other indications (610 (21.4%) females, 2234 (78.6%) males, Total n = 2844).

Age in Years	Number of Tests	Pathogenic (% Yield)	VOUS (% Yield)	Normal (% Yield)
0–3.4 *	735	30 (4.1%)	156 (21.2%)	549 (74.7%)
3.5–5.4	630	34 (5.4%)	114 (18.1%)	482 (76.5%)
5.5–10	710	60 (8.5%)	132 (18.6%)	518 (72.9%)
10.1–18	657	49 (7.5%)	126 (19.2%)	482 (73.3%)
18+	112	11 (9.8%)	24 (21.4%)	77 (68.8%)
Total	2844	184 (6.5%)	552 (19.4%)	2108 (74.1%)

* Due to the typical age of clinical recognition and diagnoses for ASD, the range of 0–3.4 years was used for the youngest grouping in this Table.

Table 6. Diagnostic yield by age in patients with only ASD indicated (569 (20.0%) females, 2281 (80.0%) males, Total n = 2850).

Age in Years	Number of Tests	Pathogenic (% Yield)	VOUS (% Yield)	Normal (% Yield)
0–3.4 *	701	24 (3.4%)	126 (18.0%)	551 (78.6%)
3.5–5.4	661	21 (3.2%)	119 (18.0%)	521 (78.8%)
5.5–10	768	32 (4.2%)	160 (20.8%)	576 (75.0%)
10.1–18	631	44 (7.0%)	110 (17.4)	477 (75.6%)
18+	89	5 (5.6%)	14 (15.7%)	70 (78.7%)
Total	2850	126 (4.4%)	529 (18.6%)	2195 (77.0%)

* Due to the typical age of clinical recognition and diagnoses for ASD, the range of 0–3.4 years was used for the youngest grouping in this Table.

The most common pathogenic findings detected in this series of individuals evaluated by CMA are shown in Figures 1–3. We observed, in some cases, striking differences in the frequencies of pathogenic findings when patients are grouped by testing indications and/or gender. For example, the 22q11.2 deletion and, to a lesser extent, the proximal 16p11.2 deletion, were far more prevalent in the non-ASD group than in the combined ASD group, suggesting that indications other than ASD in these patients are common or that ASD is less readily diagnosed in these subgroups (Figure 1). However, the 15q11.2 BP1–BP2 deletion (also known as the Burnside-Butler susceptibility locus) and the proximal 16p11.2 duplication were equally likely to be detected if ASD was indicated or not (Figure 1). In contrast, *NRXN1* gene deletions were much more common when ASD was indicated in comparison to when it was not, by a factor of nearly 4-fold (Figure 1). Figure 2 displays some similarities and differences between the ASD+ and ASD only populations; for example the 15q11.2 BP1–BP2 deletion is the most common finding for both cohorts, but detection frequencies vary significantly for other findings, with 47,XXY being the next most common for the ASD-only cohort while the proximal 16p11.2 deletions and duplications are the next most frequent finding in the ASD+ cohort.

Males outnumbered females in our study population, and the rate of abnormality differed significantly with females having higher rates of pathogenic findings across all diagnostic groupings

($p < 0.001$ for non-ASD and ASD+ groups as well as overall); ASD only detection rates in females vs. males were not statistically different ($p = 0.22$) (Table 7). In the combined ASD group, in addition to specific sex-limited diagnoses like 47,XXY and 47,XYY, there were excesses by gender in the prevalence of several common abnormalities, notably with the 15q11.2 BP1–BP2 deletion, 15q duplication, 15q13.3 deletion, proximal 16p11.2 duplication, 16p12.2 deletion, and 22q11.2 deletion all skewed toward a female preponderance by up to 2–3-fold (Figure 3).

Table 7. Rates of diagnostic findings on CMA by gender and diagnostic referral codes grouping.

CMA Result Type Rates by Gender	Non-ASD	ASD+	ASD only	All
Female				
Pathogenic	14.4%	8.5%	5.3%	11.4%
VOUS	20.9%	19.5%	17.2%	19.9%
Normal	64.7%	72.0%	77.5%	68.7%
Male				
Pathogenic	11.4%	5.9%	4.2%	7.5%
VOUS	19.6%	19.4%	18.9%	19.3%
Normal	69.0%	74.7%	76.9%	73.2%

3. Discussion

CMA is the guideline-recognized first-tier test in the evaluation of individuals with DD/ID, MCA, and most recently ASD [4,6–10,15]. CMA yields significant rates of pathogenic or potentially pathogenic (VOUS) results [2,11–20], which have clinical utility for the case-by-case clinical management of individuals with these individually rare disorders [23–34].

Since the introduction of CMA technology, the total genomic content with probe coverage has progressively increased leading to higher diagnostic yields and better resolution of chromosomal abnormalities. Collectively this trend has resulted in corresponding increases in the clinical value of CMA testing [11–21,24–34]. In addition to guidelines on the clinical indications for CMA, the American College of Medical Genetics and Genomics (ACMG) has issued guidance on the appropriate content and design of such arrays and specifically opined that, "It is desirable to have enrichment of probes targeting dosage-sensitive genes known to result in phenotypes consistent with common indications for a genomic screen (e.g., intellectual disability, developmental delays, autism, and congenital anomalies)" [22]. We report here on over four years of clinical experience with a real-world referral base for testing on an ultra-high resolution chromosomal microarray specifically designed to extend the scope of detection for individuals with ASD and other neurodevelopmental disorders. This microarray was optimized through the addition of probes targeting genomic regions more recently identified to have pathogenic relevance for DD, ID, and ASD [21,35,36].

The overall detection rate in this series for clinically established pathogenic CNVs of 8.6% is comparable to other reported series/platforms [2,11–20], despite the inherent bias toward lower rates based on the real-world referral base and higher percentage of individuals with ASD in this population. When ASD is not among the testing indications, the rate of pathogenic findings is 12.5% and the overall diagnostic yield is 32.6%, both of which are at the upper end of reported diagnostic rates. We have previously shown that diagnostic yield varies significantly on a multivariate basis including but not limited to: referring physician specialty, age of patient at testing, patient gender, and referring indication or combination of indications for testing [20]. When we look in this study at the influence of an ASD diagnosis on pathogenic diagnosis rates by practitioners, geneticists have the highest detection rate when there is no indication of ASD for testing, but also the lowest rate for individuals with ASD only.

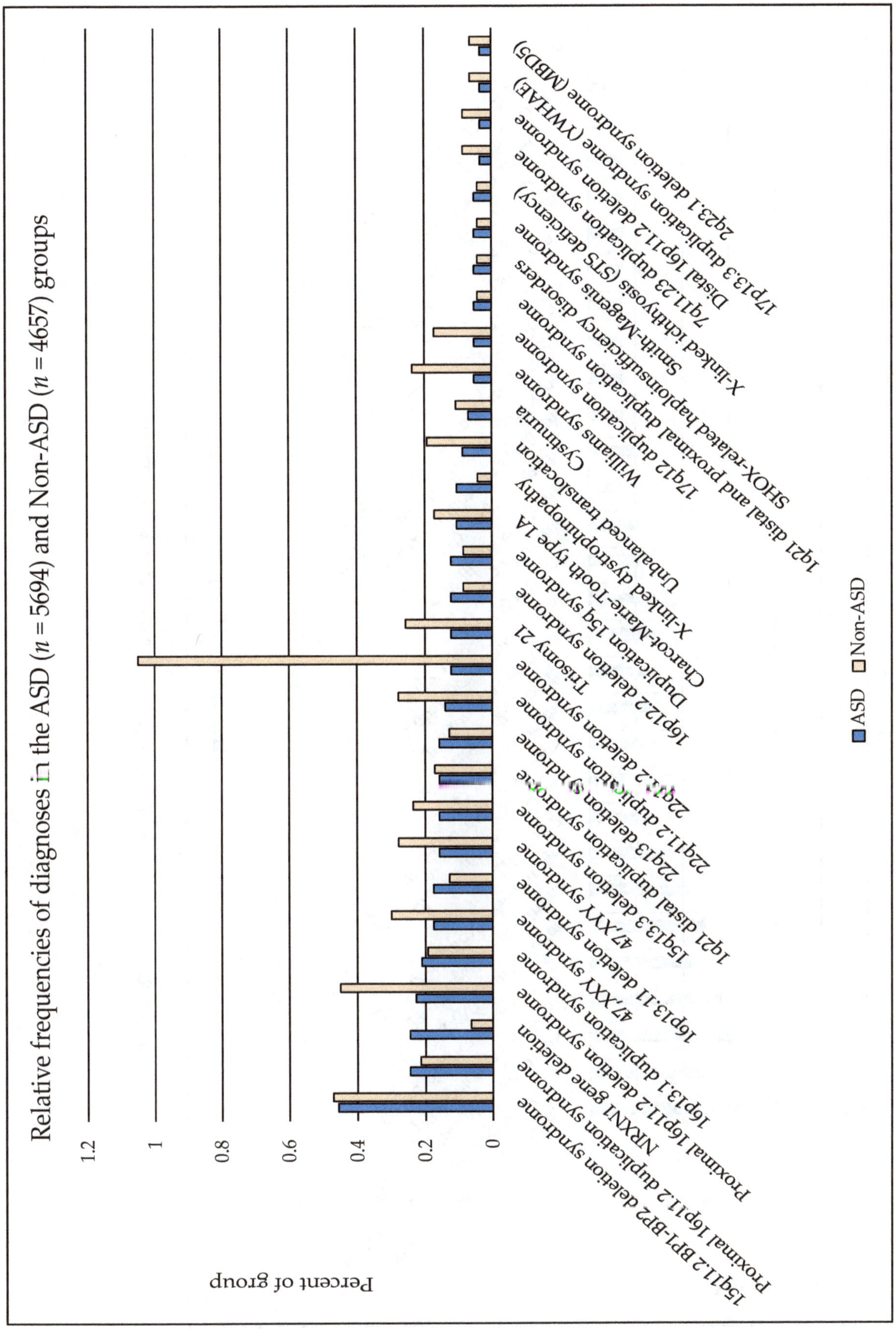

Figure 1. Relative frequencies of diagnoses in the combined ASD ($n = 5694$) and Non-ASD ($n = 4657$) groups.

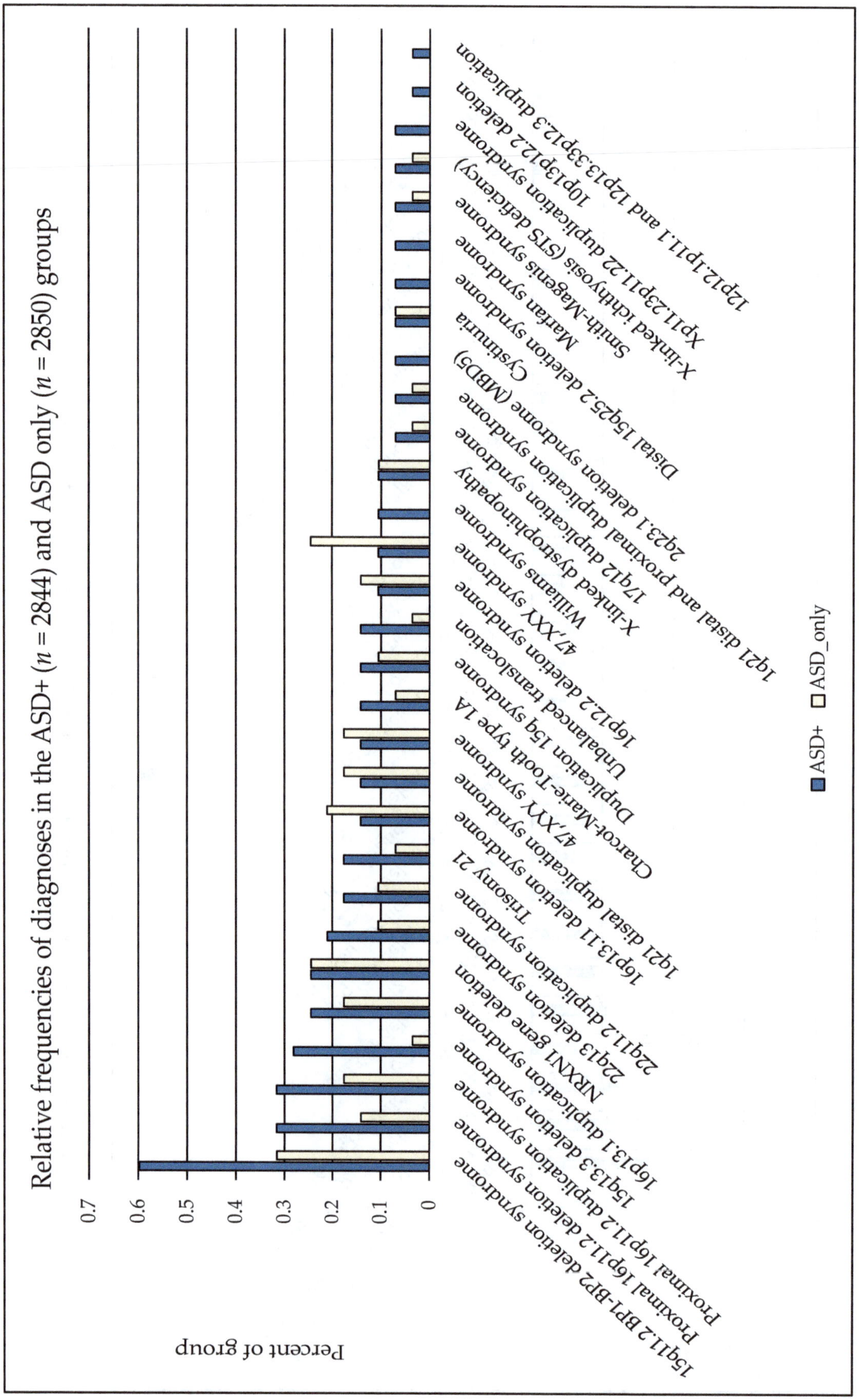

Figure 2. Relative frequencies of diagnoses in the ASD+ ($n = 2844$) and ASD only ($n = 2850$) groups.

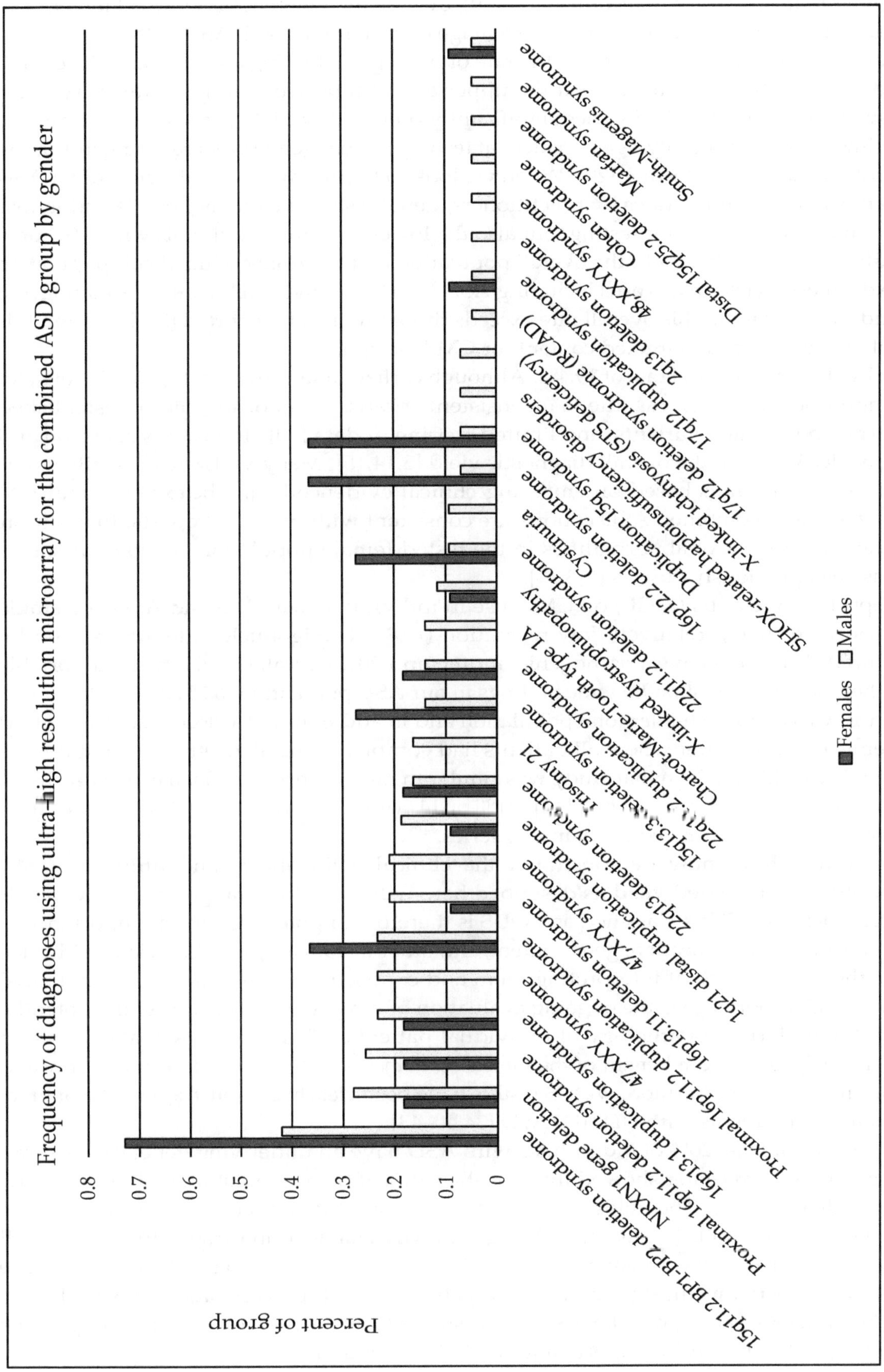

Figure 3. Frequency of diagnoses for combined ASD group by gender. Total females = 2929; total males = 7422.

The overall detection rate in this series for clinically established pathogenic CNVs of 8.6% is comparable to other reported series/platforms [2,11–20], despite the inherent bias toward lower rates based on the real-world referral base and higher percentage of individuals with ASD in this population. When ASD is not among the testing indications, the rate of pathogenic findings is 12.5% and the overall diagnostic yield is 32.6%, both of which are at the upper end of reported diagnostic rates. We have previously shown that diagnostic yield varies significantly on a multivariate basis including but not limited to: referring physician specialty, age of patient at testing, patient gender, and referring indication or combination of indications for testing [20]. When we look in this study at the influence of an ASD diagnosis on pathogenic diagnosis rates by practitioners, geneticists have the highest detection rate when there is no indication of ASD for testing, but also the lowest rate for individuals with ASD only.

While significantly lower than both the overall population and the ASD-excluded sub-population ($p < 0.0001$), the diagnostic yield in all cases including ASD (ASD only and ASD+) are 5.4% pathogenic, 19.0% VOUS, and 24.4% overall. This overall rate exceeds those previously reported [3,14–17] and this supports the value of incremental targeted content for CMA design.

We detected VOUS at an overall rate of 19.4%. Although earlier literature did not typically consider VOUS in the diagnostic yield, this was due to inconsistent criteria for reporting, lack of established databases of normal population variants, and limited sharing of data [10]. Today, it is common and reasonable to consider VOUS in the overall diagnostic yield [3,14,15]. Many VOUS results will evolve into clearly pathogenic findings based on emerging clinical evidence [37]. The excess of males to females in our overall and combined ASD cohorts are consistent with previous reports. In addition, we confirmed the higher rates of abnormalities in the tested female populations in comparison to males, which has been previously observed [3,14].

A recent report by one of us (MGB) on CMA use in individuals with DD and ASD at a single midwest genetics center using relatively low resolution (<180 K) oligonucleotide arrays found 6 of 65 patients with ASD (9%) to have a pathogenic finding and 20% overall (13/65) had a reportable CNV. This is higher than the rate of pathogenic findings in our ASD population (6.7% ASD+; 4.4% ASD only); however, this was a much smaller total population and in addition was a closely-studied cohort within an academic medical center where all patients had complete clinical genetics evaluations [3]. The overall diagnostic yield of 20% in that study was similar to rates reported by Shen et al. [14] (18.2% in 932 patients with ASD) and Schaefer et al. [15] (21% or 14 patients 68 with ASD) but is lower than the 24.4% observed with the optimized array in this series.

Numerous studies have now demonstrated the clinical actionability and utility of CMA testing [23–28,38,39], and increased yield as described here will extend the range and scope of this utility. The increased rate of CNVs classified as VOUS is therefore of potential clinical importance in this setting and consideration of location, gene content, and other factors may help clinicians with such patients despite the complexities of interpreting them and counseling families as to their potential significance. Of critical importance is the ongoing evaluation of novel methods to assess the potential role of VOUS in the underlying pathology of individual patients. This process will allow us as a community to realize the maximum benefit of the increased detection rate achieved through array and interpretation optimization. Furthermore, VOUS results have been clearly demonstrated to be of great importance to parents of patients with DD/ID/ASD [34,40–43].

It is estimated that at least 20% of individuals with ASD have an underlying genetic syndrome, but a survey of a large autism center showed that less than 10% of their population had received any form of genetic evaluation [44]. The evidence here also supports that patients with a diagnosis of ASD remain under-tested overall. The fact that the age of CMA diagnosis in those with ASD is a full standard deviation greater than the potential age of clinical diagnosis speaks to the delay or reticence in taking critical steps to better medically manage these patients. The direct correlation between higher rate of detected abnormalities and age in the ASD cohort suggests that earlier use of CMA and perhaps other genetic testing methods may be important for early intervention.

While still a relatively small sub-cohort, it is remarkable that adults (>18 years old) tested also have the highest pathogenic CNV rate of all diagnostic groups examined. This could be reflective of severity in that particular age group. For example, clinicians/families might believe that testing isn't as valuable for adults but perform it anyway when the individual is considered to be relatively severely impaired. In addition, this may also reflect the desire for adults (or adult siblings of the individual with clinical features) to define recurrence risk to their potential offspring.

Even before prior CMA was introduced into clinical use, the most common chromosome abnormalities associated with apparently isolated ASD were duplication of the 15q11–q13 region (typically of maternal origin) [45] and large microdeletions in the chromosome 16p11.2 and 22q regions reportedly accounting for as many as 1%–5% of ASD related abnormalities each [3,23]. Although these well-described recurrent abnormalities were prominent and relatively more abundant in our ASD cohorts, their prevalence was not as high as predicted by the literature; however, some of the reports suggesting high rates may have been biased by multiplex families.

Partial deletions involving the *NRXN1* gene are now well-described abnormalities, and impairment of the function of the synaptic adhesion protein it encodes, leading to a potential loss of synaptic integrity, is thought to be central to the pathogenesis of ASD [46,47]. *NRXN1* gene deletions were significantly over-represented in both our ASD+ and ASD only groups but were also observed at least occasionally in the non-ASD group. The latter may be due to either early testing for some other clinical feature prior to the formal recognition of ASD-related features, the indubitable inadequacies of relying on physician coding on test requisitions for phenotypic data, or true overlap into other neurodevelopmental conditions without ASD.

The observational study of a large consecutive series of genetic testing for neurodevelopmental disorders, over half of which had feature of ASD highlights the significant value of CMA in defining not merely the underlying etiology but in directing future research into the underlying pathophysiology for improved and ultimately targeted treatments. While it is not ideal to rely on ICD-9/10 coding on test requisitions to define the phenotypic sub-groups of this population and parse the results relevant to ASD, the comparability and trends of this large data set suggest that the conclusions are neither random nor merely directional, and likely reflects a reasonable picture of the scope of abnormalities in these populations. Improved diagnostic tools will lead to increased clinical utility and in the end better clinical management.

4. Materials and Methods

4.1. Patient Ascertainment

A consecutive series of 10,351 real-world samples referred for CMA to a CLIA-licensed clinical laboratory for etiological diagnosis of DD/ID/ASD and MCAs between July 2012 and September 2016 was reviewed for clinical characteristics and related diagnoses. The overwhelming majority of samples were buccal swabs, however 1037/10351 (~10%) cases were conducted on blood specimens. Testing indications were delineated based on International Classification of Diseases, Clinical Modification, Revisions 9 or 10, (ICD-9, ICD-10) (Centers for Medicare & Medicaid Services (cms.gov)).

4.2. Microarray Design

The FSDX PLUS® microarray utilized in this study, and its analytical and clinical validation, have been described in detail elsewhere [21]. It is an expanded whole genome chromosome microarray (CMA) built upon the ultra-high resolution Affymetrix CytoscanHD® platform (Santa Clara, CA, USA) plus 88,435 custom probes targeting genomic regions strongly associated with DD/ID/ASD [14–24]. Both copy number (CNV) and single nucleotide polymorphic (SNP) probes are included in the array, which is consistent with the ACMG guideline for CMA design, as is the "enrichment of probes targeting dosage-sensitive genes known to result in phenotypes consistent with common indications for a genomic screen" [22]. Such critical regions that did not contain >1 probe/1000 bp on the baseline array were supplemented with additional probe content to provide improved detection of smaller deletions and duplications. Additional probe enrichment was of genomic regions identified by our prior studies and elsewhere in the medical literature of published copy number variants and individual genes associated with DD/ID/ASD [23–36]. The increase in analytical sensitivity resulting from this additional 3.3% probe content has been calculated to be 2.6% [21].

4.3. CMA Performance and Interpretation

CMA was routinely performed on DNA extracted by standard methodologies from buccal swab samples (ORAcollect®) in a CLIA-certified laboratory. CMA reagents and equipment were as specified by Affymetrix. Established cytogenetic criteria for interpretation were routinely applied with a minimum of 25-consecutive impacted probes as the baseline determinant for deletions and 50 probes for duplications [35]. Rare CNVs (<1% overall population frequency) were determined to be "pathogenic" if there is sufficient published clinical evidence (at least two independent publications) to indicate that haploinsufficiency or triplosensitivity of the region or gene(s) involved is causative of clinical features. If only preliminary evidence for a causative role for the region or gene(s) therein was found, they were classified as variants of unknown significance (VOUS) as were areas of absence of heterozygosity (AOH) which may increase the risk for conditions with autosomal recessive inheritance or conditions with parent-of-origin/imprinting effects. Cases with only CNVs contained in databases such as the Database of Genomic Variants (DGV) [39] that document presumptively benign CNVs were reported as normal.

4.4. Statistical Methods

Chi-square tests for independence and 2-sided t-tests for normal distribution were applied to the data for determination of significance of findings.

5. Conclusions

Ultra-high resolution CMA has demonstrated great value in the clinical assessment of neurodevelopmental disorders. The diagnostic yield of the optimized CMA platform described here is dependent on many factors, including patient gender, age at testing, clinical presentation, and specialty of the ordering physician. Pathogenic findings give insights into the etiology of patients' neurodevelopmental conditions, and in many cases positively impact medical management decisions. The development of novel and accurate methods to interpret the potential pathenogenicity of VOUS will further enable patients and their physicians to realize the maximum benefits of genetic testing for clinical care.

Acknowledgments: We thank the participating providers and their patients for their dedication and support, Suresh Venkatasubramanian for developing custom code to aid in data analysis, Sean Dixon, Kenny Lentz, and Jon Thornton for database management and technical support. This study was made possible by the entire Lineagen team's remarkable energy and dedication to those with neurodevelopmental disabilities. The study was funded by Lineagen, Inc.

Author Contributions: E. Robert Wassman, Merlin G. Butler and Karen S. Ho conceived and designed the experiments; Hope Twede and Karen S. Ho performed the experiments; E. Robert Wassman, Hope Twede, and Karen S. Ho analyzed the data; Adrianne L. Baxter, Charles H. Hensel, Megan M. Martin, Aparna Prasad, and Rena Vanzo contributed to the analysis; E. Robert Wassman wrote the paper.

Abbreviations

CNV	copy number variant
CMA	chromosomal microarray
ASD	autism spectrum disorder
ID	intellectual disability
DD	developmental delay
MCA	multiple congenital anomalies

References

1. Boyle, C.A.; Boulet, S.; Schieve, L.A.; Cohen, R.A.; Blumberg, S.J.; Yeargin-Allsopp, M.; Visser, S.; Kogan, M.D. Trends in the prevalence of developmental disabilities in US children, 1997–2008. *Pediatrics* **2011**, *127*, 1034–1042. [CrossRef] [PubMed]
2. Heil, K.M.; Schaaf, C.P. The genetics of autism spectrum disorders—A guide for clinicians. *Curr. Psychiatry Rep.* **2013**, *15*, 334. [CrossRef] [PubMed]
3. Roberts, J.L.; Hovanes, K.; Dasouki, M.; Manzardo, A.M.; Butler, M.G. Chromosomal microarray analysis of consecutive individuals with autism spectrum disorders or learning disability presenting for genetic services. *Gene* **2014**, *535*, 70–78. [CrossRef] [PubMed]
4. Manning, M.; Hudgins, L. Array-based technology and recommendations for utilization in medical genetics practice for detection of chromosomal abnormalities. *Genet. Med.* **2010**, *12*, 742–745. [CrossRef] [PubMed]
5. Schaefer, G.B.; Mendelsohn, N.J. Professional practice and guidelines committee clinical genetics evaluation in identifying the etiology of autism spectrum disorders: 2013 Guideline revisions. *Genet. Med.* **2013**, *15*, 399–407. [CrossRef] [PubMed]
6. Volkmar, F.; Siegel, M.; Woodbury-Smith, M.; King, B.; McCracken, J.; State, M. American academy of child and adolescent psychiatry (AACAP) committee on quality issues (CQI) practice parameter for the assessment and treatment of children and adolescents with autism spectrum disorder. *J. Am. Acad. Child Adolesc. Psychiatry* **2014**, *53*, 237–257. [CrossRef] [PubMed]
7. Moeschler, J.B.; Shevell, M. Committee on genetics comprehensive evaluation of the child with intellectual disability or global developmental delays. *Pediatrics* **2014**, *134*, e903–e918. [CrossRef] [PubMed]
8. Michelson, D.J.; Shevell, M.I.; Sherr, E.H.; Moeschler, J.B.; Gropman, A.L.; Ashwal, S. Evidence report: Genetic and metabolic testing on children with global developmental delay: Report of the quality standards subcommittee of the american academy of neurology and the practice committee of the child neurology society. *Neurology* **2011**, *77*, 1629–1635. [CrossRef] [PubMed]
9. Battaglia, A.; Doccini, V.; Bernardini, L.; Novelli, A.; Loddo, S.; Capalbo, A.; Filippi, T.; Carey, J.C. Confirmation of chromosomal microarray as a first-tier clinical diagnostic test for individuals with developmental delay, intellectual disability, autism spectrum disorders and dysmorphic features. *Eur. J. Paediatr. Neurol.* **2013**, *17*, 589–599. [CrossRef] [PubMed]
10. Miller, D.T.; Adam, M.P.; Aradhya, S.; Biesecker, L.G.; Brothman, A.R.; Carter, N.P.; Church, D.M.; Crolla, J.A.; Eichler, E.E.; Epstein, C.J.; et al. Consensus statement: Chromosomal microarray is a first-tier clinical diagnostic test for individuals with developmental disabilities or congenital anomalies. *Am. J. Hum. Genet.* **2010**, *86*, 749–764. [CrossRef] [PubMed]
11. Bernardini, L.; Alesi, V.; Loddo, S.; Novelli, A.; Bottillo, I.; Battaglia, A.; Digilio, M.C.; Zampino, G.; Ertel, A.; Fortina, P.; et al. High-resolution SNP arrays in mental retardation diagnostics: How much do we gain? *Eur. J. Hum. Genet.* **2010**, *18*, 178–185. [CrossRef] [PubMed]
12. McGrew, S.G.; Peters, B.R.; Crittendon, J.A.; Veenstra-Vanderweele, J. Diagnostic yield of chromosomal microarray analysis in an autism primary care practice: Which guidelines to implement? *J. Autism Dev. Disord.* **2012**, *42*, 1582–1591. [CrossRef] [PubMed]
13. Howell, K.B.; Kornberg, A.J.; Harvey, A.S.; Ryan, M.M.; Mackay, M.T.; Freeman, J.L.; Rodriguez Casero, M.V.; Collins, K.J.; Hayman, M.; Mohamed, A.; et al. High resolution chromosomal microarray in undiagnosed neurological disorders. *J. Paediatr. Child Health* **2013**, *49*, 716–724. [CrossRef] [PubMed]
14. Shen, Y.; Dies, K.A.; Holm, I.A.; Bridgemohan, C.; Sobeih, M.M.; Caronna, E.B.; Miller, K.J.; Frazier, J.A.; Silverstein, I.; Picker, J.; et al. Autism consortium clinical genetics/DNA diagnostics collaboration clinical genetic testing for patients with autism spectrum disorders. *Pediatrics* **2010**, *125*, e727–e735. [CrossRef] [PubMed]
15. Schaefer, G.B.; Starr, L.; Pickering, D.; Skar, G.; Dehaai, K.; Sanger, W.G. Array comparative genomic hybridization findings in a cohort referred for an autism evaluation. *J. Child Neurol.* **2010**, *25*, 1498–1503. [CrossRef] [PubMed]
16. Edelmann, L.; Hirschhorn, K. Clinical utility of array CGH for the detection of chromosomal imbalances associated with mental retardation and multiple congenital anomalies. *Ann. N. Y. Acad. Sci.* **2009**, *1151*, 157–166. [CrossRef] [PubMed]

17. Beaudet, A.L. The utility of chromosomal microarray analysis in developmental and behavioral pediatrics. *Child Dev.* **2013**, *84*, 121–132. [CrossRef] [PubMed]
18. Mason-Suares, H.; Kim, W.; Grimmett, L.; Williams, E.S.; Horner, V.L.; Kunig, D.; Goldlust, I.S.; Wu, B.-L.; Shen, Y.; Miller, D.T.; et al. Density matters: Comparison of array platforms for detection of copy-number variation and copy-neutral abnormalities. *Genet. Med.* **2013**, *15*, 706–712. [CrossRef] [PubMed]
19. Pfundt, R.; Kwiatkowski, K.; Roter, A.; Shukla, A.; Thorland, E.; Hockett, R.; DuPont, B.; Fung, E.T.; Chaubey, A. Clinical performance of the CytoScan Dx Assay in diagnosing developmental delay/intellectual disability. *Genet. Med.* **2016**, *18*, 168–173. [CrossRef] [PubMed]
20. Ho, K.S.; Twede, H.; Vanzo, R.; Harward, E.; Hensel, C.H.; Martin, M.M.; Page, S.; Peiffer, A.; Mowery-Rushton, P.; Serrano, M.; et al. Clinical performance of an ultra-high resolution chromosomal microarray optimized for neurodevelopmental disorders. *BioMed Res. Int.* **2016**. [CrossRef]
21. Hensel, C.H.; Vanzo, R.; Martin, M.; Dixon, S.; Lambert, C.G.; Levy, B.; Nelson, L.; Peiffer, A.; Ho, K.S.; Serrano, M.; et al. Analytical and clinical validity study of FirstStepDx PLUS: A chromosomal microarray optimized for patients with neurodevelopmental conditions. *bioRxiv* **2016**. [CrossRef]
22. Kearney, H.M.; South, S.T.; Wolff, D.J.; Lamb, A.; Hamosh, A.; Rao, K.W. Working group of the American college of medical genetics american college of medical genetics recommendations for the design and performance expectations for clinical genomic copy number microarrays intended for use in the postnatal setting for detection of constitutional abnormalities. *Genet. Med.* **2011**, *13*, 676–679. [PubMed]
23. Weiss, L.A.; Shen, Y.; Korn, J.M.; Arking, D.E.; Miller, D.T.; Fossdal, R.; Saemundsen, E.; Stefansson, H.; Ferreira, M.A.R.; Green, T.; et al. Association between microdeletion and microduplication at 16p11.2 and autism. *N. Engl. J. Med.* **2008**, *358*, 667–675. [CrossRef] [PubMed]
24. Jacquemont, M.-L.; Sanlaville, D.; Redon, R.; Raoul, O.; Cormier-Daire, V.; Lyonnet, S.; Amiel, J.; Le Merrer, M.; Heron, D.; de Blois, M.-C.; et al. Array-based comparative genomic hybridisation identifies high frequency of cryptic chromosomal rearrangements in patients with syndromic autism spectrum disorders. *J. Med. Genet.* **2006**, *43*, 843–849. [CrossRef] [PubMed]
25. Saam, J.; Gudgeon, J.; Aston, E.; Brothman, A.R. How physicians use array comparative genomic hybridization results to guide patient management in children with developmental delay. *Genet. Med.* **2008**, *10*, 181–186. [CrossRef] [PubMed]
26. Coulter, M.E.; Miller, D.T.; Harris, D.J.; Hawley, P.; Picker, J.; Roberts, A.E.; Sobeih, M.M.; Irons, M. Chromosomal microarray testing influences medical management. *Genet. Med.* **2011**, *13*, 770–776. [CrossRef] [PubMed]
27. Ellison, J.W.; Ravnan, J.B.; Rosenfeld, J.A.; Morton, S.A.; Neill, N.J.; Williams, M.S.; Lewis, J.; Torchia, B.S.; Walker, C.; Traylor, R.N.; et al. Clinical utility of chromosomal microarray analysis. *Pediatrics* **2012**, *130*, e1085–e1095. [CrossRef] [PubMed]
28. Riggs, E.R.; Wain, K.E.; Riethmaier, D.; Smith-Packard, B.; Faucett, W.A.; Hoppman, N.; Thorland, E.C.; Patel, V.C.; Miller, D.T. Chromosomal microarray impacts clinical management. *Clin. Genet.* **2014**, *85*, 147–153. [CrossRef] [PubMed]
29. Henderson, L.B.; Applegate, C.D.; Wohler, E.; Sheridan, M.B.; Hoover-Fong, J.; Batista, D.A.S. The impact of chromosomal microarray on clinical management: A retrospective analysis. *Genet. Med.* **2014**, *16*, 657–664. [CrossRef] [PubMed]
30. Tao, V.Q.; Chan, K.Y.K.; Chu, Y.W.Y.; Mok, G.T.K.; Tan, T.Y.; Yang, W.; Lee, S.L.; Tang, W.F.; Tso, W.W.Y.; Lau, E.T.; et al. The clinical impact of chromosomal microarray on paediatric care in Hong Kong. *PLoS ONE* **2014**, *9*, e109629. [CrossRef] [PubMed]
31. Sdano, M.R.; Vanzo, R.J.; Martin, M.M.; Baldwin, E.E.; South, S.T.; Rope, A.F.; Allen, W.P.; Kearney, H. Clinical utility of chromosomal microarray analysis of DNA from buccal cells: Detection of mosaicism in three patients. *J. Genet. Counsel.* **2014**, *23*, 922–927. [CrossRef] [PubMed]
32. Martin, M.M.; Vanzo, R.J.; Sdano, M.R.; Baxter, A.L.; South, S.T. Mosaic deletion of 20pter due to rescue by somatic recombination. *Am. J. Med. Genet. A* **2016**, *170*, 243–248. [CrossRef] [PubMed]
33. Ho, K.S.; South, S.T.; Lortz, A.; Hensel, C.H.; Sdano, M.R.; Vanzo, R.J.; Martin, M.M.; Peiffer, A.; Lambert, C.G.; Calhoun, A.; et al. Chromosomal microarray testing identifies a 4p terminal region associated with seizures in Wolf-Hirschhorn syndrome. *J. Med. Genet.* **2016**, *53*, 256–263. [CrossRef] [PubMed]

34. Gurrieri, F. Working up autism: The practical role of medical genetics. *Am. J. Med. Genet. C Semin. Med. Genet.* **2012**, *160*, 104–110. [CrossRef] [PubMed]

35. Matsunami, N.; Hensel, C.H.; Baird, L.; Stevens, J.; Otterud, B.; Leppert, T.; Varvil, T.; Hadley, D.; Glessner, J.T.; Pellegrino, R.; et al. Identification of rare DNA sequence variants in high-risk autism families and their prevalence in a large case/control population. *Mol. Autism* **2014**, *5*, 5. [CrossRef] [PubMed]

36. Matsunami, N.; Hadley, D.; Hensel, C.H.; Christensen, G.B.; Kim, C.; Frackelton, E.; Thomas, K.; da Silva, R.P.; Stevens, J.; Baird, L.; et al. Identification of rare recurrent copy number variants in high-risk autism families and their prevalence in a large ASD population. *PLoS ONE* **2013**, *8*, e52239. [CrossRef] [PubMed]

37. Palmer, E.; Speirs, H.; Taylor, P.J.; Mullan, G.; Turner, G.; Einfeld, S.; Tonge, B.; Mowat, D. Changing interpretation of chromosomal microarray over time in a community cohort with intellectual disability. *Am. J. Med. Genet. A* **2014**, *164*, 377–385. [CrossRef] [PubMed]

38. South, S.T.; Lee, C.; Lamb, A.N.; Higgins, A.W.; Kearney, H.M. Working group for the American college of medical genetics and genomics laboratory quality assurance committee ACMG standards and guidelines for constitutional cytogenomic microarray analysis, including postnatal and prenatal applications: Revision 2013. *Genet. Med.* **2013**, *15*, 901–909. [CrossRef] [PubMed]

39. MacDonald, J.R.; Ziman, R.; Yuen, R.K.C.; Feuk, L.; Scherer, S.W. The database of genomic variants: A curated collection of structural variation in the human genome. *Nucleic Acids Res.* **2014**, *42*, D986–D992. [CrossRef] [PubMed]

40. Reiff, M.; Bernhardt, B.A.; Mulchandani, S.; Soucier, D.; Cornell, D.; Pyeritz, R.E.; Spinner, N.B. "What does it mean?": Uncertainties in understanding results of chromosomal microarray testing. *Genet. Med.* **2012**, *14*, 250–258. [CrossRef] [PubMed]

41. Reiff, M.; Giarelli, E.; Bernhardt, B.A.; Easley, E.; Spinner, N.B.; Sankar, P.L.; Mulchandani, S. Parents' perceptions of the usefulness of chromosomal microarray analysis for children with autism spectrum disorders. *J. Autism Dev. Disord.* **2015**, *45*, 3262–3275. [CrossRef] [PubMed]

42. Jez, S.; Martin, M.; South, S.; Vanzo, R.; Rothwell, E. Variants of unknown significance on chromosomal microarray analysis: Parental perspectives. *J. Community Genet.* **2015**, *6*, 343–349. [CrossRef] [PubMed]

43. Wilkins, E.J.; Archibald, A.D.; Sahhar, M.A.; White, S.M. "It wasn't a disaster or anything": Parents' experiences of their child's uncertain chromosomal microarray result. *Am. J. Med. Genet. A* **2016**, *170*, 2895–2904. [CrossRef] [PubMed]

44. Wenger, T.L.; Kao, C.; McDonald-McGinn, D.M.; Zackai, E.H.; Bailey, A.; Schultz, R.T.; Morrow, B.E.; Emanuel, B.S.; Hakonarson, H. The role of mGluR copy number variation in genetic and environmental forms of syndromic autism spectrum disorder. *Sci. Rep.* **2016**, *6*, 19372. [CrossRef] [PubMed]

45. Cox, D.M.; Butler, M.G. The 15q11.2 BP1–BP2 microdeletion syndrome: A review. *Int. J. Mol. Sci.* **2015**, *16*, 4068–4082. [CrossRef] [PubMed]

46. Pak, C.; Danko, T.; Zhang, Y.; Aoto, J.; Anderson, G.; Maxeiner, S.; Yi, F.; Wernig, M.; Südhof, T.C. Human neuropsychiatric disease modeling using conditional deletion reveals synaptic transmission defects caused by heterozygous mutations in NRXN1. *Cell Stem Cell* **2015**, *17*, 316–328. [CrossRef] [PubMed]

47. Prasad, A.; Merico, D.; Thiruvahindrapuram, B.; Wei, J.; Lionel, A.C.; Sato, D.; Rickaby, J.; Lu, C.; Szatmari, P.; Roberts, W.; et al. A discovery resource of rare copy number variations in individuals with autism spectrum disorder. *G3* **2012**, *2*, 1665–1685. [CrossRef] [PubMed]

Permissions

All chapters in this book were first published by MDPI; hereby published with permission under the Creative Commons Attribution License or equivalent. Every chapter published in this book has been scrutinized by our experts. Their significance has been extensively debated. The topics covered herein carry significant findings which will fuel the growth of the discipline. They may even be implemented as practical applications or may be referred to as a beginning point for another development.

The contributors of this book come from diverse backgrounds, making this book a truly international effort. This book will bring forth new frontiers with its revolutionizing research information and detailed analysis of the nascent developments around the world.

We would like to thank all the contributing authors for lending their expertise to make the book truly unique. They have played a crucial role in the development of this book. Without their invaluable contributions this book wouldn't have been possible. They have made vital efforts to compile up to date information on the varied aspects of this subject to make this book a valuable addition to the collection of many professionals and students.

This book was conceptualized with the vision of imparting up-to-date information and advanced data in this field. To ensure the same, a matchless editorial board was set up. Every individual on the board went through rigorous rounds of assessment to prove their worth. After which they invested a large part of their time researching and compiling the most relevant data for our readers.

The editorial board has been involved in producing this book since its inception. They have spent rigorous hours researching and exploring the diverse topics which have resulted in the successful publishing of this book. They have passed on their knowledge of decades through this book. To expedite this challenging task, the publisher supported the team at every step. A small team of assistant editors was also appointed to further simplify the editing procedure and attain best results for the readers.

Apart from the editorial board, the designing team has also invested a significant amount of their time in understanding the subject and creating the most relevant covers. They scrutinized every image to scout for the most suitable representation of the subject and create an appropriate cover for the book.

The publishing team has been an ardent support to the editorial, designing and production team. Their endless efforts to recruit the best for this project, has resulted in the accomplishment of this book. They are a veteran in the field of academics and their pool of knowledge is as vast as their experience in printing. Their expertise and guidance has proved useful at every step. Their uncompromising quality standards have made this book an exceptional effort. Their encouragement from time to time has been an inspiration for everyone.

The publisher and the editorial board hope that this book will prove to be a valuable piece of knowledge for researchers, students, practitioners and scholars across the globe.

List of Contributors

Silvia Busti Ceccarelli, Maria Nobile, Massimo Molteni and Alessandro Crippa
Child Psychopathology Unit, Scientific Institute, IRCCS E. Medea, 23842 Bosisio Parini, Italy

Camilla Ferrante, Erica Gazzola and Gian Marco Marzocchi
Department of Psychology, University of Milano-Bicocca, 20126 Milan, Italy

Natascia Brondino, Stefano Damiani and Pierluigi Politi
Department of Brain and Behavioral Sciences, University of Pavia, via Bassi 21, 27100 Pavia, Italy

Roberto Keller, Silvia Chieregato, Stefania Bari and Romina Castaldo
Adult Autism Center, Mental Health Department, Health Unit ASL Città di Torino, 10138 Turin, Italy

Filippo Rutto
Department of Psychology, University of Turin, 10100 Turin, Italy

Annalisa Chiocchetti and Umberto Dianzani
Department of Health Sciences, Universita' del Piemonte Orientale, 28100 Novara, Italy

Syed K. Rafi, Waheeda Hossain and Ann M. Manzardo
Departments of Psychiatry & Behavioral Sciences, University of Kansas Medical Center, 3901 Rainbow Boulevard, MS 4015, Kansas City, KS 66160, USA

Dietrich A. Stephan
Department of Human Genetics, University of Pittsburgh, Pittsburgh, PA 15260, USA

Oded Oron and Evan Elliott
Molecular and Behavioral Neurosciences Lab, Bar-Ilan University, Faculty of Medicine, 13215 Safed, Israel

Martina Landini, Ivan Merelli, Nadia Galluccio, Luciano Milanesi and Alessandra Mezzelani
Institute of Biomedical Technologies, National Research Council, Via Fratelli Cervi 93, 20090 Segrate, Italy

M. Elisabetta Raggi, Laura Villa, Francesca Ciceri, Arianna Bonfanti and Massimo Molteni
Scientific Institute, IRCSS Eugenio Medea, 23842 Bosisio Parini, Italy

Serena Camposeo and Angelo Massagli
Scientific Institute, IRCSS Eugenio Medea, 72100 Brindisi, Italy

Erika Salvi
Department of Health Sciences, University of Milan, 20142 Milan, Italy

Daniele Cusi
Institute of Biomedical Technologies, National Research Council, Via Fratelli Cervi 93, 20090 Segrate, Italy
Sanipedia srl, via Ariosto 21, 20091 Bresso, Italy

Anna Marabotti
Scientific Institute, IRCSS Eugenio Medea, 23842 Bosisio Parini, Italy
Department of Chemistry and Biology, University of Salerno, Via Giovanni Paolo II 132, 84084 Fisciano, Italy

Yasin Panahi, Mandana Hadi Jafari and Mehrdad Pedram
Department of Genetics and Molecular Medicine, School of Medicine, Zanjan University of Medical Sciences (ZUMS), Zanjan 45139-56111, Iran

Fahimeh Salasar Moghaddam and Zahra Ghasemi
Department of Medical Biotechnology, School of Medicine, Zanjan University of Medical Sciences (ZUMS), Zanjan 45139-56111, Iran

Reza Shervin Badv
Department of Pediatric Neurology, School of Medicine, Tehran University of Medical Sciences (TUMS), Tehran 14176-13151, Iran
Children's Medical Center, Pediatric Center of Excellence, Tehran University of Medical Sciences (TUMS), Tehran 14176-13151, Iran

Mohamad Reza Eskandari
Metrowest CNS Research Center, Natick, MA 01760, USA
Department of Psychiatry, School of Medicine, Zanjan University of Medical Sciences (ZUMS), Zanjan 45139-56111, Iran

Naveen S. Khanzada and Ann M. Manzardo
Department of Psychiatry and Behavioral Sciences, University of Kansas Medical Center, Kansas City, KS 66160, USA

Merlin G. Butler
Department of Pediatrics, University of Kansas Medical Center, Kansas City, KS 66160, USA
Departments of Psychiatry & Behavioral Sciences, University of Kansas Medical Center, 3901 Rainbow Boulevard, MS 4015, Kansas City, KS 66160, USA

Austen B. McGuire, Syed K. Rafi and Ann M. Manzardo
Departments of Psychiatry & Behavioral Sciences and Pediatrics, University of Kansas Medical Center, Kansas City, KS 66160, USA

Pamela Papangelo, Martina Pinzino and Maddalena Fabbri-Destro
Institute of Neuroscience, National Research Council (CNR), Via Volturno 39/E, 43125 Parma, Italy

Susanna Pelagatti
Department of Informatics, University of Pisa, 56126 Pisa, Italy

Antonio Narzisi
IRCCS Stella Maris Foundation, 56126 Pisa, Italy
IRCCS Stella Maris Foundation, 56018 Pisa (Calambrone), Italy

Ettore Caterino
Azienda USL Sudest Toscana, Centro Autismo UFSMIA di Grosseto, Ospedale di Castel del Piano, 58033 Grosseto, Italy

Maria Luisa Gava
Associazione Nazionale Famiglie di Persone con Disabilità Intellettiva e/o Relazionale (ANFFAS), 18100 Imperia, Italy

Fabio Uscidda and Mariasole Bondioli
Department of Informatics, University of Pisa, 56127 Pisa, Italy

Francesca Pardossi
Unit of Odontostomatology and Oral Surgery, University Hospital of Pisa, 56126 Pisa, Italy

Lucia Billeci and Alessandro Tonacci
Institute of Clinical Physiology, National Research Council of Italy, (IFC-CNR), 56124 Pisa, Italy

Maria Claudia Buzzi, Marina Buzzi and Caterina Senette
Institute of Informatics and Telematics, National Research Council of Italy, (IIT-CNR), 56125 Pisa, Italy

Martina Pinzino
Institute of Neuroscience, National Research Council of Italy of Italy, (IN-CNR), 56125 Pisa, Italy

Valentina Semucci
UFSMIA, Zona Livorno, Azienda USL Toscana Nord Ovest, 57124 Livorno, Italy

Benedetta Vagelli
UFSMIA, Zona Pisana, Azienda USL Toscana Nord Ovest, 56121 Pisa, Italy

Maria Rita Giuca
Unit of Odontostomatology and Oral Surgery, University Hospital of Pisa, 56126 Pisa, Italy
Department of Surgical, Medical and Molecular Pathology and Critical Care Medicine, University of Pisa, 56126 Pisa, Italy

Susanna Pelagatti
Department of Informatics, University of Pisa, 56127 Pisa, Italy
Autismo Pisa APS, Autism Parents Association, 56100 Pisa, Italy

Valentina Bianco
Laboratory of Cognitive Neuroscience, Department of Languages and Literatures, Communication, Education and Society, University of Udine, 33100 Udine, Italy

Alessandra Finisguerra
Scientific Institute, IRCCS E. Medea, Pasian di Prato, 33037 Udine, Italy

Cosimo Urgesi
Laboratory of Cognitive Neuroscience, Department of Languages and Literatures, Communication, Education and Society, University of Udine, 33100 Udine, Italy
Scientific Institute, IRCCS E. Medea, Pasian di Prato, 33037 Udine, Italy

Sonia Betti
Laboratory of Cognitive Neuroscience, Department of Languages and Literatures, Communication, Education and Society, University of Udine, 33100 Udine, Italy
Department of General Psychology, University of Padova, 35131 Padova, Italy

Giulia D'Argenio
Laboratory of Cognitive Neuroscience, Department of Languages and Literatures, Communication, Education and Society, University of Udine, 33100 Udine, Italy
PhD Program in Neural and Cognitive Sciences, Department of Life Sciences, University of Trieste, 34128 Trieste, Italy

Angela Caruso, Letizia Gila, Francesca Fulceri, Tommaso Salvitti, Martina Micai and Maria Luisa Scattoni
Research Coordination and Support Service, Instituto Superiore di Sanità, Viale Regina Elena 299, 00161 Roma, Italy

Walter Baccinelli and Maria Bulgheroni
Ab.Acus srl, Milano, via F. Caracciolo 77, 20155 Milano, Italy

E. Robert Wassman, Adrianne L. Baxter, Charles H. Hensel, Megan M. Martin, Aparna Prasad, Hope Twede and Rena J. Vanzo
Lineagen, Inc., Salt Lake City, UT 84109, USA

Karen S. Ho
Lineagen, Inc., Salt Lake City, UT 84109, USA
Department of Pediatrics, University of Utah, Salt Lake City, UT 84132, USA

Index

www.ingramcontent.com/pod-product-compliance
Lightning Source LLC
LaVergne TN
LVHW060551210926
848485LV00005B/1297
* 9 7 8 1 6 3 9 8 7 8 0 0 0 *